Between Separation and Symbiosis

Language Contact
and Bilingualism

Editor
Yaron Matras

Volume 20

Between Separation and Symbiosis

South Eastern European Languages and Cultures in Contact

Edited by
Andrey N. Sobolev

ISBN 978-1-5015-2072-3
e-ISBN (PDF) 978-1-5015-0925-4
e-ISBN (EPUB) 978-1-5015-0921-6
ISSN 2190-698X

Library of Congress Control Number: 2021936703

Bibliographic information published by the Deutsche Nationalbibliothek
The Deutsche Nationalbibliothek lists this publication in the Deutsche Nationalbibliografie;
detailed bibliographic data are available on the internet at http://dnb.dnb.de.

© 2022 Walter de Gruyter Inc., Boston/Berlin
This volume is text- and page-identical with the hardback published in 2021.
Cover image: Anette Linnea Rasmus/Fotolia
Typesetting: raumfisch.de/sign, Berlin
Printing and binding: CPI books GmbH, Leck

www.degruyter.com

Editor's Preface

The book deals in detail with previously understudied *language contact settings* in the Balkans (South Eastern Europe) that present a continuum between ethnic and linguistic separation and symbiosis among groups of people. The studies in this volume achieve several aims: they critically assess the Balkan Sprachbund theory, they analyse general contact theories against the background of new, original, representative field and historical data, they employ and contribute to recent methods of research on linguistic convergence in bilingual societies, they propose new general assessments of extra- and intralinguistic factors of Balkanization over the centuries, and they outline prospects for future research. The factors relevant to contact scenarios and linguistic change in the Balkans are identified and typologized through models such as those related to a *balanced* or *unbalanced* (socio)linguistic situation.

Each new language on the Balkan Peninsula emerges as a result of migration of (a part of) its native speakers and thus is the result of, so it seems, linguistic Balkanization – the inclusion of this language in processes of convergent structural development with its new neighbours. Balkanization as such yields similar results and occurs with apparent regularity among different languages in different periods. This, in turn, raises the question of the general and particular, internal and external, causes of such development, their particular weight, as well as the degree of determinism of language change on the basis of internal and external parameters.

As for external causes, reexamining the *sociolinguistic situations* so well-known to the field and pertinent to the region's past and present history does not allow us to identify particular circumstances that could be termed "responsible" for convergence in Balkan languages. For example, consider the well-known situation of intense sociolinguistic domination that occurs when the language of state and religion is combined with the mass population of its native speakers. This is reflected in the Balkans with the replacement of a subdominant L1 by a socially dominant L2. This is evident in the paleo-Balkan peoples of antiquity and the Middle Ages when populations adopted Greek, Latin and Slavic languages; when in the Middle Ages and the modern period Romance speakers of the Adriatic coast, West Balkans and Bulgaria adopted Slavic languages; when in middle, modern and recent times Slavic speakers of Wallachia, Albania and Greece adopted Romanian, Albanian and Greek. Nevertheless, the materials and structures of these languages reveal that the linguistic results of such language change differ profoundly. In certain cases substrates can leave deep substantial and functional traces up to wholescale restructuring of the language type (as in, for example, the so-called Balkan Romance and Balkan Slavic language area, especially in the west Macedonian version of the latter). In other cases these traces are, as such, absent (as in the Tosk dialects of Southern Albania), even with respect to lexical borrowings (as in the Serbo-Croatian Neo-Štokavian dialect). Similarly, in some cases L1 can be preserved against L2 despite high levels of social dominance with large-scale substantial and functional restructuring of L1 at all linguistic levels (as in the Aromanian Farsherot subdialects of Albania), while in other cases evince an absence of significant change (as in the Pindian Aromanian subdialects of Greece). Quite often no more than structurally insignificant linguistic change can follow severe external divisions as wrought by the separation of large ethnic groups (as in the Muslim Slavs of Greece, the Dropull Greeks in Albania, and the Slavs of Eastern Albania). Yet including a small foreign-language-speaking ethnic group in the midst of a larger one can also preserve the first language and not lead to serious structural changes (for example, the "Vlach" dialects of Eastern Serbia). As a result, it is impossible to point directly to a particular set of sociolinguistic circumstances that could either directly cause or significantly contribute to convergence or its absence among Balkan languages. This thus leads to the appearance of speculative models in the discourse of Balkan studies that are not supported by "the world of things", i.e. by the facts of the language. With these facts in tow, the search in the contemporary Balkan landscape for more rare and, perhaps, even unique situations of language contact is an important task. And should such situations be observed, they confront our discipline with new methodological challenges.

The first part of this volume makes use of new and existing knowledge to examine in linguistic terms the dialects (idioms) of multiethnic, multilingual South Eastern European communities (that is, it provides syntheses and analyses of new experimentally confirmed and existing knowledge). The focus is on the idioms of bi- and multilingual speakers of the following groups in different contact settings:

- **Greek** as L1 or L2 (Tsakonian on the Peloponnese, Greece; Himariotika in South Albania),
- **Albanian** as L1 or L2 (Dibra dialect in Golloborda, Albania; Laberia dialect in Himara, South Albania; Ana e Malit idiom in Montenegro; Prespa idiom in North Macedonia),
- **Romanian** as L1 (Iabalcea idiom in Karashevo, Romania),
- **Aromanian** as L1 (Prespa idiom in the Republic of North Macedonia),
- **Macedonian** as L1 or L2 (Golloborda dialect in Albania; Prespa dialect in North Macedonia),
- **Serbo-Croatian** as L1 or L2 (Krashovani Slavic dialect in Romania; Mrkovići idiom in Montenegro; Croatian Glagolitic data from the Island of Krk, Croatia, representing contacts of Slavic with varieties of Romance since 11th ct.)

The theoretical and methodological approach for this part of the volume is given in the introduction "Contemporary Language Contacts in the Balkans: Situations and Outcomes" by Alexander Yu. Rusakov and conclusion "Balkan Sprachbund Theory as a Research Paradigm" by Andrey N. Sobolev. Each of these presents its own contribution in accordance with the major research interests of the authors. The research framework adopted in this volume is a functional linguistic approach to the major *levels of language structure* that have been taken into consideration. These include phonetics/phonology, grammar, lexicon and text, as well as the verbalization of traditional culture. Questionnaires have been used to collect previously unrecorded data from bilingual informants, data have been extracted from mediaeval written sources; the examples (words, phrases, texts) are presented in the traditional orthography of each of the respective languages along with an IPA transcription when standard orthography is not phonemically contrastive. Glossing is provided.

Research has been focused on neglected aspects of the language situations under investigation. These are:

1. linguistic competences of bilingual informants in L1 and L2;
2. dialectical attribution of bilingual speech;
3. phonetics/phonology of L1 and L2 (including inventories of vowels, consonants, sound clusters, and phonological rules);
4. grammar (including verbal tense, aspect, and modality systems with special attention to perfect tense and pattern borrowings in syntax);
5. the lexica of L1 and L2 (semantic groups such as "Kinship", "Family", "Body parts", "Animal breeding", "Administration", "Construction", "Christian spirituality", "Moslem spirituality", "Traditional calendar", "Mythology", "Marriage", among others, as well as anthroponomastics and toponomastics, among others, are studied in sufficient detail);
6. authentic, transcribed dialect texts in L1 and L2 showing different effects of code switching/mixing, and the like.

This part of the book, produced by authors from the Institute for Linguistic Studies of the Russian Academy of Sciences in Saint Petersburg, presents the findings of two subsequent research projects supported by a grant from the Russian Science Foundation ("From Separation to Symbiosis: languages and cultures of South Eastern Europe in contact", No. 14-18-01405 and "Balkan bilingualism in dominant and equilibrium contact situations in diatopy, diachrony and diastraty", No. 19-18-00244). Significant contributions have been made by the doctoral research of Anastasia L. Makarova, Vyacheslav V. Kozak and Daria V. Konior for the partial completion of the *kandidat nauk* degree, the PhD equivalent in the Russian

Federation. In general, it has taken more than a decade to educate a new generation of specialists in Balkan linguistics in Saint Petersburg capable of doing original research in Balkan multilingual communities.

A very important paper by an invited author from Ohio State University, USA, extended the coverage to include **Judezmo**, according to recommendations of the anonymous reviewers. This volume's editor can only regret that the shortage of resources in the current Russian research landscape did not permit him to follow other recommendations and enrich the book in a similar way with articles on Turkish and Romani.

The individual contributions to this volume are as follows. The introductory chapter "Contemporary Language Contacts in the Balkans: Situations and Outcomes" by Alexander Yu. Rusakov gives an overview of the individual cases scrutinized in the volume through the lens of a contemporary theory of contact linguistics. Two main issues are addressed: the microtypology of the (socio)linguistic situations found on the ground and the types of the language changes observed.

The chapter "Separation and Symbiosis between Slavs and Albanians as a Continuum of Linguistic Contact Situations: New Challenges for New Data" by Andrey N. Sobolev deals with the concept of a Sprachbund as an interlinguistic continuum with no barriers, where contact-induced changes need to be distinguished from internal development. General and special issues are addressed, such as linguistic interference, integration and dis-integration in contemporary contact situations of separation and symbiosis. These are observed directly in areas of contact with dominant and non-dominant Albanian-Slavic bilingualism in Albania and Montenegro.

Anastasia L. Makarova's contribution, "Mutual Understanding among Albanians, Slavs and Aromanians in Prespa, North Macedonia: Perfect Tense as a Perfect Tool", compares verbal past tense systems in Macedonian, Albanian and Aromanian varieties of the Prespa lake region. These forms have developed over time in intimate contact within a geographically closed territory. Several types of grammatical parallelism are described and classified, as well as general information on the ethnic and sociolinguistic composition of the region.

The chapter "Balanced Language Contact in Social Context: Velja Gorana in Southern Montenegro" by Maria S. Morozova investigates the sociolinguistic conditions and linguistic outcomes of an Albanian-Slavic language contact situation without dominance existing in a small ethnically mixed village on the border of Montenegro and Albania. The author uses an innovative approach to the description of the present-day situation, considering the individual scenarios of bilingual speech behaviour that co-occur in the community of Velja Gorana and attributing the contact-induced changes observed in both languages to specific classes of bilingual speakers. From this she goes on to make projections about the contact situation that could have existed in the whole southern Montenegrin area in the past.

The chapter "Symbiosis Suspectus: Palasa in Himara, Albania" by Andrey N. Sobolev presents field data on a less studied Greek dialect of a Greek-Albanian community with non-dominant bilingualism.

In her chapter "Minority within a Minority: Iabalcea and Carașova in Romania", Daria V. Konior examines the origins and functioning of terminology related to spiritual culture under the conditions of intimate language contact. The example of bilingualism among the Krashovani demonstrates that a specific social and historical setting established in the Romanian Banat has been favoring symbiotic relationships between Slavic and Romanian communities, languages and cultures.

The chapter "Evidence for Past Coexistence: The Romance Stratum in Croatian Glagolitic Sources from Krk, Croatia" by Vyacheslav V. Kozak reconstructs the Croatian-Romance and Croatian-Latin written language contacts on the island of Krk by summarizing and interpreting examples of Romance and Latin influence on Old Croatian Glagolitic texts from late mediaeval and early modern periods. Despite the political dominance of Venice on Krk, the reconstruction based on the etymological and quantitative analysis of loanwords within different semantic fields and the examination of replicated grammatical structures show no more than an average level of language influence.

The situation described by Maxim L. Kisilier in his chapter "Reconstructing Past Coexistence: Problems and Mysteries in the Multilingual History of Tsakonia, Greece" is rather enigmatic. The Tsakonian dialect is not in contact with any other language or dialect apart from Standard Modern Greek. Some peculiarities of Tsakonian seem to have nothing to do with interaction with other languages and dialects while others cannot be persuasively explained from the point of view of the internal history of the dialect itself and the influence of Standard Modern Greek alone. It is almost impossible to demonstrate from where each feature could have been borrowed, but the contact-oriented approach may help to find at least typological parallels to some mysterious phenomena and thus to explain them.

Brian D. Joseph, in "Convergence and Failure to Converge in Relative Social Isolation: Balkan Judezmo", examines the factors affecting whether Judezmo shows convergence or not to Balkan structural features and lexicon, ultimately arguing that time, social setting and the dynamics of interaction are responsible for the resulting unique constellation of convergent and nonconvergent features in the language.

Finally, Andrey N. Sobolev elaborates the "Balkan Sprachbund Theory as a Research Paradigm" and argues that substantializing theoretical concepts through high-quality dialect data from bilingual communities is a better way of exiting the aporia that dominates what is now called areal linguistics than engaging in a discursive deconstruction of terminology. A research paradigm is developed upon the theoretical background that regular correspondences in the function of linguistic units provide the Balkan Sprachbund theory with the best predictive force.

This publication is aimed at specialists in general linguistics, language variation and change, dialectology, bilingualism, multilingualism, language contact, borrowing, Balkan Sprachbund, cultural anthropology, Orthodoxy, Catholicism, Islam, Judaism, language policy, history, political science, minority and subaltern studies, Balkan studies, Croatia, Montenegro, Serbia, North Macedonia, Romania, Greece, Albania and their respective languages. A broader readership interested in issues of language and cultural contact in South Eastern Europe is addressed as well.

The editor wishes to express his gratitude to Walker Trimble for patient editing and proofreading.

Andrey N. Sobolev
Bad Nauheim, 13 July 2020

Contents

Editor's Preface —— V

Alexander Yu. Rusakov
Contemporary Language Contacts in the Balkans:
Situations and Outcomes —— 1

Andrey N. Sobolev
Separation and Symbiosis between Slavs and Albanians as Continuum of
Linguistic Contact Situations: New Challenges for New Data —— 27

Anastasia L. Makarova
Mutual Understanding among Albanians, Slavs and Aromanians in Prespa,
North Macedonia: Perfect Tense as a Perfect Tool —— 59

Maria S. Morozova
"Balanced Language Contact" in Social Context:
Velja Gorana in Southern Montenegro —— 89

Andrey N. Sobolev
Symbiosis Suspectus: Palasa in Himara, Albania —— 135

Daria V. Konior
Minority within a Minority: Iabalcea and Carașova in Romania —— 157

Vyacheslav V. Kozak
Evidence for Past Coexistence: Romance Stratum in Croatian Glagolitic Sources
from Krk, Croatia —— 189

Maxim L. Kisilier
Reconstructing Past Coexistence: Problems and Mysteries in the Multilingual
History of Tsakonia, Greece —— 215

Brian D. Joseph
Convergence and Failure to Converge in Relative Social Isolation:
Balkan Judezmo —— 265

Andrey N. Sobolev
Balkan Sprachbund Theory as a Research Paradigm —— 285

Abbreviations —— 315

Index of names —— 317

Index of places —— 322

Authors' profiles —— 327

Alexander Yu. Rusakov
Contemporary Language Contacts in the Balkans: Situations and Outcomes

Abstract: This chapter[1] contains an overview of the individual cases scrutinized in the volume through the lens of the current theory of contact linguistics. The notions of language maintenance and language shift, language dominance (with the emphasis on the so-called "balanced language contact" situation) will be discussed along with the sorts of linguistic consequences that result from processes of contact. These, in turn, include the different types of transfer phenomena (matter and pattern borrowings) and code switching. This chapter has two interrelated goals: to analyse the cases considered in this book from the point of view of contact linguistics, and to speculate about the instructiveness of these cases for a clearer understanding of the contact processes which have led to the creation and development of the Balkan language area.

1 Preliminary remarks: chronological outlines

1.1 Chronological depth and possibility of extrapolation

It is well known that the last two centuries have marked a drastic reduction in the level of multilingualism in the Balkans. This has been due, in the first place, to the tendency to create monolingual "European-like" states (see Sobolev 2013; Joseph & Friedman 2017). We should ask whether the cases studied in this book (except for the Krk situation) are the real remnants of the more or less typical multilingual situations that *had existed* in the Balkans in the past, or whether they represent rather *new* situations characteristic for the Balkans of our time and, thus, are of little interest for the reconstruction of the processes that characterize Balkan linguistic history.

To answer these questions we have two kinds of sources. First there are historical data (often indirect) which may help us to determine the chronological depth of our current (socio)linguistic situations. Secondly, we have the linguistic

---

[1] This research was made possible by a grant from the Russian Science Foundation (the projects "From Separation to Symbiosis: South Eastern European languages and cultures in contact", No. 14-18-01405 and "Balkan bilingualism in dominant and equilibrium contact situations in diatopy, diachrony and diastraty", No. 19-18-00244).

data, namely the results of the contact-induced language change in the dialect systems involved.

Let us consider very briefly our cases from the point of view of their historical depth:

- Among all our cases the situation in *Velja Gorana* has minimal chronological depth – we know that the village was founded in the end of the 19th century. However, the Velja Gorana case itself is especially indicative. The matrimonial patterns characteristic for this respectively new village (and crucial for preserving the bilingual situation here) continue *mutatis mutandis* the situation which had been characteristic, presumably, for the larger *Mrkovići* region (as well as for some other parts of the Montenegrin-Albanian border zone), and which had ceased to exist long before the 20th century (see Morozova, below; Morozova & Rusakov 2018). Thus, Velja Gorana provides a unique opportunity to study processes that were characteristic in the past for a rather big part of the Western Balkans on the "micro-level" (the zone of regeneration and preservation of tribal organization) which developed from the beginning of Ottoman domination (the time when the process of Balkanization "achieved its current state", Friedman & Joseph 2017: 80). It is important that Velja Gorana's marriage practises continued to exist (almost unchanging) despite dramatic political and socio-economic changes on the macro-level (the fall of Austro-Hungarian and Ottoman empires, two World Wars, creation of the Kingdom of Yugoslavia, communist rule and its fall, various changes of borders, and so on). The comparison of the contemporary Slavic idioms of Velja Gorana and Mrkovići allows us to trace the development of contact-induced language change in this part of the Albanian-Montenegrin linguistic border zone.
- Contacts between the Albanian, Aromanian, Greek and Slavic population in the *Prespa* region, which is considered as one of the main irradiation centers of the Balkanisms,[2] are likely to begin here no later than in the first centuries of the second millennium. The imposition of modern borders might serve to change some traits of the region's linguistic landscape. Thus, currently we have no active Greek element in the North Macedonian region of Prespa while Albanian and Macedonian became sociolinguistically dominant in their respective areas. But the main tendencies of the linguistic development have

---

[2] See, for example: "The epicentre of Balkanisms seems to be somewhere south of the lakes Ohrid and Prespa, where the Greek, Albanian, Macedonian, Aromanian, and Romani languages meet [...], their local forms being clearly more similar to each other than the five language groups taken as wholes" (Lindstedt 2000: 234).

not changed. These are, first of all, tendencies towards language maintenance among Albanians and Macedonians and towards rather slow language shift among Aromanians (see Gołąb 1997). We have here the continuation of the development of the multilingual situation which had existed over several centuries.

- We do not know when contact between Albanians and Greeks began in the *Himara* region.[3] Nevertheless, it could hardly be later than the 13th or 14th century. Despite the changing sociolinguistic position of both languages (compare, for example, the high prestige of Greek in the Byzantine period and of Albanian in the 20th century), the Greek language maintained its important role as a language of culture and religion, which was perhaps crucial for maintaining the whole situation.[4]

- The exact time of arrival of the Krashovani (a Catholic Slavic-speaking people) into the territory of the Romanian Banat also is not known (probably there were several waves of the migration, see Konior, below). The case of *Carașova* is a typical example of the long-term maintenance of the island dialect, and that of *Iabalcea* is a no less typical example of a nearly completed language shift. Such situations – more or less documented – are quite widespread in the Balkans (and elsewhere).

- The Slavic-Albanian coexistence in the *Golloborda* region is documented from the end of the 15th century in such sources as Ottoman defters and in the biographies of Skanderbeg (see Sobolev & Novik 2013). We cannot draw from these documents strong evidence of the character of Slavic-Albanian relations but may suppose that the contemporary situation (with Albanians living in the peripheral parts of Golloborda) continues the Albanian-Slavic border contact of the past. Supposition concerning long-term but rather superficial contact is supported by the respectively modest linguistic results of contact in this area.

- The case of the *Tsakonian* idiom presents more difficult issues for interpretation. We have here at least two different contact situations. The first is contact of Tsakonian with the Modern Greek – two closely related idioms that have developed over the last few centuries. The second situation is the emergence of a Tsakonian language that demonstrates deep and unique differences from all other Modern Greek dialects. We may only suppose that Tsakonian arose "many centuries ago" as a result of contact with some language or languages (probably Albanian, Macedonian / Bulgarian, Italian or Balkan Romance

---

[3] We have here two unknowns: we know neither the time of the arriving of Albanians into this part of the Balkans nor when the ancestors of Himara Greeks appeared in the region.
[4] See, for example, Sobolev (2017: 427).

since the lexical results of contacts with all these languages can be found in Tsakonian, as Kisilier attests below, or with some other language unknown now to us). These contacts might have an extreme character (interrupted language shift, or something else, see below).
– The contact of Judezmo with the languages of the Balkan Peninsula and Anatolia began in the end of the 15th century and continues till now, despite the drastic diminishing of the number of Judezmo speakers during the Holocaust. It seems that the principal traits of this contact – first of all, the social isolation and one-way bilingualism (see Joseph, below) – did not alter significantly during the whole of this period.

Thus it seems that the cases this book examines[5] may be treated as a continuation of situations which previously existed and, in some degree, have been typical for the Balkans rather than examples of the "new" situations due to contemporary socio-economic conditions. Modern realities (media, state schooling and so on) do influence, of course, the character of bilingual processes and their results, but their influence does not change the basic traits of these processes. See, for example, the case of Velja Gorana where Albanian women entering the village after the marriage claim that, despite the formal study of "Serbo-Croatian" in the Montenegrin state schools, they really learned the Slavic idiom only in their new families.

1.2 Diachronic and diatopic "borders" of Balkanization

The common opinion in Balkan linguistics over the last decades has been that the study of contact processes in the Balkans should not be limited to the time of when classical Balkanisms appeared and were primarily dispersed, but should include all observable contact processes between Balkan idioms.[6] These processes began before the arrival of some "idiom-participants" into the Balkans

---

[5] I did not discuss in this section the case of the past Slavic-Romance contacts reflected in the written sources of Krk. Its chronological depth (10th to 18th centuries) coincides with the period of activity of the "main" Balkanization process.
[6] See, for example: "To exclude Debar Macedonian and Albanian from consideration in the overall convergence of Macedonian and Albanian, and to treat their localized phonological convergence as irrelevant to convergences found across other Balkan languages, would simply be an arbitrary decision rooted in an aprioristic minimum number of languages needed for a sprachbund" (Friedman, Joseph 2017: 74); and further: "Ongoing contact among speakers of regional varieties of Greek, Macedonian, Balkan Romance, Romani, Albanian, and so on, continue to occur in northern Greece, in the Republic of North Macedonia, in parts of Albania and elsewhere

(Romani, Ladino, some Turkic idioms, Slavic in some fashion)[7] and continue into the future.[8]

Let us bring as an example the dispersion of the *volo*-future in the Albanian Gheg zone. *Volo*-future is one of the classical Balkanisms, represented in all "major" Balkan languages. Nevertheless, in the majority of the reference works we read that *volo*-future is represented only in the Tosk Albanian dialect (where it should be stabilized no later than in 16th century)[9], which is more "Balkan" than the Gheg one. In reality, nearly all Gheg varieties have now, along with the "old" *habeo*-future, the "Tosk" *volo*-future forms which penetrated into the Gheg zone from the Tosk one. This occurred, most likely, in a gradual way from the 18th to the 20th centuries (Gjinari et al. 2007: map 305; see also Demiraj 1985: 825–826; Fiedler 2004: 531–532). It seems more reasonable to regard the difference between the spread of the *volo*-future through the "core" Balkan languages ((Tosk) Albanian, Greek, Balkan Slavic, and Balkan Romance) on one hand, and into Gheg Albanian on the other, as being largely chronological.[10]

---

in the Balkans, in cities and in rural areas. ... In that sense, the Balkan Sprachbund is alive and developing as contact among speakers continues" (Friedman & Joseph 2017: 88).

7 We have no grounds, of course, to exclude from the scope of interest in Balkan linguistics contacts which took place centuries before the Common Era between Greek and the ancient Balkan languages (including proto-Albanian). Unfortunately, we have no reliable data about their results.

8 We will not examine here the problem of the definition of the linguistic area in general (see the exhaustive treatment of this problem in respect of the Balkans in Friedman & Joseph 2017). I agree with Lyle Campbell (2006) that the linguistic area (i.e., Sprachbund) is a rather vague notion and tends to conceive of linguistic areas as layered contact superposition zones in the sense of Koptjevskaja-Tamm and Wälchli (2001: 728), see also (Wiemer & Wälchli 2012: 15).

9 *Volo*-future is represented in the Tosk varieties of Bulgaria and Ukraine, the speakers of which left Albanian territories presumably no later than in the 16th century.

10 A rather important question, however, is why some of the contact phenomena in the Balkans spread through all or nearly all Balkan languages whereas others remained on the level of the contacts of two languages/dialects or covered relatively smaller regions. Many answers that have been proposed are based usually on the ideas of the more preferable character of some types of contact-induced language change. See for example, the increase of the possibility of "intertranslatability" among languages involved in the contact (Linstedt 2000), the increase of "redundancy" (Sobolev 2012), and so on. Such ideas seem acceptable but they are either tautological (all contact-induced changes do increase "intertranslatability"), or explain only some of the "Balkanisms" (see, for example, Joseph 1983: 249; Tomić 2006). Considering that contemporary historical linguistics is unable to answer the majority of the *why*-questions, it seems more reasonable to explore all the contact-induced changes in the Balkans in a purely historical way (see an example of such an approach in Drinka (2017), on the spread in the Balkans of the *habeo*-perfect; see also Makarova, below).

Another aspect of the "borders" of the "linguistic Balkans" has a rather geographic character. Our materials concerning linguistic contacts involving different dialects of the BCMS, or Daco-Romanian dialects convincingly demonstrate that there is absolutely no reason to exclude any dialects spoken in the Balkans and adjacent territories outside the scope of interests of Balkan linguistics (see Morozova, Kozak, Konior in this volume).

2 Types of contact situations and scenarios: language maintenance vs. language shift, language dominance vs. balanced bilingualism

The majority of the situations analyzed in this book (as well as in the Balkan linguistic area as a whole) are the clear examples of a *language maintenance* situation (see Thomason & Kaufman 1988).[11]

Yet the linguistic history of the Balkans still demonstrates many clear cases of *language shift*. Some of them are reconstructed, first of all, on the basis of the historical data and cover larger population groups. Among them we have the shift of the Illyrians, Thracians and other ancient Balkan people to Latin, the shift of the Romance population of Dalmatia to Slavic, the shift of the Slavic population to the other languages, mostly to Greek in the central and southern Balkans, the shift to various Balkan languages on the part of the early Turkic population of the Balkans, and the shift to different Balkan languages of some groups among the Balkan Romani population (which sometimes led to the formation of new ethnic groups). The linguistic consequences of these shifts are, as a rule, not clear.[12] Other "substrate" situations are reconstructed on the basis of linguistic data confirmed by (or not in contradiction to) historical facts and have a rather

---

[11] This thesis has, however, a nearly tautological character: all living bi- or monolingual situations are – at the moment of observation – cases of language maintenance, at least at the macro-level. We may thus only reconstruct situations of completed language shift for the past or predict such development for the future.

[12] One of the reasons for this is the very diverse character of potential constellations of different sociolinguistic patterns (the size of the shifting group in its relation to the surrounding population, the duration of the period of shift, and so forth (see Thomason & Kaufman 1988)), which may lead to the language shift exerting minimal linguistic results. Sometimes we do not have sufficient (or even any) data on the shifting languages (Illyrian, Thracian), or are not able to differentiate their potential impact from the impact of closely related languages (e.g., early Turkic dialects and Ottoman Turkish).

presumptive character. See, for example, Agniya V. Desnitskaya's hypothesis regarding the massive language shift of the Slavic population to Albanian in the modern Northern Tosk zone. Here we have, on one hand, some linguistic traits that distinguish Northern Tosk dialects from both Gheg and Southern Tosk dialects. On the other hand, there is some historical evidence (place names and so on) attesting to the massive presence of the Slavic population on this territory (see Desnitskaya 1976, and the counterarguments in Ismajli 2015). Another example, perhaps more important from linguistic point of view, is the assumed shift of the Aromanians to Macedonian (Gołąb 1997): this shift explains some linguistic features characteristic of Macedonian dialects and is confirmed by the historical data. More local language shift situations are also found in many Balkan microregions.

For a better understanding of the different scenarios for both language maintenance and shift, the notion of language dominance (or its absence) is of great importance. Following Weinreich (1953) and van Coetsem, we will distinguish *linguistic* (the greater degree of the proficiency in one of the language used by the speaker,[13] see van Coetsem 1988: 13) and social or *sociolinguistic* (dominant language is the language of power and prestige) dominance. Sociolinguistic dominance acts on the level of the speech community. It influences, of course, the linguistic behaviour of individuals. Linguistic dominance is a characteristic of speakers' linguistic competence. However we may speak about the linguistic dominance of the given language in the speech community as a sum of dominance configurations among community members or as a prevailing tendency among these members. These sociolinguistic and linguistic dominations do not need to coincide (see below). Very useful is also the notion of the *pragmatically dominant language* elaborated by Yaron Matras.[14]

We may find in language contact studies of the last decades some kind of deconstruction of the notion *language shift*. Thus, in Thomason (2001) the cases of language shift are considered (under the notion "imperfect learning") together with situations where the collective acquisition of the second language (characterized by imperfect learning and – as a consequence – by the creation of a new variant of the target language) is not accompanied by the loss of the first language.

---

[13] This degree of proficiency may have, in turn, a different character. The subdominant position of the language may be expressed in the low level of its proficiency, or by the smaller role of the one of the competing languages in communication. In the latter case the proficiency in the subdominant language may have a full character.

[14] "The pragmatically dominant language is "the language that the speaker associates most closely at the moment of interaction with routine implementation of communicative tasks that are similar to the ongoing task" (Matras 2009: 98; see also Matras 1998).

So, the mechanism and the character of the linguistic results in the development of the second language, for example, of "Indian English", do not principally differ from those of "Irish English", the first language arising as a result of massive language shift (see, e.g. Winford 2003: 224–225). Another problem is that when the concrete situation is viewed at the microlevel it turns out that "some speakers can be involved in shifting languages (possibly with imperfect learning) while at the same time other speakers are borrowing, as native speakers" (Campbell 2006: 22). Nevertheless, we will maintain this notion as a characteristic of the community linguistic behavior.

On should note that the movement to (real) language shift passes usually through a stage of change of linguistic dominance – the target language becomes the dominant one and the first language takes a subordinate position. In some cases, however, movement towards the shift may be stopped and the situation with the dominance of the surrounding language may continue over a long time. Thus, for example, we have some grounds to suppose that Russian became the dominant language among the North Russian Romani in the end of the 19th century and this situation – with the maintenance of the Romani dialect – continues up to the present (Rusakov 2001). The reason should be the high level of the group's inclination towards preserving the native language together with the growing functional load of the surrounding language. The fact that the surrounding language becomes the dominant language of the given group does not mean that the "ethnic" language ceases to be the first language acquired by children. Thus, the dominance change repeats permanently over the life span of each generation and of each speaker. The linguistic consequences of such a situation are very similar to those of "imperfect learning" cases (language shift and the creation of the second language variants as Indian English) – the more or less serious change in phonology and grammar (first of all, in syntax). The main difference is that in the cases of the maintenance of the "native" language as a subordinate one we have also heavy contact-induced changes in its lexicon (Thomason & Kaufmann 1988; Haspelmath 2009).[15]

Let us thus examine the situations described in this volume from this point of view. We may characterize the linguistic situation in *Velja Gorana* as an example of a balanced language contact: "a long-standing linguistic area and stable multilingualism without any dominance relationships" Aikhenvald (2007: 42). These situations are often defined in the modern multilingual studies as "small-scale

---

15 In the case of dominance change we have the increase of the donor language's activity, according to van Coetsem's (1988) terminology. Friedman and Joseph define such cases as reverse interference (Joseph 2010).

multingualism" (Lüpke 2016; Singer & Harris 2016).[16] The long-term coexistence of Albanian and BCMS in Velja Gorana is supported by the constant influx by Albanian wives from neighbouring Albanian-speaking areas, a practise existing at least since the beginning of the 20th century (see Jovićević 1922; Morozova & Rusakov 2018; Morozova, below). As a result, this community may be characterized by the nearly equal functional use of both languages – BCMS and Albanian – despite the sociolinguistic dominance of "Montenegrin" as a state language. The microanalysis of bilingual communication in the families of Velja Gorana, together with the study of the "linguistic history" of individual speakers, clearly demonstrates that the supposed balanced language contact situation results from some different micro-situations, themselves having a rather unbalanced character. The development of linguistic competence configurations on the part of individual speakers (when they are not bilinguals since their childhood) tends to be from monolingual or nearly monolingual to the bilingual often without the clear dominance of one or other language (Albanian women brought to the village acquire BCMS, and Slavic-speaking women learn Albanian, see Morozova & Rusakov 2018; Morozova, below). At a given time in the community there are both speakers with a "balanced" competence in both languages and speakers with linguistic dominance in one of them. From the linguistic point of view, language contact in Velja Gorana leads rather slowly to the rise of a number of lexical and syntactic calques in both languages and does not result in any "radical change" of their structure. The latter are prevented in Velja Gorana by the "balanced" character of the contact situation, along with the "open" character of the community (Morozova, below).

The presence of the Albanian element for the whole *Mrkovići* region in the 15th century (fixed in the Ottoman defters) as well as evidence about the spreading of the mixed Albanian-Montenegrin marriages over a considerable part of the Mrkovići territory (Morozova & Rusakov 2018; Morozova, below) allows us to assume that the bilingual situation described for Velja Gorana might characterize the previous situation for the whole region of the Mrkovići. Now the main part of Mrkovići (except its periphery, including Velja Gorana) has ceased to be bilingual. So we have here a kind of shift (from bilingualism, maybe of the balanced type, to monolingualism), and one of its immediate causes had to be the refusal of matrimonial ties with the neighbouring Albanian population.[17] Different sce-

---

[16] See also "four-M", or "multi-lateral, multi-directional, mutual multilingualism" (Friedman & Joseph 2017: 70), or "nondominant bilingualism" (Sobolev 2017: 420).
[17] We do not know the concrete details of this shift (see, for example, Curtis 2012: 39–40; Sobolev 2015) but may suppose that it had a slow and gradual character. A very slight tendency towards language shift may be noted even in Velja Gorana, where some of the elder Albanian

narios combining language maintenance and language shift are not alien to other parts of the Albanian-Montenegrin border zone as well, witness, for example, the emergence of "blood-related" *fises* some of which unite the Albanian-speaking people, whereas the others consist of speakers of BCMS.

The case of Velja Gorana poses a very important problem of the role of mixed marriage in the appearance and maintenance of multilingual situations. The importance of this problem was noted in various contactological studies (see e.g., Aikhenvald et al. 2010) but was not considered seriously in relation to the Balkan languages. We have in Velja Gorana (and formerly in the *Mrkovići* region) a kind of linguistic exogamy which apparently represents an epiphenomenal consequence of tribal exogamy. The question arises, however, whether this situation (the widespread presence of exogamy and its influence on multilingual situations) is characteristic only for this part of the Western Balkans, with the preservation (or regeneration) of tribal structures, or does it play a more or less important role also for other parts of the Balkan dialect continuum?[18]

Golloborda shows us a rather strong separation between the two ethnic (and linguistic) groups inhabiting this *krajina*. This separation is based on and maintained by geographical separation: the Albanophones of Golloborda live in villages that form the geographical periphery of the *krajina*. The Golloborda Slavophones demonstrate the linguistic dominance of their Slavic L1 idiom. The rather modest influx of Albanian-speaking wives has not changed (at least until now) this situation, Albanian wives have acquired the community's language and Albanian plays a very small (if any) role in interfamily communication (Steinke & Ylli 2008: 29). The role of the sociolinguistically dominant Albanian state language consists in maintaining bilingualism among the majority of Golloborda Slavophones (nonetheless even now a part of them – mainly elderly women – are monolingual, see Sobolev & Novik 2013: 80).[19] The linguistic results of such a situation are very modest: the contact influence of Albanian is limited to lexical loans, rare code switching phenomena, and the maintenance of some Albanian phonetic and phonological features by adaptation and use of Albanian

---

(according to their origin) women demonstrate a tendency towards reversing the linguistic dominance of Albanian to BCMS.

18 We may only claim with confidence that the mixed marriages do not provide the necessary prerequisites for deep grammatical changes, including these of the metatypical character (see below). There are cases of such changes where we may be sure of the absence of widespread intermarriage, see, for example, the case of the North Russian Romani dialect mentioned above.

19 The inhabitants of the Golloborda Albanian-speaking villages do not know the Slavic idiom or know it to a very modest degree.

borrowings. We may characterize the Golloborda case as the situation of a dialect island with a high level of L1 maintenance.[20]

We may state preliminarily that the situations in *Velja Gorana* and *Golloborda* have a quite different character. The community of Velja Gorana arose as a bilingual one (see Morozova, below), so bilingualism was and remains its *inner*, *intrinsic* feature, the bilingual situation continues up to the present thanks to the kind of linguistic exogamy which is also an intrinsic social feature. The community itself combines unity and stability with a kind of inner ethnic and linguistic heterogeneity. The cluster of traits characteristic for Velja Gorana – the absence of linguistic dominance, functional equality of the language, and bilingualism inside the community – are typical, as seems, for small-scale bi- or multilingual communities. On the contrary, the emergence of the bilingual situation in the community of Golloborda Slavs was prompted by border contact with the neighbouring Albanians[21] and is maintained by the current role of Albanian as a state language, thus, by the *external* factors in respect to community itself, factors which reflect circumstances imposed from the outside. It should be noted that the mountainous *Golloborda* region lies outside the zone that preserves tribal structures. The community is rather homogeneous and is characterized by the strong dominance of L1 and the functional distribution of the languages. We have here a typical example of a polyglossic community with "hierarchical relationships holding between languages and functional differentiations for them" (Lüpke 2016: 41), opposed to the non-polyglossic communities with small-scale multilingualism (as in *Velja Gorana*).

The other situations described in this volume also demonstrate the features, which put them close to one or another pole; i.e. "small-scale multilingual" or "polyglossic" communities.

The situation of the long-standing coexistence of Albanian and Greek in *Himara* has its own peculiarities. One of them is that both languages used by Himara Hellenophones[22] have high status in respect of their sociolinguistic dominance. Albanian is the state language, Greek is the language of religion, high culture, and, more recently, the state language of a more economically developed

---

[20] Strictly speaking, Golloborda became a kind of linguistic island after the imposition of the strong border between Albania and Yugoslavia after World War II. Previously it amounted to the peripheral zone of the Macedonian dialects, so we had here border-contacts instead.

[21] These contacts and very formation of bilingualism among the Golloborda Slavs could be facilitated by the fact of the religious identity of the Slavic and Albanian population of the region.

[22] We will not comment here – as elsewhere in this chapter – on an important question of the coexistence (different in the various cases) of the standard and vernacular forms of the languages considered.

neighbour where the considerable part of the active population of the region earns their living.[23] The "Greek" population of Himara demonstrates also near equal proficiency in Greek and Albanian (although there are now some "Greek" monolinguals among the older generation). This fact may be explained by the presence of Albanian elements among the ancestors of Himara "Greeks", i.e. by mixed marriages (Sobolev 2017). The participation of the Albanian elements in the formation of the contemporary Himara population is confirmed by historical data and by testimonies of individual speakers. However to answer the question of the role of mixed marriages in the formation of the current linguistic (and ethnic) landscape of Himara will be possible after a more detailed study of this problem.[24] Another source of continuous preservation of a situation with a high level of mastery in both languages might be the processes of Hellenization of the Albanian population encouraged by the Orthodox church till the time of the founding of the Albanian independent state and supported in some way by the cultural differences between the Orthodox and Muslim parts of the Albanian population. Questions about the functional distribution of both languages in the daily communication of the Himariotes as well as the phenomena of grammatical contact changes need also more detailed analysis. The answers to these questions will allow us to make more strong considerations of the potential intrinsic character of the bilingualism in the Himara community and its profile of linguistic dominance.

The (socio)linguistic situation in the *Prespa* region was briefly characterized above. Now we have in the region a rather separated (from the point of view of the ethnic and linguistic consciousness) Slavic and Albanian population with the linguistic domination of their respective L1s. There is also a mismatch of the linguistic and sociolinguistic dominance (Macedonian and Albanian are sociolinguistically dominant languages in the corresponding parts of the Prespa region). Here (as in Golloborda) the influence of the state language is realized in the asymmetry of the bilingual situation: Macedonians as a rule are monolingual in North Macedonia and bilingual in Albania and vice versa.[25] So, we have rather polyglossic

---

[23] This does not mean that the situation did not change at all. A particularly difficult the position for the Greek language must have been between 1946 and 1990 when the Greek population of Himara did not study in the native language, religion was prohibited and any ties with Greek were cut (Zheltova 2015).
[24] It may be noted that the problem of Greek-Albanian linguistic (and ethnic) relations is more loaded with political and ideological overtones than, for example, Albanian-Montenegrin relations (see Sobolev 2017: 427).
[25] The example of mixed villages Arvati and Krani in North Macedonia where both Muslim Albanians and Orthodox Macedonians (mainly men) are bilingual is rather exceptional (see Makarova, below about the possible reasons for such a sociolinguistic development). It should be

situations on the both sides of the Albanian-Macedonian border. Over the history of this region, Aromanians, as was said above, exhibit a strong tendency towards language shift. The groups of Aromanians who maintain their language are characterized by the reversal of language dominance: now their dominant language is the language of the surrounding population.[26] The linguistic consequences of such a complicated situation (the fourth participant of this multilingual situation has also been Greek, which is now practically absent in the Macedonian and Albanian parts of the Prespa region) is demonstrated in the book by the example of the development of the preterital system in Macedonian, Aromanian and Albanian dialects of Prespa (Makarova, below; Makarova 2018). All three idioms demonstrate the respectively high degree of "isomorphism" in this fragment of the verb system, first of all, in the subsystem of the analytical perfect. It is interesting, however, that a higher level of contact-influenced change may be observed in the perfect system of Macedonian, which shows very striking deviations from the prototypically Slavic perfect. These deviations (mainly the invasion of the possessive perfect in the functional sphere of the *esse*-perfect of the Slavic type) increase as approaching to the presumed centre of contact with Albanian-Aromanian-Macedonian innovations in the Ohrid-Prespa region (Friedman 1976; Drinka 2017). The development of the possessive perfect in Macedonian (and, maybe, partly in Albanian) may be explained as a result of the complex and multilateral contacts in the region. One of the important components of these contacts might be the shift of the Aromanian population to Macedonian (see Makarova, below).[27] As a result of these contact processes, Macedonian developed a rather complex perfect system (more complex than in the neighboring Balkan idioms). Such a process of increased complexity may be partially explained by linguistic accommodation between different groups of the Macedonian population ("former" Aromanians and "native" Macedonians) during and after the shift (about such processes see, for example Thomason 2001: 75). As a result of such accommodation, the heterogeneous system of the (Western) Macedonian perfect may have arisen.

---

noted that both groups of the Arvati population are separate from a matrimonial point of view (see Makarova 2018). Thus, we have in each of these two villages rather two language communities with Albanian and Macedonian as the dominant L1, respectively.

26 Bilingualism becomes an internal characteristic of the community in such situations while its polyglossic character to a certain extent remains.

27 In the case of Albanian some facts (first of all, the high level of grammaticalization of the possessive perfect in the both Gheg and Tosk dialects) may indicate an earlier period of the Albanian-Balkan Romance contact situation. This may have begun in second half of the first millennium A.D., a time of intensive contact between the ancestors of Albanians and Daco-Romanians (and Aromanians?), see Rusakov 2013.

Caraşova and *Iabalcea* demonstrate two different variants of the linguistic fate of island idioms or, perhaps, two stages of linguistic development. The situation in *Caraşova* is characterized by the linguistic domination of the first (Slavic) language, with the sociolinguistic domination of Romanian. In this respect the situation in *Caraşova* is rather like the Golloborda situation. The Romanian influence on the Krashovani Slavic idiom is reflected in the simplification of the accent and vocalic systems, some syntactic calques and numerous borrowings and calques in cultural lexical fields. Thus, we have here a clear example of language maintenance. A quite different situation is observed in one of the Krashovani villages – Iabalcea. This situation may be described as a nearly completed language shift. The middle-aged and younger generation demonstrate partial proficiency in the Slavic and acquire it, as seems, not since their birth. The reasons why language shift happened in a single Krashovani village remains unknown; the narratives of the local inhabitants about the role of mixed marriages in this process can be neither confirmed nor rejected (see Konior, below). The marriage strategies both in Caraşova and Iabalcea require further research.

The Judesmo situation is another example of a linguistic island.[28] We may observe here the strong separation of Jewish speakers from the neghbouring population. Judezmo was L1 during the period of the existence of the substantial groups of Judezmo speakers in the Balkans.

The goal of the chapter dealing with Romance influence on the island of *Krk* was not in any way to study the dynamics of the multilingual situation in this part of Dalmatia. The general path of linguistic development in Krk was a slow process of language shift (ending in the second half of the 19th century) among the Romance population. The materials analyzed in the chapter show us the rather low level of Romance influence on the Slavic (Čakavian) written idiom (both in inscriptions and in the official judicial documents).

About the *Tsakonian* situation see above (1.1). It is very tempting to explain the striking differences in the grammatical system of Tsakonian (first of all, in the verb conjugation) by the shift (with a comparatively low level of the language learning) to Greek of some unknown population (or by the insufficient learning of Greek with the maintenance of its first language) and then by the longstanding contact of this population with the speakers of the "standard" Greek dialects. Unfortunately, there is not sufficient data to arrive at such conclusions (see Kisilier, below).

---

28 The notion "linguistic island" (as well as other "areal phenomena", cf. Dahl 2001: 1460) should not be understood in an exclusively geographical sense.

3 Some preliminary conclusions

We may conclude that the bi- and multilingual situations studied in this book may be divided into the two main types: the non-polyglossic situations of small-scale multilingualism and polyglossic ones. In the cases of the first type, multilingualism arises and is maintained by the community's internal properties, in the cases of the second type by the need to develop contacts outside the community. The most obvious example of the first type is *Velja Gorana*. The analysis of the Velja Gorana community showed that the main factor in the preservation of long-standing bilingualism are interethnic marriages between Albanians and Muslim Slavs. The situation in *Himara* is perhaps also close to this type. It is possible that the continuous inflow of Albanians in the Greek-speaking community via mixed marriages might be the reason for the high level of linguistic domination of both languages. Without a doubt, multilingualism has been also supported in both cases by the need to carry out communication outside the community, but internal factors prevailed.

On the contrary, in the situations of the second type the main cause of the emergence and preservation of the bi- or multilingualism is the need for communication outside the community. The cases of *Karashevo, Golloborda*, and *Prespa* region belong to this type. The first two situations are currently examples of island dialects in an alien linguistic surrounding (Golloborda, however, had previously been a border-zone). The situation in Prespa resulting from the numerous population migrations represents now (after establishing the modern state borders) a case of "border-area multilingualism" (Matras 2009: 48).

From the historical point of view, both small-scale multilingual and polyglossia situations may develop into monolingual ones. In cases of small-scale multilingualism this development takes place when the causes of maintaining the language balance within the given community cease to operate. Such a situation we have probably in some parts of the *Mrkovići* region where interethnic marriages between Slavs and Albanians were abandoned and the functional load of Albanian had to be diminished. We do not know whether the polyglossic situation was in this case an intermediate stage on the way towards monolingualism.

The cases of some communities of *Prespa Aromanians,* and maybe of *Iabalcea,* show us one of the possible courses of development for originally polyglossic situations. After the change of the linguistic dominance, "interiorization" takes place and L2 is used more and more inside the community. The next stage in this development is thus language shift while the bilingual situation may be maintained, however, for a long time (see, above on the North Russian Romani dialect, also Konior, below).

4 Types of changes

What are linguistic consequences of the sociolinguistic situations described in this volume? Can these phenomena be distinguished from classical Balkanisms, or do they resemble them? For this we must consider two points.

First, the linguistic results of contact in a given community cannot always be distinguished from the consequences of linguistic interaction within the broader diachronic and diatopic context. So we may assume that the language contacts in Velja Gorana are a direct continuation of the Slavic-Albanian contacts in the *Mrkovići* region and – more broadly – across the whole Albanian-Montenegrin border zone. The Greek-Albanian contacts in Himara likely began some centuries before when the sociolinguistic profile of this zone might have been quite different.

Secondly, in some of our cases language change and the solidification of its results may be blocked (or, at least, slowed down) now by the instant access of community members to the forms of both (or only one) of the contacting languages outside the community. So the inhabitants of Velja Gorana have such an access both to the Montenegrin and Albanian, Himariotes to Greek and Albanian, Krashovani people to Romanian, and so on.

Nevertheless, we shall try to summarize the main types of language change described in this volume.

The spare *phonetic* data show us various phenomena attesting to the simplification of the phonetic system. This takes place, first of all, in the prosodic sphere, e.g., "simplification of the accent system; loss of intonation and of qualitative and quantitative characteristics of stress" in the Slavic idiom of Karashevo (Konior, below).[29] In the field of segment phonetics we see nearly everywhere the use of the "alien" phonemes in the borrowings.

We also see some cases of the loss of phonemic contrasts (absent in BCMS) in the speech of Velja Gorana's BCMS monolinguals acquiring Albanian. These potential changes are mostly blocked due to influence of the Albanian spoken both inside and outside the community.

Interesting is "an analogical extension of the devoicing of final obstruents, which is typical for the majority of Albanian varieties [...], to the words with a historical, non-pronounced final vowel *ë*" (Morozova, below). The fact that this feature (the blocking of the Albanian "ë-rule") exists only in the speech of "the

---

[29] This fact conforms well with the typological generalizations of Yaron Matras (2009: 232) who mentioned that various prosodic phenomena belong to the potentially most contact-induced phonetic features (prosody > stress > vowel length).

older bilingual" men may show that the Albanian influence from outside the community might be not so strong in the time of their childhood.

Another phenomenon of a phonological character – the replacement in *Mrkovići* dialect of the BCMS opposition /ļ/ : /ʎ/ by the Albanian one /ł/ : /l/ – is realized only partially because intensive contact with Albanians on the greater part of the Mrkovići territory had ceased. See also the "shift from *ty/dy ... to ky/gy*" in Judezmo in Bosnia and Macedonia under local Slavic (and, perhaps, Albanian) influence (Joseph, below). Generally, we may conclude that language contacts did not lead in these cases to the systematical restructuring of the phonological systems of the languages involved.

The more rich material in the *grammatical* field shows us that the absolute majority of registered changes represents different cases of calques – semantic and structural (or combinations of the both types); i.e. clear cases of *pattern replication* (see Matras 2009). Some of these calques may be treated as an extension of "classical Balkanisms" into new idioms: the merger of locative and directive constructions, analytical comparative and superlative, reduplication of personal pronouns in accusative and dative (all in the Slavic idiom of Karashevo, Romanian > Slavic (Konior, below)). The minimal syntactic phenomena observed in Judezmo have a similar character (some trends in the development of the object reduplication; the slight diminishing of the infinitive (see Joseph, below)). So, we may draw on some additional material concerning details of the process of Balkanization. Other changes reflect phenomena limited to certain contact situations: the arising of constructions with prepositions governing the nominative case (Mrkovići and Velja Gorana, Albanian > Slavic, see Morozova, below), the merger of comitative and instrumental constructions (Mrkovići and Velja Gorana, Albanian > Slavic; Karashevo, Romanian > Slavic), marking of the external possessor by accusative with the verbs of pain and sensation (Velja Gorana, Slavic > Albanian (Morozova, below)), occasional postposition of some attributes (Slavic idiom of Karashevo, Romanian > Slavic (Konior, below)), the use of pluperfect as a non-confirmative past by "some Judezmo speakers of Istanbul" (Joseph, below).

In Velja Gorana we have some cases of mutual contact influence: see the development of "genitival constructions" where the original development of the contact influence was from Albanian to BCMS (and this influence is characteristic for the whole Montenegrin-Albanian contact zone), but then the BCMS construction (modelled under Albanian influence) began to be copied in the Albanian speech of Velja Gorana bilinguals (see Morozova, below).

One should note that both in the situations of balanced bilingualism (current Velja Gorana) and in the polyglossic situations (for example, Karashevo) we have only certain cases of moderate structural borrowing, limited mainly to the calquing of certain grammatical constructions.[30] It is rather difficult to reconstruct real scenarios for the emergence and spread of specific grammatical innovations. So, we may suppose that in the BCMS idioms of Mrkovići and Velja Gorana we have some kind of imposition (according to van Coetsem (1988); see Morozova, below; and Morozova (2019a) on the restructuring of the lexicon) or imperfect learning (according to Thomason 2001) phenomena and the main actors of these phenomena were Albanian women acquiring BCMS. It is more difficult to determine the exact character of the process of the development of the grammatical calques in Karashevo. We should keep in mind, as has been said above, that we do not know the state of the Slavic dialect of Karashevo exactly at the time when its contacts with Romanian were initiated. Nor do we know the (socio)linguistic situation in the early periods of these contacts.

The development of the verbal system in the Prespa region, the perfect tenses first of all, demonstrates an example of a more heavy contact change, especially in the case of the western Macedonian dialects, which may be characterized by the substantial enrichment of the perfect system which has now three different perfect constructions. From the formal point of view, we have here also the case of structural calques with a high level of grammaticalization. Nevertheless, the very fact that new categories arise leads us to conclusions about the different character of the situation in this case. The more or less massive shift of the Aromanian population to Macedonian (and then the processes of the linguistic accommodation between the different groups of Macedonian speakers) might be the key component of the development of the region's perfect system (see also above Section 2.).

The cases of the *matter replication* are nearly absent in our material. It is well-known that the matter replication is a much rarer phenomenon than pattern replication. Its realization in the contact situations is determined by various special factors. We may mention among them: intensive intrasententional code-switching, a high level of metatypy (see below), the emotional-pragmatic character of the said category (see Gardani 2008, Gardani et al. 2015). However, the general condition which makes matter replication possible (but not necessarily) is the very high level of bi- or multilingualism with the strong dominance of the donor language (see Gardani et al. 2015; Morozova & Rusakov 2019). This condition is

---

[30] In our cases we have also examples of contact-induced change in the frequency of some constructions, for example, the predominance of the analytical future in Judezmo (Joseph, below). Such phenomena ("frequential code-copying" in the terminology of Lars Johansson (2002 et al.)) are sometimes indistinguishable from semantic or/and structural calques (the use of the construction in new contexts increases its frequency).

absent in the majority of our cases.[31] Maybe the only type of the matter replication which does not require a high level of the donor language dominance is the borrowing of the derivational afffixes (Sobolev, below; Joseph, below).

We have in our material a various types of contact phenomena at the *lexical level*: the borrowing of lexical items, lexical calques and phenomena intermediate between the lexical interference and code switching ("nonce-borrowings", code-mixing, insertional code-switching, according the different terminological and methodological approaches).

We have in our material cases of massive borrowing processes (both loanwords and semantic and structural calques) in the kinship term "system" in such different situations as the Mrkovići / Velja Gorana, Golloborda (Morozova, below; Sobolev, below; Morozova 2019a) and Carașova and Iabalcea (Konior, below). The essential difference is that in the Mrkovići / Velja Gorana case we have a more deep "semantic restructuring" of this part of the lexicon; e.g. the Albanian difference between paternal and maternal ancestor is introduced into the BCMS idiom (Morozova, below; Morozova 2018). A version of such restructuring we also have in the Slavic dialect of Karashevo (where the notions "grandson" and "nephew" match under Romanian influence) but not in Golloborda. The reason of the difference is the very character of the contacts in the first area, which included and include the partial shift from Albanian to BCMS and, as a consequence, the imposition of this semantic difference (Morozova, below). Such changes in Karashevo may be the indices of the beginning of a change in language dominance or, to the contrary, results of older processes.

It should be noted that in the field of the lexical phenomena the notion of E.R.I.C. loans ("Essentially Rooted In Conversation") introduced by Victor Friedman and Brian Joseph (Friedman & Joseph 2014; 2017) may be helpful: "ERIC loans include closed classes and generally borrowing-resistant items including kinship terms, numerals, and pronouns, conversationally based elements such as greetings, idioms, and phraseology, and discourse elements such as connectives and interjections. These are important as they are precisely the lexical items that depend on – and thus demonstrate – close, intimate, and sustained everyday interactions among speakers" (Friedman & Joseph 2015: 78).

---

31 We might expect – to some degree – cases of matter replication in Aromanian dialects – the highly interfered idioms with nearly absolute dominance of L2. In fact we do have such a case in the Aromanian dialect of Gorna Belica (outside but rather close to the Prespa zone), where the Albanian admirative suffix was borrowed and, in consequence, a new evidential grammatical category was created (Friedman 1994). The matter replication might be supported here by the trilingual sociolinguistic history of the Aromanian dialect of Gorna Belica (Arumanian-Albanian-Macedonian, see Morozova & Rusakov 2019).

There are rather terminological and/or closed lexical classes where the contact influence is especially strong: names of the months (Mrkovići, Albanian > BCMS, structural calques; Morozova, below), animal breeding (Golloborda, Albanian > BCMS, lexical loan; Sobolev, below), wedding terminology (Iabalcea, Slavic > Romanian, preserving the semantic structure of terminological system; Konior, below).

In cases of certain thematic lexical groups we have a high level of similarity among the lexicons of the two languages with respect to such groups: BCMS and Albanian kinship terminology in Velja Gorana; Romanian (with Slavic loans) wedding terminology in Iabalcea and Slavic wedding terminology in Carașova. The question is whether we can extrapolate this similarity beyond the limits of such thematic groups. This question needs further research, foremost in the sphere of the distribution and combinatory features of the potential inter-language equivalents, their use in the indirect meanings and so on.

Another group of E.R.I.C. loans in our materials is represented by "discourse markers, particles, and connectors" (Morozova, below) which may be called "utterance modifiers" as in (Matras 1998), i.e., elements which are often borrowed from the pragmatically dominant language. Such elements (from Romanian) are used, for example in the Slavic speech of Krashovani Slavic speakers (Konior, below). It is interesting that in Velja Gorana BCMS utterance modifiers are used in the Albanian speech of both Mrkovići women originally monolingual in Slavic and young Albanian women acquiring BCMS, but not in the speech of bilingual men. This illustrates very clearly, on the one hand, the thesis (discussed in detail in Morozova, below, and Morozova & Rusakov (2019)) that balanced bilingualism results from many individual micro-situations which may have a rather unbalanced character, and, on the other hand, that some Gorana speakers (the bilingual Gorana men) truly do demonstrate balanced bilingual language competence.

The use of "utterance modifiers" belongs to the zone between lexical borrowings and code switching. As for *code switching* in general, our materials demonstrate a wide spectrum of such phenomena dependent on the character of specific (socio)linguistic situations. They include:

– Intensive intrasentential code switching in the case of the strong linguistic dominance of the one language and the need to speak another one. The clearer example of this situation is the Aromanian speech in Prespa (with the linguistic dominance of L2, see Makarova, below). To a lesser degree a similar situation is described by Morozova (below) for middle-aged Mrkovići women originally monolingual in Slavic while speaking Albanian (Velja Gorana, with the linguistic dominance of L1).

- The near absence of intrasententional code switching, motivated (but unmarked!) inersententional codeswitching by "balanced bilinguals" in Velja Gorana (Morozova, below; Morozova 2018; 2019b) and Himara (Sobolev, below).
- The code switching of the insertional type (nonce-borrowings hardly distinguished from the real lexical loans) in the cases of lexical deficiency in the intra-group communication in the situation of L1 dominance (Golloborda in Sobolev, below; Morozova (2018; 2019b); Caraşova in Konior, below).

Two points pertaining to both grammar and vocabulary (and to a certain extent to phonetics) should be added.

1. Communicative-pragmatic moments play a big role in the rapid spread of contact phenomena, witness the discussion of utterance modifiers above. With respect to grammar, the differences in the development of Balkan evidentiality represented in our volume (the use of the the pluperfect with evidential meaning in Judezmo (Joseph, below)) belong to this sphere. In all Balkan languages (Turkish, Albanian, Bulgarian, Macedonian, Romanian), evidential meanings are expressed very differently (both semantically and formally). It seems that the very means by which discourse is organized is copied (see Aikhenwald 2007: 26–28); yet each language builds the system of evidential markers from the improvised material at its disposal. Thus what we have here is something resembling grammatical loan creations (Weinreich 1953: 51).[32]
2. We may note that – even in cases of respectively heavy modification of the grammatical system – we still do not observe anything which might be interpreted as metatypy.[33] Therefore, even the contact-influenced dialects of Aromanian, Albanian and Macedonian described in the book fail to demonstrate full similarity in their perfect system (Makarova, below). I think that cases of "total" metatypy do not exist and (probably) cannot exist. As for cases of partial metatypy (see, for example the Takia and Waskia cases described in Ross 1996, or the North Russian Romani dialect, see Heine and Kuteva 2005:

---

[32] See also the different ways to express the evidential meanings in the Romani varieties on the Balkans (see Asenova, Marku 2020; Friedman 2013).

[33] Over recent years Malcolm Ross has modified the very notion of metatypy. Now he understands metatypy rather as a syntactic reordering of the elements of syntactic construction; i.e. as a second stage of the process of syntactic calquing (Ross 2007). Changes in word order are comparatively rare in our sample, as elsewhere (see Matras 2007: 60). The interlanguage identification of two constructions does not imply the necessity of reordering their elements. In this connection, cases of optional word order changes in Karashevo are of the great interest (Konior, below).

185), all of them are characterized by the strong linguistic dominance of the donor language (L2).[34]

5 Some conclusions

All our main situations demonstrate a rather modest scale of contact-influenced change. We have here neither cases of matter replication, nor cases of deep metatypic change.[35] Nevertheless, we have no reason to state that the processes described in this book for Golloborda, Mrkovići and Velja Gorana, Himara, the Prespa region, Carașova and Iabalcea differ principally from the spreading of the majority of "classical" grammatical Balkanisms which represent the different types of calques along with processes of grammaticalization.[36] The case of the development of "genitival constructions" in Velja Gorana with its mutual "ping-pong" like contact influence is here especially instructive.

It is interesting also that none of our cases exhibit instances of real linguistic simplification. To the contrary, there are here some examples of clear increases in complexity: the development of the perfect system in Western Macedonian dialects, lexical borrowing which coexists along with the "native" words (e.g., in Mrkovići / Velja Gorana (Morozova, below)), insertion of "alien" phonemes with lexical borrowings. These facts may be explained by the long-standing contacts inside or between relatively closed communities (see Trudgill 2011).

Doubtlessly not all Balkanisms developed in such a way. For example, the deep similarity of the nominal system between Albanian and Balkan Romance languages needed, so it seems, more intensive contact (perhaps with processes of partial language shift and imposition on a greater scale). The situations described in this book do not exhaustively reflect all the possible types of situations that existed in the Balkans in the past, but we may suppose that they might be quite *typical* for those of the past.

---

[34] I do not use here the rather vague notion of *convergence* (see Wiemer and Wälchli 2012: 36–42).
[35] This may be explained by the fact that among our cases (save for the Prespa Aromanians) there are no situations of L2 dominance. Such situations are, however quite widespread in the Balkans, see, for example, Megleno-Romanian communities, some Slavic communities in Albania and Greece, and some Romani communities.
[36] I do not discuss the problem of the contact-induced grammaticalization in this paper. It should be noted only that often it is very difficult to distinguish cases of parallel grammaticalization and those of the contact induced gramamticalizaton (see discussion in Wiemer & Wälchli 2012: 18–44).

References

Aikhenvald, Alexandra Y. 2007. *Grammars in Contact. A Cross-Linguistic Perspective*. In Alexandra Y. Aikhenvald & Richard M.W. Dixon (eds.), *Grammars in Contact. A Cross-Linguistic Typology* (Explorations in Linguistic Typology 4), 1–66. Oxford, UK: Oxford University Press.

Aikhenvald, Alexandra Y. 2010. *Language Contact in Amazonia*. Oxford: Oxford University Press.

Asenova, Petia & Marku, Xristina. 2020. K probleme evidencialnosti v jazykah balkanskogo jazykovogo sojuza [On the problem of the evidentiality in the Balkan languages]. *Acta Linguistica Petropolitana* 16 (2). 11–53.

Campbell, Lyle. 2006. Areal linguistics: A closer scrutiny. In Yaron Matras, April McMahon & Nigel Vincent (eds.), *Linguistic Areas. Convergence in Historial and Typological Perspective*, 1–31. Houndsmills: Palgrave Macmillan.

Coetsem, F. van. 1988. *Loan Phonology and the Two Transfer Types in Language Contact*. Dordrecht: Foris.

Curtis, Matthew Cowan. 2012. *Slavic-Albanian Language Contact, Convergence, and Coexistence*. Ohio State University Doctoral Dissertation.

Dahl, Östen. 2001. Principles of areal typology. In Martin Haspelmath, Ekkehard Konig, Wulf Osterreicher & Wolfgang Raible (eds.), *Language Typology and Language Universals*, Vol. 2, 1456–1470. Berlin: de Gruyter.

Demiraj, Shaban. 1985. *Gramatikë historike e gjuhës shqipe* [Albanian Historical Grammar]. Tirana: "8 Nëntori".

Desnitskaya, Agniya V. 1976. Evoliutsiia dialektnoi sistemy v usloviiakh etnicheskogo smesheniia (iz istorii sloviano-albanskikh iazykovykh kontaktov) [Evolution of a dialectical system under conditions ethnic mixing (from the history of Albanian-Slavic language contacts)]. *Voprosy etnogeneza i etnicheskoi istorii slavian i vostochnykh romantsev* [Issues of ethnogenesis and ethnic history of Slavs and Eastern Romance speakers], 186–197. Moscow: Nauka.

Drinka, Bridget. 2017. *Language Contact in Europe: The Periphrastic Perfect through History*. Cambridge: Cambridge University Press.

Fiedler, Wilfried. 2004. *Das albanische Verbalsystem in der Sprache des Gjon Buzuku (1555)*. Prishtinë: Akademia e shkencave e arteve e Kosovës.

Friedman, Victor. 1976. Synchrony and Diachronic Syntax: The Macedonian Perfect. In Sanford B. Steever, Carol A. Walker & Salikoko S. Mufwene (eds.), *Papers from the Parasession on Diachronic Syntax, Chicago Linguistic Society*, 96–104.

Friedman, Victor. 1994. Surprise! Surprise! Aumanian has had an admirative. *Indiana Slavic Studies* 7. 79–89.

Friedman, Victor. 2013. The Use of *li* as a Marker of Evidential Strategy in Romani. *Săpostavitelno Ezikoznanie / Contrastive Linguistics* 38 (2–3). 253–261.

Friedman, Victor & Brian Joseph. 2014. Lessons from Judezmo about the Balkan sprachbund and contact linguistics. *International Journal of the Sociology of Language* 226. 3–23.

Gardani, Francesco. 2008. *Borrowing of Inflectional Morphemes in Language Contact*. Frankfurt am Main: Peter Lang.

Gardani, Francesco, Peter Arkadiev & Nino Amiridze (eds.). 2015. *Borrowed Morphology*. Berlin: Walter de Gruyter.

Gjinari, Jorgji, Bahri Beci, Gjovalin Shkurtaj & Xheladin Gosturani. 2007–2008. *Atlasi dialektologjik i gjuhës shqipe* [Albanian dialect atlas], Vol. 1–2. Napoli, Italy: Universita degli studi di Napoli l'Orientale, Tirana: Akademia e shkencave e Shqipërisë.

Gołąb, Zbigniew. 1997. The ethnic background and internal linguistic mechanism of the so-called Balkanization of Macedonian. *Balkanistica* 10. 13–19.

Haspelmath, Martin. 2009. Lexical borrowing: Concepts and issues. In Haspelmath, Martin & Uri Tadmor (eds.), *Loanwords in the world's languages: A comparative handbook*, 35–54. Berlin: De Gruyter Mouton.

Heine, Berndt & Tania Kuteva. 2005. *Language Contact and Grammatical Change*. Cambridge: Cambridge University Press.

Johansson, Lars. 2002. Contact-induced change in a code-copying framework. In Mari C. Jones & Edith Esch (eds.), *Language Change (The Interplay of Internal, External and Extra-Linguistic Factors)*, 285–313. Berlin: De Gruyter Mouton.

Joseph, Brian D. 1983. *The synchrony and diachrony of the Balkan infinitive: a study in areal, general, and historical linguistics*. Cambridge: Cambridge University Press.

Joseph, Brian. 2010. Language contact in the Balkans. In Raymond Hickey (ed.), *The Handbook of Language Contact*, 618–633. Malden, MA: Wiley-Blackwell.

Joseph, Brian & Victor Friedman. 2017. *Reassessing sprachbunds: A view from the Balkans*. In Raymond Hickey (ed.), *The Cambridge Handbook of Areal Linguistics*, 63–90. Cambridge: Cambridge University Press.

Jovićević, Andrija. 1922. Crnogorsko primorje i Krajina [The Montenegro coast and Krajina]. *Srpski etnografski zbornik*, 11. Beograd: Srpska kraljevska akademija.

Ismajli, Rexhep. 2015. Rreth sllavizmave të shqipes [On Slavicisms in Albanian]. In Rexep Ismajli (ed.), *Studime për historinë e shqipes në kontekstin ballkanik*, 469–511. Prishtinë: Akademia e shkencave dhe e arteve të Kosovës.

Koptjevskaja-Tamm, Maria & Bernhard Walchli. 2001. The Circum-Baltic languages. An areal-typological approach. In Östen Dahl & Maria Koptjevskaja-Tamm (eds.), *Circum-Baltic languages*, Vol. 1, 313–337. Amsterdam & Philadelphia: John Benjamins.

Lindstedt, Jouko. 2000. Linguistic Balkanization: Contact-induced change by mutual reinforcement. In Dicky G. Gilbers, John Nerbonne & Jos Shaeken (eds.), *Languages in Contact (= Studies in Slavic and General Linguistics)*, Vol. 28, 231–246. Amsterdam & Atlanta, GA: Rodopi.

Lüpke, Friederike. 2016. Uncovering Small-Scale Multilingualism. *Critical Multilingualism Studies* 4 (2). 35–74.

Makarova, Anastasia L. 2018. *Preterital'naia sistema govorov regiona Prespa – makedonskogo, albanskogo i arumynskogo* [The Preterite system in the subdialects of the Prespa region: Macedonian, Albanian and Aromanian]. St. Petersburg: Institut lingvisticheskikh issledovanii RAN Dissertation.

Matras, Yaron. 1998. Utterance modifiers and universals of grammatical borrowing. *Linguistics* 36. 281–331.

Matras, Yaron. 2007. The borrowability of structural categories. In Yaron Matras & Jeanette Sakel (eds.), *Grammatical Borrowing in Cross-Linguistic Perspective*, 31–73. Berlin: Mouton de Gruyter.

Matras, Yaron. 2009. *Language Contact*. Cambridge: Cambridge University Press.

Morozova, Maria S. 2018. "Problema vybora": perekliuchenie kodov v balkanskom poliloge ["The problem of choice": code-switching in the Balkan polilogue]. *Kruglyi stol Tsentra lingvokul'turnykh issledovanii BALCANICA "Balkanskii polilog: kommunikatsiia v kul'turno-slozhnykh soobshchestvakh", Pamiati Viacheslava Vsevolodovicha Ivanova*, 49–67. Moscow: Institut slavianovedeniia RAN.

Morozova, Maria S. 2019a. Language contact in social context: Kinship terms and kinship relations of the Mrkovići of southern Montenegro. *Journal of Language Contact* 12 (2). 305–343.

Morozova, Maria S. 2019b. Osobennosti kommunikatsii v slavianskikh soobshchestvakh Albanii: interferentsiia i perekliuchenie kodov pri neravnovesnom bilingvizme [Features of communication in the Slavic communities of Albania: interference and code-switching under conditions of unequal bilingualism]. In Irina A. Sedakova, Maxim M. Makartsev & Tatiana V. Tsiv'ian (eds.), *Balkanskii tezaurus: kommunikatsiia v slozhno-kul'turnykh obshchestvakh na Balkanakh* (Balkanskie chteniia vol.15), 82–88. Moscow: Institut slavianovedeniia RAN.

Morozova, Maria S. & Alexander Yu. Rusakov. 2018. Albansko-chernogorskoe iazykovoe pogranich'e: v poiskakh "sbalansirovannogo iazykovogo kontakta [The Albanian-Montenegrin language boundary: in search of "balanced language contact"]. *Slověne* 2, 258–302.

Morozova, Maria S. & Alexander Yu. Rusakov. 2019. Iazykovye kontakty v usloviiakh trilingvizma: zaimstvovanie materii (matter borrowing) v balkanskikh dialektakh [Language contact under trilingual conditions: matter borrowing in Balkan dialects]. In Irina A. Sedakova, Maxim M. Makartsev & Tatiana V. Tsiv'ian (eds.), *Balkanskii tezaurus: kommunikatsiia v slozhno-kul'turnykh obshchestvakh na Balkanakh*, (Balkanskie chteniia vol. 15), 75–81. Moscow: Institut slavianovedeniia RAN.

Ross, Malcolm D. 1996. Contact-induced change and the comparative method: Cases from Papua New Guinea. In Mark Durie & Malcolm D. Ross (eds.), *The comparative method reviewed: Regularity and irregularity in language change*, 180–217. New York: Oxford University Press.

Ross, Malcolm. 2007. Calquing and metatypy. *Journal of language contact*. Theme 1, 116–143.

Rusakov, Alexander Yu. 2001. The North Russian Romani Dialect: Interference and Code Switching. In Östen Dahl & Maria Koptjevskaja-Tamm (eds.), *Circum-Baltic languages*. Vol. 1, 313–337. Amsterdam & Philadelphia: John Benjamins.

Rusakov, Alexander Yu. 2013. Nekotorye izoglossy na albanskoi dialektnoi karte (k voprosu o vozniknovenii i rasprostranenii balkanizmov albanskogo iazyka) [Some isoglosses on the Albanian dialectical map (toward the question of the emergence and distribution of Balkanisms in Albanian)]. In Viacheslav V. Ivanov (ed.), *Issledovaniia po tipologii slavianskikh, baltiiskikh i balkanskikh iazykov [Research on typology of Slavic, Baltic and Balkan languages]*, 113–174. St. Petersburg: Aleteia.

Singer, Ruth & Salome Harris. 2016. What practices and ideologies support small-scale multilingualism? A case study of Warruwi Community, northern Australia. *International Journal of the Sociology of Language* 241. 163–208.

Sobolev, Andrey N. 2012. On redundancy in Albanian. In Domosiletskaia, Marina V., Alvina V. Zhugra, Maria S. Morozova & Alexander Yu. Rusakov (eds.), *Sovremennaia albanistika: dostizheniia i perspektivy* [Contemporary Albanology: Achievements and Perspectives], 407–412. St. Petersburg: Nestor-Istoriia.

Sobolev, Andrey N. 2013. *Osnovy lingvokul'turnoi antropogeografii Balkanskogo poluostrova. Tom I. Homo balcanicus i ego prostranstvo* [Foundations of linguocultural anthropogeography on the Balkan peninsula. Vol. 1. Homo balcanicus and his space]. St. Petersburg, München: Nauka, Otto Sagner Verlag.

Sobolev, Andrey N. 2015. Mrkovichi (i Gorana): iazyki i dialekty chernogorskogo Primor'ia v kontekste noveishikh balkanisticheskikh issledovanii [Mrkovići (and Gorana): Languages and dialects of the Montenegro coast in the context of recent Balkan research]. In Demiraj Bardhyl (ed.), *Sprache und Kultur der Albaner: Zeitliche und räumliche Dimensionen. Akten der 5. Deutsch-albanischen kulturwissenschaftlichen Tagung (Albanien, Buçimas bei Pogradec, 5.–8. Juni 2014)*, 533–556. Wiesbaden: Harrassowitz.

Sobolev, Andrey N. 2017. Iazyki simbioticheskikh soobschestv Zapadnykh Balkan: grecheskii i albanskii iazyki v sele Paliasa v kraine Himara, Albaniia [Languages in the Western Balkan Symbiotic Societies: Greek and Albanian in Palasa, Himara, Albania]. *Vestnik Sankt-Peterburgskogo gosudarstvennogo universiteta. Iazyk i literatura* 14 (3). 421–442.

Sobolev, Andrey N. & Aleksandr A. Novik. 2013. *Golo Bordo (Gollobordë), Albaniia. Iz materialov balkanskoi ekspeditsii RAN i SPbGU 2008–2010 gg.* [Golo Bordo (Gollobordë) Albania. From the materials of the RAS and SPSU expedition of 2008–2010]. Munich: Otto Sagner Verlag, St. Petersburg: Nauka.

Steinke, Klaus & Xhelal Ylli. 2008. *Die slavischen Minderheiten in Albanien (SMA). Vol. 2. Teil Golloborda – Herbel – Kërçishti i Epërm.* Munich: Verlag Otto Sagner.

Thomason, Sarah Grey. 2001. *Language contact.* Edinburgh: Edinburgh University Press.

Thomason, Sarah Grey & Terrence Kaufman. 1988. *Language Contact, Creolization, and Genetic Linguistics.* Berkeley: University of California Press.

Tomić, Olga Mišeska. 2006. *Balkan Sprachbund. Morpho-Syntactic Features.* Dordrecht: Springer.

Trudgill, Peter. 2003. Modern Greek dialects. A preliminary classification. *Journal of Greek Linguistics* 4. 45–64.

Weinreich, Uriel. 1953. *Languages in Contact. Findings and Problems.* New York: Linguistic Circle of New York.

Wiemer, Björn & Bernhard Wälchli. 2012. Contact-induced grammatical change: Diverse phenomena, diverse perspectives, In Björn Wiemer, Bernhard Wälchli & Björn Hansen (eds.), *Grammatical Replication and Borrowability in Language Contact*, 3–64. Berlin & Boston: Mouton de Gruyter.

Winford, Daniel. 2003. *An Introduction to Contact Linguistics.* Oxford: Blackwell Publishing.

Zheltova, Ekaterina A. 2015. *Diskursivnye strategii konstruirovaniia identichnosti v grekogovoriashchikh soobshchestvakh Albanii (Khimara i Dervichani)* [Discursive strategies of identity construction in the Greek dialect communities of Albania (Himara and Dervicani)]. St. Petersburg: Evropeiskii universitet v Sankt-Peterburge. Master's Thesis.

Andrey N. Sobolev

Separation and Symbiosis between Slavs and Albanians as Continuum of Linguistic Contact Situations: New Challenges for New Data

Abstract: This chapter[1] addresses issues of general relevance for the book as a whole, including linguistic interference, integration and dis-integration in a continuum of linguistic contact situations from separation to symbiosis, and within polylingual and polyethnic societies. The determinant linguistic features of the Balkans are the result of structural language change induced by language contact and directed towards a Sprachbund as a particular, convergent group of languages and an interlinguistic continuum with no impermeable barriers. We need to account for and distinguish prior structural changes that have resulted from contact from those which have resulted from internal development. The chapter addresses extremely rare cases that allow the Balkan linguist to observe immediately at least a phase of the integration process at work among significantly large groups of people in zones of ongoing direct intense and intimate language contact. The paradigm of field research into non-dominant bilingualism in the Balkans is presented. This chapter is based on recent field data from areas of contact with dominant and non-dominant Albanian-Slavic bilingualism in Albania and Montenegro. The data from a Macedonian L1 Muslim community in Golloborda (Eastern Albania) with no official ethnic minority status is presented. The dialect is identified clearly as a Macedonian Debar variety. Phonetics/phonology, morphology, morphosyntax, syntax and vocabulary of the idiom reveal the whole vitality and local dominance of Slavic L1 under some influence of Albanian L2, which is otherwise dominant in the region and in the country as a whole. Texts in Macedonian L1 are published, showing absence of code switching and language hybridization. Sufficient data from the neighbouring Albanian-speaking community is provided, evincing the absence of any intimate language contacts in the area which could be interpreted as ethnic and linguistic separation. No strong correlations between the qualities of bilingualism, code switching strategies, bilateral linguistic accommodation, past language change situation and social praxis can be identified. Two phonologies and two grammars coexist

---

1 This research was made possible by a grant from the Russian Science Foundation (the projects "From Separation to Symbiosis: South Eastern European languages and cultures in contact", No. 14-18-01405 and "Balkan bilingualism in dominant and equilibrium contact situations in diatopy, diachrony and diastraty", No. 19-18-00244).

https://doi.org/10.1515/9781501509254-002

in bilingual individuals, whereas parts of the lexicon tend to form a joint stock of highly semantically specialized lexical items. There is a gap between the language of our bilingual informants and their speech behaviour. In speech behaviour involving actual interference, the 'alien' L2 substance can be used both with 'alien' L2 or 'one's own' (L1) rules with very different degrees of integration into 'one's own' L1. The data from the Slavic-Albanian symbiotic polylingual community in the Mrkovići area in Montenegro is used to provide a base comparison, with bilingualism of a non-dominant type with functional balance between L1 and L2 in language practice and competency. It is claimed that, at the present state of research, there is no possibility of finding out any strong correlation between the types of language change and the types of language contact situations, including the possibility of balanced bilingualism without dominance. Some outlines for future research are provided.

1 Introduction

Unlike Slavic or Romance linguistics, which deal with closely related Slavic or Romance languages, Balkan linguistics might be understood as both the sum and the derivative of several academic disciplines as they apply to the languages and cultures of the Balkan Peninsula. Though these languages are not closely related to each other, they form, or have formed, either a geographic (areal) or a convergent group with areal features; i.e., a Sprachbund (see contradictory approaches in Bisang (2006); Campbell (2006); Friedman (2006); Thomason (2006); Sobolev (2012; 2013; 2016); Friedman & Joseph (2017); Drinka (2017), among others).

So long the historical and linguistic sources on natural Balkan language evolution over the last two thousand years are insufficient or utterly inadequate, we have, generally speaking, only the contemporary linguistic **results of language change** that can be set against our knowledge regarding the proto-stages of some language families (Latin for Balkan Romance, Proto-Slavic and Old Church Slavonic for Balkan Slavic), yet no comparable historical evidence for Albanian. It is widely accepted, that the *facts* of language change observed in the Balkans are the outcome of linguistic interference, integration and dis-integration that must be *reconstructed* for historical situations (Hinrichs, Büttner 1999). The crux of the question is, nevertheless, how to make use of linguistic methods to account for and distinguish prior structural changes that have resulted from contact from those which have resulted from internal development.

The linguistic development of the Balkans sets before the student of *Slavic languages* basic questions related to Slavic studies that are both general and particular to the field. General questions involve determining the main principles behind the formation of the Balkans' linguistic landscape and the establishment of the specific contact situations that were "responsible" for the occurrence of individual phenomena and groups. These questions include: which languages were involved in the contact, what the character of the interaction between groups of speakers of these languages was, and the chronological and geographical scope of contact. There are particular questions aimed at establishing the role that Slavic languages and their speakers play in the formation of the linguistic and cultural landscape of the Balkan Peninsula. For example, in which cases were Slavic languages and cultures donors, in which cases were they recipients for other Balkan languages and cultures, and in which cases were they neither? When engaging in an analysis of innovations which are attributable to an indexable contact internal to the language's system, it is important to ascertain: the changes that occur as a result of contact and in which languages they occur, the features they exhibit and the extent to which they are fixed, and the causes of unevenness within the internal system.

Until the field develops its own unified method and approach, there will remain different ways to present *results* of contact-induced language change in different genres. These include monographs (the most recent English ones being Curtis (2012), Dombrowski (2013), Wahlström (2015), Prendergast (2017)), or highly time and labour-consuming elaborations of pan-Balkan etymological dictionaries (Domosiletskaia 2002; Sukhachev, in preparation), cross-linguistic areal-typological dialect studies (Cyxun 1981) and linguistic atlases. From the end of the 20th to the beginning of the 21st century, the compilers of the *Minor Dialectological Atlas of Balkan Languages* (Domosiletskaia et al. 1998; MDABL 2003–2018) attempted to confirm the hypothesis that a Balkan Sprachbund exists as a particular, convergent group of languages and an interlinguistic continuum with no barriers. To this end we have directed our research toward living territorial dialects[2] and attempted to establish, describe and chart the maximum number of similarities and differences between the most *representative* dialects of the principal Balkan languages. In particular, our attempt was to:

---

[2] The relevance of the approach we have been taking since 1995 has been confirmed by the most recent conclusions of our American colleagues in a particular case related to Slavic-Albanian language contact in the Western Balkans. They write: "Because contact is ongoing and the effects of contact also continue into the present, it is not only historical accounts of the languages that must consider the inheritance of Slavic-Albanian contact, but also synchronic descriptions of these languages, particularly those documenting the living manifestations of the languages: the dialects" (Curtis 2012: 286).

1. resolve the problem of identifying interlingual linguistic units and the way in which they functioned in the language contact situation;
2. resolve the problem of linguistic signs being systemically consistent and mutually implicative in their internal and external aspects and to establish a hierarchy of these characteristics;
3. determine the units of language structure that were sustainable and susceptible to contact-induced innovation. This involved determining the inherent linguistic features behind the processes and results of contact as well as contributing to a typology of contact-induced changes at the language level and establishing a relative hierarchy;
4. describe the role of each language group (and/or language) as a donor and recipient in the Balkan linguistic community. This required focusing on small or already extinct languages of the peninsula;
5. establish the relationship of the socio-linguistic situation and the patently observable results of contact;
6. answer questions about the relationship between the presence of a linguistic community of the convergent type and the presence of common properties between respective ethnic groups at other non-linguistic levels (especially with respect to material and non-material culture);
7. answer the question as to whether the absence of dominant/subordinate relations between speakers of contact languages and between the cultures and languages (prestigious and non-prestigious languages and language forms) themselves are a necessary condition for the formation of a convergent linguistic group;
8. examine the problem of the unlimited permeability of languages and cultures and the unlimited possibilities of mutual understanding on the part of their human instantiations.

We came to the conclusion that the necessary and adequate conditions for including a language in a *convergent group* (e.g., a Sprachbund) involved determining regular correspondences between the functions of linguistic units at all language levels (substantial convergence in this case would be an unavoidable accompanying symptom). If languages whose speakers are in direct territorial proximity do not demonstrate such systematic, regular correspondences, they should be recognized as a (geographic) areal group. One may allow that a (geographic) areal group can be integrated into a convergent group and the opposite – that a convergent group be de-integrated into a (geographic) areal group – as, apparently, is happening and has happened in the Balkans (Rusakov & Sobolev 2008). The principal stimulus for including a group of languages in a convergent group is not the widespread concept of "close, or intimate linguistic contact" but the long-term bilingualism of large groups of people and their subsequent monolingualization.³ This must be correlated to the constant and dominant geographical, political, economic and religious features of the Balkan societies and *peninsula in general*.⁴

Recent research has produced extremely valuable lists of phenomena for theoretical interpretation. Consider, for example, the data illustrating contact-induced changes in substance and function (with regard to matter and pattern, see Rusakov & Sobolev (2008)) in phonology and morphosyntax in four areas of Slavic-Albanian contact (as compiled in Curtis (2012)). In contrast with the *results* of contact, the causes, actors, drivers, mechanisms, and stimuli of language integration and dis-integration, on the one hand, and barriers to these *processes*, on the other, often cannot be directly *observed*, but must in the main be *reconstructed* through different procedures of linguistic research. Specialists in language contact, however, find it difficult to "tease apart" the processes which led to the emergence of a Sprachbund, leaving the issue unresolved (Muysken 2013: 726).

Nevertheless, there are extremely rare cases that allow the Balkan linguist to observe immediately the integration process at work among significantly large groups of people at least at some phase, such as those in the zones of ongoing direct language contact. Immediate observation of "contact at work" is possible

---

3 It is well known, for example, that part of the Slavic population of different regions of Albania, Kosovo and Western Macedonia were Albanianized in the Middle Ages and in the Modern period. A portion of the Aromanian population was Slavicized and Albanianized, among others (see the most recent publications of, for example Curtis (2012; Dombrowski 2013). The field can be home to even more generalizing statements, witness Curtis' assessment: "As the historian John Fine rightly remarks, "The Albanians did not have a single ancestor in one or the other of these pre-Slavic peoples; the present-day Albanians, like all Balkan peoples, are an ethnic mixture and in addition to this main ancestor they contain an admixture of Slavic, Greek, Vlach, and Romano-Italian ancestry" [1983: 11–12]. The same precaution applies to *all Balkan peoples*, including the Slavic populations discussed here as well. Although names for languages and communities may overlap, there is no stable, persistent connection between biological descent and linguistic descent." (Curtis 2012: 18).

4 One can, in particular, consider this prominent feature to be an incessantly productive element in the Balkan linguistic area: "…it appears that, when the southwest Slavic area (Slovenia, Croatia, and Serbian dialects, as well as an eastern Serbian dialect and western Bulgaria) is examined with an areal-typological view to the general Balkan context, there emerges a Balkan linguistic **west** (this includes Albanian and Aromanian dialects, along with some Slavic dialects of Western Macedonia). This western area is quite obviously opposed to the Balkan east and southeast (predominantly Greek-Bulgarian-east Macedonian). Indeed, this testifies to the depth of divisions within the peninsula's linguistic landscape which have been sustained over the whole of its known history. This extends from the Illyrian-Thracian and the Latin-Greek opposition to the well-known division of Turkic Balkan dialects into western and eastern groups)" (Sobolev 2003: 23).

in the examination of *speech behaviour*, when sufficient amounts of spontaneous speech; i.e. texts produced by representative bi- and monolingual informants, are available (see Adamou 2016). But still this kind of research remains a qualitative investigation of processes that are not easily quantified.

Particular consideration in research on linguistic *results* of language change is given to the significance of Balkan states' language politics through history. This includes, among others, the rejection of polycentric proscriptive rules, the elimination of sub-standard options, the assimilation of linguistic and ethnic minorities, the struggle for recognition of the global value of individual ethnic languages.

2 Convergence and synthesis vs. separation

The long-standing bilingualism among relatively large groups of people can be observed at present in different regions of the Western Balkans where we can collect and analyse necessary and sufficient material on ethnocultural interferences in order to answer the question: in which aspects are the surveyed regions (the minimum anthropo-geographical units that we have called *krajinas* 'micro-regions; ethnic enclaves') places of ethnic, linguistic and cultural convergence and synthesis in general and in which aspects they are such in particular.

For example, the well-known fact that the *krajinas* Malësia, Metohija and Debar are to this day zones of contact and convergence (and perhaps symbiosis) between rather large groups of Slavs and Albanians is worthy of close attention. Among others, of great heuristic value is the answer to the question as to whether the region of Debar and Golloborda was a place of ethnic, linguistic, and cultural convergence in the past and whether it is so at present. We addressed this question in the monograph *Golo Bordo, Albania* (Sobolev & Novik 2013). Albanian and Slavic speaking inhabitants of the region represented language groups that are clearly opposed to each other both historically and synchronically. Thus the only correct designation for these respective populations is Golloborda Albanians and Golo Brdo Slavs. Likewise the region's (Orthodox) Christians and (Sunni) Muslims have been and continue to be clearly historically and synchronically opposed as confessional groups and, in this sense, their respective designations conform to the actual state of affairs.

Golloborda's language convergence takes place while both communities of speakers maintain the source language (which is subjected to phonetic, grammatical and lexical influence) as well as by taking on the character of language shift (a transition of some peripheral part of the community of Albanians to Slavic and Slavic-speakers to Albanian). Ethnic convergence can be observed between representatives of both the Muslim Albanian and the Slavic members of the population. Its basic factors can be attributed to a single religion (Sunni Islam), Slavic speakers' knowledge of Albanian, and loyalty to Albanian culture and statehood. The result of Slavic-Muslim and Albanian convergence is the Albanianization of the former.

The large-scale impression of the Debar region and the Golloborda micro-region as a locus of ethnic, linguistic and cultural convergence must at least be reassessed. Differentiating groups of people along confessional and linguistic grounds is as relevant here as it is everywhere, and the only way to resolve contradictions, apart from emigration, remains the integration of an individual into the dominant and more prestigious group. Successful integration is possible only by rejecting such clear markers as «outsider» – the set of such markers being arbitrary. Divergence is observed between representatives of different religious groups and most clearly manifested in the almost complete emigration of Orthodox from the region. Golloborda nowadays represents a region of de facto linguistic and confessional *separation* between large groups of people.

Starting from our knowledge of Golloborda, our recent observation in the Western Balkans has identified new subjects of research which we had previously anticipated. This was a *symbiotic polylingual community*, whose characteristics were, so it seems, unknown to contemporary Balkan studies.[5] The existence of such communities can be presumed also for previous stages in West Balkan regional history and new research on them allows one to address the problem of the mechanisms of formation and functioning in a Sprachbund. To this purpose, one must synchronically and comparatively examine linguistic elements (idioms) of different ethnic, polylinguistic groups in areas where linguistic and ethnic symbiosis can be found between Slavs, Romanians, Albanians and Greeks.

In particular, we must:

1. identify and give a precise linguistic description of all idioms used (or used in the past) in the given symbiotic, multi-ethnic communities;
2. reveal the degree of mutual isophoneticism, isogrammatism and isosemantism in these idioms;
3. determine the inherited and acquired elements in the speech of bi- and multilingual speakers of Balkan languages in selected areas of ethnic symbiosis while specifying the theoretical content of such attributes as "ancestral"

---

[5] That is to say, the characteristics and patterns of linguistic and ethnic interactions of the members of such a community with each other and the community as a whole with other groups of people were unknown.

and "derived" in relation to structural elements and linguistic units of such idioms;
4. determine the sociolinguistic, cultural, confessional and other parameters influencing the course of the ongoing linguistic and social processes of separation and integration in such communities;
5. critically evaluate the thesis of creolization of the Balkan languages in their history, a thesis which was actively promoted in the 2000s without any basis in the linguistic data (Uwe Hinrichs (2004a; 2004b; 2010), Dieter Stern (2006), and others);
6. objectively assess the pertinent, targeted monolingualization on the part of so-called "titular" ethnic groups (in particular, the monolingualization of Ukrainians, Croats, Albanians in Albania and Kosovo, Romanians, Greeks, and others) against the background of the polylingual symbiotic communities of South Eastern Europe (including the value judgments of the members of such groups with respect to languages).

We can assume that idioms deriving from symbiotic multiethnic, polylingual (Slavic-Romance, Slavic-Albanian, Graeco-Roman, Graeco-Albanian, etc.) groups of people in South Eastern Europe share approximately the same allophone, allogrammatical, allolexical, etc., features at the same degree that the other idioms of these languages do. In addition to internal structural linguistic parameters, the anthropological features that help to constitute the symbiotic community play, in all likelihood, a key role in the failure of mixoglossia.[6] Also important are the relative levels of prestige of belonging to different languages, ethnic and confessional groups and their respective cultures.

3 Research questions

In **synchrony** we are interested in establishing:

1. the features of bilingualism in Balkan pre-industrial symbiotic societies;
2. the number of grammars and lexicons of bilingual speakers (note the well-known claim that "the Balkan languages possess one grammar but different lexicons", see Kopitar (1829 (1945));

---

[6] In particular, membership or non-membership of the core as part of a group is joined to the notion of blood-kinship and in practise requires exo- or, respectively, endogamy for members of that group.

3. the possibility of determining the lexicons and grammars of bilingual speakers using linguistic methods of language and speech behaviour;
4. code-switching strategies;
5. the level of bilateral linguistic accommodation of subdialects in contact;
6. the degree of alloglossy in the framework of closely related dialects.

In **diachrony** we are attempting to distinguish between the past language change situation and a past language maintenance situation that persists despite intensive contact with another language.

Balkan historical linguistics is engaged with the question of whether it was important or just peripheral that bilingual symbiotic societies subsisted in mixoglottic processes of the remote past (Pavlović 1970) in the light of the claim that "linguistic areas emerge exclusively out of contact with multilateral diffusion without any relationship of dominance" (see Bisang 2006: 96).

We intend to reconstruct the process of language change while remaining sceptical about the possibility of finding out any strong correlation between *the types of language change* and *the types of language contact situations*, including the possibility of balanced bilingualism without dominance. From the viewpoint of cultural anthropology, the role of exogamy can be of crucial importance, followed by the questioning of borders or delimitation between partially shared cultures.

4 The paradigm of field research into non-dominant bilingualism in the Balkans

Balkan linguistics does not employ methods of research exclusive to it, nor is its *methodological toolbox* entirely unique. However, a) going beyond individual ethnic languages and the restrictive discourse of nationalist philology, b) appealing not to standard forms of languages but to dialects, c) accounting for speakers' personal histories, including migration, polyglossia and language change, and, finally, considering the language landscape of the peninsula as an interlinguistic continuum in synchrony and in diachrony is the methodological core that dominates engaged Balkan studies. Any approach to linguistics that allows us to a) reveal, consistently describe, and explain the system of interlinguistic similarities and differences among Balkan languages, b) establish which individual languages and dialects are substrates, superstrates and adstrates and, in turn, which are donors and recipients of Balkanization, c) identify and study the isomorphism, isosemanticism and isofunctionality of individual members of a language inventory requires that we appropriately state our object of investigation.

Yet beyond the fact that practically all Balkan languages lack complete etymological and historical dictionaries, dialectological atlases, large collections of dialect texts, and historical texts "in the vernacular", the Balkan linguist is still confronted by the small, fragmentary, and unsystematic, nature of the descriptions that are available. And this is compounded by the often utter incompatibility of material accumulated between languages in ethnically-centred dialectologies, including data in major national language archives and catalogues. In this case *one's own fieldwork* is the only means of resolving these issues in a manner aimed toward attaining high-quality, systematic, and comparable data in suitable quantities that can reveal often extraordinary and irreplaceable facts of these different languages. In the forefront here are methods implemented along the course of the work: selecting sites (point grids), researching and establishing a programme (a linguistic questionnaire and subjects for an open interview), developing criteria for selecting informants, organizing and conducting field research making use of various interview techniques, archiving, transcription and publication of materials.

The bilingualism of a non-dominant type with functional balance between L1 and L2 in language practice and competency is a rare linguistic situation that could amount to causes of convergence of each of the languages without a loss of identity in either. Developing a *paradigm of field research into bilingualism* of this type was new challenge and an important task by itself. It was initially not clear whether it were possible at present for non-dominant or balanced dialect bilingualism to inhabit a traditional, local Balkan society. Nor was it clear what characterized such a society in social and cultural terms, or whether any changes that might take place as a result of contact be subject to observation. We might propose that balanced bilingualism played some role in the emergence and spread of Balkan Sprachbund. This would be evidenced by a higher degree of comprehensive *mutual accommodation of dialects* manifested in the speech of community members in comparison to the speech of monolinguals of the same dialects. *Bilinguals' speech strategies* could, for their part, reveal the mechanisms behind adstrate innovations in L1 and L2 dialects that lead to their divergent development in relation to others.

The field research paradigm was developed on the basis of material obtained in three rural anthropogeographic micro-regions: Mrkovići in Montenegro (Sobolev 2015; Morozova 2019; Morozova & Rusakov 2019), Karashevo in Romania (Konior 2017) and Himara in Albania (Sobolev 2017), where the situation of balanced bilingualism is reproduced for a long period of time without one language replacing the other. The first step in such research is to advance a hypothesis of the existence of the desired linguistic situation in a concrete local community. In the first case, the starting point was an ethnographic report concerning regular penetration of Albanian L2 into the Slavic environment as a result of exogamy (Jovićević 1922). The second was a dialectologist's assumption regarding the exchange of a Slavic language with Romanian in some part of an ethnic group (Syrku 1899). In the third, an acute scientific and public controversy regarding ethnicity and native language (L1 Albanian or Greek?) in a region's population (Nasi et al. 2004). The hypothesis was enforced by the fact that all three of these micro-regions lie along a borderline or, in the case of Karashevo, what once had been one. *The hypothesis was tested* upon high-quality primary materials attained in dialectological expeditions in rural areas. These have been preceded by a survey of the literature and official statistics on the ethnicity, languages and dialects of each microregion, data related to the structure of the contact dialects at all levels, local traditional cultures and religious confession. The research programme was based on a modified version of the lexicographic, syntactic, and ethnographic survey associated with the MDABL. These surveys are distinguished by the completeness of the functional and semantic grid, queries from the respondent in the form of both inter-dialect and inter-language translation, and the attentively-selected range of ethnolinguistic subject matter that is relevant to the Balkan situation and that allows for attaining dialect narratives with extensively interconnected materials and content. The materials obtained by these surveys are thus always to be regulated by the facts of informants' spontaneous speech themselves.

Before *field work* is initiated, researchers need to make contact with local administrative bodies, teachers, cultural workers, and clerics in order to clarify the aims and content of the project and to receive recommendations as to how to conduct interviews with some of the local residents. It is more than just desirable to avoid all contact with members of political parties. The process of searching for and selecting informants undergoes a set approach: an expert assessment of their linguistic competencies takes place with the aim of getting as full and as complete a picture of each of the multi-level markers of the local dialect in their speech. This, in part, means a coherent presentation of the phonetic, morphological, and lexical features of the dialect. No less important is the fullness and precision of their knowledge regarding local traditional culture (folk calendars, family rituals, mythology, traditional craft and industry). Among these, however, it is very important that informants have the capacity to generate well-connected, improvised speech. The informant must be taken as a unique, free, creative personality, i.e., as a subject and not an object of material and social forces. Despite scarce resources, the preference is for a more qualitative than quantitative approach, while some balance in representing speakers from different generations and both sexes is essential.

The *interview* process must avoid suggestive and prejudiced questions as well as questions related to identity. At the same time, inclusion on the part of the interviewer can be quite valuable, with the use of local discourse markers and an active and deep immersion in the topic of conversation. It is perfectly acceptable to employ the main features of both contact languages in their local dialect forms so as to create one's own research idiolect that can then be adapted to specific communicative situations to reduce the "outsider effect". A particular feature of Russian Balkan studies is that it tends not to use local native speakers as collectors of primary research materials. Hidden recording is not permitted. Audio and video recording, as well as the recording and further publication of informants' personal information, is allowed only with express consent. So as to penetrate more deeply into the process and content of the conversation, it is useful for an interviewer to make use of a written dialectologists' notebook and not to rely solely on recording technology and their own short-term memory.

Should it be established that the whole society in question is completely monolingual, its linguistic situation is not of interest. Should it be established that the society in question is, in whole or in part, bilingual and is subject to examination, then the *prepared programme* begins. For members of the monolingual part of the community the recording takes place in one language, for those of the bilingual in both. In any case it is essential to conduct an expert assessment of speakers' linguistic competencies. A useful recommendation is to first record a narrative related to traditional culture appealing to the speech patterns of elder informants. It is better to work with single speakers and not with a group at once. It is usually the case in patriarchal Balkan communities that the first informants are men. They can be asked about the origins and history of the locality, krajina, tribe, their own kind, traditions, the languages used in that microregion and those used by neighbouring ethnic groups. Aside from the researcher showing respect for the numerous rules of Balkan etiquette, this allows one to find reliable reference points for subsequent conversations with both the same informant and with others. Narratives should be given a preliminary analysis at the end of the same working day. Then one can go on to record lexical information (for example the lexical and semantic groups which are well-known to all those in rural communities: "body parts", "terms of kinship", "animal husbandry in sheep and goats", "days of the week and months", "calendar rituals", "family rituals", "mythology", and the like). This involves the elicitation of grammatical examples, records of new narratives along with the personal history of the interlocutor, his or her marriage and family members. Researchers must be sensitive to the informant's time and his or her stamina. During the first expedition, it is enough to examine the speech of two monolingual informants and four bilingual ones, making 10 hours of high-quality audio or video recordings. At the same time, it is necessary to conduct an initial survey of the linguistic situation as it exists in churches, mosques and tekke, in schools, in local government, in political organizations and in local media. It is also important to photograph public markers that give evidence to the language situation, including official and private announcements, placards, advertising, inscriptions, signs with the names of localities, streets, etc. It is also useful to conduct an anthroponomastic survey of local cemeteries. There is also good reason to get a hold of locally-produced literature about the region that may not be available elsewhere.

If there is promise for future research, a detailed programme for ongoing *thematic expeditions* can be developed, for example: "microvariativity in contact dialects and bilingual speech behaviour under circumstances of linguistic exogamy in the Mrkovići tribe", or "the language code of the wedding ceremony in the Karashevo bilingual community", or "code switching in the spontaneous speech of bilinguals in Himara". Then a sociolinguistic analysis of the parameters of the language situation must be undertaken. This includes establishing the domains of each of the contact dialects as well as the orthographic systems of their respective standard languages (including the actual domains of those languages). The extent to which the written forms of both languages are used must be determined, including the use of modern communication systems, radio, television, books and periodicals of both secular and religious content. The languages of folklore are important in both in singing and story-telling. It is also worthwhile to record official narratives about the community as generated by clerics and teachers and to establish the extent of external linguistic, religious, cultural and political influence (Albania in the case of the Mrkovići, Croatia in Karashevo, Greece in Himara), and to note the possible existence of a political problem related to the recognition of an ethnic minority and its linguistic rights. Finally, the accumulation of enough quantitatively significant material will make it possible to create digital corpora of bilingual dialect speech.

When deciding on whether the language situation being studied qualifies for research (whether dominance is present or absent), and when determining how L1 and L2 communities are distributed, one must take into account the differences between *social, pragmatic and cognitive dominance*. It is important to a) conduct sociolinguistic profiling of speakers according to gender, age, origins, L1, L2, b) describe the individual scenarios that characterize their bilingual speech behaviour, and 3) establish their speech strategies when communicating with family members, their community and representatives of the outside world. It is possible that language variation or change may turn out to be associated with a particular speech practise on the part of a particular informant or type of informant.

Beyond the *contact-induced* phonetic, morphonological, morphosyntactic, syntactic and lexical phenomena of both dialects under examination, it is necessary to establish the group's own linguonyms and microlinguonyms in their relation to official forms and those accepted by linguists. Endo- and exoethnonyms are important, as well as ktetics. When collecting anthroponyms, Christian and Moslem names, clan and family names, given names and nicknames must be distinguished from each other as well as the forms they might take in different languages. Nor should one ignore the names of localities in the krajina and tribal region in both languages and microtoponyms (hydronymy, oronymy, the names of fields, gardens, pastures, forests, and the like), including their translations. This will aid in reconstructing the stages of the territory's settlement with data from medieval monastic charters, Venetian, Ottoman and Austrian censuses. If possible, the degree of linguistic and geographical variability of the findings in a number of localities in the microregion should also be determined.

The collection of *cultural and anthropological references*, including the group's cultural markers, cannot cover all aspects of the life of the community and its members, but should be limited to those most relevant for the analysis of the local language situation. These include traditional clothing, religious practice, genealogical reconstruction, marriage patterns and, in particular, linguistic exogamy, and inter-confessional and inter-ethnic marriage. Also relevant are the economic and social niches the community occupies (in livestock, fishery, horticulture, etc.), members' economic activity outside their traditional territory (seasonal and factory work, etc.), contact groups of the community (marital ties, economic activities, religious practices), state policy towards the community (limitations, prohibitions, and privileges during different historical periods), immigration, economic stratification, and new opportunities (tourism, real estate, etc.).

The *results of influence* contact languages have on each other that are well-known to research must be compared with those obtained on the basis of these new materials. It is important to make an effort to distinguish results from synchronic language microvariation and ongoing processes of microdiachronic change. This is done by distinguishing the extent of the recipient's adaptiveness at different language levels: multi-word code switching, inserted foreign linguistic elements, occasional borrowings and the speaker's own invented borrowings. Yet different levels of language structure, such as phonetic and morphological, may show on the part of the same donor language unit a significantly different degree of adaptation and integration into the recipient language (cf. Poplack et al. 2020). For the lexicon of a semantic group, it is essential to use etymological and dialect dictionaries, and, if available, dialectological atlases, to conduct an etymological and areal analysis. If possible, this should establish the lexicon's genetic layers and the ratio of foreign borrowings. These would include foreign substitutes for native words and the coexistence of multilingual synonyms and doublets so as to determine the direction of material borrowings as well as semantic borrowings, i.e. full and partial calques.

5 Golloborda vs. Mrkovići

Our focus lies on linguistic processes in bilingual symbiotic societies in the Balkan Peninsula as a special setting for lesser-known language contact situations and a possible key to understanding the Balkan Sprachbund puzzle in accordance with our general claim that Balkan linguistic convergence might be caused by a shift from L1 to L2 after a long period of mass and perhaps symmetric bilingualism (Rusakov & Sobolev 2008; Sobolev et al. 2018). This part of the chapter sets this claim against new, recently collected field data from *two* areas of intense and intimate language contact in the Western Balkans:

1. Golloborda / Golo Bordo (Dibër / Debar, Albania (and Macedonia)) (Sobolev & Novik 2013) (the transcribed texts contain 9,500 word forms (Sobolev & Novik 2013: 186–217)) and
2. Mrkovići (Primorje and Krajina / Krajë, Montenegro) (Sobolev 2015; Morozova 2017a) (the transcribed texts contain more than 1,000 word forms).

In the first area, which is primarily under consideration here, we are concerned with the bilingualism of a minority group (where the socially dominant country's official language possesses power and prestige and the minority's language is linguistically dominant in the speaker's linguistic competence (see van Coetsem 1988: 13). In the second area, analysed in great detail in (Morozova, below), groups of people interact in alternating distributions of forms and a special non-dominant bilingualism with symmetry in power, prestige and linguistic competence of L1 and L2. This occurs accounting for the fact that some general models of language contact "may be thought to presuppose an asymmetry between L1 and L2" (Muysken 2013: 727).

The parameters of the contact including power, prestige and range (Michaelis & Haspelmath 2014; Konior 2015), and social microfactors (Adamou 2016), are presented in two tables below.

Table 1 The languages in contact

Parameters	Trebisht (Golloborda / Golo Brdo area, Albania)	Velja Gorana (Mrkovići area, Montenegro)
Languages/ dialects in contact	L1 Local Macedonian dialect; L2 Standard Albanian (with restrictions on age/gender groups = no knowledge of Albanian by elderly women and children up to 7)	*Men* L1=L2 Standard Serbo-Croatian ("Montenegrin") and local Serbo-Croatian ("Mrkovići") dialect = local Albanian dialect(s) *Women* L1 Local Albanian dialect(s) L2 Standard Serbo-Croatian ("Montenegrin") and local Serbo-Croatian ("Mrkovići") dialect
	Comments: – no Standard Slavic language in usage – almost no local Gheg Albanian dialect in usage	*Comments*: no Standard Albanian in active usage

Table 2 Power, prestige and range (attitudes not taken into account)

Parameters	Trebisht (Golloborda / Golo Brdo area, Albania)	Velja Gorana (Mrkovići area, Montenegro)
Powerful group in the country	Albanians	Orthodox Montenegrins
Powerless group in the country	Slavs	Moslem Slavs and Albanians
Modern state language	Standard Albanian	Standard Serbo-Croatian ("Montenegrin")
Prestigious language of religion	Standard Albanian	Standard Serbo-Croatian ("Montenegrin")
Prestigious emblematic language	Standard Albanian	Standard Serbo-Croatian ("Montenegrin") and Standard Albanian
Language of wider communication in the region	Standard Albanian and Local Macedonian dialect	Standard Serbo-Croatian and Albanian

Parameters	Trebisht (Golloborda / Golo Brdo area, Albania)	Velja Gorana (Mrkovići area, Montenegro)
Indigenous minor language	Local Macedonian dialect	Local Serbo-Croatian ("Mrkovići") dialect and local Albanian dialect(s)
Everyday language within the family and neighbourhood	Local Macedonian dialect	Standard Serbo-Croatian ("Montenegrin") and local Serbo-Croatian ("Mrkovići") dialect and local Albanian dialect(s)
Local language (on the *krajina*-level)	Local Macedonian dialect and local Albanian dialect(s)	Standard Serbo-Croatian ("Montenegrin") and local Serbo-Croatian ("Mrkovići") dialect and local Albanian dialect(s)

5.1 Golloborda / Golo Brdo

In phonetics and phonology there are no significant traces of any direct substantial Albanian influence on genetically Slavic lexical items. If phonetical substance is borrowed, it happens together with the Albanian lexical item. Hence, there is no linguistic change in Macedonian L1 due to contact with Albanian as L2.

Occasionally one can hear back [ɒ] and labialized [y] in words that are fully identical with Albanian ones due to common Balkan origin or borrowing from the same source such as Turkish. Their morphological properties are inherently Slavic. To this group one can add onomatopoeia and generally phonetically deviant exclamations:

[ɒ] *n'ɒːna* 'mother' (*n'ɒːna m'oja 'imat k'aʒveno* 'my mother said', generally [n'ana] or [n'əna]; *hɒ!* 'yes!';

[y] *b'yret͡si* PL 'baked filled pastry' (*i te go rab'otaet t'amo za b'yret͡si pr'aet* 'and they work it over to make *b'yret͡si*'), generally [b'urek]; onomatopeic *pr:y!*

Consonants, alien to Macedonian Slavic phonetics and phonology (/θ/, /ð/, /ʎ/, /ɫ/), can be encountered only in two cases:

— in Albanian loanwords, often integrated morphologically into Macedonian, /θ/, /ð/, /ʎ/, /ɫ/: *djaθ* 'cheese' (*a be s'ega pospr'avjime m'alo djaθ* 'and now we make some cheese', note Slavic *s'iren'e* 'cheese'); *nd'oð-e* to happen-AOR.3SG (*'ak'i i 'ak'i mi nd'oðe* 'so and so happened to me'); there are peripheral examples, such as vocatives: /λ/ *št'oprajš, o pλ'ak'e!* 'how do you do, old lady!' and personal names: /ł/ *Pəł'umb* (comp. the Macedonized variant *P'olum*), lit. 'pigeon'; *Dałend'iʃa*, lit. 'swallow'

- in code switching into Albanian /θ/, /ð/, /λ/: *ʃ'utλeʃ si e θ'uemi mak'edon'iʃt? 'oris me tə 'ambəλ?* 'what do we call *ʃ'utλeʃ* in Macedonian, rice with sweets'; – *o v'erdija! – urðər'o!* 'o, verdija! – yes!? As you wish!'

Switching from Macedonian (L1) into Albanian (L2) is triggered by pragmatic or special communicative needs. There are no unmotivated instances. The proficiency in Albanian as L2 is full. The phonetics of switching into Albanian and borrowing from Albanian is partially dialectically determined Gheg Albanian (*'ambəλ* 'sweet'; *ðom-paraḻ'om* < Alb. *dhomë paradhomë* 'chamber'; *Dałend'iʃa* personal name, lit. 'swallow') and partially Tosk or even Standard Albanian (*tə b'əftə m'irə!* 'bon appetit!'; *θ'uemi* 'we say'; *urðər'o* 'at your service!'; *'ambəλ* 'sweet'), sometimes with Macedonian accent retraction (*'oris* < Alb. *or'iz* 'rice').

Direct substantial Albanian influence in grammar is almost absent. One can give the examples of the preverb *p'ara* 'over-' (*n'e para kup'uaet* '(They) don't buy very actively'), disjunctive conjunction *'ose* 'or' (*i tɕe pom'in'it od'ovde m'etʃka, 'ose vəlk* 'And a bear will come from here, or a wolf'), the affirmative particle *po* 'yes' and negative *nuk* 'no' in prohibitive: *ej, n'uk-ajte!* no-IMPERAT.2PL, fully calquing the Albanian *mos-ni!* no-IMPERAT.2PL. The linguistic change in Macedonian L1 substance owing to contact with Albanian as L2 in the field of grammar is almost irrelevant, affecting only borrowing of synsemantical lexical units.

Hybrid phenomena in Macedonian L1 production are absolutely rare and can be met only in spontaneous speech, leaving the question of their systemic status rather unsolved until more and deeper research is done. Here are some striking examples in one short text (160 word forms) in Golo Bordo dialect of Macedonian, showing the simultaneous comprehensive interplay of Slavic, Albanian and Balkan Romance, pan-Balkan and hybrid phenomena (Sobolev 2013: 197):

Text in Golo Bordo dialect of Macedonian (man, 50-years old):

| ...s'amo 'eno d'ete 'imal. [...] mu o d'ade t'ɛ dete i mu r'etʃe, k'ei t͡ɕe se n'aprait dv'aeset g'odinʲi, 'ovoi t͡ɕe o pr'aiʃ k'urban. i toi ot'ide, k'uːrban t͡ɕe o prait. 'ama toi k'amberot naʃ, g'ospod za n'aize, za m'iie n'e sme ft'asanʲi da o f'atime, mu 'isfərlat pred nego [...] 'oven daʃ. d'eteto, v'elʲit, t'ornʲi go, v'elʲit, t͡ɕe o k'olʲiʃ 'oveno[t], d'aʃot. i s'ea d'aʃof 'izlezę za k'urban. i s'ega sv'ekoi n'ekoi, nap'imer 'ovie se br'ai ʃt 'imaet p'oːt͡ɕe... k'olʲet k'urbanʲi, i 'oviia k'urbanof se d'elvet s'ea po sirom'aite:. se d'elvet po sirom'aite napr'imer vo s'elovo zn'aime m'ie 'enʲi n'emaed br'ai. a za sv'ite za toi pr'aznʲik... t'oi vetʃer za da 'imaed m'eso, i toi t͡ɕe im p'odelʲit. [...] 'eden pies go z'evaʒ za: s'ebe, 'oviiat ʃto k'olʲit k'urbanof. a tri pi'esoi dr'ugʲi p'odelʲvet po sirom'aii. b'es pari, go d'avat t'aːka. i za toi k'urbanot t'oa i'esti s'ea. [...] ja n'emam k'olʲeno. a toi b'abo 'imat k'olʲeno, 'imat d'elʲveno na d'eʃi. 'ima 'imano br'avi p'orano toi. | '...he had only one son. ...he gave that son to him and said: When he will be twenty years old, you will sacrifice him. And he went to sacrifice him. But our God, whom we cannot understand, throws a ram in front of him. Put the son aside, he says, you will slaughter the ram. And now the ram became the sacrifice. And now everybody, for example these people (will) have lots of small livestock, they slaughter the sacrifice, and this is distributed among the poor. It is distributed among the poor. For example, we know in the village some people do not have small livestock. And for all of us for that festival... this evening for everybody to have meat... and he will distribute among them. ...one part you take for yourself, the one who slaughters the sacrifice. And three other parts they distribute among the poor. With no money, they give it for free. And as for sacrifice, that is it. I did not slaughter, but my father did. He distributed rams. He had small livestock before.' |

There are some Slavic phenomena in the text which I refer to as *antibalkanisms* – linguistic properties that never get lost in Balkan Slavic and never propagate beyond Slavic in the Balkans regardless of contact intensity (Sobolev 2011):

- stress retraction on prepositions: *b'es pari* [*b'es=pari*] WITHOUT=MONEY 'without money',
- verbal aspect of the Slavic type, marked by the verbal root itself: *f'atime* PF 'take' vs. *z'evaʃ* IPF 'take',
- the Slavic l-participle (and l-perfect): *'imal* 'to have'.

Some other phenomena show clearly the distance to Albanian:

- elisions, tolerated vowel groups, contractions: *p'oːt͡ɕe* < *p'ovet͡ɕe* 'more'; *s'ea* 'now'; *br'ai ~ br'avi* PL 'sheep and goats',
- emphatic, phonologically undistinguished length: *k'uːrban ~ k'urban* 'sacrifice of a livestock animal', *sirom'aite: ~ sirom'aite* PL 'poor people', *zaː ~ za* 'for' (note phonologically distinguished length in Gheg Albanian (Gjinari et al. 2007–2008, vol. 1: 86, Harta 18)),
- no code-switching into Albanian L2.

On the other side, there are some phenomena in the text which go back to Albanian and Balkan Romance structural and lexical influence and which make the dialect's grammar system and vocabulary more compound and sophisticated, and finally significantly more alloglottic in the dialect continuum of Macedonian:

- postposition of attribute: *k'amberot naʃ* 'our prophet'; *p̦i'esoi̦ dr'ugʲi* 'other parts',
- habeo-perfect, extended: *'ima 'imano* 'he had' (see Makarova 2017),
- esse-perfect, highly idiosyncratic: *n'e sme ft'asanʲi* 'we are not capable of' (comp. Alb. *s'jemi arritur*),
- a highly idiosyncratic prepositional direct object: *'imat d'elʲveno na d'eʃi* '(They) distributed rams',
- lexical borrowings: *p̦ies* SG, *p̦i'esoi̦* PL 'part' < Alb. *pjes*.

Hybrid phenomena, built of both a Slavic and an Albanian substance, can also be observed in grammar, lexica and phraseology.

The most striking form in our data is *na d'eʃi* ram-ACC.PL. From the lexical point of view this is a direct material borrowing from Alb. *dash* [*daʃ*] 'ram', partially integrated into the morphology of Macedonian, comp. *daʃ* SG.INDEF, *d'aʃof* ~ *d'aʃot* SG.DEF 'ram'. From the viewpoint of plural building the expected form should sound **d'aʃovi* ~ **d'aʃoi̦*, like the above attested *p̦ies* SG, *p̦i'esoi̦* PL 'part'. Instead, the speaker used two models with two substances simultaneously, taking the common Albanian morphosyntactic plural-marking model with apophony *a* ~ *e*, that is Alb. *dash* ~ *desh*, which is completely alien to Slavic and affixing the common Slavic plural marker *-i*.

The addition of the preposition *na* to mark the direct object, following the Balkan Romance model (Sobolev 2008), finalizes this extraordinary and highly redundant complex (Sobolev 2012). Our conclusion is, that the degree of phonetical and grammatical adaptation of Albanian items into spontaneous speech in Macedonian is selected by the Slavic speaker with great freedom, but no linguistic change happens, not even in *statu nascendi*. There is no doubt that the bilingual hearers had no difficulties in decoding the form, but one can be assured that it is highly unlikely to occur in monolingual speech and will never be accepted or systematically reproduced by any monolingual Macedonian community.

As for hybrid phenomena in phraseology and lexica, one can point to the first component of *t͡ʃiz g'ozica* (comp. Alb. *qish bythën* PRS IND, *qifsh bythën* OPT '*pedicabo in asino*'), while lexically the reduplication *'oven daʃ* SG.INDEF 'ram' and *'oveno[t] d'aʃot* SG.DEF 'ram' (*mu 'isfərlat pred nego 'oven daʃ... t͡ɕe o k'olʲiʃ 'oveno[t], d'aʃot* 'throws a ram in front of him… you will slaughter the ram') attracts attention. We can interpret it as a compound of Slavic hyperonym and non-Slavic hyponym like in Serbian *ruʒa ɖul* 'damask rose' with a Slavic and a Turkic word for 'rose', which is a fact of the language.

In contrast to phonetics and grammar, the lexicon – viewed through thematic groupings (see Kozak 2015; Kisilier 2017; Morozova 2017b) – behaves in a significantly different way in the sense that one and *the same set of lexical items can serve both languages in a specific semantic field*. The claim that the norm and proportion of lexical substitutes is not random (Hammarström 2016: 23) can be illustrated by the terminology of animal breeding and kinship terms, where an increasing number of lexical-semantic oppositions through material borrowing can be viewed as an immediate structural consequence of contact. Note the lexical items *ʃeʎ'ek, miʎ'or* and *daʃ* which have the same meanings in the Golo Bordo dialect of Macedonian (Sobolev & Novik 2013) and in the Skrapar dialect of Albanian (see Ylli & Sobolev 2002; Ylli & Sobolev 2003; MDABL 2013: Map 19).

Table 3 Lexicon of animal breeding. Sex and age

Meaning	Macedonian dialect of Trebisht (Golloborda / Golo Bordo area, Albania)	Albanian dialect of Leshnja (Skrapar, Albania)
Lamb	j'agnje	qengj [tɕendʑ]
one year old lamb (in autumn)	ʃ'iλeʒe	shel'ek [ʃeʎ'ek]
two year old lamb / ram	m'iλor	mil'or [miʎ'or]
ram, at least three years old	daʃ 'oven	dash [daʃ]

A similar contact-induced lexical enrichment is observed in the field of kinship terminology. The dialect of Golo Bordo makes use of various terms for grandparents: *dedo / babo star / babod͡ʑiʃ* 'grandfather', *baba / staramajka / nəna stara / nənad͡ʑiʃa* 'grandmother' (Morozova 2013). The words *babod͡ʑiʃ* and *nənad͡ʑiʃa* originate from the local Albanian dialect, where they stand only for paternal grandparents (Gjinari et al. 2007–2008: 236–237). The Map 42 in MDABL (2006: 96–97) shows, that lexicalizations of these concepts do not happen (frequently) beyond Albanian. The native term *staramajka* 'grandmother' is used in Golo Bordo along with *babo star* 'grandfather' and *nəna stara* 'grandmother', both following the Albanian structural pattern with the adjective following the noun. None of these terms expresses the distinction between the paternal and maternal side. By contrast, in the dialect of the Mrkovići, the borrowing of lexical material occurred together with the imposition of the associated structural and semantic patterns, and resulted in changes within the system of kinship terms (Morozova 2017).

5.2 Mrkovići (and Gorana)

In the phonetics and phonology of Mrkovići, aside from direct lexical borrowings from Albanian, there are significant traces of direct substantial Albanian influence on genetically Slavic lexical items (Vujović 1969; Curtis 2012; Sobolev 2015; Morozova 2017a; 2017b), for ex.:

[ʋ] zl'ʋto 'gold'; sv'ʋdba 'wedding';

[ł] kłôs 'spike'; môłi 'small'; tr̩łʋm 'to rub';

The regular devoicing of final obstruents: comp. NOM ~ ACC [grat] ~ [gr'ada] 'city', comp. [memet] ~ [memeta] 'Mohammed'.

In word formation one finds the Albanian diminutive suffix -za (Alb. qytet 'town' ~ qyte-za 'small town'), which is present in personal names and patronyms Alb. Dabza ~ Slav. Dabezit͡ɕ; Alb. Nikëza ~ Slav. Nikezit͡ɕ, and in toponyms (Šekularac & Pavlović 2012).

The question is, did these features emerge due to the balanced bilingualism we can observe at present, or due to eventual Albanian and Romance language and population shifts in the area during the Middle Ages?

The speech of bilingual informants from the Velja Gorana village in Mrkovići area reflects their full competence of both Slavic and Albanian at all levels. They master perfectly the phonetics and phonology, morphology and lexicon of Serbo-Croatian and Albanian dialects respectively as subsystems of two diasystems (Ahmetaj 2006; Bjeletić 2013; Sobolev 2015):

Serb.-Cr. r̩: k'r̩sti 'back'; ɛ: ʃup'ɛk 'arse' versus Alb. y: kr'yti 'head'; ø: b'øθa 'arse'; uⁿ: truⁿ 'brains'; ə: v'etəł 'eyebrow'; θ: θ'oni 'nail'; ɟ: i ɟat 'long';

Serb.-Cr. kuk SG ~ k'ukovi PL 'hip' versus Alb. krah INDEF ~ kr'ahi DEF 'arm'.

These diasystems are additionally distributed in the language, but *not* in spontaneous speech behaviour, where *unmotivated code switchings* can take place, as Maria Morozova's 2017 transcript of the speech behaviour in Velja Gorana shows (Albanian material marked with italics). Can these findings refute the widespread thesis that almost every case of language contact is somehow asymmetric?

Text in Velja Gorana idiom of the Mrkovići dialect (male, 80-years old)

e, da ti kʹaʒem za to. i dandanʹas se kʊʒujʹe ta zʹima. smʹrzła je ʹona u płanʹinu, u ʃarpłanʹinu u ałbʹaniju. smʹrzła je pʹoʃto ʹona se fołʹiła kæ jʹeno prolʹetɕe. iʒ ʎivdʹu pranvʹerəs. bok je pʹosłao... ja ka ʎʃʹu ftʹofin e u ɲɾi dʹeʎet e tʹəna, ajʹʌ me d͡ʑiθ dʹeʎen, me d͡ʑiθ mʹad͡ʑen n maʎ. i dandanʹas su tʹije kʹameɲe ʃto su słʹuʒeli ju. i dʹandanʹas. i ʹot toga dʹana se zʹove... kæd zʹima na izłʹas mʹʊrta kʹʊʒe bʹabe su. trʹutʃkaju se bʹabi. ʃkʹunen pʎʹakat. t͡ʃʹetiri dʹana.	'Hey, let me tell you about this. Even nowadays that (kind of) winter can happen. She iced up in the mountains, in the Shar mountains in Albania. She iced up because she boasted in the spring. *She boasted in the spring.* The God sent... *He sent coldness and her sheep iced up, she iced up with all the sheep, with a kneading trough in the mountains.* Even nowadays there are the stones that she used. Even nowadays. And from that day it is called... when winter ends in march they say, there are 'old ladies'. 'Old ladies shake'. *'Old ladies shake'*. Four days (long).'

6 Linguistic vs. social parameters

I do not believe social circumstances to be the dominant factor in determining the outcomes of linguistic contact (see Thomason 2006: 344–346). In any case, we still have insufficient data for strong correlations between the qualities of bilingualism, code switching strategies, bilateral linguistic accommodation, past language change situations and social practises. Our observations allow only for vague juxtapositions.

Table 4 Linguistic vs. social parameters

Parameters	Trebisht (Golloborda / Golo Brdo area, Albania)	Velja Gorana (Mrkovići area, Montenegro), male speakers only
qualities of bilingualism	dominant	balanced (bilingual first-language acquisition)
code-switching strategies	pragmatically motivated	unmotivated
level of bilateral linguistic accommodation in phonetics	very low	medium
level of bilateral linguistic accommodation in grammar	low to medium	low to medium
level of bilateral linguistic accommodation in lexicon	medium, with a tendency towards a joint stock of vocabulary	medium, with a tendency towards a joint stock of vocabulary

Parameters	Trebisht (Golloborda / Golo Brdo area, Albania)	Velja Gorana (Mrkovići area, Montenegro), male speakers only
microtoponyms	L1	L1 and L2
personal names	L1 and L2	L1 (Islamic)
hybrid phenomena in discourse	yes	not attested
degree of alloglossy in the framework of the closely related dialects	low	high
past language change situation	Albanian as an adstrate until 1913, as a superstrate since 1913	Albanian as a substrate in Middle Ages, as an adstrate since 1878
linguistic exogamy	unknown	in practice

7 Conclusion

We have compared the main conditions of language contact, intralinguistic processes and patterns of code-switching, as well as general results of contact-induced linguistic change, in two Slavic and Albanian bilingual societies (Golloborda and Mrkovići). These conditions have affected all levels of language structure: phonetics/phonology, grammar and lexicon (vocabulary). It is claimed that two phonologies and two grammars coexist in the same bilingual individual (e.g., a male bilingual with Slavic L1 and Albanian L2 in Montenegro shows no higher level of alloglossy in vocalic nasalism or inflection as compared to other speakers of Albanian), whereas parts of the lexicon – viewed through thematic groupings (see Kozak 2015; Kisilier 2017; Morozova 2017b) – behave in a significantly different way.[7] One and the same set of highly semantically specialized lexical items can serve both languages in a specific semantic field, basic kinship terms inclusive. Another example is provided by the colour terms used for sheep and goats in Golo Bordo. For the basic colours common Slavic words are used, whereas particular shades are denoted with special pan-Balkan terms like *b'ardʒa, k'al'eʃ(k)a, m'urga, s'orka, brez* (Sobolev & Novik 2013; MDABL 2013; Domosiletskaia 2002), which gives striking evidence for a single set of lexical items serving both Macedonian

---

[7] Note the same finding in Torres Cacoullos & Travis (2018: 172): "bilinguals' Spanish aligns with monolingual Spanish and their English with monolingual English".

and Albanian. One can even generalize that the Balkan languages sometimes seem to possess one lexicon but different grammars.

Qualitative, though not voluminous, primary data obtained during fieldwork allowed us to regard the role cognitively non-dominant bilingualism played in contact-conditioned language change as being relatively low. This particular situation is thus unlikely to be "responsible" for the deep convergence found within the Balkan languages. In this way, positive research results within the framework of the paradigm developed, in addition to the detection of actual situations of non-dominant bilingualism, can be recognized as a methodologically correct reduction in the number of hypotheses that would claim to reveal the causes and mechanisms behind the formation of a Balkan Sprachbund.

In both cases no single integrated speech community emerges with no creole, no mixed language, no emergence of new types, and there is no language death or observable abandonment of any language. The bilinguals in the Balkans seem not to be distressed by the need of "lightening the cognitive load of having to remember and use two different linguistic systems" (see Silva-Corvalán 1994: 6; Bisang 2006: 90). Our data show

a) sophisticated, not simplified grammatical categories and lexical oppositions (see Sobolev 2015a),
b) forms, following highly idiosyncratic patterns,
c) retention of synthetic archaisms.

Observations on the *language* of our bilingual informants, on one side, and their *speech behaviour*, on another side, show, however, that there is a gap with no strongly predictable or determinant relation between language and behaviour. In language the 'one's own' L1 rules are applied to the 'one's own' L1 substance which itself can be systematically sophisticated through borrowing and extended up to cross-linguistic clusters of terms. In speech behaviour involving actual interference, almost anything goes: the "alien" L2 substance can be used both with "alien" L2 or "one's own" L1 rules with a very different degree of transfer from one language to another and of integration into "one's own" L1. The effects of contact can be identified in bilingual speech behaviour only if synchronically contrasted to a monolingual one. A prior contact-induced linguistic change seems to be identifiable in retrospectively detecting and opposing prior bilingual and monolingual speech behaviour. Unfortunately, there is no adequate Balkan data available for any past period of time.

Among Balkan societies, linguistic and cultural convergence subsists alongside the preservation of ethnic and linguistic identity. The results of many years of research into this phenomenon demand that we devote the utmost scrutiny to the long-term circumstances of bilingualism among large groups of people in symbiotic, polylingual communities, in particular in the *krajina* Mrkovići and the Montenegrin Coast. In-depth monographic study must in future address the following general and specific linguistic issues of heuristic value:

1. with regard to bi- and multilingual speakers in southeast Europe: a) the quantity or, rather, degree of similarity in their lexica and grammars, b) the internal structure of their lexica and grammars (the composition of their elements, structural similarities, the presence of genetically stable segments not subjected to external influence, and segments subject to change in a contact situation);
2. the possibility of a *single grammar* with *different lexica* and its possible structure;
3. the possibility of using linguistic methods to: a) establish bi- and multilingual lexica and grammars and the development of a methodology to do so, b) reconstruct and reconstitute bi- and multilingual lexica and grammars from the past;
4. distinguishing situations of exchanging or retaining languages when: a) one language was dropped in exchange for another in the past and, b) another "native" language was preserved despite the use of different languages, c) arriving at a prognosis of whether a or b is more likely to occur;
5. a) the strategies and mechanisms behind the formation of symbiotic groups of people distinguished by language, confession, and "culture", including the idea of blood kinship as a regulating factor, b) the linguistic mechanisms that separate groups of people, among others.

References

Adamou, Evangelia. 2016. *A Corpus-driven Approach to Language Contact: Endangered Languages in a Comparative Perspective*. Boston; Berlin: Mouton de Gruyter.
Ahmetaj, Mehmet. 2006. *E folmja e Anës së Malit* [The dialect of Ana e Malit]. Prishtinë: Instituti albanologjik.
Asenova, Petya. 2016. Les interférences dans le dialecte de Golo bărdo – Albanie. *Izbrani statii po balkansko ezikoznanie* [Selected papers in Balkan linguistics], 282–309. Sofia: Faber.
Asenova, Petya. 2018. Balkan Syntax: Typological and Diachronic Aspects. In Iliana Krapova & Brian Joseph (eds.), *Balkan Syntax and (Universal) Principles of Grammar*, 13–36. Berlin: De Gruyter Mouton.
Barth, Frederik. 1969. Introduction. In Frederik Barth (ed.), *Ethnic Groups and Boundaries: the Social Organization of Cultural Difference*, 9–38. Bergen & Oslo: Universitetsforlaget.
Bisang, Walter. 2006. Contact-Induced Convergence: Typology and Areality. In Keith Brown (ed.), *Encyclopedia of Language and Linguistics*, 2nd edition, 88–101. Oxford: Elsevier.

Bjeletić, Marta. 2013. Slovenski meseceslov (od Miklošića do Spića) [Slavic words for the months of the year (from Miklošić to Spić)]. In Jasmina Grković-Mejdžor & Aleksandar Loma (eds.), *Miklosichiana bicentennalia: zbornik u čast dvestote godišnjice rođenja Franca Miklošića*, 99-128. Beograd: SANU.

Campbell, Lyle. 2006. Areal linguistics. In Keith Brown (ed.), *Encyclopedia of language and linguistics*, 455-460. Oxford: Elsevier. 2nd ed.

Coetsem, Frans van. 1988. *Loan Phonology and the Two Transfer types in Language Contact*. Dordrecht: Foris.

Curtis, Matthew Cowan. 2012. *Slavic-Albanian Language Contact, Convergence, and Coexistence*. Ohio State University Doctoral Dissertation.

Cyxun, Gennadiy A. 1981. *Tipologičeskie problemy balkanoslavyanskogo areala* [Questions of typology in the Balkan Slavic area]. Minsk: Nauka i tehnyka.

Dombrowski, Andrew. 2013. *Phonological aspects of language contact along the Slavic periphery: an ecological approach*. University of Chicago Doctoral Dissertation.

Domosiletskaia, Marina V. 2002. *Albansko-vostochnoromanskii sopostavitel'nyi poniatiinyi slovar'. Skotovodcheskaia leksika* [Albanian and East Romance comparative comprehensive dictionary. Herding vocabulary]. St. Petersburg: Nauka.

Domosiletskaia, Marina V., Anna A. Plotnikova & Andrey N. Sobolev. 1998. Malyi dialektologicheskii atlas balkanskikh iazykov [Minor Dialectological Atlas of Balkan Languages]. *Slavianskoe iazykoznanie. XII mezhdunarodnyi s"ezd slavistov. Doklady rossiiskoi delegatsii*, 196-211. Moscow: Nauka.

Dugushina, Alexandra S., Maria S. Morozova & Denis S. Ermolin. 2013. Etnograficheskie nabludeniya v oblasti Gora (Albaniya, Kosovo) [Ethnographic observations in the region of Gora (Albania, Kosovo)]. In Elena G. Fedorova (ed.), *Materialy polevykh issledovaniy MAE RAN* 13, 50-65. St. Petersburg: MAE RAN.

Fine, John V. A. 1983. *The early medieval Balkans: A critical survey from the sixth to the late twelfth century*. Ann Arbor, Michigan: University of Michigan Press.

Fleming, Luke. 2016. Linguistic exogamy and language shift in the northwest Amazon. *International Journal of the Sociology of Language* 2016. 9-27.

Friedman, Victor A. 2006. Balkans as a linguistic Area. In Keith Brown (ed.), *Encyclopedia of Language and Linguistics*, 2nd edition, 657-72. Oxford: Elsevier.

Gjinari, Jorgji, Bahri Beci, Gjovalin Shkurtaj & Xheladin Gosturani. 2007-2008. *Atlasi dialektologjik i gjuhës shqipe* [Albanian dialect atlas], Vol. 1-2. Napoli, Italy: Universita degli studi di Napoli l'Orientale, Tirana: Akademia e shkencave e Shqipërisë.

Golant, Natal'ia G. 2013. *Martovskaia starukha i martovskaia nit'. Legendy i obriady nachala marta u rumyn* [The March Crone and the March thread. Rituals and legends]. St. Petersburg: MAE RAN.

Hammarström, Harald. 2016. Linguistic diversity and language evolution. *Journal of Language Evolution* 1. 19-29.

Hinrichs, Uwe. 2004a. Ist das Bulgarische kreolisiertes Altbulgarisch? In Uwe Hinrichs (ed.), *Die europäischen Sprachen auf dem Weg zum analytischen Sprachtyp*, 231-242. Wiesbaden: Harrassowitz.

Hinrichs, Uwe. 2004b. Orale Kultur, Mehrsprachigkeit, radikaler Analytismus: Zur Erklärung von Sprachstrukturen auf dem Balkan und im kreolischen Raum. Ein Beitrag zur Entmystifizierung der Balkanlinguistik. *Zeitschrift für Balkanologie* 40(2). 141-174.

Hinrichs, Uwe (ed.). 2010. *Handbuch der Eurolinguistik*. Wiesbaden: Harrassowitz.

Hinrichs, Uwe & Uwe Büttner (eds.). 1999. *Handbuch der Südosteuropa-Linguistik* (Slavistische Studienbücher). Vol. 10. Wiesbaden: Harrassowitz.

Jackson, Jean. 1983. *The fish people: Linguistic exogamy and Tukanoan identity in northwest Amazonia*. Cambridge: Cambridge University Press.

Joseph, Brian & Victor Friedman. 2017. Reassessing sprachbunds: A view from the Balkans. In Raymond Hickey (ed.), *The Cambridge Handbook of Areal Linguistics*, 63–90. Cambridge: Cambridge University Press.

Jovićević, Andrija. 1922. Crnogorsko primorje i Krajina [The Montenegro coast and Krajina]. *Srpski etnografski zbornik*, Vol. 11. Beograd: Srpska kraljevska akademija.

Kisilier, Maxim L. 2017. Leksicheskie osobennosti tsakonskogo dialekta novogrecheskogo iazyka [Lexical features of the Tsakonian dialect of Modern Greek]. *Voprosy iazykoznaniia* 1. 105–136.

Konior (Koner), Daria. 2016. Leksicheskaya realizatsiya predmetnogo koda karashevskoi svad'by ["Objective code" of the Krashovani wedding vocabulary and its lexical manifestation]. *Acta linguistica Petropolitana (Trudy Instituta lingvisticheskih issledovaniy)* 12 (3). 629–649.

Konior (Koner), Daria. 2017. "The labalcea phenomenon" in the area of Caraşova, Romania. In Sergey Monakhov, Irina Vasilyeva, Maria Khokhlova (eds.), *Advances in Social Science, Education and Humanities Research (ASSEHR)*, Vol. 122, 318–322. Proceedings of the 45th International Philological Conference (IPC 2016). Atlantis Press.

Konior (Koner), Daria & Anastasia Makarova. 2015. Osobennosti etnoyazykovoy situacii v regione Karashevo (Rumyniya) [On the ethnolinguistic situation in the community of Karashevo (Romania)]. *Poznańskie studia slawistyczne* 8. 83–91.

Konior (Koner), Daria & Andrey N. Sobolev. 2017. Osobennosti neravnovesnogo bilingvizma u rumynoyazychnykh karashevtsev v sele Yabaltcha [On some aspects of nonequilibrium Romanian-Slavic bilingualism in the village of Iabalcea]. *Indoevropeyskoye yazykoznaniye i klassicheskaya filologiya* 21. 985–1001.

Kopitar, Jernej. 1829. Albanische, walachische und bulgarische Sprache. *Wiener Jahrbücher der Literatur* 46. 56–106.

Kozak, Vyacheslav V. 2015. Otrazhenie slaviano-romanskikh kontaktov v leksike glagolicheskikh nadpisei s ostrova Krk XI–XVIII vv. [Reflections of Slavo-Romance contacts in the lexicon of Glagolitic inscriptions of the 11th to the 18th centuries on the island of Krk]. *Indoevropeyskoye yazykoznaniye i klassicheskaya filologiya* 9. 401–410.

Makarova, Anastasia L. 2016. Neka zapažanja o etnojezičkoj situaciji u dvojezičnim makedonsko-albanskim selima u regionu Prespa: fenomen Arvati [Some observations on the ethnolinguistic situation in the bilingual Macedonian-Albanian villages of the Prespa region: the case of Arvati]. *Studia Slavica Academiae Scientiarum Hungaricae* 61 (1). 115–130.

Makarova, Anastasia L. 2017. Interferentsiia v rechi bilingval'nykh nositelei dialektov regiona Prespa (Makedoniia). [Discourse Strategies of Bilingual Speakers of Macedonian, Aromanian and Albanian Dialects, the Prespa Region]. In Sergey Monakhov, Irina Vasilyeva & Maria Khokhlova (eds.), *Advances in Social Science, Education and Humanities Research (ASSEHR)*, Vol. 122, 364–367. Proceedings of the 45th International Philological Conference (IPC 2016). Atlantis Press.

MDABL – Andrey N. Sobolev (ed.). 2003–2018. *Malyi dialektologicheskii atlas balkanskikh iazykov. Probnyi vypusk (2003). Seriia leksicheskaia. Tom I. Leksika dukhovnoi kul'tury (2005). Tom II. Chelovek. Sem'ia (2006). Tom III. Zhivotnovodstvo (2009). Tom IV. (Avtor: M. V. Domosiletskaia). Landshaftnaia leksika (2010). Tom V. (Avtor: M. V. Domosiletskaia). Meteorologiia (2012). Tom VI. Polevodstvo. Ogorodnichestvo (2013). Tom VII. (Avtor: M. V. Domosiletskaia). Pčelovodstvo (2018). Seriia grammaticheskaia. Tom I. Kategorii imeni sushchestvitel'nogo (2005)* [Minor dialect atlas of the Balkan languages. Test launch (2003).

Lexical series. Vol. 1. Cultural vocabulary (2005). Vol. 2. The person and human relations (2006). Vol. 3. Animal husbandry (2009). Vol. 4. (M. V. Domosiletskaia, author). Landscape (2010). Vol. 5 (M. V. Domosiletskaia, author). Meteorology (2012). Vol. 6. Field-tending and Gardening (2013). Vol. 7. (M. V. Domosiletskaia, author). Apiculture (2018). Grammatical series. Vol. 1. Noun categories (2005)]. St. Petersburg, München: Nauka, Verlag Otto Sagner.

Michaelis, Susanne M. & Martin Haspelmath. 2014. Introductory remarks. *Grammatical hybridization and social conditions. Workshop*. Leipzig. https://www.eva.mpg.de/linguistics/conferences/grammatical-hybridization-and-social-conditions/index.html (accessed 15 March, 2021).

Morozova, Maria S. 2013. Slavyane Golo Bordo. Yazyk. Leksika. Sistema terminov rodstva i semeynyy etiket [The Golo Bordo Slavs. Language. Lexicon. Kinship terminology and family etiquette]. In Andrey N. Sobolev & Aleksandr A. Novik (eds.), *Golo Bordo (Gollobordë), Albaniia. Iz materialov balkanskoi ekspeditsii RAN i SPbGU 2008–2010 gg.* [Golo Bordo (Gollobordë) Albania. From the materials of the RAS and SPSU expeditions of 2008–2010], 81–108. Munich: Verlag Otto Sagner, St. Petersburg: Nauka.

Morozova, Maria S. 2017a. Albanskii govor ili govory Gorany? Genezis i funktsionirovanie [Albanian subdialect or subdialects of Gorana? Origins and function]. *Vestnik Sankt-Peterburgskogo gosudarstvennogo universiteta. Iazyk i literatura* 14 (2). 222–237.

Morozova, Maria S. 2017b. Paradoks issledovatelia na Balkanakh: perekliuchenie kodov u bilingval'nykh informantov pri interv'iuirovanii [The Paradox of Balkan research: code-switching among bilingual informants during interviews]. In Maksim M. Makartsev, Irina A. Sedakova, Tatiana V. Tsiv'ian (eds.), *Balkanskii tezaurus: Vzgliad na Balkany izvne i iznutri. Balkanskie chteniia 14. Tezisy i materialy*. Moskva, 18–20 aprelia 2017 goda, 137–143. Moscow: InSlav RAN.

Morozova, Maria S. 2019. Language Contact in Social Context: Kinship Terms and Kinship Relations of the Mrkovići in Southern Montenegro. *Journal of language contact* 12 (2). 305–343.

Morozova, Maria S. & Alexander Yu. Rusakov. 2019. Montenegrin-Albanian Linguistic Border: In Search of "Balanced Language Contact". *Slověne. International Journal of Slavic Studies* 7 (2). 258–302.

Muysken, Pieter. 2013. Language contact as the result of bilingual optimization strategies. *Bilingualism: Language and Cognition* 16 (4). 709–730.

Nasi, Lefter et al. (eds.). 2004. *Himara në shekuj* [Himara over the centuries]. Tirana: Akademia e Shkencave e Shqipërisë.

Novik, Aleksandr A. & Andrey N. Sobolev. 2016. Traditional wedding costume of the Mrkovići in Montenegro: between real heritage and folk construction (materials of the Russian expeditions in 2012–2014). *Folklore* 66. 15–36.

Pavlović, Milivoj. 1970. *Govor Janjeva: Međudijalekatski i miksoglotski procesi* [The Janjevo dialect: Interdialectical and mixoglottic processes]. Novi Sad: Matica srpska.

Pešikan, Mitar. 1984. Neke zetske dijalekatske paralele pojava u makedonskom glagolskom sistemu [Some Zeta dialectal parallels in the verbal system of Macedonian]. *Makedonski jazik* 35. 117–121.

Petrović, Dragoljub. 2005. Božidar Vidoeski i istraživanje srpsko-makedonskih dijalekatskih kontakata [Božidar Vidoeski and research into Serbo-Macedonian dialectal contacts]. *Arealna lingvistika. Teorii i metodi. Meǵunarodna konferencija v pamet na Božidar Vidoeski*, 35–50. Skopje: MANU.

Pižurica, Mato. 1984. Tragovi međujezičkih dodira u govorima Crne Gore [Examination of language contacts in Montenegrin dialects]. *Crnogorski govori. Rezultati dosadašnjih ispitivanja i dalji rad na njihovom proučavanju: zbornik radova sa nauchnog skupa*, 83–95. Titograd: CANU.

Poplack, Shana & Suzanne Robillard, Nathalie Dion, John C. Paolillo. 2020. Revisiting phonetic integration in bilingual borrowing. *Language*. 96/1. 126–159.

Popović, Ivan. 1958. Slaven und Albaner in Albanien und Montenegro. Zum Problem der slavisch-albanischen Sprachchronologie. *Zeitschrift für Slawische Philologie* 26 (2). 301–324.

Prendergast, Eric Heath. 2017. *The origin and spread of locative determiner omission in the Balkan linguistic area*. Ph.D. dissertation. Berkeley, CA: University of California dissertation.

Rusakov, Alexander Yu. & Andrey N. Sobolev. 2008. *Substantsial'no-funktsional'naia teoriia balkanskogo iazykovogo soiuza i slavianskie iazyki* [A substantial and functional theory of Balkan Sprachbund and Slavic languages]. XIV Mezhdunarodnyi s"ezd slavistov v Okhride, Makedoniia. St. Petersburg: ILI RAN.

Silva-Corvalán, Carmen. 1994. *Language contact and change: Spanish in Los Angeles*. Oxford: Clarendon Press.

Smith, Norval. 2000. Symbiotic mixed languages: A question of terminology. *Bilingualism: Language and Cognition* 3. 122–123.

Sobolev, Andrey N., Maxim L. Kisilier, Viacheslav V. Kozak, Daria V. Konior, Anastasia L. Makarova, Maria S. Morozova & Alexander Yu. Rusakov. 2018. Iuzhnoslavianskie dialekty v simbioticheskikh soobshchestvakh Balkan [South Slavic dialects in symbiotic communities of the Balkans]. *Acta linguistica Petropolitana. Trudy Instituta lingvisticheskikh issledovanij RAN* 14 (2). 685–746.

Sobolev, Andrey N. 2003. *Iuzhnoslavianskie iazyki v balkanskom areale. Doklad k XIII Mezhdunarodnomu s"ezdu slavistov* (Liubliana, avgust 2003) [South Slavic languages in the Balkan linguistic area. Paper delivered at the 13th Congress of Slavists (Ljubljana, August 2003)]. Marburg: Institut für Slavische Philologie.

Sobolev, Andrey N. 2008. On some Aromanian Grammatical Patterns in the Balkan Slavonic Dialects. In Biljana Sikimić & Tijana Ašić (eds.), *The Romance Balkans*, 113–121. Belgrade: Balkanološki institut SANU.

Sobolev, Andrey N. 2011. Antibalkanizmy [Antibalkanisms]. *Južnoslovenski filolog* 67. 185–195.

Sobolev, Andrey N. 2012. On redundancy in Albanian. In Domosiletskaia, Marina V., Alvina V. Zhugra, Maria S. Morozova & Alexander Yu. Rusakov (eds.), *Sovremennaia albanistika: dostizheniia i perspektivy* [Contemporary Albanology: Achievements and Perspectives], 407–412. St. Petersburg: Nestor-Istoriia.

Sobolev, Andrey N. 2013. *Osnovy lingvokul'turnoi antropogeografii Balkanskogo poluostrova. Tom I. Homo balcanicus i ego prostranstvo* [Foundations of linguocultural anthropogeography on the Balkan peninsula. Vol. 1. Homo balcanicus and his space]. St. Petersburg, München: Nauka, Otto Sagner Verlag.

Sobolev, Andrey N. 2015. Mrkovichi (i Gorana): iazyki i dialekty chernogorskogo Primor'ia v kontekste noveishikh balkanisticheskikh issledovanii [Mrkovići (and Gorana): Languages and dialects of the Montenegro coast in the context of recent Balkan research]. In Demiraj Bardhyl (ed.), *Sprache und Kultur der Albaner: Zeitliche und raumliche Dimensionen. Akten der 5. Deutsch-albanischen kulturwissenschaftlichen Tagung (Albanien, Buçimas bei Pogradec, June 5–8, 2014)*, 533–556. Wiesbaden: Harrassowitz.

Sobolev, Andrey N. 2016. Sravnitel'no-istoričeskoe i areal'no-tipologičeskoe izučenie balkanskih dialektov: aktual'nye voprosy teorii. [Comparative-historical and areal-typological research in Balkan dialects]. *Linguistique Balkanique* 1. 53–74.

Sobolev, Andrey N. 2017. Iazyki simbioticheskikh soobschestv Zapadnykh Balkan: grecheskii i albanskii iazyki v sele Paliasa v kraine Himara, Albaniia [Languages in the Western Balkan

Symbiotic Societies: Greek and Albanian in Palasa, Himara, Albania]. *Vestnik Sankt-Peterburgskogo gosudarstvennogo universiteta. Iazyk i literatura* 14 (3). 421–442.

Sobolev, Andrey N. & Aleksandr A. Novik. 2013. *Golo Bordo (Gollobordë), Albaniia. Iz materialov balkanskoi ekspeditsii* RAN *i SPbGU 2008–2010 gg.* [Golo Bordo (Gollobordë) Albania. From the materials of the RAS and SPSU expedition of 2008–2010]. Munich: Otto Sagner Verlag, St. Petersburg: Nauka.

Stanišić, Vanja. 1995. *Srpsko-albanski jezički odnosi* [Serbo-Albanian linguistic relations]. Beograd: Srpska akademija nauka i umetnosti.

Stern, Dieter. 2004. Balkansprachen und Kreolsprachen: Versuch einer kontakttypologischen Grenzziehung. *Zeitschrift für Balkanologie* 42(1–2). 206–225.

Sukhachev, Nikolai. 2021. *Tyurkizmy v yazykakh Yugo-Vostochnoy Yevropy* [Turkic lexical items in the languages of South Eastern Europe]. St. Petersburg: Nauka.

Syrku, Polihroniy A. 1899. Narechie karashevcev [The Krashovani dialect]. *Izvestiya* ORYAS *Imperatorskoy AN* 2. 641–660.

Šekularac, Božidar & Cvetko Pavlović. 2012. *Toponimija opštine Bar* [Toponyms of the Bar municipality]. Podgorica: DANU.

Thomason, Sarah. 2006. Language change and language contact. In Keith Brown (ed.), *Encyclopedia of Language and Linguistics*, 2nd edition, 339–346. Oxford: Elsevier.

Torres Cacoullos, Rena & Catherine E. Travis. 2018. *Bilingualism in the Community. Code-switching and Grammars in Contact.* Cambridge: Cambridge University Press.

Vujović, Luka. 1969. Mrkovićki dijalekat (s kratkim osvrtom na susjedne govore) [The dialect of Mrkovići (with a brief account of neighboring subdialects)]. *Srpski dijalektološki zbornik* 18. 73–399.

Wahlström, Max. 2015. *The loss of case inflection in Bulgarian and Macedonian* (Slavica Helsingensia. Vol. 47). Helsinki: Helsinki University.

Ylli [Iully], Xhelal [Dzhelial'] & Andrey N. Sobolev. 2002. *Albanskii toskskii govor sela Leshnia (Kraina Skrapar). Sintaksis. Leksika. Etnolingvistika. Teksty.* [The Albanian-Tosk subdialect of the town of Leshnia (Skrapar Krajina). Syntax. Lexicon. Ethnolinguistics. Texts]. Marburg: Biblion Verlag.

Ylli [Iully], Xhelal [Dzhelial'] & Andrey N. Sobolev. 2003. *Albanskii gegskii govor sela Mukhurr (Kraina Dibyr). Sintaksis. Leksika. Etnolingvistika. Teksty.* [The Albanian-Gheg subdialect of the town of Mukhurr (Dibyr Krajina). Syntax. Lexicon. Ethnolinguistics. Texts]. München: Biblion Verlag.

Anastasia L. Makarova
Mutual Understanding among Albanians, Slavs and Aromanians in Prespa, North Macedonia: Perfect Tense as a Perfect Tool

Abstract: This chapter[1] deals with a polylingual community in the geographically isolated Prespa region in Republic of North Macedonia, where Macedonians, Albanians, Aromanians, Turks, and Romani have been living for several centuries. Based on the author's intensive fieldwork on the three languages since 2012, the chapter presents in detail one segment of this system – the past tenses. Special emphasis is put on the "Balkan perfect tense" phenomenon, with special attention given to the three analytical forms that convey the perfect tense meaning in the Macedonian Prespa dialect. This is, in turn, set against the background of the analogous grammatical constructions in Albanian and Aromanian. Data obtained by questionnaires and dialectal texts produced by multilingual informants are provided and analysed showing that mutual contacts of Albanian, Macedonian, and Aromanian dialects (all members of the Balkan Sprachbund) have generated **a convergent grammar system** in which the identical set of grammatical meanings is expressed by means of isomorphic forms.

1 General historical and cultural information about the region

The Prespa lakes area or, as it will be referred to here, Prespa, is a high-altitude isolated region in the geographical centre of the Balkan Peninsula. Prespa is surrounded mainly by a steep, stony, wooded and grassy mountain chain. A quarter of the territory of the Prespa basin is occupied by the Great and Small Prespa lakes. Due to its high position above sea level and natural isolation, as well as other favorable natural factors (mild climate, rich water and forest resources, fertile soils), Prespa became an attractive territory for settlement at an early stage (Jovanovski 2005: 11).

---

1 This research was made possible by a grant from the Russian Science Foundation (the projects "From Separation to Symbiosis: South Eastern European languages and cultures in contact", No. 14-18-01405 and "Balkan bilingualism in dominant and equilibrium contact situations in diatopy, diachrony and diastraty", No. 19-18-00244).

https://doi.org/10.1515/9781501509254-003

Prespa is a diverse area from a natural, geographic, and economic point of view and home to a mosaic of ethnicities, ethno-confessions and cultures. This region is now also divided by political boundaries between the Republic of Albania, the Republic of Greece and the Republic of North Macedonia. State borders pass through the waters of Great Prespa Lake. Over the past few decades, Prespa's inhabitants, separated by political boundaries, have been isolated due to the prohibition of movement from one country to another along the lake's waters and the absence of border crossings (with the exception of one crossing between Albania and North Macedonia (Sobolev 2013: 98)).

The first Slavic tribes came to Prespa in the 6th century. Having fallen under Greek influence (south of the Jireček line (Jireček 1952)), they partially replaced and partially assimilated the indigenous population, which at that time consisted of Romanized and Hellenized paleo-Balkan tribes.

During the Middle Ages, Prespa was a politically and strategically important region of the Balkan Peninsula. At the end of the 10th and the beginning of the 11th centuries, during the reign of King Samuel, the whole region became part of the medieval early feudal state of the Balkan Slavs – the First Bulgarian Kingdom, which at that time included almost the entire Balkan Peninsula (in Macedonian national historiography it is customary to call the period of Samuel's reign (971–1018) the Samuel Kingdom). Prespa became an important political and spiritual centre with a capital on the island of St. Achilles in the Small Prespa Lake (Jovanovski 2005; Mikulčić 1996). On the oldest of the ancient Bulgarian inscriptions, the inscriptions of King Samuel see Ivanov (1986: 26–27) and Georgiev (2003).

While Ottoman defters allow us to quite accurately trace the dynamics of migration processes during the Ottoman rule in the Prespa lakes region (Sokolski 1973), the first Turkish permanent settlers appeared in Prespa in the 16th century. They were, most likely, officers or officials of the administrative and judicial apparatus of the empire who had finished their service and received flax (feudal holdings) as a reward, or were invested with new responsibilities for the administration of this territory. Subsequently, Ottoman farmers, artisans, traders, clerics, and others settled in Prespa (Jovanovski 2005). In the 17th and 18th centuries, as a result of these processes, the Turkish ethnic element significantly expanded its presence in the area. According to statistics, there were 151,061 residents of the Gorna and Dolna Prespa *nahiyahs* at the end of the 19th century, among whom there were 14,370 Turks, 12,346 Albanians and 22,995 Vlachs (Kŭnčov 1900)).

We do not have reliable historical evidence regarding when Albanians began to appear around the Prespa lakes. The Macedonian historical tradition indicates that Albanian settlement only began from the second half of the 18th century, "primarily as a result of Turkish policy, whose goal was to strengthen defensive power and stability by means of militant Islamized Albanians, especially in areas where there was discontent, presence of the Haiduk movement and armed uprisings, which amounted to Prespa" (Jovanovski 2005). However, according to a study by Lumnie Jusufi (Jusufi 2012: 167–182), evidence based on personal names from medieval Ottoman documents confirms an Albanian presence in Manastir (Bitola) and Prespa from the 15th century.

Of the 46 settlements in Macedonian Prespa today, the mixed Albanian-Macedonian population lives only in six villages (besides Resen, the administrative center of the region): Krani, Nakolec, Grnčari, Arvati, Asamati and Gorna Bela Crkva. These villages are compactly located on the north-eastern shore of Prespa Lake (except for the village of Nakolec, which is located in the southeast). The Aromanian population lives in Resen and in the adjacent village of Jankovec.

Until the 20th century, Prespa's economy was based on cattle breeding (in the mountains), field crop cultivation (in the area of Resensko pole) and fishing (in coastal villages). Residents of Prespa have always engaged in beekeeping, viticulture and horticulture. After the construction of special irrigation systems, apple cultivation began to take priority among the local population (Jovanovski 2005: 24–26).

In recent years, tourism has played a significant role in the regional economy. According to our observations, ethnicity does not correlate with the distribution of occupations. Engaging in various types of agriculture, tourism, administrative, educational, medical or trade spheres can be practiced by both Macedonians and Albanians. Turks from Resen often work in the restaurant industry. Roma form a special group as most are not involved in registered labor activity.

The study presented in this chapter focused on three localities of Macedonian Prespa: Resen, Arvati and Krani.

Resen is the administrative center of the region, which was granted city status only in the middle of the 19th century (Pjanka 1970; Hadži-Vasiljević 1927). In antiquity there was the settlement of Sciritiana, which was dependent upon the Roman *Via Egnatia* trade and military route (Cvijić 1911). According to local legend, a new period of the history of Resen began at the end of the 17th century, when residents of the village of Dobrovo (2km south-east of Resen) left their land due to frequent devastating attacks and moved to safer places, including a previously small and insignificant village, first mentioned in the 16th century Slepčev codex as Resen (Jovanovski 2005; Pjanka 1970; Selishchev 1933). Today it is the largest settlement and the only town in the whole Prespa region. It is believed that the Macedonians began to migrate there in the early 19th century from the villages of Podmočani, Bolno, Malevišta, among others (Pjanka 1970). In addition to Macedonians and Albanians, a significant part of the population consisted of Turks and Roma. In the past, Resen (with the adjacent village of Jankovec) used to be one of the major Aromanian centres.

Krani is a clachan on the eastern shore of Prespa lake. Today most inhabitants are occupied with cattle breeding, apple cultivation and related trades. Archaeological evidence suggests that the settlement already existed on this site twenty centuries ago. Traces of a settlement dating from the late antiquity and remains of several medieval Orthodox churches and cemeteries were also found (Momeva 2012). The village of Krani is located 2.5 kilometers from the shore of the Prespa lake at an altitude of 987m above sea level at the foot of Mount Pelister. Today the village has 416 inhabitants, including 103 Macedonians and 305 Albanians (Jovanovski 2005).

The village of **Arvati** is located to the east of Krani at an altitude of 900m above sea level. At present, Arvati and Krani have actually merged into one settlement. However, for the local people, opposition between the two villages still exists. Inhabitants are mostly occupied with cattle breeding and handiwork. At present the village has 137 inhabitants with 51 Macedonians and 85 Albanians (Jovanovski 2005).

The Islamic residents of Krani and Arvati visit the same mosque, which is considered a formal border between Krani and Arvati and shares the same Muslim cemetery. Despite such a close neighborhood, the villages are organized in different ways. For example, in Krani, Macedonian houses are located in a separate compact area (in one of five mahallas), while in Arvati Macedonian and Albanian houses are not separated in terms of location and comprise multiethnic neighbourhoods.

2 Regional languages and idioms

2.1 The Macedonian dialect

The Prespa dialects are a western peripheral group of Macedonian dialects. They have been subject to a large amount of Balkanizing innovations and yet have also preserved a number of Slavic archaisms.[2] Meanwhile, the Macedonian dialect of the Gorna Prespa region occupies an intermediate position between the peripheral Ohrid-Strugian western dialects and the central-western dialects chosen in the middle of the 20th century as the basis for the Macedonian literary language (Vidoeski 1998: 9–33).

---

[2] Among archaic phenomena, in the field of morphosyntax one should first note the preservation of elements of syntactic declination; most of the dialects in this region have preserved dative forms for proper nouns (and also the nouns *Bog* ('God') and *Gospod* ('Lord') of the masculine gender (Koneski 1966: 115; Mindak 1987).

The only description of the Macedonian dialects of the region of Gorna Prespa (Maced.: *Gornoprespanski govor*) has been done by the Macedonian dialectologist Božidar Vidoeski (1998). Meanwhile, at present no monograph dedicated solely to the Gorna Prespa dialect or to the particular idiom of any Prespan town has been written. The six villages of the Macedonian part of the Prespa Valley (Maced.: *Leskoets, Stenje, Ljubojno, Arvati, Pretor, Tsarev Dvor*) were studied within the framework of the Macedonian dialectological atlas (Gaidova 2008).

According to the classification recognized by Macedonian dialectologists, it is precisely in the Dolna Prespa zone that the important boundary for the Macedonian dialectal differentiation lies: between the peripheral western dialect group and the "Kostur-Lerin" group of the South Macedonian dialect zone. The description of these dialects was done by the Bulgarian dialectologist Blagoi Šklifov (1979). The dialect of the Albanian part of Prespa, which also belongs to the Dolna Prespa subgroup, is described in the work of Goce Cvetanovski (2010).

2.2 Albanian dialects

The Albanian dialects of southwestern Macedonia, including those of the Prespan Albanians, belong to the Tosk dialect group and show similarities with the idioms of the northern Tosk zone (Osmani 1996). The whole of the Tosk zone exhibits weak phonetic and grammatical dialectal differentiation (Desnitskaya 1968: 260), while the Prespan dialect stands out in terms of a vocabulary characterized by a large number of Slavic borrowings (Poloska 2003). The vowel system consists of seven phonemes (*a, e, ë, o, u, i, y*) and represents the standard for the North-Eastern Tosk dialect situation (Osmani 1996: 19; Jusufi 2012: 173).

There is neither quantitative opposition of vowels, nor reduction. In the idioms of the villages Krani and Gorna Bela Crkva, there is a tendency to move forward the articulation of the vowel *ë* in the position in front of the nasal consonant: *dhembë, kengë* (Osmani 1996: 23; Gjinari 2007–2008). In some Slavic borrowings *u* is observed, corresponding to *o* in Albanian (*gumë < gomë; pumpë < pompë*).

The village of Krani is one of the survey points of the Albanian dialectal atlas (Gjinari et al. 2007–2008). The description of the Albanian Prespa dialect was carried out by Zihni Osmani (Osmani 1996, 1997, 2001). Agim Poloska (2003, 2014) was engaged in collecting and analyzing the dialect lexicon of the Albanian villages of Prespa (with special attention to Slavic lexical borrowings). A similar study on the Macedonian dialectal lexicon of the Prespa region was not carried out at that time.

2.3 Aromanian

The dialect of the Prespan Aromanians has not yet been recorded and described in the scientific literature up to the present, but the ethnolinguistic situation of the Resen Vlachs was presented in September 2015 at the 11th Congress on the Study of the Countries of South Eastern Europe (Sofia), based on materials from field research conducted between 2013 and 2015 (Konior & Makarova 2015b; 2017). The dialect of the Prespan Aromanians is related to the idiom of the Krushevo Vlachs (both groups are descendants of the Moskopole Vlachs[3] who fled to North Macedonia). This dialect was described by Gołąb in his monograph (1984). At the same time, there is historical evidence that confirms the presence of Vlachs in the Prespa and Pelister regions even before the destruction of Moskopole and resulting migration. In fact, the first explicit historical testimony in this regard dates back to 976 (in that year some "Vlach thieves" killed the brother of King Samuel David (Winnifrith 1987: 100)). The Vlach villages of southwestern Macedonia in the Pelister and Prespa regions appear to be some of the most ancient Aromanian settlements on the territory of Vardar Macedonia (Kukudis 2013), which is confirmed by the local oral tradition. It is believed that the original dialect of the Prespan Vlachs was significantly different from that of the Moskopole people who had migrated to the country (Weigand 1895: 39–40) on a massive scale. By the beginning of the 19th century, however, local Vlachs had mixed with Moscopole Vlachs and Macedonians had contracted marriages between Krushevian and Prespan Aromanians – all leading to linguistic differences between the groups becoming insignificant.

3 Observations on the language situation in the multi-ethnic communities of Prespa

3.1 The Aromanians

From the second half of the 20th until the beginning of the 21st century, Aromanians who, according to 19th century data (Kŭnčov 1900), were a significant part of the population of Resen and the village of Jankovets, left Prespa and moved to Skopje or abroad. At present only one Aromanian family lives in Resen. The members of this family served as informants for this study. Aromanian is used by

---

[3] Moskopols had fled from a city of that name in southern Albania, destroyed in 18th century by the Muslim Albanians, to North Macedonia and to Northern Greece (Narumov 2001a: 638).

the informants only in the limited speech context of their own family life. In other situations, they use Macedonian (acquired as a second language, but dominating in almost all domains (Konior & Makarova 2017)).

Working with various questionnaires (phonetic, lexical and grammatical), we found out that the language competence of the informants in Aromanian is significantly lower than their competence in Macedonian, especially on the lexical level. Thus, a study conducted using the lexical questionnaire regarding the 'body parts' semantic field showed that our informants know only basic vocabulary in Aromanian ('tongue', 'hand', 'hair'), while a more specific lexicon remains beyond their competence ('earlobe', 'auricle', 'Adam's apple', etc.):

Table 1 "Body parts" in Aromanian and Macedonian dialects of Prespa

Number	English	Macedonian	Aromanian
3.053	tongue	jazik	limba/linba
3.054	sky	nepče	—
3.055	ear	uvo	urekle | urekli
3.056	outer ear	ušna školka	—
3.057	earlobe	mekoto na uvo	—
3.058	tragus or the ear	—	—
3.059	neck	vrat	guše
3.060	front portion of the neck	til	—
3.061	rear portion of the neck	guša	—
3.062	throat	grlo	gurmadz
3.063	Adam's apple	petle	—
3.064	hair on the head	kosa	perče
3.065	beard	brada	barba
3.066	mustache	mustakji	mustaki/ mustac
3.067	hand/arm	răka	măn(ă) | măń
3.068	palm of the hand	kiska | šaka	—

The speech of the Aromanian informants, both oral and written, abounds with frequent cases of code switching (switching to the second language or its subvariant in the process of speech production, depending on the peculiarities of the language situation and the degree of language competence). Thus, in the text of a prayer recorded by the Aromanian informant in the Macedonian Cyrillic alphabet, we see the Macedonian lexeme "blessed". In the absence of an audio recording, we cannot be sure what phonetic reality hides behind this way of transmitting the Prespa dialect, thus we give the text exactly in the form in which it was written by our informant, Figure 1:

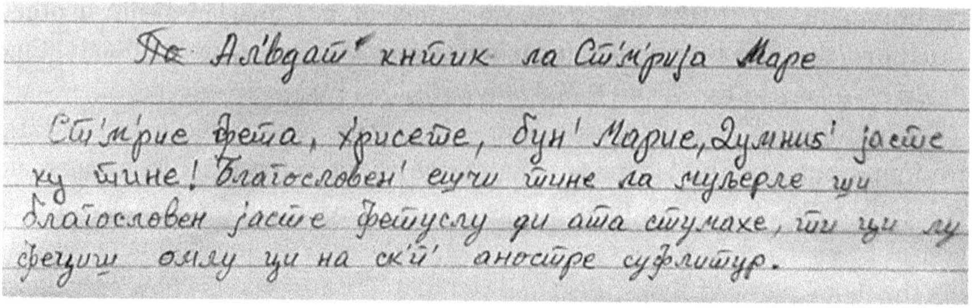
Ал'вдат' кнтик ла Ст'м'рија Маре
Ст'м'рие фета, х'рисете, бун' Марие, Думнис' јасте
ку тине! Благословен' ешчи тине ла муљерле ши
благословен јасте фетуслу ди ата стумахе, ти ци лу
фетиш омлу ци на ск'п' аностре суфлитур.

...Благословен' *ешчи тине ла муљерле ши* ***благословен*** *јасте фетуслу ди ата стумахе...*[4]
'...Blessed are you among women, and blessed is the son of your womb...'

Figure 1 "Hail Mary" prayer.[5]

The oral speech of the Aromanian informants is replete with examples of code switching and spontaneous Macedonian translations. According to the typology developed by P. Muysken (2000, 2013), all interference phenomena occurring in their speech can be divided into three groups: a) insertion, b) alternation and c) congruent lexicalization.

a. **Insertion.** Insertion is the introduction of certain elements from language B (here Macedonian) into a sentence spoken in language A (here Aromanian).

(1) Arom.

K	*feati*	*iram*	*multu*	*skromni.*
As	girl.PL	be.IMPF.1PL	very	modest.PL

'We were very modest girls.

The Macedonian lexeme *skromni* appears in the Aromanian sentence without morphological adaptation (with a full flexion of plural -*i*). It seems that the absence of diachronic morphological and phonetic adaptation is a parameter that distinguishes code-switching from lexical borrowing (Haspelmath 2009: 38; Adamou 2016: 41–42).

b. **Alternation.** Elements of languages A and B fall in a sentence that cannot be uniquely identified as being said in A or B:

4 From a "Hail Mary" prayer (written by our informant in Macedonian Cyrillic).
5 Ал'вдат кнтик ла Ст'м'рија Маре. Ст'м'рие фета, х'рисете, бун' Марие, Думнис' јасте ку тине! Благословен' ешчи тине ла муљерле ши благословен јасте фетуслу ди ата стумахе, ти ци лу фетиш омлу ци на ск'п' аностре суфлитур.

(2) Arom.
Avea   un' muleari ci   ne zapozna.
have.IMPF.3SG a.F woman that us introduce.AOR.3SG
'There was one woman who introduced us'

(3) Arom.
Iram   na odmor.
be.IMPF.1PL in vacation
'We were on vacation'

To this type of code switching, we can also add transitions from A to B at the text level, that is, when the bilingual informant alternates sentences in two languages, as well as cases of spontaneous translation:

(4) Maced./Arom.
Kako da   počnam   ne znam.   K' feati   iram
how PART.CONJ begin.PRS.1SG not know.PRS.1SG as girl.PL be.IMPF.1PL
multu skromni.
very modest.PL
'I do not know how to begin. We were very modest girls.'

(5) Maced./Arom.
Š   bana   mi   ira   multu buna. Životot   mi   beše
and life.DEF me.DAT be.IMPF.3SG very good. life.DEF me.DAT be.IMPF.3SG
ubaf.   Četiriest os'm sme   vo brak.   Fala
beautiful forty   eight be.PRS.1PL in marriage thank
mu   na   Gospo šo   se   vika.   Di   tute
he.DAT on (IO marker) God   what REFL say.PRS.3SG from all.F.PL
ira   bune.   Am   feat   š' fičor. Fičorlu lu
be.IMPF.3SG good.F.PL have.PRS1SG daughter and son   son.DEF he.ACC
vidzuši.   Feata   e   m'rtata.
see.AOR.2SG daughter.DEF be.PRS3SG married
'And my life was very good. (Arom.) I had a good life. (Maced.) For forty-eight [years] we have been married. Thank God, as they say. (Maced.) All was good. I have a daughter and a son. You saw my son. My daughter is married. (Arom.) …'

c. **Congruent lexicalization.** Lexical elements of language B are used in a grammatical structure that is fully or partially represented in both languages. This type of code switching is possible only if the languages are typologically close to each other and demonstrate isomorphism of grammatical structure. "Switching" essentially involves the insertion of a foreign lexical element into a common grammatical construction.

(6) Arom.
 ...nu *puteam* da *prodolžime*
 not can.IMPF.1PL PART.CONJ continue.PRS.1PL
 'We could not continue.'

In the example (6), code switching occurs in a common construction for the Aromanian and Macedonian languages, expressing the category of factivity (modal particle + conjunctive).

The narratives generated by Prespan Aromanian informants so abound with varying examples of code switching that their speech gives the impression of a complete "hodgepodge of languages". This circumstance, as well as the decreased language competence of children (in comparison with their parents), coupled with the fact that grandchildren know Aromanian only passively or do not know it at all, illustrates the process of gradual transition of a large group of people from one language to another (thus a language shift amounts one of the possible outcomes of long-term contact situations (Thomason & Kaufman 1988)). The fact that such a transition took place can be testified by official statistics: if at the end of the 19th century there were more than twenty thousand Vlachs (Kŭnčov 1900) in the Gorna Prespa region, then the data of the population censuses of the 20th century show a gradual decrease in their number up to one dozen at the beginning of the 21st century (Jovanovski 2005), among whom only four people who still remember the Aromanian language.

3.2 The case of Arvati

A language situation atypical to western Macedonia has been recorded in the mountain village of Arvati. Macedonian-Albanian bilingualism is a characteristic of the whole of western Macedonia, with the only bilinguals being Albanians (except for single cases when Macedonian Muslims fall into an Albanian-speaking environment). For the Macedonians of the Orthodox faith, the Albanian language is not prestigious, and the geography of Macedonian towns and villages does not allow one to learn the language in a natural way, such as communicating with foreign-speaking peers in childhood: usually the population is divided into "Albanian" and "Macedonian" zones, which are often divided by a significant physical boundary (such as a river). In the village of Arvati there are no zones based on an ethno-linguistic principle, and bilingualism is a characteristic of each of the ethno-confessional groups: Albanian-Muslims speak the Macedonian language, Macedonian-Orthodox speak Albanian. At the same time, it should be stipulated that such confessionally unbound bilingualism is widespread only among the Macedonian men who were born and grew up in the village of Arvati and in the village of Krani adjacent to it. Macedonian women in these villages usually do not speak Albanian, as most marriages are exogamous (the Orthodox Macedonians of the older and middle generations brought brides usually from other, monoethnic Macedonian villages of Prespa). It can be assumed that the reason for this type of bilingualism was the geographical position of the villages of Arvati and Krani: the settlements are located higher than other villages of the Prespa basin, and earlier, before the paved road, they had been quite isolated from the main communication routes and from the administrative center of the region. Thus Macedonian Orthodox inhabitants, being unable to leave the village on a regular basis, preferred to learn the language of the Albanian Muslim majority as that which determined communication in the village: at the local market, in the shops, at the cafe on the main square in Krani, at public transport stops, or on the bus.

Given that all Albanians also speak Macedonian, one would expect that Macedonian men could also use their mother tongue in talking to Albanians as the women do. However, this does not happen, as the Macedonians prefer to speak Albanian, which, as one can conclude from conversations with bilingual Macedonian informants, is a kind of "honour" for them (as one informant said: *mos mësosh shkip, turpu, aq popull ishte shkiptar* ("If you don't learn Albanian, it is a shame because so many people were Albanians here.")). Such a statement speaks to the high prestige of Albanian.

3.3 Separation and/or symbiosis?

Today on the territory of the Macedonian Prespa, apparently, a symbiotic community is formed by a population of bilingual Macedonian-Albanian villages, where the language of Albanian Muslims – isolated from representatives of other faiths and strictly endogamous community – has a high prestige among Macedonian neighbors of the Orthodox faith. The Aromanian population of Prespa, as the language situation of Resen shows, after a possible centuries-old symbiosis, has survived, but continues to experience another scenario of ethnic and linguistic contact: gradual assimilation and language shift. Unlike the Albanian community, the Prespa Aromanian community was not ethnoconfessional; its representatives freely entered Macedonian families through marriages, and did not necessarily transfer the Aromanian language to their children.

In the present section, the problem of "separation and/or symbiosis" is proposed to be resolved by comparing the grammatical structures of the three idioms in contact. The centuries-old situation of contact in a geographically-isolated territory suggests that the same processes that led to the emergence of the Balkansprachbund on the micro level of dialect contact allowed idioms to undergo greater convergence and develop a greater number of correspondences on all linguistic levels. In the following paragraphs we shall analyze the contact phenomena on the morphosyntactic level, namely the convergence of the preterite systems and the isofunctionality of past verb forms.

4 Sources

Material was collected in accordance with the principles applied in the framework of the MDABL project: the recording of authentic dialect texts based on an ethnolinguistic questionnaire (Plotnikova 1999) and using a special grammatical questionnaire, which is a set of contexts illustrating particular grammatical phenomena. Informants were selected in accordance with the following recommendation: "For this work suitable informants are fluent in both the colloquial and literary language and are able to make a clear distinction between the two." (Sobolev et al. 1997: 14). Some data on our informants is given below.

Monolingual informant

N.T. was born 1953 in the Prespan village of Braichino, North Macedonia. She spent her childhood in Resen and received a medical education in Skopje. She is a dialect speaker who can clearly distinguish between the dialectal and standard form of Macedonian and participates creatively in the study over the course of an interview involving the grammatical questionnaire while noting dialectal features. In her twenties, she had been to Germany where she was able to speak Macedonian (the dialect form) only with her family – with her husband and son. After retirement, she settled permanently in Resen.

Bilingual informants

D.S., of Albanian ethnicity, was born in 1963 in the village of Krani. He graduated from the Department of Philology in Skopje and now teaches Albanian in primary and secondary schools and can clearly distinguish between the dialect and standard form. He studied dialectology of the Albanian language, knows grammatical and dialectological terminology and understands the principle and tasks of the study. During the interview, he draws attention to the features of using verbal forms and phonetic differences between the standard and dialect variants of the language.

The representatives of the only Aromanian family in the town became informants for the Aromanian language: V.A., born in 1954, a woman from Krushevo, has lived in Resen since the age of 19. N.A., born in 1948, Aromanian, is originally from the village of Jankovec. The family owns a tailoring workshop. Their children – a daughter and a son – know Aromanian and speak it with their parents, but in their own families and with their own children they speak only the language of their spouses; i.e., Macedonian.

When answering the questions from the grammatical questionnaire, our Aromanian interlocutors experienced difficulties in translating some words from the meta language (Macedonian) into Aromanian. Taking this fact (and several other practical reasons) into account, the informants were asked to fill out the questionnaire in writing within a few days. Thus, we received a manuscript of the translation of the grammatical questionnaire from Macedonian into the Aromanian language, made in Macedonian Cyrillic. Below, presenting the results of the study, we give its Latin transliteration.

With these informants, we worked using the grammatical questionnaire. In addition, a number of interviews with other bilingual and monolingual interlocutors were recorded. Thus, a corpus of dialect narratives was obtained, which also served as a source for the study of grammatical systems.

The grammatical categories investigated

Temporal and aspectual temporal (perfect) grammatical preterite meanings:
meaning 1.1 simple preterite: a situation that occurred in a particular period (or moment) in the past and ended before the moment of speech; **meaning 1.2 recent past**: a situation that took place just before the moment of speech; **meaning 1.3 long past**: a situation that took place in the distant past; **meaning 1.4 resultative perfect**: the situation took place in the past, but its result is relevant for the present moment; **meaning 1.5 experiential perfect**: meaning refers to the life experience of the subject: the situation has already occurred at least once;

Evidential grammatical meanings of the preterite:
meaning 2.1 evidentiality: the speaker is aware of the situation from an indirect source; **meaning 2.2 admirative**: the speaker expresses surprise at the fact that the situation has occurred; **meaning 2.3 re-narrative**: a consistent story of events in the past. The speaker drew information from an indirect source.

5 Data. General characteristics

The material of our study consists of dialect texts collected over the course of three expeditions between 2014 and 2016: a grammatical questionnaire filled out by three informants (a monolingual Macedonian informant, a bilingual Aromanian informant and an Albanian informant). In addition to the questionnaire, we analysed narratives collected during interviews with the residents of Prespa. Of particular interest are narratives produced by bilingual informants in both languages with the aim of determining whether bilinguals chose the same grammatical strategies when generating the same text in different languages. We also used dialectal texts published earlier in the descriptions of the Macedonian and Albanian dialects of Prespa (see Vidoeski 2000; Osmani 1996).

5.1 Convergence of the verbal systems of nuclear Balkansprachbund languages

Considering the general similarity of the verbal systems of the Balkan languages, most attention has been drawn to such phenomena as the loss of the infinitive and the formation of the common model of the future tense form. These phenomena have been included in the list of Balkanisms since the very first works on Balkan linguistics (Kopitar 1829:106; Miklosich 1861; Sandfeld 1930), and extensive literature has been devoted to them (Asenova 2002: 141–152 lit.; Demiraj 1994: 161–188). Meanwhile, in the verbal system of the Balkan languages, many other regular correspondences can be met, both in local dialects and on the general level of the whole peninsula (or its major regions). Observations on such correspondences allowed Jouko Lindstedt (2002) to ask a specific question: is there a general Balkan verbal system in which forms are shared by different languages, and in which lexical content is unique for every case? The mechanism for the development of such system is identical to the appearance of the remaining Balkanisms: two (or more) closely connected linguistic systems in long-term contact, and gradually adapting to each other owing to the bi- and multilingualism of their speakers, become structurally identical (isomorphic). Most often such convergence will occur on the level of dialectal microcontacts, which can be illustrated by the example of the development of aspectual oppositions in the Romance dialects, where they occupy a subdominant position in relation to the Slavic dialects. Thus, the aspect category was developed by the Aromanian dialects of Ohrid (Marković 2011: 140), and the Istroromanian dialects borrowed some verbal prefixes from the Croatian language (Narumov 2011b: 665).

Development of forms denoting values of the epistemic modality (such as the evidential, optative, etc.) has often been described in general work on Balkan linguistics (Asenova 2002: 220–240), but they are not usually included in the list of Balkanisms (Schaller 1975). This is explained by the fact that these characteristics are shared by many other Indo-European languages genetically related to Balkan ones. From the point of view of areal approach, they can be described more as "Europeanisms" (Hinrichs, Büttner 1999) – features shared by the languages outside the Balkan region (Lindstedt 2002: 332–233; Haspelmath 2001).

Separate examples of the convergence of linguistic systems observed in the contacting idioms of the Balkan Peninsula suggest that long-term contact among several dialects in a closed geographic space could lead to such profound structural changes as the development of an isomorphic (in the wide sense) grammatical system. As a result, the same set of forms expresses a single set of grammatical values. Table 2 shows the set of verbal forms possible for the preterital system of three corresponding macrodialect groups: Macedonian peripheral-western, Albanian-Toskan and the dialect of the Moscopole Aromanians settled in North Macedonia (the table does not list the forms of the pluperfect (for the Albanian pluperfect and supercomplex forms see (Rusakov 2015, 2016)) and a separate "non evidential" paradigm of the Macedonian verb, homonymous to *l*-perfect (Makartsev 2014)).

Table 2 Past tense system in Macedonian, Albanian and Aromanian

Verb form (past tense)	Macedonian language	Aromanian language	Albanian language
imperfect	slušav	askultam	dëgjoja
aorist	slušnav	askultai	dëgjova
esse-perfect (Slavic type)	sum slušal/slušnal		
esse-pluperfect (Slavic type)	bev slušal/shlušnal		
habere-perfect	imam slušano/slušnato	amᵘ ascultatᵊ	kam dëgjuar (*act.*)
habere-pluperfect	imav slušano/slušnato	avemᵘ ascultatᵊ *avui (*aor. of auxiliary verb*) ascultatᵊ (*only in Aromanian dialects of Ohrid and Struga (Marković 2014)	kisha dëgjuar (*act.*) *pata (*aor. of auxiliary verb*) dëgjuar (Rusakov 2016)

Verb form (past tense)	Macedonian language	Aromanian language	Albanian language
esse-perfect	(dial.) sum slušan/ slušnat (act.) sum slušan {od site}(pass.)	esk^u vănit^ă 'I have come' derived only from intr. verbs	jam dëgjuar (pass. only)
esse- pluperfect	(dial.) bev slušan/ slušnat (act.) bev slušan {od site} (pass.)	avem^u vănit^ă *plusquampf. of this type in Aromanian dialects of North Macedonia derived only from intr. verbs	isha dëgjuar (pass. only)
admirative		* In the Aromanian dialect of Gorna Belica village an admirative has been recorded Tini **avuska** mari kasă! 'It turns out you have a big house!'	dëgjuakam (presence) dëgjuakësha paskam dëgjuar (pf.) paskësha dëgjuar (plusquampf.)

The "original" verbal systems of macrodialect groups cannot be called parallel, as not all forms in all three languages have a complete correspondence.[6] However, having found themselves in close contact in a closed geographic space (Prespa), the systems, as the results of the survey and data of dialect texts show, exhibit a tendency to become equal and similar to each other. Further, examples of an isomorphic expression of grammatical meanings will be given, as well as cases of exception from this trend.

5.2 Means of expressing grammatical meanings are isofunctional and isomorphic

Isomorphism is meant here, following Björn Wiemer (2020: 280), as a "blueprint for specific structures whose slots can be filled with material from several varieties which are related at different degrees. If such blueprints accumulate in some region, because changes are mutually reinforced, isogrammatism results". The temporal grammatical meanings (see Section 3) are expressed isomorphically in

---

[6] Speaking of the isomorphism of verbal forms, we stick to a broad, maximal understanding of this term.

the studied varieties. Thus, the meaning of a simple past is regularly expressed by resorting to the aorist and imperfect, depending on the aspectual nature of the situation:

(7) Maced.
I plivaf, i lovef, sea ne, ne, tolku
and swim.IMPF.1SG and hunt.IMPF.1SG now no no so much
umorvaf, ne možef pojḱe da oda.
feel tired.IMPF.1SG not can.IMPF.1SG more PART.CONJ walk.PRS.1SG
'And I swam, and went for hunt, now no, no, I felt so tired, could not walk anymore.'

(8) Alb.
Edhe ashu e kalova atë rrezik.
and so it.ACC.SG cross.AOR.1SG this.ACC danger
'And so I went through this danger.'

(9) Arom.
Atunčel nă aduneam tuci tu măhălă fečori, fete
at that time REFL.1PL gather.IMPF.1PL all.PL in mahala boy.PL girl.PL
mări, nic, tuci nă džucam.
adult.PL small.PL all.PL REFL.1PL play.IMPF.1PL
'At that time we all gathered together, the whole mahala. Boys, girls, adults, children, we all played.'

The grammatical meaning of recent past is isomorphically expressed in all three dialects by means of the aorist form (10–12):

(10) Maced. *Samo što umre.*
Only that die.AOR.3SG
'He has just died'

(11) Alb. *Sapo vdiq.*
just die.AOR.3SG
'He has just died'

(12) Arom. *Samo (Maced.) ci mori.*
only that die.AOR.3SG
'He has just died'

The meaning of the long-past can be expressed either by means of the aorist, or by the imperfect, depending on the aspectual character of the situation (examples 9, 10, 12), or by the forms of pluperfect. Iterative and habitual meanings in the examples modeled from the questionnaire are expressed in all three languages with the use of imperfect forms. However, in spontaneous narratives Macedonian informants often choose a special form *ḱe + imperfect* (future in the past) – a grammaticalized construction, marking a series of modal and temporal meanings: 1) the action, following respective to another action in the past; 2) irreality in the apodosis of the conditional period; 3) assumption; 4) habituality / iterative (Koneski 1990: 147–201). In the Albanian and Aromanian languages, where there is no specialized form for expressing habituality, the iterative meaning is expressed by the imperfect. So the form *ḱe zemeše* in example (13) corresponds to the imperfects in example (14).[7]

(13) Maced.
Porano imaše vampiri, vampirite gi šetat
earlier have.IMPF.3SG vampire.PL vampire.PL.DEF they.ACC walk.PRS3PL
po kuḱite, vlegoa vo kuḱata šo nemaše
along house.PL.DEF enter.AOR.3PL in house.DEF that not have.IMPF.3SG
tavan ḱe zemeše koj šo imaše.
ceiling PART.FUT take.IMPF.SG who that have.IMPF.3SG
'There used to be vampires, vampires went to their houses, entered houses where there was no ceiling, they took what they had.'

(14) Alb.
Unë zhdo muaj shkonja në Stamboll.
I every month go.IMPF.1SG in Istanbul
'I used to go to Istanbul every month.'

(15) Arom.
Io kati mes nizem tu Stambol.
I every month go.IMPF.1SG in Istanbul
'I went to Istanbul every month.'

The grammatical meaning of resultative perfect is usually expressed using *habere*-perfect forms in all three languages, as shown in the following examples:

---

[7] Examples 13 and 14 are excerpts from stories in Albanian and Macedonian from one of the informants (Albanian bilingual, the bearer of Albanian and Macedonian dialects of Prespa).

(16) Maced.
   Site   ovie   knigi   gi   *imam*   *pročitano*.
   all.DEF   these   book.PL   they.ACC have.PRS.1SG   read.PART.PASS.N.SG
   'I have read all these books.'

(17) Alb.
   Gjita   këto   libra   i   *kam*   *lexuar*.
   all   these.F   book.PL   they.ACC have.PRS.1SG   read.PART
   'I have read all these books.'

(18) Arom.
   Tute   aiste   kărc   l=   *em*   *ğuvusită*.
   all.PL.F these.F   book.PL   they.ACC have.PRS.1SG   read.PART.PSS.F.SG
   'I have read all these books.'

5.3 Means for expressing grammatical meanings are isofunctional, but not isomorphic

In the western Macedonian dialects, there is a verbal form that does not have isomorphic parallels in other Balkan idioms: the "old" *l*-perfect (*esse*-perfect Slavic type, see table 6), inherited from the common Proto-Slavic language. In eastern Macedonian dialects, the *l*-perfect is used in typical perfect contexts (Fielder 2000); in the western ones, the semantics of the form have undergone profound changes (Graves 2000). The semantics of this form in the modern Macedonian standard language are mainly associated with the category of evidentiality: "Forms of the non-affirmative past tense serve to retell actions that we did not personally perceive, but which were communicated to us from another source, while forms of the affirmative past tense [aorist and imperfect] always assume the performance of action in our presence and personal perception..." (Koneski 1982: 459–475; Curtis 2012: 358). Any information obtained from an indirect source (indirect evidential) is drawn up as an *l*-perfect. In addition, this form can express a number of other meanings of the category of evidentiality: the admirative, the dubitative, the conclusive (Makartsev 2014: 109).

Thus, the verbal systems of the Prespa dialects do not show isomorphism in expressing the values of the epistemic modality. However, the forms that are used in each language are most often regularly isofunctional to the forms used by the other languages. Thus, in the examples (19)–(21) the Macedonian *l*-perfect naturally corresponds to the possessive perfect in Albanian and Aromanian when expressing the admirative meaning:

(19) Maced.
Tolku mnogu nikogaš ne sum prodala!
so much never not be.PRS.1SG sell.PART.PAST.F
'I've never sold so much!'

(20) Alb.
Aq shumë asnjëherë nuk kam shitur!
so much never not have.PRS.1SG sell.PART
'I've never sold so much!'

(21) Arom.
Ahắt multu pute n= om vindută!
so much never not have.PRS.1SG sell.PART.PASS.F.SG
'I've never sold so much!'

In some cases, for example, in case of the verb 'to be' with the meaning 'to visit', there can be seen a competition between all three forms of the perfect tense: *sum bil Stambol/Stambol imam odeno/Stambol sum biden* "I've been to Istanbul". As a rule, the competition of three perfects is observed when expressing the experiential meaning. In this case, the Macedonian *l*-perfect also will regularly correspond to the possessive perfect in Albanian and to the possessive or the *esse*-perfect in Aromaian (the latter will often be chosen with intransitive verbs), as in examples (22)–(24):

(22) Maced.
Da, jas sum bil tamu nekolku pati.
yes I be.PRS.1SG be.PART.PAST.M there several time.PL
'Yes, I've been there several times.'

(23) Alb.
Po, un kam qan[8] atje disa erë.
yes I have.PRS.1SG be.PART.PAST.M there several time.PL
'Yes, I've been there several times.'

---

8 Forms of participle from the verb "to be" in the speech of our Albanian informant: *qenë, k'en, k'enë, qan.*

(24) Arom.
   Da, jo esku   dusă   aklo   multu or.
   yes I be.PRS.1SG depart.PART.PAST.M there several time
   'Yes, I've been there several times.'

It should be noted that, in the narratives of the Prespa dialect of Albanian, there are phenomena that give evidence to the drift of the meaning of the possessive perfect form towards the simple preterite (Fryd 1998). Thus, in the example from Krani, the perfect form is accompanied by an indication of the exact date of the event:

(25) Alb.
   Gjashtëmbëdhjetë kollozheg kam   rënë   në mest
   sixteen   January   have.PRS.1SG fall.PART in middle
   të   gjolit.
   ART.LINK lake.GEN
   'On the sixteenth of January I fell into the water in the middle of the lake.'

The prohibition on employing the Macedonian possessive perfect to indicate the moment of committing an action is still valid (Velkovska 1998). However, in the speech of the bilingual Albanians of North Macedonia, this prohibition can be violated under the influence of the Albanian grammatical model and the perfect tense form loses the semantic component of current relevance, as it can be observed in the following example (upon our request, the informant translated the story of his fall into the lake (example 26) into Macedonian):

(26) Maced.
   Osumdeset i   prva   godina šesnaeseti januar   imam
   eighty   and first.F   year   Sixteen.M   January   have.PRS.1SG
   frleno   ovie   mrežite   v   ezero.
   throw.PART.PASS.M   these net.PL.DEF in lake
   'In year eighty-one on the sixteenth of January, I threw these nets into the lake.'

We see that the perfect here does not fulfill two conditions determining the perfect meaning (Lindstedt 2002): 1) prohibition of being used as a narrative verb form (see example 27, i.e., the story of the events of the distant past, as in 28 and 29); 2) inability to use with a temporary determinant.

(27) Alb.
   Aty   ka   një   kishë. Më   ka   zënë
   there have.PRS.3SG one   church me.ACC have.PRS.3SG catch.PART
   shiu.   Isha   me   dhëntë   dhe   kam   vënë
   rain.DEF be.IMPF.1SG with sheep.PL.DEF and   have.PRS.1SG   put.PART
   kokën   te   pragu   i   kishës   aty
   head.ACC.DEF to   Threshol.NOM.DEF ART.LINK church.GEN.DEF   there
   dhe... S= kam   patur   frikë,   as   pej   ije,
   and   not have.PRS.1SG have.PART   fear   neither   from   shadow.PL
   as pej   lugati.
   neither from   vampire
   'There is one church there. I was caught in the rain. I was with the sheep, and I leaned my head against the threshold of the church there and ... I was not afraid neither of shadows nor of a vampire.'

5.4 Means of expressing grammatical meanings are isomorphic, but allofunctional

Exceptions to general isomorphism will also apply to the use of the *esse*-perfect in the Aromanian and Macedonian dialects in the active sense. In such cases, the standard Albanian active form of the *habere*-perfect will correspond to these forms in Albanian, examples (28)–(30):

(28) Maced.
   Ne e   doma   sega,   izlezena   e.
   not be.PRS.3SG at home   now   go out.PART.PASS.F   be.PRS.3SG
   'She's not at home now, she's gone out.'

(29) Alb.
   Nuk është   në shtëpi, ka   dalë.
   not   be.PRS.3SG in house   have.PRS.3SG go out.PART
   'She's not at home now, she's gone out.'

(30) Maced.
   Nu   e   akas,   tora inšită   e.
   not be.PRS.3SG at home   now   go out.PART.PASS.F be.PRS.3SG
   'She's not at home now, she's gone out.'

Albanian forms such as *jam larë* are able to express the values of both the passive actional perfect ("I was washed.") and the static object resultative ("I am washed") (Buchholz & Fielder 1987: 186; Massey 2000).

This form is isomorphic and isofunctional to the Macedonian constructions, expressing a passive result (Veklovska 1998), but is allofunctional with respect to the *esse*-perfect in the active meaning like *sum dojden*.

However, when expressing a passive meaning using these forms, the system becomes completely isomorphic, as in examples (31)–(33):

(31) Maced.
 Mnogu sum umoren.
 much be.PRS.1SG tire.PART.PASS.M
 'I am very tired'

(32) Alb.
 *Shum i lodhur jam.*⁹
 much ART.LINK tire.PART be.PRS.1SG
 'I am very tired'

(33) Arom.
 Multu esku kurmată.
 much be.PRS.1SG tire.PART.PASS.F
 'I am very tired'

The Macedonian *esse*-perfect has a complete isomorphic parallel in the Aromanian Macedonian dialects: the perfect of the *esk^u vinit^ă* type in the Aromanian dialects of North Macedonia. Such a perfect is attested neither in the Aromanian dialects of Greece and Albania, nor in the idiom of the Aromanians who moved to Dobrudja (Papahagi 1974; Vrabie 2000; Bara, Kahl & Sobolev 2005; Saramandu & Nevaci 2013: 130–153; Nevaci 2011).

This perfect is described in Gołąb's monograph (1984) focusing on the grammar of the Krushevo dialect, and in the works of Marjan Marković (2007, 2011, 2014), who reviewed the idioms of the Ohrid Aromanians. At the same time, it is interesting that in the "Aromanian grammar" published in Krushevo in 2001, only the forms of possessive perfect are given (Ianachieschi-Vlahu 2001), while the form is used by the Aromanians of Resen.

---

9 The form *i lodhur jam* (as well as the Macedonian *сум уморен* and the Aromanian *esku kurmată*) can be characterized as a passive of state: *Zustandspassiv* (Buchholz & Fielder 1987: 192).

(34) Arom.
Samo un oră tu bană esku   dusă   tu Stambol.
only one time in life be.PRS.1SG go.PART.PASS.F in Istambul
'Only once in my life did I go to Istanbul.'
(compare to Maced. *sum oden vo Stambol*).

In our data from the town of Resen, the use of a perfect type of esk^u $vinit^ă$ from transitive verbs in the active voice is not recorded, with the exception of one lexical-semantic group: food intake (compare to Maced. *salata sum jaden*, see Graves (2000)):

(35) **Arom.** *Esk măkat.* = (**Maced.**) *Sum jaden* "I have eaten."
Arom. *Esk bit.* = (**Maced.**) *Sum pien* "I have drunk."
Arom. *Esk činat.* = (**Maced.**) *Sum večeran* "I have had supper."

Verbs which can form this type of perfect usually refer to the lexical group of verbs of movement and state change, which makes the situation typologically similar to the common opposition of perfects with the auxiliary verbs 'to be' and 'to have' in European languages (Sichinava 2008). In the Aromanian language, the construction of 'to be' + passive participle from the transitive verb, as a rule, expresses value of the statal objective resultative:

(36) Arom.
Anostru căsăbă e   multu vekl'u.
our town be.PRS.3S much old
Tu rimskul   di kiro e   adrată.
in Roman.M.DEF from time be.PRS.3S build.PART.PASS.F
'Our town [Resen] is very old. It was built in the Roman era.'

The use of the transitive verbs of the lexico-semantic group 'food intake' in the structure of this construction, apparently, should be considered a lexicalized exception.

Like the forms of a possessive perfect, a perfect type esk^u $vinit^ă$ is rarely found in free narratives (more often in spontaneous dialogues), which indicates that this form is also at the first stage of evolution in the resultative constructions (Lindstedt 2000); most of the examples of its use in the dialect of the Aromanian Resen were obtained through the grammatical questionnaire.

6 Conclusion

As shown by the above examples, the formal means of expressing grammatical meanings in the dialects of the Prespa region can be divided into three groups.

The first group includes *isofunctional* and *isomorphic* means of expressing grammatical sense. These include the resultative perfect markers (*habere-* and *esse-*perfect), the simple past, the long-past and the recent past. The iterative meaning is expressed isomorphically (through the forms of the imperfect) in isolated utterances; in long narratives the Macedonian idiom prefers a specialized form that does not find isofunctional parallels in contacting languages.

The second group includes *isofunctional*, but *non-isomorphic*, means of expressing grammatical sense. Thus, for example, often in the expression of the meaning of the experiential perfect, the Macedonian informant chooses the perfect of the Slavic type. At the same time in Aromanian and Albanian this regularly corresponds to the *habere-*perfect or *esse-*perfect, depending on the verb's transitivity. In addition, this group includes cases of expressing the values of the epistemic modality of the admirative, evidential and dubitative, for which a special modal paradigm is usually chosen in the Macedonian dialect – the homonymous *esse-*perfect of the Slavic type. The analogous form in the Albanian and Aromanian is the *habere-*perfect (the Albanian dialect of Prespa at one point lost the actual Albanian means of expressing the admirative meaning; i.e. the admirative mood (Osmani 1996)).

Forms of *esse-*perfect in Aromanian and Macedonian expressing the active meaning are *isomorphic*, but *allofunctional* towards the *esse-*perfect in Albanian, which expresses only a passive meaning.

Thus, we see that the grammatical systems demonstrate a high degree of convergence when expressing the same set of modal and temporal grammatical meanings of the past tense system. Such an isomorphic system could be formed because of a prolonged direct contact of dialects in a relatively enclosed territory and with mass bilingualism: the Prespan Aromanians have always known Aromanian and Macedonian, the Albanians Albanian and Macedonian, and the Macedonians Macedonian and Albanian.

Exceptions from isomorphism appear, as expected, in situations where the language systems demonstrate the most profound formal inconsistencies that date back to the pre-contact period. For example, most cases of "non-isomorphism" arise in the expression of evidential meanings, where the *esse-*perfect is used in the Macedonian dialect of the (common) Slavic type. The Slavic active past participle of the past tense ending in *-lъ* is considered to be one of the antidonational elements, that is, one of those linguistic phenomena that "*do not go beyond the original language*" under the Balkan linguistic convergence and are most difficult to be traced and borrowed (Sobolev 2011). Structurally isomorphic verb forms (that is, all forms other than the *esse*-perfect of the Slavic type) are generally isofunctional in the Prespa dialects. The exception is the form of the *esse*-perfect in Albanian, which is used only for expressing the passive voice, while in Macedonian they have become unmarked due to the loss of the voice distinction in the Slavic participle in -n/-t (Sobolev 1999). Possibly, resulting from the calquing of the corresponding Aromanian construction (see Gołąb 1984), the *esse*-perfect appeared in the sense of the active voice.

Thus, the example of the Prespa convergent dialect group shows that grammatical systems – under conditions of language contact and in a geographically isolated territory – can change and adapt to each other acquiring and shedding some of their pre-contact elements.

References

Adamou, Evangelia. 2016. *A Corpus-driven Approach to Language Contact: Endangered Languages in a Comparative Perspective*. Berlin & Boston: Mouton de Gruyter.
Asenova, Petya. 2002. *Balkansko ezikoznanie* [Balkan linguistics]. Sofia: Faber.
Bara, Maria, Thede Kahl & Andrey N. Sobolev. 2005. *Die südaromunische Mundart von Turia (Pindos)*. München: Biblion Verlag.
Buchholz, Olga & Wilfried Fielder. 1987. *Albanische Grammatik*. Leipzig: Verlag Enzyclopädie.
Curtis, Matthew C. 2012. *Slavic-Albanian Language Contact, Convergence, and Coexistence*. Ohio State University Doctoral Dissertaton.
Cvetanovski, Goce. 2010. *Govorot na Makedoncite vo Mala Prespa* [The dialect of Macedonians in Mala Prespa]. Skopje: Institut za makedonski jazik "Krste Misirkov".
Cvijić, Jovan. 1911. *Osnove za geografiju i geologiju Makedonije i Stare Srbije* [Foundations of the geography and geology of Old Serbia]. Beograd: Srpska Kraljevska Akademija.
Demiraj, Shaban. 1994. *Balkanska lingvistika* [Balkan linguistics]. Skopje: Logos-A.
Desnitskaya, Agniya V. 1968. *Albanskii iazyk i ego dialekty* [Albanian and its dialects]. Leningrad: Nauka.
Fielder, Grace E. 2000. The perfect in Eastern Macedonian dialects. In Vera Stojčevska-Antić et al. (eds.), *IV makedonsko-severnoamerikanskata slavistička konferencija za makedonistika* [IVth North-American-Macedonian Conference: Studies related to Macedonian language, literature, and culture], 137–146. Skopje: Univerzitet "Sv. Kiril i Metodij".
Fryd, Marc. 1998. Present perfect et datation: Une dérive aoristique. In Andrée Borillo, Carl Vetters & Marcel Vuillaume (eds.), *Regards sur l'aspect*, 29–50. Amsterdam & Atlanta: Rodopi.
Gaidova, Ubavka (ed.). 2008. *Makedonski dialekten atlas. Prolegomena* [Macedonian dialect atlas. Prolegomena]. Skopje: Institut za makedonski jazik "Krste Misirkov".
Georgiev, Petŭr. 2003. Prespa. In *Kirilo-Metodievska Entsiklopediia* [The Cyril and Methodius Encyclopedia] 3, 327–331. Sofia: BAN.
Gjinari, Jorgji, Bahri Beci, Gjovalin Shkurtaj & Xheladin Gosturani. 2007–2008. *Atlasi dialektologjik i gjuhës shqipe* [Albanian dialect atlas], Vol. 1–2. Napoli, Italy: Universita degli studi di Napoli l'Orientale; Tirana: Akademia e shkencave e Shqipërisë.

Gołąb, Zbigniew. 1984. *The Arumanian dialect of Kruševo. SR Macedonia, SFR Yougoslavia.* Skopje: MANU.
Graves, Nina. 2000. Macedonian – A language with three perfects? In Dahl, Östen (ed.), *Tense and Aspect in the Languages of Europe*, 479–494. Berlin: de Gruyter.
Hadži-Vasiljević, Jovan. 1927. Resen i njegova okolina [Resen and its surroundings]. *Brastvo* 21. 40–55.
Haspelmath, Martin. 2001. The European linguistic area: Standard Average European. In Martin Haspelmath, Ekkehard König, Wulf Oesterreicher & Wolfgang Raible (eds.), *Language typology and language universals* (Handbücher Zur Sprach- und Kommunikationswissenschaft), Vol. 2, 1492–1510. Berlin & New York: Mouton de Gruyter.
Haspelmath, Martin. 2009. Lexical borrowing: Concepts and issues. In Haspelmath, Martin & Uri Tadmor (eds.), *Loanwords in the world's languages: A comparative handbook*, 35–54. Berlin: De Gruyter Mouton.
Haspelmath, Martin et al. (eds.). 2005. *The World Atlas of Language Structures*. Oxford & New York: Oxford University Press.
Hinrichs, Uwe. 1999a. Balkanismen – Europäismen. In *Eurolinguistik – ein Schritt in die Zukunft. Beiträge zum Symposion von 24–27 März 1997*, 85–110. Wiesbaden: Harrassowitz.
Hinrichs, Uwe. 1999b. *Handbuch der Südosteuropa-Linguistik*. Wiesbaden: Harrasowitz Verlag.
Ianachieschi-Vlahu, Iancu. 2001. *Gramaticã armãneascã* [Grammar of Aromanian]. Krushevo: Drushtvo za kultura I umetnost ART-KUL Krushevo.
Ivanov, Iordan N. 1986. *Bŭlgarite v Makedoniia. Fototipno izdanie* [Bulgarians in Macedonia]. 2nd ed. Sofia: Nauka i izkustvo.
Jireček, Konstantin. 1952. *Istorija Srba* [The History of Serbs]. Beograd: Naučna knjiga.
Jovanovski, Vlado. 2005. *Naselbite vo Prespa (mestopoložba, istorijski razvoj i minato)* [The populated places in Prespa (localities, historical development and the past)]. Skopje: Ǵurǵa.
Jusufi, Lumnije. 2012. Historische Migrationen im Spiegel der Dialektlandschaft von Manastir. In Bardhyl Demiraj (ed.), *Aktuelle Fragestellungen und Zukunftsperspektiven der Albanologie*, 167–181. Wiesbaden: Harrassowitz.
Konior (Koner), Daria V. & Anastasia L. Makarova. 2015a. Osobennosti etnoyazykovoy situacii v regione Karashevo (Rumyniya) [On the ethnolinguistic situation in the community of Karashevo (Romania)]. *Poznańskie studia slawistyczne* 8. 83–91.
Konior (Koner), Daria V. & Anastasia L. Makarova. 2015b. Arumynskii iazyk v Prespanskom regione [Aromanian in the Prespa region]. (manuscript).
Konior (Koner), Daria V. & Anastasia L. Makarova. 2017. Arumynskii iazyk v Prespanskom regione (Republika Makedonija) segodnia [The Aromanian language in the Prespa region (Republic of Macedonia) today]. *Studia Slavica Academiae Scientiarum Hungaricae* 59 (2). 291–303.
Koneski, Blaže. 1966. *Istorija makedonskog jezika* [History of the Macedonian Language]. Beograd: Prosveta.
Koneski, Blaže. 1982. *Gramatika na makedonskiot literaturen jazik* [Grammar of the Macedonian standard language]. Skopje: Kultura.
Koneski, Kiril. 1990. *Glagolskite konstruktsii so kje vo makedonskiot jazik* [Verbal constructions with kje in the Macedonian language]. Skopje: Institut za makedonski jazik "Krste Misirkov".
Kopitar, Jernej K. 1829. Albanische, walachische und bulgarische Sprache. *Wiener Jahrbücher der Literatur* 46. 56–106.
Kukudis, Asterios J. 2013. *Vlasite. Metropoli i dijaspora* [The Vlakhs. Metropolises and diaspora]. Skopje.
Kŭnčov, Vasil. 1900. *Makedoniia. Etnografiia i statistika* [Macedonia. Ethnography and statistics]. Sofiia: Dŭržavna pechatnitsa.

Lindstedt, Jouko. 2000a. Linguistic Balkanisation: Contact-induced change by mutual reinforcement. In Dicky Gilbers, John Nerbonne & Joe Schaeken (eds.), *Languages in contact* [Studies in Slavic and General Linguistics 28], 231–246. Amsterdam & Atlanta: Rodopi.

Lindstedt, Jouko. 2000b. The perfect – aspectual, temporal and evidential. In Östen Dahl (ed.), *Tense and aspect in the languages of Europe*, 365–383. New York: Mouton de Gruyter.

Lindstedt, Jouko. 2002. Is there a Balkan Verb System? *Balkanistika* 15 (2002). 323–336.

Makartsev, Maksim M. 2014. *Evidentsial'nost' v prostranstve balkanskogo teksta* [Evidentuality in the Balkan textual space]. Moscow & St. Petersburg: Nestor-Istoriia.

Marković, Marjan. 2001. *Dijalektologija na makedonskiot jazik* [Dialectology of Macedonian]. Skopje: Filološki fakultet "Blaže Koneski".

Marković, Marjan. 2007. *Aromanskiot i makedonskiot govor od ohridsko-struškiot region vo balkanski kontekst* [Aromanian and Macedonian dialects in the Ohrid-Struga region in the Balkan context]. Skopje: MANU.

Marković, Marjan. 2011. Konstrukcii so 'esse' i 'habere' vo aromanskiot [Esse and habere constructions in Aromanian]. In Zuzana Topolinjska (ed.), *Perifrastični konstruktsii so "esse" i "habere" vo slovenskite i vo balkanskite jazitsi = Periphrastic constructions with "esse" and "habere" in Slavic and Balkan languages*, 123–144. Skopje: Makedonska akademija na naukite i umetnostite.

Marković, Marjan. 2014. Od ponovite balkanski inovacii vo makedonskiot gramatički sistem [On new Balkan innovations in the Macedonian grammatical system]. *Prilozi na Oddelenieto za lingvistika i literaturna nauka* 38 (1–2). 110–118.

Massey, Victoria W. 2000. Perfect, Passive and Reflexive in Albanian. *University of Pennsylvania Working Papers in Linguistics* 7 (1). 159–170.

MDABL – Andrey N. Sobolev (ed.). 2003–2018. *Malyi dialektologicheskii atlas balkanskikh iazykov. Probnyi vypusk (2003). Seriia leksicheskaia. Tom I. Leksika dukhovnoi kul'tury (2005). Tom II. Chelovek. Sem'ia (2006). Tom III. Zhivotnovodstvo (2009). Tom IV. (Avtor: M. V. Domosiletskaia). Landshaftnaia leksika (2010). Tom V. (Avtor: M. V. Domosiletskaia). Meteorologiia (2012). Tom VI. Polevodstvo. Ogorodnichestvo (2013). Tom VII. (Avtor: M. V. Domosiletskaia). Pčelovodstvo (2018). Seriia grammaticheskaia. Tom I. Kategorii imeni sushchestvitel'nogo (2005)* [Minor dialect atlas of the Balkan languages. Test launch (2003). Lexical series. Vol. 1. Cultural vocabulary (2005). Vol. 2. The person and human relations (2006). Vol. 3. Animal husbandry (2009). Vol. 4. (M. V. Domosiletskaia, author). Landscape (2010). Vol. 5 (M. V. Domosiletskaia, author). Meteorology (2012). Vol. 6. Field-tending and Gardening (2013). Vol. 7. (M. V. Domosiletskaia, author). Apiculture (2018). Grammatical series. Vol. 1. Noun categories (2005)]. St. Petersburg, München: Nauka, Verlag Otto Sagner.

Miklosich, Franz R. 1861. *Die slavischen Elemente im Rumunischen*. Wien: K. K. Hof- und Staatsdruckerei.

Mikulčić, Ivan. 1996. *Srednevekovite gradovi i tvrdini vo Makedonia* [Mediaeval towns and fortifications in Macedonia]. Skopje: MANU.

Mindak, Jolanta. 1987. Morfosintaksički zapadnomakedonsko-albanski paraleli [Parallels in West Macedonian and Albanian morpho-syntax]. *Makedonski jazik* 38. 151–163.

Momeva, Viktorija. 2012. *Selskite naselbi i kukji v Potpelisterieto: kulturno nasledstvo na Bitolsko-Prespanskiot region* [Rural residents and houses in Pelister lowlands: cultural inheritance in the Bitola-Prespa region]. Bitola: NU, zavod i muzej.

Muysken, Pieter. 2000. *Bilingual Speech. A Typology of Code-mixing*. Cambridge: Cambridge University Press.

Muysken, Pieter. 2010. Scenarios for Language Contact. In Raymond Hickey (ed.), *The Handbook of Language Contact*, 265–281. Malden, MA: Wiley-Blackwell.

Muysken, Pieter. 2013. Language contact as the result of bilingual optimization strategies. *Bilingualism: Language and Cognition* 16 (4). 709–730.

Narumov, Boris P. 2001a. Arumynskii iazyk/dialekt [The Aromanian language/dialect]. In Irina I. Chelysheva, Boris P. Narumov & Ol'ga I. Romanova (eds.), *Iazyki mira. Romanskie iazyki* [Languages of the World. Romance languages], 636–656. Moscow: Academia.

Narumov, Boris P. 2001b. Istrorumynskii iazyk/dialekt [The Istro-aromanian language/dialect]. In Irina I. Chelysheva, Boris P. Narumov & Ol'ga I. Romanova (eds.), *Iazyki mira. Romanskie iazyki* [Languages of the World. Romance languages], 656–671. Moscow: Academia.

Nevaci, Manuela. 2011. *Graiul aromânilor fărşeroţi din Dobrogea* [The Aromanian farsherot dialect in Dobruja]. București: Editura universitară.

Osmani, Zihni. 1996. *E folmja shqipe e Prespës* [The Albanian Dialect of Prespa]. Shkup: Flaka e vëllazërimit.

Osmani, Zihni. 1997. *E folmja shqipe e Manastirit dhe e qarkut të tij* [The Albanian dialect of Bitola and its surroundings]. Shkup: Logos-A.

Osmani, Zihni. 2001. *Prespa dhe zhvillimi i arsimit shqip* [Prespa and the development of Albanian education]. Shkup: Fine art.

Papahagi, Tache. 1974. *Dicţionarul dialectului aromân general şi etimologic* [Dictionnaire Aroumain (Macédo-Roumain) général et étymologique]. 2nd ed. București: Editura Academiei Republicii Socialiste România.

Pjanka, Vloǵimjež. 1970. *Toponomastika na Ohridsko-Prespanskiot bazen* [Toponomastics in the Ohrid-Prespa basin]. Skopje: Institut za makedonski jazik "Krste Misirkov".

Poloska, Agim. 2003. *Leksiku dialektor në regjionin e Prespës: studim krahasimtar* [Dialect lexicon in the Prespa region: a comparative study]. Shkup: Asdreni.

Poloska, Agim. 2014. *Leksička interferencija na makedonskiot i albanskiot dijalekten jazik* [Lexical interference in Macedonian and Albanian dialects]. Skopje: Menora.

Rusakov, Alexander Yu. 2015. Albanian Supercompound Verb Forms: a Corpus-based Study. *Balcanistica* 28. 435–469.

Rusakov, Alexander Yu. 2016. *Pliuskvamperfekt s aoristom vspomogatel'nogo glagola v sovremennom albanskom iazyke* [Pluperfect with the aorist of an auxiliary verb in modern Albanian]. *Indoevropeiskoe iazykoznanie i klassicheskaia filologiia* 20 (2). 910–919.

Sandfeld, Kristian. 1930. *Linguistique balkanique. Problèmes et résultats*. Paris: Champion.

Saramandu, Nicolae & Manuela Nevaci. 2013. *Sinteze de dialectologie română* [Synthesis of Romanian dialectology]. București: Editura universitară.

Schaller, Helmut W. 1975. *Die Balkansprachen. Eine Einführung in die Balkanphilologie*. Heidelberg: Carl Winter Universitätsverlag.

Selishchev, Afanasii M. 1931. *Slavianskoe naselenie v Albanii* [The Slavic population in Albania]. Sofia: Makedonskii nauchnyi institut.

Sichinava, Dmitrii V. 2008. Sviaz' mezhdu formoi i semantikoi perfekta: odna neizuchennaia zakonomernost' [Connections between forms and the semantics of the perfect: one unstudied principle]. In Bondarko, Alexandr V. (ed.), *Dinamicheskie modeli: Slovo. Predlozhenie. Tekst*, 711–749. Moscow: Iazyki slavianskikh kul'tur.

Sobolev, Andrey N. 1999. O zalogovykh znacheniiakh slavianskikh prichastii na -n/-t [On the genus verbi of the participles in -n/-t in Slavic]. *Wyraz i zdanie w językach słowiańskich* 4. 209–215.

Sobolev, Andrey N. 2011. Antibalkanizmy [Antibalkanisms]. *Južnoslovenski filolog* 67. 185–195.

Sobolev, Andrey N. 2013. *Osnovy lingvokul'turnoi antropogeografii Balkanskogo poluostrova, Tom I. Homo balcanicus i ego prostranstvo* [Foundations of linguocultural anthropogeography on the Balkan peninsula, Vol. 1. Homo balcanicus and his space]. St. Petersburg: Nauka, Munich: Otto Sagner Verlag.

Sobolev, Andrey N., Iurii A. Lopashov, Irina I. Voronina & Alexander Yu. Rusakov (eds.). 1997. *Malyi dialektologicheskii atlas balkanskikh iazykov. Sintaksicheskaia programma* [Minor dialectological atlas of Balkan languages. Syntactic program]. St. Petersburg: ILI RAN.

Sokolski, Metodija. 1973. *Turski dokumenti za istorija na makedonskiot narod (Opširni popisni defteri od XV vek)* [Turkish documents related to the history of the Macedonian people (General *defter* documents from the 15th century)] Vol. 2. Skopje: Arhiv na Makedonija.

Šklifov, Blagoi St. 1979. *Dolno-Prespanskiiat govor: prinos kŭm proučvaneto na iugozapadnite bŭlgarski govori* [The Dolno-Prespa subdialect: approaching the study of southwestern Bulgarian dialects]. Sofiia: BAN.

Thomason, Sarah Grey & Terrence Kaufman. 1988. *Language Contact, Creolization, and Genetic Linguistics*. Berkeley: University of California Press.

Velkovska, Snežana. 1998. *Izrazuvanje na rezultativnosta vo makedonskiot standarden jazik* [Expression of the resultative in standard Macedonian]. Skopje: Institut za makedonski jazik "Krste Misirkov".

Vidoeski, Božidar. 1998. *Dijalektite na makedonskit jazik* [Dialects of the Macedonian language]. Vol. 1. Skopje: Filološki fakultet "Blazhe Koneski".

Vidoeski, Božidar. 2000. *Tekstovi od dijalektite na makedonskiot jazik* [Texts in Macedonian dialects]. Skopje: Institut za makedonski jazik "Krste Misirkov".

Vrabie, Emil. 2000. *An English-Aromanian Dictionary*. Oxford, MS: University of Mississippi.

Weigand, Gustav. 1895. *Die Arumunen*. Bde I–II. Leipzig: Johann Ambrosius Barth.

Wiemer, Björn. 2020. Convergence. In Evangelia Adamou & Yaron Matras (eds.), *The Routledge Handbook on Language Contact*, 276–299. London: Routledge.

Winnifrith, Tom J. 1987. *The Vlachs: The History of a Balkan People*. New York: St. Martin's.

Maria S. Morozova
"Balanced Language Contact" in Social Context: Velja Gorana in Southern Montenegro

Abstract: This chapter[1] investigates the case of Velja Gorana, a multilingual village in southern Montenegro, located in the area between the towns of Bar and Ulcinj. This area of Montenegro has a mixed Muslim Slavic, Muslim Albanian, Orthodox Slavic, and Catholic Albanian population. The people in Gorana associate themselves with the Slavic-speaking Muslim community of Mrkovići in the highlands of Bar; but they also speak Albanian because local men marry Albanian women from neighbouring areas. All children in mixed families of Velja Gorana learn two languages from their parents and grandparents: the local variety of Bosnian-Croatian-Montenegrin-Serbian (BCMS) and the Northwestern Gheg subdialect of Albanian. The village community can be thought to represent a good example of a *"balanced language contact"* situation which does not result in a shift towards either Albanian or Slavic. The chapter presents the history and the present-day sociolinguistic situation based on the data from the author's fieldwork starting from 2012. Particular attention is given to the role population shifts and mixed marriages have in the creation of this community. Subsequent sections describe and analyze the linguistic evidence for phonological, grammatical and lexical interference among bilinguals in Velja Gorana. The author attempts to relate the social and historical processes taking place in this community to particular linguistic outcomes (contact-induced change in both interacting languages), and to explain the greater implications of a "balanced language contact" situation and how individual choices of the speakers in such situations become part of a commonly-shared code.

---

[1] This research was made possible by a grant from the Russian Science Foundation (the projects "From Separation to Symbiosis: South Eastern European languages and cultures in contact", No. 14-18-01405 and "Balkan bilingualism in dominant and equilibrium contact situations in diatopy, diachrony and diastraty", No. 19-18-00244). I am grateful to prof. Alexander Yu. Rusakov (Institute for Linguistic Studies of the Russian Academy of Sciences (ILS RAS), Saint Petersburg University (SPbU)) for the helpful comments on an earlier draft of this chapter.

1 Introduction

Balkan linguistics devotes considerable attention to a certain number of features (called linguistic Balkanisms) exhibited in many, but not necessarily all, Balkan languages and documents numerous instances of local diffusion of features shared by only two languages or even dialects.[2] It is generally accepted that most of these features in Balkan languages and dialects are contact-induced rather than internally motivated and that they may have emerged in a particular type of multilingual contact situation. Thomason and Kaufman (1988: 95–96) described the Balkans as "a long-term multilateral Sprachbund" which is constituted "without asymmetrical dominance relations or large-scale shifts, and with multilateral rather than one-way bi- and multilingualism". This common, though not universal, contact situation in this area has been since defined in various studies as "active bilateral bilingualism" (Rusakov 2007: 84), "intense, intimate, and mutual multilingualism" (Joseph 2010: 625), and most recently as "four-M", or "multi-lateral, multi-directional, mutual multilingualism" (Friedman & Joseph 2017: 70), "nondominant bilingualism" (Sobolev 2017: 420), and "balanced language contact"[3] (Morozova & Rusakov 2018). Due to the permanent bi- or multilateral replication processes ("mutual reinforcement of change" according to Lindstedt (2000: 242)), this situation has brought about the linguistic state of affairs for which Balkan languages and dialects are well known. These include: widespread (but by no means extreme) structural isomorphism, non-systematic phonological correspondences, an abundance of loan-translation parallels, shared cultural vocabulary, and some shared "conversationally based" vocabulary (Joseph 2010: 621–623, 626–629; Friedman & Joseph 2017: 55).

Contactologists and Balkan linguists are unanimous in adhering to the view that language change begins at the level of an individual language user (Lindstedt 2000: 241; Matras & Sakel 2007: 849; Muysken 2010: 267) and that actual speaker-to-speaker contacts are responsible for the diffusion of the convergent linguistic features across the area (Rusakov 2007: 84; Lindstedt 2016: 52; Friedman & Joseph 2017: 69–70). On the one hand, in the sociolinguistic history of the Balkans such contacts have happened within large groups of speakers with stable prestige relations and different types of asymmetry between their languages. On the other hand, an important role has been played by small and close-knit speech communities, which have been the main loci of the bi- or multilingual contact

---

[2] See, for example, a list of the best-known works and a sampling of features in Joseph (2010).
[3] According to Alexandra Aikhenvald (2007: 43), "...in a situation of a long-standing linguistic area and stable multilingualism without any dominance relationships, language contact is 'balanced'".

situations without a clear dominance among any of the languages involved (situations of this type are referred to as "small-scale multilingualism" in the recent literature, see e. g. Lüpke 2016; Morozova & Rusakov 2021). Careful observation of such communities in the modern Balkans may be helpful for the reconstruction of the processes governing the ethnic and linguistic convergences that took place in the past as well as for the prediction of future developments (Sobolev & Novik 2013: 10).

This chapter examines the case of Velja Gorana, a small bilingual village in southern Montenegro. The population of the village is ethnically mixed and speaks varieties of Albanian and BCMS. Velja Gorana makes part of the territory inhabited by a Slavic-speaking Muslim community, or "tribe" (BCMS *pleme*) of the Mrkovići/Mrkojevići, also known as Mërkot in Albanian.[4] Most villages of the Mrkovići are currently monolingual, but it is possible that their population was (partially) bilingual in the past. Between 2012 and 2016, a team of linguists and anthropologists from Saint Petersburg, in which I participated, conducted fieldwork in this region. My linguistic materials from Velja Gorana, as well as the sociolinguistic and some historical data used in this chapter were gathered during these field trips.[5] Additional information about the past of the region was obtained from old censuses and publications of Serbian and Albanian historians and ethnographic research (Jovićević 1922; Pulaha 1974; Pejović & Kapisoda 2009 [1879]) as well as that of local researchers (Metanović 2012). My knowledge about the variety of the Mrkovići comes from its first, and quite complete, description by Vujović (1969) as well as personal observations.

The geographic, historical, and ethnographic data about the Mrkovići and Velja Gorana is given in this chapter's section 2. Section 3 is dedicated to the sociolinguistic conditions of the past and present contact, with particular attention to the balanced language contact situation in modern Velja Gorana. Section 4 describes the contact-induced features in the dialectal variety of the Mrkovići and shows what is happening in the ongoing contact situation in Velja Gorana, where the emerging changes can be easily attributed to specific bilingual speakers. In conclusion, I sum up the observations from Section 4 and describe the different

---

[4] The toponyms and anthroponyms in this chapter are given in the BCMS Latin alphabet when they are of Slavic origin and in standard Albanian script when they are Albanian. If a proper or place name has distinct forms in each of the languages, both are cited in their corresponding orthographies (BCMS/Albanian).

[5] The participants of the field trips guided by Andrey N. Sobolev (ILS RAS, SPU) were: Aleksandr A. Novik (Peter the Great Museum of Anthropology and Ethnography "Kunstkamera" (MAE RAS), SPU), Maria S. Morozova (ILS RAS, SPbU), Aleksandra S. Dugushina (MAE RAS), Denis S. Ermolin (MAE RAS), and Anastasia L. Makarova (ILS RAS).

individual scenarios of bilingual behaviour[6] that co-occur in the community of Velja Gorana. After that, by extrapolating from what happens in Velja Gorana to the Mrkovići, I make assumptions about the language contact situation that could have existed in the Mrkovići area in the past.

2 Velja Gorana and the Mrkovići in southern Montenegro

2.1 The Mrkovići and their neighbours

The community of the Mrkovići lives in the area between the towns of Bar and Ulcinj, in the southern part of Montenegro (see Map 1). The natural boundaries of the area are Lake Skadar in the north, the Adriatic in the south, and the river Bojana/Bunë, which forms the border between Montenegro and Albania in the east. The population is Muslim Slavic, Orthodox Slavic, Muslim Albanian, and Catholic Albanian. The regions to the east and south of Bar are inhabited mainly by Slavic-speaking Muslims (Tuđemili, Poda, Mrkovići), while those to the northwest by Orthodox Montenegrins. The regions of Kraja, Shestan, Ana e Malit, and Ulcinj are dominated by Muslim and Catholic Albanians.

The territory of the Mrkovići lies between the Rumija and Lisinj mountain ranges in the north and the mountain of Možura in the south. The villages of Mali Mikulići and Velji Mikulići are set high on Rumija mountain, and Dobra Voda, Pečurice, Grdovići, Velje Selo (together with the hamlet of Lunje), Dabezići (with the hamlet of Dapčevići), Ljeskovac, and the currently abandoned Međureč are situated near Lisinj, or on its slopes. Kunje, Mala Gorana, and Velja Gorana

---

[6] In the scenario approach given by Pieter Muysken, a scenario is defined as "the organized fashion in which multilingual speakers, in certain social settings, deal with the various languages in their repertoire" (2010: 267). Muysken (2010) proposes a variety of scenarios with different linguistic outcomes (borrowing, grammatical convergence under prolonged stable bilingualism, simultaneous acquisition of two languages by children, metatypy, insertional and alternational codeswitching, language attrition and death, among others). Most are asymmetrical from the point of view of the relations between the languages involved. This approach may be combined with others that exist in the theoretical framework devoted to language contact, including: 1.) Thomason and Kaufman's (1988) basic types of interference (borrowing and interference through shift) and 2.) van Coetsem's (1988) schematic dichotomy between borrowing and imposition based on whether bilingual speakers are cognitively dominant in the recipient language or the source language. These may serve to create a more detailed picture of the processes occurring on the microlevel and individual level in contact situations.

"Balanced Language Contact" in Social Context —— 93

are located in the other part of the region, near Možura. Two small settlements, Vukići and Pelinkovići, lie between the two clusters of villages. Some of the villages, such as Međureč, Ljeskovac, Vukići, Pelinkovići, and Velja Gorana, are situated on the "boundary" with the Albanian-speaking region of Ana e Malit (Sobolev et al. 2018: 28).

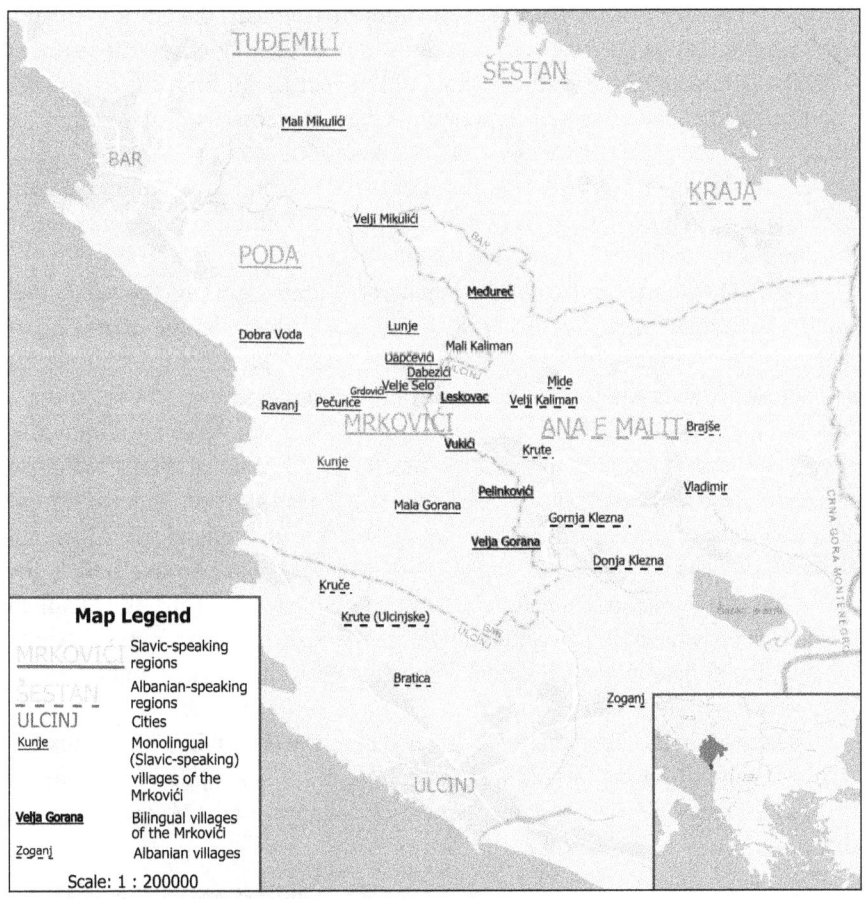

Map 1 The Mrkovići and Velja Gorana in southern Montenegro[7]

---

[7] The map is drawn using the Sasgis SAS.Planet (v. 190707.9476 Stable) and Inkscape Drawing Software (v. 0.92.1 r15371) software. The coordinates of the settlements are taken from Map Carta Interactive Map (https://mapcarta.com/).

2.2 The Mrkovići and Velja Gorana in the history of the area

The Mrkovići are first mentioned in 15th century Venetian documents as *Li Marchoe* (1409) and *de Marchois* (1449) near Bar (Metanović 2012). The Venetian Republic controlled the port of Bar during Balšići rule in Montenegro (1402–1412), and took possession of Bar and Ulcinj after the death of Balša III in 1421. By the end of the 15th century, during the rule of the Crnojevići dynasty, the quickly expanding Ottoman Empire absorbed almost all territory of the modern Montenegro. In 1571, the Ottomans conquered the ports of Bar and Ulcinj from the Venetians, and exercised control over southern Montenegro for more than three centuries (Đurović 1970: 130–131, 150; Đurović 1975: 58; Fine 2009: 49–53, 389–392, 414–421, 595–603). Throughout this period, a part of the Slavic and Albanian population in the region remained Orthodox (Montenegrins) and Catholic (Albanians), while the other part gradually converted to Islam.

The 1485 Ottoman census of the Sanjak of Scutari mentions the subdistrict *Nahija Mërkodlar*,[8] with the village of *Mërkojeviqi* (rather, a group of villages or hamlets) consisting of 140 households. The names of heads of the households are mainly of Slavic and Christian Slavic origin: *Milosh, Ivza, Ivan, Gjuro, Andrija, Damjan, Dabzhiv/Dabo*. Many names in the list bear the Albanian diminutive suffix *-z(ë)*, as in Alb copë-z, DEF copë-z-a 'small piece' and shtëpi-zë, DEF shtëpi-z-a 'small house' (from *copë* 'piece', *shtëpi* 'house'): *Dabza, Nikëza, Malëza, Miloza, Mladoza, Kalza*.[9] Several names in the census are unambiguously Albanian: *Dabza, i biri i **Gjonit** 'Dabza, the son of **Gjon**', Nuliçi, i biri i **Bukmirit** 'Nulich, the son of **Bukmir**', Lekëza, Radiç Kolzini* (Pulaha 1974: 141–143). Thus, the Albanian element likely existed in the community of the Mrkovići at least from the beginning of the Ottoman period, but later Albanians likely assimilated and intermingled with Slavic speakers.

The names in the Ottoman census show that by the end of the 15th century the Mrkovići had not yet converted to Islam. In 1614, in his description of the Sanjak of Scutari, Mariano Bolizza also mentioned some villages of the Mrkovići. As seen

---

8 The manuscript was transcribed in Albanian characters, translated, and published by an Albanian historian Selami Pulaha (1974). The personal names and place names in this paragraph are cited after his publication.

9 Mitar Pešikan notes that the Albanian suffix *-z(ë)* is found in the toponyms of Old Montenegro (*Mareza, Releza, Đeđeza*) and in modern Montenegrin patronymics (*Kalezić, Nenezić, Nikezić*) in the areas of past and present Slavic-Albanian contact, for example in the regions Piperi, Kuči, Zetska Ravnica, and Krajina to the north-east of Lake Skadar. Such cognomena are even more widespread in the Mrkovići than in these regions (Pešikan 1981: 419–420, 423). Compare, for example, the Mrkovići village name *Dabezići* and patronymics such as *Nikezić* in Mala Gorana and *Kalezić* in Velje Selo.

from the names of their headmen, the Mrkovići had yet to be Islamicized: *Marco Nicou* is the headman in *Marchoeuich* (Mrkojevići, 260 houses), *Luca Matuscou* in *Michulichi* (Mikulići, 25 houses), *Giuro Marcou* in *Gradojevich* (Grdovići, 50 houses), *Rado Giurou* in *Dobra Voda* (40 houses), *Schuchi Giurou* in *Cumgni* (Kunje, 20 houses), *Guiro Strepieu* in *Racé* (Ravanj?, 25 houses), and *Dumo Luchi* in *Gorana*, with 20 houses (Bolizza 1866 [1614]: 297). The real turning point likely happened when, in 1717, the Mrkovići joined Montenegrins and Venetians in their unsuccessful attempt to seize Bar. Many later began to convert to Islam for fear of Ottoman reprisal (Jovićević 1922: 22; Vujović 1969: 78).

In 1878, Montenegrins conquered Bar from the Ottomans and incorporated it into their state. The Congress of Berlin (13 June to 13 July 1878) recognized the full independence of Montenegro from the Ottoman Empire and officially established the border between the two states in the treaty bearing its name. The area between Bar and Ulcinj was split in two parts: Ulcinj and the Albanian-speaking Ana e Malit remained in the Ottoman Empire, while Bar and the Mrkovići joined Montenegro (*Traktat*" 1906: 87). According to the 1879 census of the population of Montenegro, *Mrkovska kapetanija* 'the captaincy of the Mrkovići' included the villages of *Kunje*, *Mala Gorana*, *Kriči* (now the village of Kruče), *Grdovići*, *Dabezići*, *Ulići* (now the hamlet of Vulići), *Dobčevići* (now Dapčevići), *Kalimani* (Mali or Velji Kaliman), *Ljeskovac*, *Velje Selo*, *Ravanj*, *Pečurice*, *Dobra Voda*, *Velji* and *Malji Mikulići*. Almost all population was Muslim, with the exception of a few Catholic (likely Albanian) families in Kruče, Pečurice, Dobra Voda, and Mali Mikulići, and several Orthodox families in Kruče, Dobra Voda, and Velji Mikulići (Pejović & Kapisoda 2009 [1879]: 413–450).

Since the place name *Mala Gorana* (lit. "small Gorana") was mentioned as such in the census, it can be assumed that some *Velja Gorana* (lit. "big Gorana") also existed in the neighbourhood, but the establishment of the Montenegrin-Ottoman border in 1878 left it in the Ottoman empire (Sobolev 2015: 541, footnote 10). Velja Gorana may have joined the Mrkovići at the earliest in 1880, when the town of Ulcinj with the surrounding area was transferred to independent Montenegro. The Albanian-speaking regions of Ana e Malit, Shestan, and Kraja (and likely the now-Mrkovići villages of Međureč, Vukići, and Pelinkovići, which were missing in the 1879 census) were incorporated into Montenegro only after the Balkan Wars of 1912–1913 and the proclamation of Albanian independence, with the Albanian-Montenegrin border being established on the river Bojana/Bunë.

During the Italian and the subsequent German occupation of Montenegro from 1941 to 1944, the Albanian-speaking regions of southern Montenegro, like all territories in Yugoslavia inhabited by Albanians, were placed under Albanian rule. The neighbouring Slavic-speaking region of the Mrkovići, except for the village of Dobra Voda, then also became part of Albania (Sobolev 2015: 540, footnote 8). After World War II, the border was returned to where it was in 1913 and Montenegro was included into the Socialist Federal Republic of Yugoslavia. Soon after that, in 1948, Socialist Albania retreated into political isolation from Yugoslavia, which had been hindering people's contacts across the border for over four decades. From 1992 to 2003, Montenegro comprised part of the Federal Republic of Yugoslavia, and later the State Union of Serbia and Montenegro. In 2006, the Republic of Montenegro became an independent state.

2.3 Interethnic marriages and population movements. The foundation of Velja Gorana

A study of marriage behaviour of the Mrkovići (Dugushina & Morozova 2016; 2020) showed that community members may marry both inside and outside of their group. Residential endogamy is possible because many of the Mrkovići families are not closely related to each other. Some families are descended from the old population of the area, while the ancestors of the others were non-related persons who came from different areas and settled in the region in the 19th century. For example, Ivanovići and Lakovići in Dobra Voda came from the Kuči. Dapčevići arrived from Cetinje, Dibre in Dobra Voda migrated from the Macedonian Dibra in approximately 1840, and Rackovići came from Lješanska Nahija after 1878 when Montenegrins took control of Bar and its surroundings (Jovićević 1922: 77–85). The newcomers were eventually incorporated into existing social networks, and often created marriage ties with their closest neighbours in the village.

Exogamous marital ties of the Mrkovići were established (or, more likely, reinforced) during the period of Islamization in the area between Bar and Ulcinj (Jovićević 1922: 113; Vujović 1969: 79). The modern Mrkovići have matrimonial bonds not only with the neighbouring Muslim Slavic communities of Tuđemili and Poda, but also with Albanians.[10] Albanian women from Ana e Malit, Shestan, Kraja and Ulcinj, as well as from northwestern Albania, can be met with in many of the Mrkovići villages. However, such ethnic and, as it were, linguistic exogamy seems to be a prevailing pattern that has existed for a long time rather than one

---

[10] Residential and occasional ethnic exogamy was a tradition among the Montenegrin tribes of the region Brda (BCMS *brda* 'mountains') and in some of the *fises* (Alb *fis* 'kin', 'descent group') of Northern Albania. The best-known example in Serbian ethnography is that of the Kuči who never married women from their own community, but often took Albanian wives and gave their daughters to Albanians (Rovinskii 1897: 239). In Albania, as late as the 1950s, men from one *fis* took wives only from the region inhabited by another *fis*, while their daughters were always married into the third *fis*, from which they never took brides (Ivanova 1988: 183–184).

that has emerged fairly recently only in the villages located near the unofficial boundary with Albanians. For example, in Velja Gorana, almost all families have Albanian-speaking wives, daughters-in-law or grandmothers.

The origin of the situation in Velja Gorana can be found in the genealogies and history of its inhabitants (see the reconstructed genealogies in Morozova & Rusakov (2018)). The village community consists of a big family of *Kovačevići* and two smaller families, *Vučići* and *Osmanovići*. The modern Kovačevići family actually includes two nonrelated relatives. The "real" Kovačevići are said to be descended from a person called Danila Kovačević, who arrived to the region of the Mrkovići in an attempt to escape from a blood feud, joined the local Muslim community, and converted to Islam (Morozova & Rusakov 2018: 289). He originated from the area of Grahovo, a town in the Nikšić municipality in the west of the present-day Montenegro. Nikšić belonged to the Ottoman Empire for several centuries and became Montenegrin after the 1858 battle of Grahovac. The approximate time of his migration to Velja Gorana, roughly estimated from the birth years of his successors, seems to be close to the date of this battle. The second descent group in the now-Kovačevići family was called *Tahirovići/Tahiri* (i.e. descendants of Tahir), and its founder(s) came to Velja Gorana from the Albanian village of Mide/Millë in Ana e Malit, probably toward the latter part of the 19th century. There are several versions of the story about how the Tahirovići changed their surname, but the exact time and reason remains unclear.

Vučići likely settled in Velja Gorana in the very beginning of the 20th century or a little earlier, since marriages between them and Kovačevići appear approximately at that time in their genealogies. It is said about the Vučići that they were Catholic when they came to Velja Gorana, and that their men used to marry Catholic women, so the family probably had Albanian origin (Morozova & Rusakov 2018: 288). The first Osmanović, an Albanian from the village of Vladimir/Katërkollë (Ana e Malit), married a woman from Vučići and moved to Velja Gorana in the 1930s.

The community of Velja Gorana clearly represents a recent case of small-scale population movement, a factor in Slavic-Albanian interaction and intermingling throughout the Ottoman period.[11] It is important that, from the very beginning, the village was populated by monolingual Muslim Slavs and monolingual or bilingual Albanians. The common tendency to make use of matrimonial bonds to

---

11 Compare with the Kuči who had been an Orthodox Serbian tribe until the 15th century. Through the 15th to 17th century several Albanian (Catholic) and Serbian (Orthodox and Catholic) groups from other areas settled in their tribal territory. The population in the region had been a long time bilingual, but shifted to monolingualism due to the gradual Slavicization of Albanians. A bilingual situation now exists only in the small area of Koći/Kojë, which is inhabited by Albanians and Albanized Serbs (Erdeljanović 1981 [1907]: 117, 158–172).

assure good relations with near neighbours can be regarded as a prerequisite for the natural (re-)emergence of ethnic (and "linguistic") exogamy in Velja Gorana. The next section will show the effects of mixed marriages on the past and present bilingual situation in the community.

3 The (socio)linguistic situation in the Mrkovići and Velja Gorana

3.1 Bilingualism in the Mrkovići in time and space

The majority of the residents of modern Mrkovići are monolingual in BCMS. The young, school-aged children, and most middle-aged people tend to speak *crnogorsko* 'Montenegrin', a variant of the Eastern Herzegovinian dialect of Ijekavian Neo-Štokavian (Ivić 1985: 132) spoken across most of Montenegro and used as the basis for the standardized Montenegrin language. Older and some middle-aged people may speak the local variety of the Old-Štokavian Zeta-Sjenica dialect, which is spoken in the southeast of Montenegro and the southwest of Serbia (Ivić 1985: 157). The dialectal variety spoken by the Mrkovići (BCMS *mrkovićki dijalekat*, *mrkovićki govor*) was described by Luka Vujović as having both relics and innovations due to contact with Venetian, Ottoman Turkish, and Albanian (Vujović 1969: 78–79). An important distinctive feature of this variety is the Ekavian development of the long jat /ě/: *dete / dejte* 'child'; comp. the Ijekavian *dijete* in most areas of Montenegro and the Ikavian *dite* among Muslim Slavic speakers in Plava and Gusinje, and near Podgorica (Ivić 1985: 159). In fact, both Ekavian and Ijekavian variants may occur in the speech of virtually everyone in the Mrkovići (Vujović 1969: 100), and this variability may be the result of some late dialect mixing.

In our fieldwork, people in the majority of modern Mrkovići villages do not speak or understand Albanian and insist that their (great-)grandparents were also monolingual in BCMS. However, in the remote past the Mrkovići region could have been totally or partially bilingual. According to Matthew Curtis (2012: 39), "[i]t is likely that both the population shifts and bilingualism with surrounding Albanian speakers are responsible for the penetration of Albanian features on the Slavic dialect spoken by the Mrkovići". Historical documents provide sustainable grounds for claims that the situation of Slavic-Albanian ethnic and linguistic contact, with migrations, population mixing, mutual bilingualism, and shifts into either Albanian or Slavic, existed throughout this area of Montenegro in the Middle Ages (see Sobolev 1990). Pastures shared by the Mrkovići and Albanians from Ana e Malit, and trade in the markets of the two urban centres of the area,

Shkodra and Bar, could have played an important role in the development and maintenance of the bilingual situation (Vujović 1969: 79). Moreover, as shown in Section 2.2, during the Ottoman period Albanians made up part of the population of the Mrkovići villages, and this could be amenable to intimate contact and mutual bilingualism within the village communities.

The easternmost Mrkovići villages, such as Pelinkovići, Vukići, Ljeskovac, and Velja Gorana, are now bilingual in BCMS and Albanian. This is undoubtedly due to their closeness to the Albanian-speaking regions and marriages between the local men and Albanian women (see 2.3). At the beginning of the 20th century, Andrija Jovićević claimed that "the Mrkovići, who lived close to Albanians, did not abandon their language, even though they had converted to Islam 200 years before. Only the population of Pelinkovići, Vukići, Klezna, and partly of Gorana, acquired Albanian because they used to marry women from the villages of Ana e Malit" (Jovićević 1922: 113). In the 1930s and 1940s, according to Luka Vujović, bilingualism was not widespread among the Mrkovići, but the inhabitants of Međureč, Ljeskovac, Vukići, and the "lower" part of Gorana could use Albanian in communication (Vujović 1969: 82–83). Nowadays in Velja Gorana, the local bilingual men tend to bring Albanian wives from Ana e Malit, Ulcinj, and from the nearby parts of Albania (Dugushina & Morozova 2016; 2020; Morozova 2017a: 67). Consequently, all children in Velja Gorana learn two languages in the family, and "the long-term bilingual condition of sufficiently big groups of people is reproduced and does not result in a consequential shift from one language to another" (Sobolev 2015: 542).

3.2 Bilingualism in Velja Gorana from the perspective of individual speakers

Using the variationist approach taken on the (socio)linguistic situation of Velja Gorana in (Morozova & Rusakov 2018), the members of the village community can be classified into six "sociolinguistic profiles" according to their sex, age, origin, and spoken language(s). Profiles 1 and 2 include, respectively, elder and middle-aged bilingual men who were born and live in Velja Gorana (BCMS SG *goranac*, PL *goranci*). Profiles 3 and 4 involve elder and middle-aged women who came to Velja Gorana after marriage from the monolingual villages of the Mrkovići (BCMS SG *mrkovka*, PL *mrkovke*) or from the neighbouring Albanian-speaking regions.[12]

---

[12] Marriages within the village have not occurred over the last few decades and marriageable girls usually leave the community. For this reason the women born in Velja Gorana are not taken into account in this survey.

Finally, a distinction is made between elder and younger children, which belong, respectively, to Profiles 5 and 6. It should be observed that different speakers demonstrate different "histories" of acquisition and usage of the two languages spoken in the community of Velja Gorana, BCMS and Albanian, and use these languages to varying degrees (see details in Morozova & Rusakov 2018; 2021).

Most *elder* and *middle-aged men* were exposed to both languages in their families at a very young age. Their (grand)fathers were bilingual natives of the village, while the (grand)mothers could be either monolingual in Albanian or bilingual. In addition, both Albanian and BCMS were actively (but not necessarily equally) used in communication among neighbours of different ages, as all families in Velja Gorana were mixed to a greater or lesser extent. Only one of my elder informants remarked that he did not speak Albanian as a child. His mother was monolingual in BCMS and it was the only language spoken in the home. However, he acquired Albanian in adolescence, when he grazed livestock in the pastures near Velja Gorana and communicated with young Albanians from the neighbouring villages (Morozova & Rusakov 2018: 287; 2021). At present he does not seem to be less proficient in Albanian than the other bilingual men in the community.

In their childhood, all men from Velja Gorana attended school, where teaching was given in BCMS and no Albanian was taught or spoken by the teachers. After school they served in the Yugoslav army, in which BCMS obviously was the preferred language of communication. At present, elder men rarely leave the village, while the middle-aged men work mostly in Ulcinj, where the majority of the population speaks Albanian as a native language.

As described in (Morozova & Rusakov 2018; 2021), at home bilingual men may use the languages from their repertoire to varying degrees. They normally speak Albanian with their Albanian wives or daughters-in-law and BCMS with their sons or grandsons. Daughters or granddaughters are addressed either in both languages or only in BCMS. Communication between an elder and a younger man occurs mainly in BCMS, but Albanian can be chosen when the Albanian wife/daughter-in-law participates in the conversation. The situation is different in the families where the elder woman is a native Albanian, while the younger one comes from a monolingual Mrkovići village. In such families, the bilingual men and women prefer BCMS even when they speak with one another. The everyday interaction of bilingual men with neighbours can be carried on both in BCMS and Albanian. In communication with a wife's/daughter-in-law's relatives, male bilinguals from Velja Gorana obviously prefer BCMS if they belong to the BCMS-speaking community of the Mrkovići (or another one), and choose Albanian if they are native speakers of that language.

Elder and *middle-aged women* went at least to primary school and were taught only in BCMS, but almost all Albanian women insist that they mastered BCMS well only in Velja Gorana. The Albanian women in Velja Gorana are bilingual (the two languages may be known to different degrees and used with different frequency). The women from the Mrkovići villages sometimes learn Albanian as a second language after getting married and coming to Velja Gorana. Some Mrkovići women, according to their own words and the estimations of their neighbours, "understand Albanian, but do not speak it" (as passive bilinguals) or "do not want to speak Albanian" (Morozova & Rusakov 2018: 283). During the fieldwork, I did not investigate the degree of "understanding" of Albanian speech by such informants. However, I observed some conversations with Albanian women speaking their native language and a woman from the Mrkovići "understanding" them and responding to them in BCMS, with all speakers acting as passive bilinguals.

Most women are involved only in domestic activities and rarely leave Velja Gorana, but some of my bilingual female informants work or sell dairy products in Ulcinj and use both of their languages (Albanian is preferred) in communication with co-workers, local administration, and tourists. When the bilingual women visit their relatives in the native villages, they obviously speak their first language. Within the community of Velja Gorana, middle-aged and elder Albanian women use the two languages from their repertoire in different ways. The middle-aged are fluent in both languages and choose Albanian in the majority of situations, while the elders often switch to BCMS in the conversation and insist that they start "forgetting" Albanian after several decades in Velja Gorana (Morozova & Rusakov 2018: 287; 2021).

Children in mostly bilingual families begin to acquire the two home languages in early childhood. Small girls improve their competence in Albanian more quickly as they communicate more with their mothers, who usually speak in their native language with their daughters. Boys start speaking Albanian when they are approximately five years old, which does not exclude the possibility of passive bilingualism at an earlier age. For the children of the school age, BCMS is the only language of school education and communication with classmates and teachers from the other villages of the Mrkovići. Albanian remains a home language, and, according to some parents, their adolescent children may use it more rarely in the family, and give their preference to BCMS.

It is apparent that the linguistic situation in Velja Gorana includes a range of different micro-situations, with different degrees of knowledge and usage of BCMS and Albanian in close networks of family members, neighbours, and friends. The bilingual competence of the community's members may change over their lifespan, depending on their social position, linguistic preferences, and choices. However, as noted in (Morozova & Rusakov 2018: 295), the development from monolingualism towards bilingualism with further maintenance of bilingual competence remains a prevailing pattern, and the fact that the community is "open" both for BCMS and Albanian speakers (due to mixed marriages) ensures the stability of the bilingual situation in Velja Gorana over a sufficiently long period of time.

4 Mutual influence and contact-induced language change in Velja Gorana and the Mrkovići

This section considers the linguistic interference in phonetics, morphosyntax, and lexicon in the the Mrkovići variety and in (the versions of) Albanian and BCMS spoken in Velja Gorana. The dialectological material from the Mrkovići and the other areas of Montenegro is taken mainly from (Vujović 1969; Sobolev 1988; 1990, with bibliography). Analysis of the contact-induced language change in Velja Gorana is based on the data from my questionnaires[13] and interviews in BCMS and Albanian which were conducted in three field trips between 2014 and 2015. In my description of the linguistic innovations that can be found in the bilingual community of Velja Gorana I follow the idea that "every change is both structurally and socially embedded", as formulated by Pieter Muysken in his scenario framework (Muysken 2010: 272), and make an attempt to identify the mechanisms, or paths of development, for each of the contact-induced features from the standpoint of the bilingual individuals in whose speech such features emerge and crystallize.

4.1 Phonetic and phonological interference

Contact-induced changes in the Mrkovići variety. The variety of the Mrkovići has phonetic and phonological innovations that are likely induced by foreign influence, but in some cases the exact source of this influence cannot be identified. For example, Luka Vujović (1969: 122–126) argued that the labialized

---

[13] I investigated the phonetic and phonological features of the Albanian speech in Velja Gorana using a bilingual questionnaire, which was created by myself and Alexander Rusakov on the basis of the more general monolingual questionnaire of the Albanian Dialectological Atlas (Gjinari et al. 2007: 439–445). In gathering the data on the morphosyntactic features of the contact varieties of BCMS and Albanian in Velja Gorana, I used our bilingual questionnaire, which focuses on several potentially interesting aspects of morphosyntax, such as clitic doubling, the main types of actant marking, among others. The material on kinship terminology was gathered using the lexical questionnaire of Minor Dialectological Atlas of Balkan Languages (MDABL vol. 2, 2006).

pronunciation of the long *a* (*zl'aᵒto* 'gold', BCMS *zl'ato*) in the Mrkovići variety, which is also found in the Montenegrin coastal areas of Kotor, Budva, and Bar, is due to contact with Venetian. However, the labialization of the nasal *ã* and the nonnasal long stressed *a:* is widespread in Gheg Albanian, in particular in its northwestern varieties, including those spoken in the south of Montenegro (Desnitskaya 1968: 82–83, 86; Gjinari & Shkurtaj 2000: 115, 120; Morozova 2017a: 229).

Among the phonetic innovations that can be attributed to contact with Albanian, Luka Vujović mentions the change of articulation of the BCMS laterals. BCMS has two lateral approximants, apical denti-alveolar /l̪/ and dorsal palatal /ʎ/ (Simić & Ostojić 1996: 182–183; Petrović & Gudurić 2010: 167, 179), while Albanian has two apical alveolar laterals, the velarized /ɫ/ and the non-velarized /l/ (Memushaj 2011: 79–80). In the Mrkovići variety the velarized /ɫ/ occurs in Albanian borrowings, e.g. [bˈoɫa] 'grass snake' from Alb DEF *b'olla*. Besides that, it can be found in in some native BCMS words, replacing the non-velarized apical denti-alveolar /l̪/ ([kɫas] 'spike', comp. BCMS *klas* [kl̪as]) and the dorsal palatal /ʎ/ before back vowels: [debeɫˈan], comp. BCMS *deb'eljak* [debˈeʎak] 'fatty'. In the other positions the palatal /ʎ/ of BCMS can be replaced by the Albanian alveolar /l/: [kral] 'king', comp. BCMS *kralj* [kraʎ]. The mixing of laterals in the native BCMS words is subject to a high degree of variation between individuals (Vujović 1969: 156–162); while in the Albanian loanwords like [bˈoɫa] 'grass snake' the Albanian laterals are consistently maintained.

Some other Albanian loanwords adopted in their original phonetic form can be found in modern monolingual Mrkovići. Consider, for example, [ðˈokun] 'waterhole, small puddle' in the speech of an elderly woman in Mala Gorana (BCMS *lokanj*, Alb *llokajë* 'watery mud', most probably borrowed from BCMS), which contains the Albanian interdental fricative /ð/. The alternation of /ð/ and /ɫ/ has received diverse accounts in the literature on Albanian dialects. According to Gjinari et al. (2007–2008: map 23, 25), in Northwestern Gheg varieties the interdental /ð/ and the velarized lateral approximant /ɫ/ occur as "free variants", while Desnitskaya (1968: 84) considers that, in most cases, /ɫ/ replaces /ð/. However, in the variety of Kraja, a mountainous region near Lake Skadar, /ð/ may replace /ɫ/; e.g. *modha* instead of *molla* 'apple' (Desnitskaya 1968: 84). In our case, a dialectal /ð/ and /ɫ/ merger might be reflected in the local Albanian variant of *llokajë*, which could be equated with the corresponding Slavic lexical item in the speech of bilinguals from the Mrkovići and preserved in their local variety.

Contact-induced changes in Albanian: observations from Velja Gorana. In contemporary Velja Gorana some observations were made about the manner in which different bilinguals speak the Albanian language and reproduce its sounds. Local men and Albanian women preserve the phonemic oppositions in the vowel and consonant system of the Albanian language, such as the dialectal Gheg opposition of long and short vowels: *plak* [plak] 'old man' — *plakë* [pla:k] 'old woman' and the general Albanian contrast between the flap /ɾ/ and trill /r:/: Standard Albanian *ruaj*, Gheg *ru:j* [ɾu:j] 'I guard' — Standard Albanian *rruaj*, Gheg *rru:j* [r:u:j] 'I shave'. These phonemic contrasts can become more vague or disappear in the speech of women from the Mrkovići who learned Albanian after they were brought to Velja Gorana: [nˈana plaks] 'grandmother's (lit. "old woman's") mother'.

The Albanian interdental consonants /θ/ and /ð/ are pronounced by the majority of the elder and middle-aged bilingual speakers from Velja Gorana. It should be observed that in the speech of the local Albanians the interdental /ð/ is often, though not always, replaced by /ɫ/ (Morozova 2017a: 230). It is not surprising that the Albanian speech of men in Velja Gorana may show similar variation, because they likely produce their mothers' versions of lexical items. Consider [ðˈija] (Alb *dhi*, DEF *dhia* 'goat', pronounced as [ðˈija] or [ɫˈija] by different native Albanians) and [ɫˈanər] (Alb *dhëndër*, DEF *dhëndri* 'bridegroom', which can be either [ɫˈanri] or [ðˈanri]) in the speech of an elder man in Velja Gorana.

Children have more innovations in their Albanian speech than do their older relatives. They may eliminate the phonemic opposition between the Albanian flap /ɾ/ and trill /r:/ and substitute both sounds by the trill /r/, which is typical for the Balkan Slavic phonological systems: [ruj] 'I guard; I shave' (Morozova 2017a: 232). The Albanian interdental stop /θ/ can be substituted by fricative /f/, which is present both in Albanian and BCMS: [fˈave] 'you said', a dialectal form of aorist from the verb *them* [θem] 'I say' (Ibid.). One of the adolescent informants said that she could not pronounce the Albanian interdental /ð/ like her Albanian mother, even though the other members of the family, including the smaller sister and brother, could articulate it. One of the middle-aged male informants, whose mother was from a monolongual Mrkovići village, also noted that he could not pronounce the interdental sound articulated by his Albanian wife in the words like *dhelpër* [ðˈelpər] 'fox' (DEF *dhelpra*) and pronounced [ɫˈelpna]. On the one hand, such phenomena in the speech of bilinguals from Velja Gorana are results of imperfect learning, which are unlikely to be propagated among the Albanian-speaking community. On the other hand, given the fact that girls from Velja Gorana participate in interethnic marriages, they may contribute to the Albanian language change on the local level.

The local bilinguals may initiate some changes in the application of the phonological rules that regulate the positional alternation of phonemes. For example, in the Albanian speech of an elder bilingual man of Velja Gorana, I observed analogical extension of the devoicing of final obstruents – typical for the majority of Albanian varieties (*i madh* [i maθ] 'big', *zog* [zok] 'bird') – to words with a historical, non-pronounced final vowel *ë*: *i verdhë* [i verθ] 'yellow' and *lugë* [lu:k] 'spoon' (Morozova 2017a: 232). Comp. [i verð] and [lu:g] in Standard Albanian, in the majority of Albanian dialects (Gjinari et al. 2007–2008: maps 44, 45), and in the speech of the Albanian women in Velja Gorana. It can be assumed that the above feature may have emerged in the speech of this informant in his childhood, because of the non-acquisition of the Albanian ë-rule and the extension of the scope of the word-final devoicing pattern.

4.2 Grammatical interference

Prepositions governing the nominative case. One of the innovations of the Mrkovići that undoubtedly results from contact with Albanian is the construction with the preposition *ge/gi* 'at; to' that takes the object in nominative and encodes either static location (1a) or goal of motion (1b), on the model of the Albanian *te(k)* 'at; to', Gheg *ke* (2a–b).[14]

(1) BCMS (THE MRKOVIĆI)
    a. *Njeg'ov-a   s'esr-a   je   **ge**   **đev'ojk-a***
       his-F.NOM.SG sister-NOM.SG be.PRS.3SG PREP girl-NOM.SG
       m'oj-a.
       my-F.NOM.SG
       'His sister is at my daughter's place.' (Vujović 1969: 270)
    b. *Pođ-'osmo **ge** **dž'aᵒmi-ja** na K'unje.*
       go-AOR.1PL PREP mosque-NOM.SG PREP Kunje.ACC.SG
       'We went to the mosque in Kunje.' (Vujović 1969: 270)

(2) a. ALBANIAN
      *'Ish-a   **te**   **m'iq-të**.*
      be.IPF-IPF.1SG PREP friend.PL-NOM.PL.DEF
      'I was at my friends' place.' (Thomai et al. 2002: 1327)
    b. ALBANIAN (VELJA GORANA)
      *Vjet   k'e-na   ʃku   **ke**   **ʃp'i-ja***
      last.year have-PRS.1PL go.PTCP PREP house-NOM.SG.DEF
      baːb-s.
      father-GEN.SG.DEF
      'Last year we went ('have gone') to the father's house.'

---

14 Many languages do not overtly encode the distinction between goal of motion and static location, source of motion and location or between all these meanings (Nikitina 2009). As shown in Sobolev (1988), neutralization of the distinction between the goal of motion and location in case marking, prepositions, and interrogative and relative adverbs is a Balkanism shared by some varieties of BCMS, including those spoken in Montenegro.

The use of the nominative case with prepositions in the variety of the Mrkovići is restricted to this construction. The preposition *ge* is derived from the question and relative adverb *ge* (3a, 3b), BCMS *gde* 'where (at/to what place)' (Vujović 1969: 269). Given that the preposition *te(k)*, Gheg *ke* in Albanian can be used as conjunction, or relative adverb with the meaning 'where (at/to what place)' (4), the use of the Mrkovići adverb *ge* as preposition was likely triggered by the polyfunctionality of its Albanian counterpart. As suggested by Curtis (2012: 319), "it is also possible that the [phonetic] similarity with the Slavic form facilitated the borrowing of the structure associated with the Albanian form".

(3) BCMS (THE MRKOVIĆI)
    a. ***Ge***   ti   e   b'aᵒbo?
         where 2SG.DAT be.PRS.3SG father.NOM.SG
         'Where is your father?' (Vujović 1969: 269)
    b. 'Odž-a   ***gi***   e,   t'amo.
         hodzha-NOM.SG where be.PRS.3SG there
         'There where the hodzha is.' (Vujović 1969: 270)

(4) ALBANIAN
     Ja   ***tek***   'është.
     here where be.PRS.3SG
     'Here's where it is.' (Thomai et al. 2002: 1327)

In Velja Gorana some elder men and elder women from the Mrkovići may use the construction with *ge*, while the majority of speakers of the middle and younger generation prefer the more frequent preposition *kod* of BCMS. In the standard language this preposition takes genitive case objects and encodes the meaning of static location. In the varieties of Montenegro and Southern Serbia, as well as in Bačka and Banat, it is used for both location and the goal of motion (Sobolev 1988: 56), as in my examples (5a) and (5b) from the speech of an old man born in Velja Gorana. Example (6) shows the construction with *kod* undergoing a more radical change in the speech of an Albanian woman in Velja Gorana who learned BCMS as second language. In the phrase *kod moji* 'to my people (i.e. close relatives)' (BCMS *kod mojih*) the preposition *kod* governs the nominative case on the model of *te(k)* in Albanian.

(5) BCMS (VELJA GORANA)
   a. *Jer   je   b'i-l-a   tu   j'en-a   k'ut͡ɕ-a*
      because be.PRS.3SG be-PTCP-F.SG here one-F.NOM.SG house-NOM.SG
      kod ɲih,   *j'en-a   k'ut͡ɕ-a   **kod nas**.*
      PREP 3PL.GEN   one-F.NOM.SG house-NOM.SG PREP 1PL.GEN
      'Because there was here one house on their side, one house on our side.'
   b. *D'oʃ-l-i   su   **kod nas,**   **kod** m'oj-ega*
      come-PTCP-M.PL be.PRS.3PL PREP 1PL.GEN   PREP   my-M.GEN.SG
      d͡z'ed-a.
      grandfather-GEN.SG
      'They came to us, to my grandfather.'

(6) BCMS (VELJA GORANA)
   *'Ide-ʃ   **kod   m'oj-i.***
   go-PRS.2SG PREP my-M.NOM.PL
   'You go to my people.'

Merger of comitative and instrumental. The other contact-induced innovation in the variety of the Mrkovići is the merger of comitative and instrumental constructions. In Standard BCMS the bare instrumental case encodes the instrumental (7a) and several other meanings, while the same form with the preposition *s(a)* 'with' stands for comitative (8a). In Albanian these meanings are expressed by prepositional constructions with *me* 'with' and the accusative (7b, 8b).

(7) a. BCMS
       P'iše-m   'olovk-om.
       write-PRS.1SG pencil-INSTR.SG
       'I write with a pencil.' (Piper & Klajn 2013: 375)
   b. ALBANIAN
       *E   pr'e-u   **me   th'ikë.***
       3SG.ACC cut-AOR.3SG PREP knife.ACC.SG.INDF
       '(S)he cut it with a knife.' (Thomai et al. 2002: 759)

(8) a. BCMS
       *Š'eta   **sa**   s'estr-om.*
       walk.PRS.3SG PREP sister-INSTR.SG
       '(S)he walks with sister.' (Piper & Klajn 2013: 375)
   b. ALBANIAN
       *L'ua-n   **me**   sh'ok-ë-t.*
       play-PRS.3SG PREP friend-PL-ACC.PL.DEF
       '(S)he plays with friends.' (Thomai et al. 2002: 759)

In many Montenegrin varieties the construction with *s(a)* extends its functional scope and covers both comitative and instrumental meanings. The non-prepositional construction disappears or continues to exist in parallel to the prepositional one. Serbian dialectologists agree that this innovation developed in contact with non-Slavic languages, Albanian and Romanian. As seen in the examples taken from in the speech of children (9), elder (10) and middle-aged men (11–12), all natives of Velja Gorana prefer the prepositional construction both for comitative and instrumental meanings. During field work, one of the male informants explained that the bare instrumental like *gad͡z'ao sam k'amenom* 'I have thrown a stone' is possible, but the prepositional structure of the kind *gad͡z'ao sam sa k'amenom* 'I have thrown (with) a stone' (12) sounded more correct to him; the functional difference between the two constructions, thus, was not perceived by this speaker.

(9) BCMS (VELJA GORANA)
  Z'emλ-a   se   'ore   sa   b'ik-ov-ima.
  land-NOM.SG REFL plow.PRS.3SG PREP OX-PL-INSTR.PL
  'The land is plowed with oxen.'

(10) BCMS (VELJA GORANA)
  'Ide-m   u   plan'in-u   sa   'ov͡ts-ama.
  go-PRS.1SG PREP mountain-ACC.SG PREP sheep-INSTR.PL
  'I go to the mountains with sheep.'

(11) BCMS (VELJA GORANA)
  'Ubi-o   ga   s   n'oʒ-em.
  kill-PTCP.M.SG M.3SG.ACC PREP knife-INSTR.SG
  'He killed him with a knife.'

(12) BCMS (VELJA GORANA)
  Gad͡z'a-o   sam   sa   k'amen-om.
  throw-PTCP.M.SG be.PRS.1SG PREP stone-INSTR.SG
  'I threw a stone.'

By contrast, in the variety of the Mrkovići, according to Vujović (1969: 300–308), prepositional constructions were rarely used by the speakers, while the distribution of the non-prepositional instrumental form was extended to cover comitative meaning (13). In my recent observations in the monolingual Mala Gorana, the elder generation also prefers non-prepositional constructions to the prepositional ones (14–15). An example similar to (15) is found in the speech of an old woman from Mala Gorana who has been living in Velja Gorana for several decades (16).

(13) BCMS (THE MRKOVIĆI)
 Gr'ede **koz-'ama.**
 go.PRS.3SG goat-INSTR.PL
 '(S)he goes with goats.' (Vujović 1969: 306)

(14) BCMS (MALA GORANA)
 N'osi-m d'ȓvo **k'oɲ-om** i **tɕ'er-om.**
 carry-PRS.1SG wood.ACC.SG horse-INSTR.SG and ox-INSTR.SG
 'I carry wood with the horse and ox.'

(15) BCMS (MALA GORANA)
 'Ona kren'u-l-a **kor'it-ima** i **st'ok-om**
 F.3SG.NOM set.off-PTCP-F.SG trough-INSTR.PL and livestock-INSTR.SG
 i **kutʃ'itɕ-om.**
 and dog-INSTR.SG
 'She set off with troughs and livestock, and the dog.'

(16) BCMS (VELJA GORANA)
 Da sm'ȓzne b'ab-u u plan'in-u
 SBJV freeze.PRS.3SG old.woman-ACC.SG PREP mountain-ACC.SG
 kutʃ'itɕ-ama, i **t'ikvits-ama** i **'ovts-ama.**
 dog-INSTR.PL and marrow-INSTR.PL and sheep-INSTR.PL
 '[...] to freeze the old woman in the mountains, with the dogs, marrows, and sheep.'

Thus it seems that, both in Velja Gorana and the Mrkovići, the same convergence mechanism is responsible for the merger of instrumental and comitative categories. In the framework of pattern replication in language convergence elaborated by Yaron Matras, "it is often the case that the syncretization will selectively target a pivotal point of reference which is perceived as 'carrying' the construction" (Matras & Sakel 2007: 836). The distributional pattern of the preposition meaning 'with' in Albanian was perceived as a pivot in both cases. In the Mrkovići this resulted in the generalization of the bare instrumental, having more abstract meaning and a broader range of distribution. For Velja Gorana, the structural pattern 'preposition + noun' was probably taken as the other pivotal feature. The prepositional construction of BCMS was more easily identified with the Albanian equivalent, and its distribution, though quite limited and regular in the beginning, began to replicate the distribution of the model.

Mutual influence: the case of "genitival" constructions. Another example of the change of functional rather than structural patterns involves the constructions consisting of the head noun and its attribute, which is normally encoded by the genitive noun phrase in BCMS. In the standard BCMS the periphrastic construction with the preposition *od* 'from' can be also used as attribute in this structure specifying the material out of which the object named by the head noun is made (17a) and some other relations between the head and the dependent noun (17b). With kinship terms, the lexicalized *od*-construction expresses kinship relations of the kind *brat od strica* 'paternal cousin (lit. "brother from the side of the paternal uncle")' (Miloradovich 2011: 17).[15]

(17) BCMS
    a. *čaj*   *od*   *n'an-e*
       tea.NOM.SG   PREP   mint-GEN.SG
       'mint tea' (Piper & Klajn 2013: 336)
    b. *klj'uč-ev-i*   *od*   *st'an-a*
       key-PL-NOM.PL   PREP   apartment-GEN.SG
       'keys from the apartment' (Piper & Klajn 2013: 339)
    c. *brat*   *od*   *str'ic-a*
       brother.NOM.SG   PREP   paternal.uncle-GEN.SG
       'paternal cousin'

In the variety of the Mrkovići and some other Montenegrin varieties of BCMS, the *od*-construction expresses much wider range of relations between the head and the dependent. Andrey Sobolev (1990) maintains that the expansion of usage of this construction can be connected with the influence of Albanian, where the structure of the genitival phrase necessarily contains a connecting element, called "article" in the Albanian grammatical tradition, which agrees with the head of the construction and indicates that the following genitive noun is an attribute to the head. "Under conditions of advanced bilingualism, [...] [w]hen such constructions are calqued into Serbo-Croatian, the position of this marker is occupied by a Slavic morpheme with the most similar structure and syntactic function in the noun phrase, namely the preposition" (Sobolev 1990: 17–18).[16] Example (18) shows the (non-standard) Mrkovići construction (18a) replicating the Albanian pattern (18b). A similar pattern 'noun (kind of geographical object)

---

15 In Albanian the same relation is expressed by means of a different semantic pattern: *djali i xhaxhait* 'paternal cousin (lit. "son of the paternal uncle")'.
16 According to Serbian dialectologists, Romance influence on BCMS is also possible (Pižurica 1984: 93). Sofiia Miloradovich (2011: 22) suggests that this construction may be considered as "Adriatism" in the peripheral north- and southwestern dialects of BCMS, and as "Balkanism" in the Prizren-Timok and Kosovo-Resava dialects.

+ relationship marker + genitive attribute (place name)' is found in the microtoponymics of the Mrkovići region (19a). Given the fact that such model is typical for place names only in Albanian (19b) and extremely unusual for BCMS, the Albanian influence on the functional diffusion of the Mrkovići *od*-construction seems to be plausible explanation.

(18) a. BCMS (THE MRKOVIĆI)
 ml'ek-o   o   kr'av-e
 milk-NOM.SG PREP COW-GEN.SG
 'cow's milk' (Vujović 1969: 298)
 b. ALBANIAN
 q'umësht-i   i   l'opë-s
 milk-NOM.SG.DEF M.NOM.SG COW-GEN.SG.DEF
 'cow's milk'

(19) a. BCMS (THE MRKOVIĆI)
 p'otok   o   Šk'urt-e
 stream.NOM.SG PREP Shkurta-GEN.SG
 'river Shkurta, or the stream of Shkurta' (Vujović 1969: 298)
 b. ALBANIAN
 l'um-i   i   **Shkumb'in-it**
 river-NOM.SG.DEF M.NOM.SG Shkumbin-GEN.SG.DEF
 'river Shkumbin' (Thomai et al. 2002: 708)

In my observations, the *od*-construction describes a diverse set of genitival relations and replaces the standard BCMS non-prepositional genitive construction in the speech of the older bilinguals in Velja Gorana. See the examples from the speech of an old man (20a), a middle-aged man (21a), and a woman from the Mrkovići (22a), as well as the (nearly) correspondent Albanian expressions proposed by the same informants (20b–22b). It should be noted that the prepositional article can be omitted (or may never appear) after some forms of the head noun (the definite nominative singular, for example) in many varieties of Albanian (see Gjinari et al. 2007–2008: map 198, 199, and the example (20b) below).

(20) a. BCMS (VELJA GORANA)
 k'oʒ-a   ot   r'uk-e
 skin-NOM.SG PREP hand-GEN.SG
 'skin of the hand'

b. ALBANIAN (VELJA GORANA)
lik'ur-a **dor-s**
skin-NOM.SG.DEF hand-GEN.SG.DEF
'skin of the hand'

(21) a. BCMS (VELJA GORANA)
sin **od** *s'in-a br'at-a mi*
son.NOM.SG PREP son-GEN.SG brother-GEN.SG 1SG.DAT
'son of the son of my brother'
b. ALBANIAN (VELJA GORANA)
dj'al-i i m'otrə-s nɒn-s
son-NOM.SG.DEF M.NOM.SG sister-GEN.SG.DEF mother-GEN.SG.DEF
'son of sister of mother'

(22) a. BCMS (VELJA GORANA)
ʃkrap **o** *n'os-a*
nostril.NOM.SG PREP nose-GEN.SG
'nostril of the nose'
b. ALBANIAN (VELJA GORANA)
bir'uts-a-t e h'un-it
nostril-PL-NOM.PL.DEF NOM.PL.DEF nose-GEN.SG.DEF
'nostrils of the nose'

In the contexts where Albanian allows several synonymic constructions the elder bilinguals of Velja Gorana are likely to give preference to those that are structurally similar to the *od*-construction. By contrast, schoolchildren who speak the general Montenegrin variant rather than the Mrkovići variety do not necessarily choose such structural doublets and may use other constructions acquired from their Albanian mothers. For example, Albanian has several ways to encode cause with the predicates 'to fear', 'to be afraid of': (i) bare accusative doubled by a pronominal clitic; (ii) prepositional constructions of the kind '*nga* + nominative' (in the standard language) and '*p(r)ej* + ablative' (mainly in the Gheg dialect); (iii) construction 'I have fear of...' in which the cause is expressed by the genitival case form preceded by the article and dependent on the noun for 'fear'. The last two constructions may be equated with the *od*-construction of BCMS: (ii) involves the preposition meaning 'from' and the ablative case form, which has the same inflections as the genitive in Albanian and can be easily identified with the genitive, while (iii) may be seen as structurally parallel to the *od*-construction, as it was described above. In my fieldwork with the bilingual questionnaire, where many stimuli with 'fear' predicates were proposed to the informants, the bilingual men and children preferred to use the prepositional construction with *p(r)ej* (ii), which is intertranslatable with the *od*-construction of BCMS (23). The construction like (iii), which is also replicating the BCMS construction with *od* (24b), was found only in the speech of the bilingual men (24a). The accusative construction (i) was rare in their speech, while children extensively used it, as their mothers probably do (25).

(23) a. ALBANIAN (VELJA GORANA)
fm'ij-a ka-jn fr'igə-n **pej dʑ'ærpn-it.**
child-NOM.SG.DEF have-PRS.3PL fear-ACC.SG.DEF PREP snake-ABL.SG.DEF
'The children are afraid of the snake.'
b. BCMS
d'eca 'ima-ju strah **od zm'i-je.**
children.NOM.SG have-PRS.3PL fear.ACC.SG PREP snake-GEN.SG
'A brave man is not afraid of death.'

(24) a. ALBANIAN (VELJA GORANA)
tr'im-i s=kʋ frik
brave.man-NOM.SG.DEF NEG=have.PRS.3SG fear.ACC.SG.INDF
t dek-s.
ACC.SG.INDF death-GEN.SG.DEF
'A brave man is not afraid of death.'
b. BCMS
j'unak n'ema strah **od sm'r̩t-e.**
brave.man.NOM.SG NEG.have.PRS.3SG fear.ACC.SG PREP death-GEN.SG
'A brave man is not afraid of death.'

(25) ALBANIAN (VELJA GORANA)
tʃ'un-i frig'o-het **dʑiɲ t huj.**
boy-NOM.SG.DEF fear-INACT.PRS.3SG people.ACC.PL.INDF PL.INDF alien
'The boy is afraid of strange people.'

Marking of external possessor with the verbs of pain and sensation. An example of more or less exact grammatical calquing, or replication of the structural pattern is found in Albanian phrases with verbs of pain and sensation used by middle-aged men and children in Velja Gorana, where the possessor appears as an accusative complement of the verb (26a, 27a) on the model of BCMS (26b, 27b). By contrast, in the speech of native Albanians (28) and the elder men (29) I observed only dative external possessor constructions which are typical for the Albanian language.

(26) a. ALBANIAN (VELJA GORANA)
 As'an-in   e   ɫemp   kr'yt-i.
 Asan-ACC.SG.DEF 3SG.ACC hurt.PRS.3SG head-NOM.SG.DEF
 'Asan's head hurts.'
b. BCMS
 'Asan-a   b'oli   gl'av-a.
 Asan-ACC.SG hurt.PRS.3SG head-NOM.SG
 'Asan's head hurts.'

(27) a. ALBANIAN (VELJA GORANA)
 E   kru-n   h'un-i.
 3SG.ACC itch-PRS.3SG nose-NOM.SG.DEF
 'His/her nose is itching.'
b. BCMS
 Sv'r̥bi   **ga**   nos.
 itch.PRS.3SG M.3SG.ACC nose.NOM.SG
 'His nose is itching.'

(28) ALBANIAN (VELJA GORANA)
 As'an-it   i   ðem   kr'ye-t.
 Asan-DAT.SG.DEF 3SG.DAT hurt.PRS.3SG head-NOM.SG.DEF
 'Asan's head hurts.'

(29) ALBANIAN (VELJA GORANA)
 Pl'ak-ut   i   kr'u-het   ʃp'in-a.
 old.man-DAT.SG.DEF 3SG.DAT itch-INACT.PRS.3SG back-NOM.SG.DEF
 'The old man's back is itching.'

It should be observed that the sentences (26a, 27a) do not show total word-by-word intertranslatability with the corresponding BCMS phrases (26b, 27b). The model language (BCMS) does not require the clitic doubling of the definite direct object, but it is doubled in (26a) in accordance with the rules of the replica language (Albanian). The short pronominal forms normally follow the verb in BCMS (27b), but the word order of BCMS is not replicated in the Albanian speech of the bilinguals of Velja Gorana, and in (27a) the pronominal object expressed by a short form of pronoun stands in front of the verb.

4.3 Lexical borrowing and codeswitching

As indicated by Thomason and Kaufman (1988: 74–76), lexical borrowing is likely to happen in any kind of contact situation, and it is not surprising that many loanwords from different languages are found in the lexicons of the Albanian and BCMS varieties spoken in southern Montenegro, where various situations of casual to intense contact within symmetrical or asymmetrical dominance relations between the donor-language and the recipient-language speakers have taken place over time. The Mrkovići variety has some words of Romance origin which may pertain to the times of Venetian rule in the town of Bar and the surrounding area (1402–1412, 1422–1429, 1443–1571), a considerable number of borrowings from Ottoman Turkish which occurred during the Ottoman rule and socio-cultural dominance in this part of Montenegro (1571–1878), as well as loanwords and calques from Albanian (Vujović 1969: 81, 353–356; Sobolev 2015; Novik & Sobolev 2016; Morozova 2019).

This section treats the results of the Albanian-Slavic interaction in the Mrkovići region. Some of these examples have been cited also in (Sobolev et al. 2018; Morozova 2019), but no detailed analysis was provided. To start with, I consider lexical calques in both directions, Slavic to Albanian and Albanian to Slavic, with particular attention to the speech of different bilinguals in Velja Gorana. After that I concentrate on the Albanian loanwords in the variety of the Mrkovići, which are largely due to past contact, and discuss the situation in Velja Gorana, where language contact is ongoing. This involves a description of both codeswitching and the borrowing of content and function words in the speech of bilinguals.

Lexical calquing. Some noteworthy calques, or loan translations, from Albanian in the variety of the Mrkovići are reported in the sources. As given by Vujović (1969: 355) and Sobolev (2015: 544), the names of the autumn months *p'rvi j'eseni* 'September', *dr'ugi j'eseni* 'October', and *tr'eći j'eseni* 'November' seem to reproduce the semantic pattern of the corresponding Albanian expressions *vj'eshtë e p'arë*, *vj'eshtë e d'ytë*, and *vj'eshtë e tr'etë* (lit. "first/second/third autumn"). It should be observed that Albanian and BCMS have different word order patterns in noun phrases: the former has the attribute following the noun it modifies and the latter tends to have the attribute preceding the noun (inverted order is possible in both languages, but it is used for purely stylistic purposes). As seen in the example below, the word order pattern of Albanian (31) is not replicated in the variety of the Mrkovići; rather the elements of the expression are adapted to the syntactic pattern of the recipient language (30). Moreover, the noun *j'esen* 'autumn' is feminine in BCMS and requires gender agreement with the attribute as in (32). In the Mrkovići phrase the cardinal number *p'rvi* 'first' has masculine ending, as if it agreed with the grammatical gender of a masculine noun (e.g.

BCMS *m'esec* 'month' in a tentative construction "the first month of autumn"). It may therefore be concluded that the Mrkovići *p'rvi* (*dr'ugi, tr'eći*) *j'eseni* falls in the category of loan renditions, "in which the model compound only furnishes a general hint for the reproduction" (Weinreich 1979: 51). The possibility for the bilinguals of Slavic origin being responsible for this calque in the variety of the Mrkovići is quite strong, and this example can be interpreted as a transfer of foreign material to the recipient language (the variety of the Mrkovići) in which the speakers are more proficient than in the donor language (Albanian).

(30) BCMS (THE MRKOVIĆI)
p'rv-i   j'esen-i
first-M.NOM.SG autumn-GEN.SG
'September' (lit. "the first [month] of autumn")

(31) ALBANIAN
vj'eshtë   e   p'arë
autumn.NOM.SG.INDF F.NOM.SG first.F.SG
'September' (lit. "first autumn")

(32) BCMS
p'rv-a   j'esen
first-F.NOM.SG autumn.NOM.SG
'first autumn'

Calquing occurs in the kinship terminology of the Mrkovići. For example, their variety developed an innovative distinction of grandparents from the father's and mother's sides, which is conveyed by means of native terms for grandparents, calques, and loanwords from Albanian (see Morozova 2019 for detail). The term for paternal grandfather, *babov'ejlji*, where *b'abo* 'father' is a borrowing from Turkish which is very common for the Muslim population of the Balkans, reproduces the semantic pattern 'big + father/mother' of Albanian (comp. *babam'adh* and *tatm'adh* 'paternal grandfather', *nanm'adhe* 'paternal grandmother' in Gjinari et al. (2007–2008: 234–237)). The other Mrkovići terms for grandparents from the father's side, *babost'ari* 'paternal grandfather' and *nanast'ara* 'paternal grandmother', show the Balkan Slavic semantic pattern 'old + mother/father', originally standing for grandparents in general (comp. BCMS *stari'otac* 'grandfather' and *staram'ajka* 'grandmother'). As shown below, the structural pattern of Albanian (35) is copied into the variety of the Mrkovići (33a–b), and the structure of the BCMS compounds (34) changed. In (Morozova 2019) the calques in the kinship terminology of the Mrkovići are interpreted as the result of imposition;

i.e. the conservation of linguistic structures from the native language by speakers who acquire a new language (van Coetsem 1988). Some of these speakers were probably Albanian women, who learned BCMS after marriage in the Mrkovići families and transferred it to their children, as well as Albanian families living in the villages of the Mrkovići who shifted to BCMS.

(33) BCMS (THE MRKOVIĆI)
    a. *babo=v'ejlj-i*
       father=big-M.NOM.SG
       'paternal grandfather' (lit. "big father")
    b. *babo=st'ar-i*
       father=old-M.NOM.SG
       'paternal grandfather' (lit. "old father")

(34) BCMS
    stari='otac
    old=father.NOM.SG
    'grandfather' (lit. "old father")

(35) ALBANIAN
    baba=m'adh
    father=big.NOM.SG.INDF
    'paternal grandfather' (lit. "big father")

In Velja Gorana, I observed calques from both directions, Albanian to BCMS and vice versa, in the speech of bilingual members of the community (see also Sobolev et al. 2018: 32; Morozova 2019). Some expressions were registered in the speech of one individual, which does not preclude the possibility of wider distribution, while the others are used by different informants or can be found in the other areas of Slavic-Albanian contact (according to Omari 2012; Stanišić 1995 and their sources).

    The examples (36a–37a) show calques from Albanian into the local variety of BCMS, which are found in the speech of an older bilingual man from Velja Gorana (the expression shown in (36a) also occurred in a story told by a monolingual female informant in the village of Lunje, see Sobolev (2015: 544)). The example (38a) was met in a spontaneous text in BCMS recorded from a middle-aged Albanian woman in Velja Gorana. The expression (39a) from the Albanian speech of a previously monolingual woman from the Mrkovići is a calque from a common BCMS colloquial expression (40b) found in many northern Albanian varieties in contact with BCMS.

(36) a. BCMS (VELJA GORANA)
    tr'uʃka-ju   *se*   *b'ab-e*
    shake-PRS.3PL   REFL   old.woman-NOM.PL
  b. ALBANIAN (VELJA GORANA)
    ʃk'und-en   *pl'ak-a-t*
    shake-INACT.PRS.3PL   old.woman-PL-NOM.PL.DEF
    'it is raining and snowing [in the end of March] (lit. "the old women are shaking").'

(37) a. BCMS (VELJA GORANA)
    na   *ul'as*   *apr'il-a*
    PREP   entrance.ACC.SG   April-GEN.SG
  b. ALBANIAN
    në   *h'yrje*   *të*   *pr'ill-it*
    PREP   entrance.ACC.SG.INDF   ACC.SG.INDF   April-GEN.SG.DEF
    'in the beginning of April'

(38) a. BCMS (VELJA GORANA)
    Ne   **t͡s'epa-m**   **gl'av-u**   **za**   **k'uhiɲ-u.**
    NEG   split-PRS.1SG   head-ACC.SG   for   kitchen-ACC.SG
    'I do not care about the kitchen.' (lit. "My head does not crack over the kitchen.")
  b. ALBANIAN
    Nuk   **ça-j**   **k'okë-n.**
    NEG   split-PRS.1SG   head-ACC.SG.DEF
    'I do not care.' (lit. "I do not split my head.")

(39) a. ALBANIAN (VELJA GORANA)
    S=kʋ   *l'iðje.*
    NEG=have.PRS.3SG   connection.ACC.SG.INDF
  b. BCMS
    N'ema   *v'ez-e.*
    NEG.have.PRS.3SG   connection-GEN.SG
    'Never mind (lit. "there is no connection").'

The example (40a) shows the construction 'I am two (sic!) years old' (lit. "I have two"), with the auxiliary 'to have' as in BCMS (40b) instead of the Albanian construction with the auxiliary 'to be' (40c), in the speech of a 5-year old boy in a bilingual family. The use of the auxiliary 'to have' served as pivotal feature of the BCMS construction, which was taken by the child to the replica language. As nothing similar was observed in the speech of elder bilinguals, this innovation is unlikely to be propagated further among the community of Velja Gorana.

(40) a. ALBANIAN (VELJA GORANA)
    Ka-m   dy.
    have-PRS.1SG two
  b. BCMS
    'Ima-m   dve   g'odin-e.
    have-PRS.1SG two.F.NOM.PL year-ACC.PL
  c. ALBANIAN
    Ja-m   dy   vjeç.
    be-PRS.1SG two years.old.M
    'I am two years old.'

Loanwords from Albanian to the variety of the Mrkovići are not substantial in number. Most of them are nouns, which belong to different semantic fields, but some examples of borrowed verbs also can be found. Table 1 shows several examples of such borrowings cited after (Vujović 1969; Sobolev 2015; Novik & Sobolev 2016).

Table 1 Albanian loanwords in the variety of the Mrkovići

semantic field	sample	Mrkovići word	origin
kinship terms	grandfather (BCMS *ded/đed*)	*đuš*	Alb *gjysh*
landscape	hill (BCMS *brež'uljak*)	*k'odra*	Alb *k'odër* (DEF *k'odra*)
crop farming and vegetation	red pepper (BCMS *p'aprika*) tomato (MS *parad'ajz*)	*sp'eca* *mulat'arti, dom'atija*	Alb *spec* (PL *sp'eca*) Gheg Alb *mollat'art* (DEF *mollat'arti*), Alb *dom'ate* (DEF *dom'atja*)
animals	bat (BCMS *sl'epi miš*) magpie (BCMS *švr'aka*) weasel (BCMS *l'asica*)	*lakur'ić* *gr'išeza* *b'ukulica*	Alb *lakur'iq* Alb *gr'ishëz* (DEF *gr'ishëza*) Alb *b'ukël*
household terms	steps (BCMS *pr'eslo*) water tank (BCMS *'ubao*) water keg (BCMS *žbanj*) roof rafter (BCMS *gr'eda na kr'ovu*)	*kaprc'ol* *pus* *buc'ela* *grš'aneza*	Alb *kapërc'ell* Alb *pus* Alb *buc'elë* (DEF *buc'ela*) Alb *gërsh'ërëz* (DEF *gërsh'ërëza*)

semantic field	sample	Mrkovići word	origin
body parts	back (BCMS k'ičma)	kor'is	Alb kurr'iz
	milt (BCMS sl'ezina)	špan'etka	Gheg Alb sh(p)n'etkë (DEF sh(p)n'etka)
abstract nouns	oath (BCMS kl'etva)	b'esa	Alb b'esë (DEF b'esa)
verbs	set off (BCMS kr'enuti)	n'išnjat	Alb nis
	mistake (BCMS gr'ešiti)	gab'onjat	Alb gab'ohem
	disappear (BCMS izg'ubiti se)	tr'etnjat, 'umjat	Alb tr'etem, humb

The traditional dichotomy of core borrowings, for which the recipient language "has viable equivalents", and cultural borrowings, which serve to "fill the gaps in the recipient language's store of words, because they stand for objects or concepts new to the language's culture" (Myers-Scotton 2006: 212, 215; see also Haspelmath 2009: 46) is problematic in the case of the Mrkovići. Part of the Albanian loanwords in Table 2 stand for cultural objects, such as household items and cultural plants, but these words do not seem to "fill the gaps" in the lexical stock of the variety of the Mrkovići because the corresponding items have probably already been familiar to the speakers, and native words for them could very well have already existed in their lexicon. The loanword b'esa 'oath', which is found in many BCMS varieties in Montenegro (Omari 2012: 385; Stanišić 1995: 59–60), can be considered a cultural borrowing, because it describes one of the most important concepts of the Northern Albanian tribal society, an oath that protected the alliances between tribes, guaranteed the truce between the parties of a blood feud, etc. However, this concept cannot be said to be completely unknown to the Montenegrin tribes of the past. In the modern varieties in Montenegro the borrowed word b'esa can be used in the expressions like 'give (someone) your word' along with the native rij'eč 'word'.

The effect of the Albanian loanwords on the lexicon of the recipient variety of the Mrkovići can be best described in terms of the categorization proposed for the World Loanword Database by Martin Haspelmath et al., which includes the following types: "insertion (the word is inserted into the vocabulary as a completely new item), replacement (the word may replace an earlier word with the same meaning that falls out of use, or changes its meaning), or coexistence (the word may coexist with a native word with the same meaning)" (Haspelmath 2009: 49). It can be seen from Table 2 that the Albanian loanwords typically coexist with the native words or the other borrowings with the same meaning. The word for tomato, which is obviously a novel term in all languages of Europe, is a potential cultural borrowing from the neighbouring Northwestern Gheg variety of Albanian (*mollat'art* or *dom'ate*) inserted into the vocabulary of the Mrkovići as a new item. However, as no information about the way and time of the spread of tomatoes in the region is available, it is equally possible that the Albanian term appeared in the variety of the Mrkovići later than the other borrowing from the Austrian German word *parad'ajz*, and also coexisted with it.

Some cases of replacement of the earlier words can be found in such semantic fields as body parts. This is salient for other bilingual communities of the Balkans where Albanian is spoken. For example, the Greek dialect of Palasa, a village in the southern Albanian Himara district, shows a moderate number of borrowings from Albanian, e.g. words for body parts: *s'upi* 'shoulder' from Alb *sup* (DEF *s'upi*), in contrast to *ómos* in Standard Greek (Sobolev 2017: 432). However, it should be noted that replacement of the native items may be confined to several villages of the Mrkovići or even several individual speakers. For example, the BCMS word *sl'ezina* 'milt' seems to be replaced with the Albanian borrowing *špan'etka* in the speech of two elder informants in Velja Gorana, while in the version of the informant from Dapčevići the two words coexisted as shown in Sobolev (2015: 552) and our field work.

Table 2 Coexistence of borrowings and native words in the variety of the Mrkovići

semantic field	sample	Mrkovići word	origin
crop farming and vegetation	tomato	*parad'ajz*	MS *parad'ajz*, from Germ *Parad'eiser*
		mulat'arti	Gheg Alb *mollat'art* (DEF *mollat'arti*), a calque from It *pomod'oro* ("golden apple")
		dom'atija	Alb *dom'ate* (DEF *dom'atja*) from Gr *domáta* (borrowing via Spanish *tom'ate* in most European languages)
		frenk	Tr *Frenk* 'foreigner'
household terms	steps	*pr'eslo*	BCMS *pr'eslo*
		kaprc'ol	Alb *kapërc'ell*
		sk'ala	It *sc'ala*
body parts	milt	*sl'ezina*	BCMS *sl'ezina*
		špan'etka	Gheg Alb *sh(p)n'etkë* (DEF *sh(p)n'etka*)

Borrowing and codeswitching in Velja Gorana. Some of the Albanian loanwords treated in this section are better known in Gorana than in other Mrkovići villages. For example, *kaprc'ol* 'steps' is more often used in Mala and Velja

Gorana, according to (Vujović 1969: 354; Sobolev 2015: 556). The kinship term *đuš* 'grandfather' mentioned by Vujović (1969: 353) as pertaining to Mrkovići can be found today only in Velja Gorana, where bilingual children use it when they address their grandfathers in BCMS (41). Such items as *đuš* 'grandfather' (with a vocative variant *d͡zʼiʃo*) come from day-to-day contacts of bilingual speakers, with both languages used in family communication, as described in 3.2 (see Morozova & Rusakov 2018 for more detail).

(41) BCMS (VELJA GORANA)
    ş'utra   k'iʃ-a,   **d͡zʼiʃ-o!**
    tomorrow rain-NOM.SG grandfather-VOC
    'There will be rain tomorrow, grandfather!'

As to be expected, the Albanian speech of bilinguals shows a considerable number of loanwords from BCMS. As noted by Matthew Curtis (2012: 383), "borrowings from Slavic may be found in every dialect of Albanian, [...], as well as around 450 words incorporated into standard Albanian". It is important that along with Slavicisms that have broader diffusion in Albanian or in its Northwestern Gheg subdialect, there are some lexical items that get transferred from one language to another in the ongoing bilingual situation of Velja Gorana. Compare, for example, the BCMS word *z'emljotres* 'earthquake' in the Albanian speech of an older bilingual man (42) and the local Mrkovići word *piɲ'ata* 'pot', from It *pignʼat(t)a*, used by an older Albanian woman who tells how her mother-in-law spoke to her in the variety of the Mrkovići (43). Both lexemes are adapted to the structure of the Albanian language. It is possible, however, that the speaker in (42) does not know the Albanian word *tërm'et* 'earthquake' and quite naturally substitutes by the corresponding lexeme from his second language (in contrast, some other male bilinguals in Velja Gorana know the Albanian word and do not tend to borrow its equivalent from BCMS). The borrowed localism in (43) can be seen as a linguistic consequence of integration of the previously monolingual Albanian women into the community of Velja Gorana. As it was mentioned in 3.2, acquiring the language of the in-laws and neighbours was the necessary condition for the Albanian brides to join the community, and after their shift to bilingualism the "old words" of the Mrkovići could occur as fully integrated items in their Albanian speech as well.

(42) ALBANIAN (VELJA GORANA)
Kto   i   k'e-na   gad'it   taʃ,   mas
this.F.ACC.PL 3PL.ACC have-PRS.1PL build.PTCP now   after
zemljotr'es-it.
earthquake-ABL.SG.DEF
'We built them [these houses] now, after the earthquake.'

(43) ALBANIAN (VELJA GORANA)
θ'o-tə,   ma   nep   **pɲ'atə-n.**
say-PRS.3SG 1SG.DAT:3SG.ACC give.IMP.2SG pot-ACC.SG.DEF
'She says: "Give me the pot".'

It should be noted that Albanian women may also use loanwords from general BCMS, especially those denoting the cultural items and concepts that appeared in Yugoslavia or in recent times. For example, one of my elder informants told how she worked in the state-owned farm when she was young, using the BCMS words like *poljopriv'ed* 'agriculture' (BCMS *poljopr'ivreda*, Alb *bujqës'i*), *preduz'etɕe* 'enterprise' (BCMS *preduz'eće*, Alb *ndërm'arrje*), *p'ensija* 'pension' (BCMS *p'ensija*, Alb *pensi'on*).

The transfer of discourse markers, particles, and connectors — which may be called "utterance modifiers", as in (Matras 1998) — seems to be more widespread in the bilingual speech of Velja Gorana than the borrowing of content words. Yaron Matras characterized the donor language, which lends its discourse markers, as being "pragmatically dominant" from the point of view of "the role [...] in regulating mental processing activities" and noted that "the statistical relevance of discourse markers might indeed decrease for balanced bilinguals simply because of their ability to switch elsewhere as well" (Matras 1998: 286–287). In Velja Gorana I did not observe much use of discourse markers from one contact language in utterances in the second language among balanced bilinguals who were born in the village. Rather, such cases occur among the previously monolingual women from the other villages. The examples (44–46) below show that BCMS plays the role of the pragmatically dominant language both for its native speakers who learn Albanian as adults and the native speakers of Albanian who acquire BCMS during their first years in Velja Gorana. Example (44) is taken from the speech of a young Albanian woman who has lived in the village for about seven years; and examples (45–46) contain fragments from the speech of a middle-aged Mrkovići woman (items from BCMS are in bold). The bilingual variation is seen for the adversative conjunction (BCMS *'ali* 'but') in (44–45) and the discource-connecting adverbs *'isto* 'too' (45) and *stv'arno* 'really' (46).

(44) ALBANIAN (VELJA GORANA)
'Ali maj men ɲih'erən kuɾ i kam θ'ye ða:mt.
'**But** I remember a case when I broke my teeth.'

(45) ALBANIAN (VELJA GORANA)
*Po, pl'aku perf'ekt ka fol serb'iʃt. 'Eɫe pl'aka ka fol serb'iʃt bɔɫ... pak aʃt'u, s ka dit mir, **'ali** aj'ʌ ka fol se n'ana plaks aj'ʌ **'isto** ka ken pej **Mr̩koj'evit͡ɕa**, aj'ʌ ka fol serb'iʃt **perf'ektno**. Kn'ene, kn'ena **Mr̩koj'evit͡ɕi**, **zn'at͡ʃi L'aʃkit͡ɕ se prez'ivala**, **'ali** aj'ʌ ma t'epər ka fol ʃt͡ʃip.*
'Yes, grandfather spoke Serbian. And grandmother spoke a lot of Serbian... a little bit so, she did not know it well, **but** she spoke, because the grandmother's mother, she **also** was from **the Mrkojevići**, she spoke Serbian **in a perfect way**. There, there are **the Mrkojevići**, **so, her surname was Laškić**, **but** she spoke mostly Albanian.'

(46) ALBANIAN (VELJA GORANA)
*A jan mart'u me daʃur'i, nuk kam **p'ojma**, **stv'arno** nuk e di.*
'I have no **idea**, whether they got married for love, **really**, I don't know.'

Examples (45–46) also provide evidence of the codeswitching patterns that occur in the Albanian speech of a bilingual woman from the Mrkovići village of Kunje, who lives in Velja Gorana (switches from Albanian into BCMS are marked in bold and underlined). In the example (45) the non-adapted genitival form of the BCMS patronym *Mr̩koj'evit͡ɕi* 'Mrkojevići' is used after the Albanian preposition *prej*, Gheg *pej* 'from'. This preposition takes ablative case objects, but the ablative case in Albanian has the same inflections as genitive, and because of that it could be identified by the speaker with the genitive in BCMS. In the same sentence the BCMS adverb *perf'ektno* 'in a perfect way' is inserted into the Albanian clause, instead of finding an Albanian equivalent. It should be noted that the root *perfekt-* is known in Albanian, but there are no adverbs containing it; adverbial phrases like *shumë mirë* 'very good' were probably rejected by the speaker because of the perceived lack of emphasis. In the next sentence the speaker again inserts the BCMS patronym *Mr̩koj'evit͡ɕi*, now in the nominative case, instead of its Albanian version *Mërk'ot*. Finally, a fragment in BCMS, *zn'at͡ʃi L'aʃkit͡ɕ se prez'ivala* 'so, her surname was Laškić', is cited in the otherwise Albanian sentence in (45). The example (46) shows the expression *nuk kam p'ojma* 'I have no idea', where the BCMS word *p'ojam* 'idea' in the non-adapted genitival form is inserted into the Albanian phrase.

The speech of male bilinguals and older women who have been living in Velja Gorana for a long time shows (almost) none of the codeswitching strategies described above. Rather, intersentential codeswitching may occur, as in an example of switching from Albanian into BCMS and back (BCMS bolded) by an old man from Velja Gorana (47, partially cited in Sobolev et al. 2018: 32).

(47) ALBANIAN (VELJA GORANA)
D'imni i ka kərk'u z'otit me mi ła tri dit uh'ʋ. Tri dit uh'ʋ me e myt pl'akən me d͡ʑiθ t͡ʃa kʋ. **I bog ga da tri d'ana od z'ime.** *Kʋ dal pranv'era iʒ lut...*
'Winter asked the god to give three days on loan. Three days on loan to freeze the old woman with everything she had. **And the god gave three days from winter.** Spring went out and begged...'

The linguistic behaviour shown in (47) may be observed in the situations in which the bilinguals are aware that their interlocutor possesses both of their languages, but cannot be sure which language is preferred because (s)he does not belong to their community. As for the community members, they are addressed in accordance with the community norms (see Morozova 2018 for a detailed description). One of the expected (and unmarked) conversational strategies in Velja Gorana, though not the only one, is codeswitching, which "conveys the message of dual identities or memberships in both of the cultures that the languages index" (Myers-Scotton 2006: 167). Bilingual speakers may switch between their languages in accommodating different interlocutors or in addressing the outsider. The former kind of linguistic behaviour is characteristic of the older Albanian women, while the latter is especially typical for the local men who are intended to convey the local identity (see Morozova 2017b). Non-accommodative behaviour on the part of different speakers, either bi- or monolingual, each speaking his or her native language, is also tolerated by the community. As it seems, the coexistence of the two languages in Velja Gorana without the articulated dominance of either is the main factor for the development of such "tolerance", or acceptability of different linguistic behaviour strategies, and one of the cornerstones of the prolonged bilingualism in the community.

5 Conclusion

5.1 The ongoing contact in Velja Gorana: an overview

As can be seen from the above, the linguistics of the contact situation in Velja Gorana do not include extreme instances of contact-induced change in (the local versions of) Albanian and BCMS. The greatest number of borrowed items are discourse markers from BCMS. Borrowing of content words from BCMS into

Albanian is moderate and involves mainly words borrowed in modern times and localisms, while the transfer of lexical items from Albanian into the local version of BCMS (see 4.3) in speech behaviour is avoided. Lexical calquing occurs both in the Albanian and BCMS speech of virtually all members of the community (4.3). Phonetic and phonological interference in Albanian includes the loss of some phonemic contrasts and morphophonemic rules in the speech of late bilinguals and some local bilinguals (4.1). Even though the phonology of (the local version of) BCMS was not thoroughly investigated, it may be concluded from field observations that the effects of contact influence in this domain are either absent or confined to subphonemic changes in articulation and do not result in change of the phonological system. In morphosyntax, mutual influence of Albanian and BCMS involves a degree of replication in functional patterns, and structural similarity of model and replica constructions serves as one of the pivotal features in this process (4.2). As a result, new functional restrictions may emerge for already-existing constructions in either language. For example, the prepositional construction with *s(a)* in BCMS extends its functional scope by modelling the Albanian prepositional construction with *me*. From the various Albanian constructions with verbs of fear, bilingual speakers more often use those that have structural parallels in BCMS. Replication of structural patterns is confined to a few constructions that have limited diffusion in the model language and maintain the same scope of distribution in the replica language. See, for example, the accusative government of verbs of pain and sensation in the local version of Albanian on the model of BCMS and the nominative government of the BCMS preposition *kod* on the model of Albanian *te(k)*.

It has also been shown in Section 3 that a situation of balanced language contact among individual speakers of different ages and origins may contribute to the process of linguistic convergence. Taking the effects of contact-induced language change in the speech of bilinguals observed in Velja Gorana, it is apparent that the paths of development of these features can be related to the profiles of bilingual speakers described in Section 3.2, based on the findings in (Morozova & Rusakov 2018).

Profile 1. *Older men* may occasionally use lexical borrowings from BCMS in their Albanian speech, while their version(s) of BCMS contain(s) lexical calques from Albanian, which are likely inherited rather than spontaneously created. In other respects they seem to be balanced bilinguals, with neither of the two languages playing a dominant role on the individual level. Consequently, the effects of contact-induced change in their speech do not include heavier lexical borrowing in either direction, syntactic pattern replication, or shared discourse markers from a "pragmatically dominant" language.

Profile 2. *Middle-aged men* do not tend to borrow discourse markers and content words in either direction from one language to another. Some phonetic and phonological innovations in (their version of) Albanian are probably owing to a disbalance in their acquisition of the two languages. For example, the men whose mothers originated from the monolingual villages of the Mrkovići may not acquire the certain Albanian phonemes. It is significant that the speech of middle-aged men in Velja Gorana contains almost all the morphosyntactic innovations described in Section 4.2 and provides a good illustration of mutual influence on the part of the two language systems, both Albanian and BCMS.

Profile 3. *Older women* in Velja Gorana usually have one native language and acquire the second language after marriage. As for the older Albanian women, their two languages do not show extensive changes in phonology and morphosyntax due to the ongoing language contact. The lexicon of their native language, Albanian, is slightly affected by contact with BCMS, and, probably for functional reasons, some modern terms from BCMS and localisms from the Mrkovići variety may occur in their Albanian speech. What is more, all Albanian women, no matter how long they have been living in Velja Gorana, tend to use discourse markers from BCMS when they speak Albanian. Such interference cannot be explained by the lack of equivalents in (their version of) Albanian or unequal power relations between the two languages in the community as a whole. Rather, it results from the change of dominance that happens at the level of individual speakers and is perceived by them as "forgetting" the native language and "speaking more BCMS than Albanian".

The Albanian speech of the older Mrkovići women, who learned Albanian only after marriage, may have some simplifying phonetic and phonological changes and contain lexical calques and loanwords from BCMS. Their BCMS speech does not demonstrate any effects of contact-induced change that may have developed in Velja Gorana either under the influence of the second language or as a result of dialect mixing with the version(s) of BCMS spoken by the locals. In contrast, they tend to maintain the version of BCMS that they learned in their native villages (as in the example (16) from the speech of an older woman from Mala Gorana who continues to use bare instrumental forms instead of the prepositional constructions to encode comitative). BCMS remains the pragmatically dominant language of the older Mrkovići women, and they may use BCMS discourse markers in their Albanian speech.

Profile 4. *Middle-aged and young women* from the Mrkovići and from Albanian villages have virtually no effects of interference in their native languages. The only exception is the tendency to borrow discourse markers from BCMS into Albanian in the speech of Albanian women, likewise an influence of the pragmatically dominant language.

As for the second language, which is acquired after marriage, it was observed that young and middle-aged Albanians may innovate in BCMS by replicating some structural patterns and calquing idiomatic phrases from Albanian. No changes of this kind were found in the speech of elder Albanian women, and it can be thus suggested that a long-term stay in the community of Velja Gorana favours better acquisition of the second language. With young and middle-aged women it is important that they are the main caregivers for children, and any of their learners' innovations may propagate directly into the children's speech or trigger a less overt change in it.

The Albanian speech of the middle-aged women from the Mrkovići has simplifying phonetic and phonological changes and some lexical calques and loanwords from BCMS. BCMS remains their pragmatically dominant language, and middle-aged women from the Mrkovići extensively use BCMS discourse markers in their Albanian speech. They do not actually innovate in grammar by means of replication of the BCMS patterns in Albanian, but in their speech this is "compensated" by the relatively lax fashion of dealing with the two languages and intensive codeswitching. It is typical for them to insert BCMS phrases and alternate between the two languages in one clause when they speak in Albanian. By contrast, native Albanians and the local male bilinguals avoid intrasentential codeswitching.

Profile 5. *Elder children* share most part of phonetic and phonological and grammatical innovations that can be found in the local version of Albanian. This is probably connected with the fact that they currently learn and extensively use BCMS at school, while Albanian takes the position of the subdominant "home language". As girls from Velja Gorana participate in interethnic marriages, their innovations may propagate to the Albanian-speaking communities of southern Montenegro if they are preserved in their speech. However, it is of high possibility that children's innovations may disappear because the children in Velja Gorana do not cease to have access to Albanian.

Profile 6. *Small children* may innovate in grammar (and probably in phonology), because their competencies in both Albanian and BCMS are not yet full. They may also acquire the innovations in both languages, such as grammatical and lexical calques, that have been created by their caregivers, especially their bilingual mothers. However, these effects are unlikely to be diffused from the speech of small children into the whole community of Velja Gorana. They may disappear when the children go to school (relevant for BCMS only) and extend their circle of contacts within the community.

The situation in Velja Gorana differs from many contact situations in which considerable interference comes about in a language through imperfect learning by nonnative speakers and through the bilingualism of the native speakers in the other language, which is politically or numerically dominant (see Thomason & Kaufman 1988: 69–71 for examples). Both languages are equally important not only in the community of Velja Gorana, but also in the whole region of southern Montenegro, even though the main official language on the state level is BCMS. In the community, norms of use of the two languages are relatively lax, and this enables a less abrupt adaptation on the part of previously monolingual speakers and exerts fewer effects of imperfect learning in their speech in the second language. On the individual level the situation of balanced language contact in Velja Gorana does not result in shifts to monolingualism in the non-native language (for example, full shift of Albanian women from Albanian to BCMS) or in one of the languages simultaneously acquired in childhood. There may be only slight changes in the individual situation over the course of one's life: a degree of imbalance between the two languages of the bilinguals may emerge when they start going to school, get married, and the like.

5.2 Past contact in the Mrkovići: several assumptions

The modern variety of the Mrkovići shows some changes that can result from previous contact with Albanian. The borrowed phonemes in loanwords in the now monolingual villages apparently show that contact may have taken place in these village communities. Phonetic and phonological interference has resulted in a few relatively widespread changes in native phonemic oppositions (4.1). In the lexicon, borrowed discourse markers are absent, while borrowing content words is quite moderate. Examples of lexical calques include kinship terms (*babost'ari, babov'ejlji*) preserving the Albanian word order. Such calques were possibly introduced by Albanian women and retained because these Albanians spoke (their version of) BCMS with their children, as argued in Morozova (2019). Grammatical interference in the variety of the Mrkovići is confined to changes in the patterns of distribution of some native constructions based on their structural similarity with Albanian ones (*od*-construction in 4.2) and a few innovative constructions that apparently replicate Albanian structures (the preposition *ge* governing the nominative case). These changes are largely similar to those found in the speech of bilinguals in the modern Velja Gorana. The other type of change, not found in modern Velja Gorana, involves replication of functional and semantic patterns without the exact replication or correspondence of structures between model and replica. Consider, for example, the lexical calques standing for the names of months (4.3) and the extended use of bare instrumental case forms of BCMS (4.2).

From the sociolinguistic point of view, the situation in the now monolingual villages of the Mrkovići could have been partially similar to that of Velja Gorana. It may have involved the bilingualism of some part of the population due to everyday contacts with the neighbouring Albanian regions, the presence of originally Albanian families, and more or less constant influx of Albanian speakers (or natively bilingual speakers, such as women from Velja Gorana) as a result of exogamous marriages. The frequency of interethnic marriages likely decreased after the population movements of the 18th and 19th centuries. At that time many monolingual newcomers came to the area and the conditions for the transition from a bilingual to a monolingual community began to take shape. The transition likely involved several generations and developed on the level of individual speakers and families, as is observed in the modern situation of Velja Gorana.

References

Aikhenvald, Alexandra Y. 2007. Grammars in Contact. A Cross-Linguistic Perspective. In Robert M. W. Dixon & Aleksandra Y. Aikhenvald (eds.), *Grammars in Contact. A Cross-Linguistic Typology*, 1–66. Oxford, UK: Oxford University Press.

Bolizza, Mariano. 1866. Relatione et descrittione. Dei Sangiacato di Scutari, dove si da piena contezza delle citta et siti loro, village, case et habitatori, rito, costumi, habere et armi di quki popoli et quanti di considerabile munitamente si contenga in quel ducato, fatia da Mariano Bolizza, nobile di Cattaro. Di Venetia, li 25 maggio 1614. In François Lenormant (ed.), *Turcs et Monténégrins*, 286–330. Paris: Didier & Co.

Coetsem, Frans van. 1988. *Loan Phonology and the Two Transfer types in Language Contact*. Dordrecht: Foris.

Curtis, Matthew Cowan. 2012. *Slavic-Albanian Language Contact, Convergence, and Coexistence*. Ohio State University Doctoral Dissertation.

Desnitskaya, Agniya V. 1968. *Albanskii iazyk i ego dialekty* [Albanian and its dialects]. Leningrad: Nauka.

Dugushina, Aleksandra S. & Maria S. Morozova. 2016. Mrkovichi i ikh sosedi: o chem mozhet rasskazat' brachnaia geografiia? [The Mrkovići and their neighbours: what can marriage geography tell us?]. In XLV *Mezhdunarodnaia filologicheskaia konferentsiia, 14–21 marta 2016 g.: Tezisy dokladov*, 544–545. St. Petersburg: Filologicheskii fakultet SPbGU.

Dugushina, Aleksandra S. & Maria S. Morozova. 2020. *Plemia* Mrkovichi na iuge Chernogorii: Izuchenie brachnoi geografii [*Pleme* Mrkovići in southern Montenegro: A study of marriage geography]. *Vestnik antropologii* 4 (52). 64–82.

Đurović, Milinko et al. (eds.). 1970. *Istorija Crne Gore. Knjiga druga. Od kraja XII do kraja XV vijeka. Tom drugi. Crna Gora u doba oblasnih gospodara* [History of Montenegro. Part 2. From the end of the 12th to the end of the 15th century. Vol. 2. Montenegro in the time of the principalities]. Vol. 2. Titograd: Redakcija za istoriju Crne Gore.

Đurović, Milinko et al. (eds.). 1975. *Istorija Crne Gore. Knjiga treća. Od početka XVI do kraja XVIII vijeka. Tom prvi* [History of Montenegro. Part 3. From the start of the 16th to the end of the 18th century. Vol. 1]. Titograd: Redakcija za istoriju Crne Gore.

Erdeljanović, Jovan. 1981 [1907]. Kuči [Kuchi]. In Jovan Erdeljanović. *Kuči, Bratonožići, Piperi*. 1–343. Beograd: Slovo ljubve. (*Srpski etnografski zbornik. Knj.* VIII. [Serbian Ethnographical Collection Vol. 8]. Beograd: Srpska kraljevska akademija, 1907).

Fine, John V. A. 2009. *The late medieval Balkans: a critical survey from the late twelfth century to the Ottoman conquest*. Ann Arbor, MI: University of Michigan Press.

Gjinari, Jorgji & Gjovalin Shkurtaj. 2000. *Dialektologjia* [Dialectology]. Tirana: Shtëpia botuese e librit universitar.

Gjinari, Jorgji, Bahri Beci, Gjovalin Shkurtaj & Xheladin Gosturani. 2007–2008. *Atlasi dialektologjik i gjuhës shqipe* [Dialectological atlas of Albanian], Vol. 1–2. Napoli: L'Università degli studi di Napoli l'Orientale, Tirana: Akademia e Shkencave e Shqipërisë.

Haspelmath, Martin. 2009. Lexical borrowing: Concepts and issues. In Martin Haspelmath & Uri Tadmor (eds.), *Loanwords in the world's languages: A comparative handbook*, 35–54. Berlin: De Gruyter Mouton.

Inkscape Drawing Software. https://inkscape.org/ru/ (accessed 15 March, 2021).

Ivanova, Iuliia V. 1988. Albantsy [The Albanians]. In Iuliia V. Ivanova, Margarita S. Kashuba & Natalia A. Krasnovskaia (eds.), *Brak u narodov Tsentral'noi i Iugo-Vostochnoi Evropy*, 182–205. Moscow: Nauka.

Ivić, Pavle. 1985. *Dijalektologija srpskohrvatskog jezika. Uvod i štokavsko narečje* [Dialectology of the Serbo-Croatian Language. Introduction and the Štokavian dialect]. 2nd edn. Novi Sad: Matica srpska.

Joseph, Brian. 2010. Language contact in the Balkans. In Raymond Hickey (ed.), *The Handbook of Language Contact*, 618–633. Malden, MA: Wiley-Blackwell.

Joseph, Brian & Victor Friedman. 2017. Reassessing sprachbunds: A view from the Balkans. In Raymond Hickey (ed.), *The Cambridge Handbook of Areal Linguistics*, 63–90. Cambridge: Cambridge University Press.

Jovićević, Andrija. 1922. Crnogorsko primorje i Krajina [The Montenegro coast and Krajina]. *Srpski etnografski zbornik*, Vol. 11. Beograd: Srpska kraljevska akademija.

Lindstedt, Jouko. 2000. Linguistic Balkanization: Contact-induced change by mutual reinforcement. In Dicky G. Gilbers, John Nerbonne & Jos Shaeken (eds.), *Languages in Contact* (= *Studies in Slavic and General Linguistics)*, Vol. 28, 231–246. Amsterdam & Atlanta, GA: Rodopi.

Lindstedt, Jouko. 2016. Multilingualism in the Central Balkans in late Ottoman times. In Maxim Makartsev & Max Wahlström (eds.), *Slavica Helsingiensia* 49. 51–67.

Lüpke, Friederike. 2016. Uncovering Small-Scale Multilingualism. *Critical Multilingualism Studies* 4 (2). 35–74.

Map Carta Interactive Map. https://mapcarta.com/ (accessed 15 March, 2021).

Matras, Yaron. 1998. Utterance modifiers and universals of grammatical borrowing. *Linguistics* 36. 281–331.

Matras, Yaron & Jeanette Sakel. 2007. Investigating the mechanisms of pattern replication in language convergence. *Studies in Language* 31. 829–865.

MDABL – Andrey N. Sobolev (ed.). 2003–2018. *Malyi dialektologicheskii atlas balkanskikh iazykov. Probnyi vypusk (2003). Seriia leksicheskaia. Tom I. Leksika dukhovnoi kul'tury (2005). Tom II. Chelovek. Sem'ia (2006). Tom III. Zhivotnovodstvo (2009). Tom IV. (Avtor: M. V. Domosiletskaia). Landshaftnaia leksika (2010). Tom V. (Avtor: M. V. Domosiletskaia). Meteorologiia (2012). Tom VI. Polevodstvo. Ogorodnichestvo (2013). Tom VII. (Avtor: M. V. Domosiletskaia). Pčelovodstvo (2018). Seriia grammaticheskaia. Tom I. Kategorii imeni sushchestvitel'nogo (2005)* [Minor dialect atlas of the Balkan languages. Test launch (2003).

Lexical series. Vol. 1. Cultural vocabulary (2005). Vol. 2. The person and human relations (2006). Vol. 3. Animal husbandry (2009). Vol. 4. (M. V. Domosiletskaia, author). Landscape (2010). Vol. 5 (M. V. Domosiletskaia, author). Meteorology (2012). Vol. 6. Field-tending and Gardening (2013). Vol. 7. (M. V. Domosiletskaia, author). Apiculture (2018). Grammatical series. Vol. 1. Noun categories (2005)]. St. Petersburg, München: Nauka, Verlag Otto Sagner.

Memushaj, Rami. 2011. *Fonetika e shqipes standarde* [Phonetics of Standard Albanian]. Tirana: TOENA.

Metanović, Mahmut. 2012. Istorija Mrkojevića [History of the Mrkovići]. *Nevladina organizacija Mrkojevići*. http://mrkojevici.me/naselja.html (accessed 15 March, 2021).

Miloradovich, Sofiia. 2011. Sposoby vyrazheniia pritiazhatel'nosti v serbskikh narodnykh govorakh na fone analitizatsii [Analysis of the means of expressing possession in Serbian subdialects in the context of analyticization]. In Motoki Nomachi (ed.), *The Grammar of Possessivity in South Slavic Languages: Synchronic and Diachronic Perspectives* (= *Slavic Eurasian Studies* 24), 13–33. Sapporo: Slavic Research Center, Hokkaido University.

Morozova, Maria S. 2017a. Albanskii govor ili govory Gorany? Genezis i funktsionirovanie [Albanian subdialect(s) of Gorana? Genesis and functioning]. *Vestnik Sankt-Peterburgskogo gosudarstvennogo universiteta. Iazyk i literatura* 14 (2). 222–237.

Morozova, Maria S. 2017b. Paradoks issledovatelia na Balkanakh: perekliuchenie kodov u bilingval'nykh informantov pri interv'iuirovanii [The Researcher's Paradox in the Balkans: codeswitching among bilingual informants during interviews]. In Maksim M. Makartsev, Irina A. Sedakova, Tatiana V. Tsiv'ian (eds.), *Balkanskii tezaurus: Vzgliad na Balkany izvne i iznutri. Balkanskie chteniia 14. Tezisy i materialy. Moskva, 18–20 aprelia 2017 goda*, 137–143. Moscow: InSlav RAN.

Morozova, Maria S. 2018. Vybor iazyka i perekliuchenie kodov v balkanskom poliloge (na primere bilingval'nogo soobshchestva Velja Gorany, Chernogoriia) [Language choice and codeswitching in the Balkan polilogue: A case of the bilingual community of Velja Gorana, Montenegro]. In Irina A. Sedakova, Maxim M. Makartsev, Tatiana V. Tsiv'ian (eds.), *Balkanskii polilog: kommunikatsiia v kulturno-slozhnykh soobshchestvakh. Pamiati V. V. Ivanova*, 49–67. Moscow: InSlav RAN.

Morozova, Maria S. 2019. Language contact in social context: Kinship terms and kinship relations of the Mrkovići of southern Montenegro. *Journal of Language Contact* 12 (2). 305–343.

Morozova, Maria S. & Alexander Yu. Rusakov. 2018. Albansko-chernogorskoe iazykovoe pogranich'e: v poiskakh "sbalansirovannogo iazykovogo kontakta [The Albanian-Montenegrin Linguistic Border: In Search of "Balanced Language Contact"]. *Slověne* 7 (2). 258–302.

Morozova, Maria S. & Alexander Yu. Rusakov. 2021. Societal multilingualisms *à la balkanique*: the Montenegrin Velja Gorana and beyond. *International Journal of Bilingualism*. In press.

Muysken, Pieter. 2010. Scenarios for Language Contact. In Raymond Hickey (ed.), *The Handbook of Language Contact*, 265–281. Malden, MA: Wiley-Blackwell.

Myers-Scotton, Carol. 2006. *Multiple Voices. An Introduction to Bilingualism*. Malden, MA: Blackwell Publishing.

Nikitina, Tatiana. 2009. Subcategorization pattern and lexical meaning of motion verbs: a study of the source/goal ambiguity. *Linguistics* 47. 1113–1141.

Novik, Aleksandr A. & Andrey N. Sobolev. 2016. Traditional wedding costume of the Mrkovići in Montenegro: between real heritage and folk construction (materials of the Russian expeditions in 2012–2014). *Folklore* 66. 15–36.

Omari, Anila. 2012. *Marrëdhëniet gjuhësore shqiptaro-serbe* [Albanian-Serbian linguistic relations]. Tirana: Botimet Albanologjike.

Petrović, Dragoljub & Snežana Gudurić. 2010. *Fonologija srpskoga jezika* [Serbian phonology]. Beograd: Institut za srpski jezik SANU; Matica srpska.

Pejović, Srđan & Marina Kapisoda (ed.). 2009. *Popis svega stanovništva Crne Gore po okružjima, varošima i selima (1879). Zbirka dokumenata* [Census of the total population of Montenegro by district, town, and village (1879). A collection of documents]. Vol. 2. Cetinje: IVPE.

Pešikan, Mitar. 1981. Nastavak -za u južnozetskim imenima XV veka [Suffix -za in the Southern Zeta names in the 15th century]. *Četvrta jugoslovanska onomastična konferencija: Portorož, od 14. do 17. oktobra 1981*, 419–425. Ljubljana: Slovenska Akademija Znanosti in Umetnosti.

Piper, Predrag & Ivan Klajn. 2013. *Normativna gramatika srpskog jezika* [Normative grammar of the Serbian language]. Novi Sad: Matica srpska.

Pižurica, Mato. 1984. Tragovi međujezičkih dodira u govorima Crne Gore [Examination of language contacts in Montenegrin dialects]. In *Crnogorski govori. Rezultati dosadašnjih ispitivanja i dalji rad na njihovom proučavanju: zbornik radova sa naučnog skupa*, vol. 12, 83–95. Titograd: Crnogorska akademija nauka i umjetnosti.

Pulaha, Selami. 1974. *Defteri i regjistrimit të Sanxhakut të Shkodrës i vitit 1485* [The register of the Sandjak of Shkodër in the year 1485]. Tirana: Akademia e Shkencave e RP të Shqipërisë.

Rovinskii, Pavel A. 1897. *Chernogoriia v" eia proshlom" i nastoiashchem". Geografiia. — Istoriia. — Etnografiia. — Arkheologiia. — Sovremennoe polozhenie. Tom" II, chast' 1* [Montenegro past and present. Geography – History – Ethnography – Archaeology – Present circumstances. Vol. 2, pt. 1]. St. Petersburg: Tipografiia Imperatorskoi Akademii nauk.

Rusakov, Alexander Yu. 2007. Slavianskie iazyki na Balkanakh: aspekty kontaktnogo vzaimodeistviia [Slavic languages in the Balkans: aspects of contact relations]. In Viacheslav V. Ivanov (ed.), *Areal'noe i geneticheskoe v strukture slavianskikh iazykov. Materialy kruglogo stola*, 77–89. Moscow: Probel.

Sasgis SAS.Planet. http://www.sasgis.org/ (accessed 15 March, 2021).

Simić, Radoje & Branislav Ostojić. 1996. *Osnovi fonologije srpskog književnog jezika* [The basics of phonology of the Serbian literary language]. Beograd: Univerzitet u Beogradu.

Sobolev, Andrey N. 1988. O nekotorykh innovatsionnykh protsessakh v sfere vyrazheniia prostranstvennykh znachenii v territorial'nykh dialektakh serbokhorvatskogo iazyka [On some innovative processes in the expression of spatial meanings in territorial dialects of Serbo-Croatian]. *Zbornik Matice srpske za filologiju i lingvistiku* 31 (1). 47–77.

Sobolev, Andrey N. 1990. Zametki o padezhnykh sistemakh serbokhorvatskikh govorov kontaktnykh zon [Notes on the case system of Serbo-Croatian subdialects in contact areas]. *Južnoslovenski filolog* 46. 13–28.

Sobolev, Andrey N. 2015. Mrkovichi (i Gorana): iazyki i dialekty chernogorskogo Primor'ia v kontekste noveishikh balkanisticheskikh issledovanii [Mrkovići (and Gorana): Languages and dialects of the Montenegro coast in the context of recent Balkan research]. In Bardhyl Demiraj (ed.), *Sprache und Kultur der Albaner: Zeitliche und raumliche Dimensionen. Akten der 5. Deutsch-albanischen kulturwissenschaftlichen Tagung (Albanien, Buçimas bei Pogradec, 5.–8. Juni 2014)*, 533–556. Wiesbaden: Harrassowitz.

Sobolev, Andrey N. 2017. Iazyki simbioticheskikh soobschestv Zapadnykh Balkan: grecheskii i albanskii iazyki v sele Paliasa v kraine Himara, Albaniia [Languages in the Western Balkan Symbiotic Societies: Greek and Albanian in Palasa, Himara, Albania]. *Vestnik Sankt-Peterburgskogo gosudarstvennogo universiteta. Iazyk i literatura* 14 (3), 421–442.

Sobolev, Andrey N. & Aleksandr A. Novik. 2013. *Golo Bordo (Gollobordë), Albaniia. Iz materialov balkanskoi ekspeditsii RAN i SPbGU 2008–2010 gg.* [Golo Bordo (Gollobordë) Albania.

From the materials of the RAS and SPSU expedition of 2008–2010]. Munich: Otto Sagner Verlag, St. Petersburg: Nauka.

Sobolev, Andrey N., Maxim L. Kisilier, Viacheslav V. Kozak, Daria V. Konior, Anastasia L. Makarova, Maria S. Morozova & Alexander Yu. Rusakov. 2018. Iuzhnoslavianskie dialekty v simbioticheskikh soobshchestvakh Balkan [South Slavic dialects in symbiotic communities of the Balkans]. *Acta linguistica Petropolitana. Trudy Instituta lingvisticheskikh issledovanij RAN* 14 (2). 685–746.

Stanišić, Vanja. 1995. *Srpsko-albanski jezički odnosi* [Serbo-Albanian linguistic relations]. Beograd: Srpska akademija nauka i umetnosti.

Thomai, Jani, Miço Samara, Josif Kole, Pavli Haxhillazi, Hajri Shehu, Thanas Feka & Kornelja Sima. 2002. *Fjalor i shqipes së sotme. Botim i dytë i ripunuar (me rreth 35.000 fjalë)* [Dictionary of Contemporary Albanian. 2nd edition. Around 35 000 words]. Tirana: TOENA.

Thomason, Sarah Grey & Terrence Kaufman. 1988. *Language Contact, Creolization, and Genetic Linguistics*. Berkeley: University of California Press.

Traktat", zakliuchennyi mezhdu Rossiei, Germaniei, Avstro-Vengriei, Frantsiei, Velikobritaniei, Italiei i Turtsiei v" Berline (1) 13 Ijulia 1878 g. [The Treaty concluded between Russia, Germany, Austria-Hungary, France, Great Britain, Italy, and Turkey on the (1) 13 July 1878]. *Sbornik" dejstvujushchikh" traktatov", konventsii i soglashenii, zakljuchennykh"Rossiei s" drugimi gosudarstvami. Izdano po rasporjazheniiu g. Ministra inostrannykh" del"*. Sankt-Peterburg": Tipogr. Trenke i Füsno, 75–98. 1906.

Vujović, Luka. 1969. Mrkovićki dijalekat (s kratkim osvrtom na susjedne govore) [The dialect of the Mrkovići (with a brief overview of neighbouring subdialects)]. *Srpski dijalektološki zbornik*. Knj. XVIII. Rasprave i građa, 73–399. Beograd: Institut za srpskohrvatski jezik.

Weinreich, Uriel. 1979. *Languages in Contact. Findings and Problems*. Ninth printing. The Hague: Mouton Publishers.

Andrey N. Sobolev
Symbiosis Suspectus: Palasa in Himara, Albania

Abstract: This chapter[1] advances the hypothesis that a Greek-Albanian symbiotic society once existed in the Himara krajina of South Albania where Greek and Albanian languages and cultures were engaged in a complementary relationship. Data derived from a lexicon and spontaneous narratives in a previously undescribed Greek dialect of the Palasa village are presented that reveal a typologically rare and underexamined form of non-dominant bilingualism with features that include a balanced and complementary functional distribution of Greek and Albanian, code switching, and language hybridization.

1 Introduction

The geographical and historical region of Epirus, divided between modern Albania and Greece, has for millennia been a melting pot of intense ethnic, cultural, religious and linguistic interaction among Balkan peoples, a condition which continues to this day. The region occupied the centre of attention in emerging Balkan studies at the beginning of the 19th century (see Leake 1814, 1835; Desnitskaya 1987 (1979)), and it continues to be of interest to linguists, ethnologists and culturologists owing to the plurality, diversity and rich mosaic of the linguistic and cultural situations that have developed there.

It is *Greeks* who have been the focus of modern research in Southern Albania (the Northern part of historical Epirus) (Kondis & Manta 1994; Spiro 2015). Their

---

[1] This research was made possible by a grant from the Russian Science Foundation (the projects "From Separation to Symbiosis: South Eastern European languages and cultures in contact", No. 14-18-01405 and "Balkan bilingualism in dominant and equilibrium contact situations in diatopy, diachrony and diastraty", No. 19-18-00244). Materials for the study were collected from 2010 to 2019 over the course of numerous expeditions conducted by the author along with Aleksandr A. Novik (Peter the Great Museum of Anthropology and Ethnography (Kunstkamera) and St. Petersburg State University). These were extended by joint Russian-Albanian and Russian-American projects led between 2014 and 2016. Research was funded by grants received from the Presidium of the Russian Academy of Sciences, the Russian Foundation for the Humanities and the Russian Science Foundation (project director: Andrey N. Sobolev). The preliminary results of the work were presented in a paper presented in Moscow (Sobolev & Novik 2016) and in a co-authored paper with B. Joseph, A. A. Novik, A. Spiro and M. Spiro presented at the University of Utah in Salt Lake City, USA. This chapter draws on Sobolev (2017).

https://doi.org/10.1515/9781501509254-005

language and traditional culture are distinguished by evident Greek and Balkan features, as well as a number of regional and local elements that have been established only over the course of a detailed scientific study *in situ*. The aim of studying this ethnic group (or, more precisely, the so-called Greek-speaking "minority" in the districts of Delvina, Saranda, Dropull, Riza, Pogon, Përmet, Himara, and Vlora) is to reconstruct the history of its ethnic and linguistic origins and to establish its place and role in the region's past and present, among other ethnoconfessional Albanian, Romance and Slavic groups.

In modern Albanian and Greek research, a major and a very lively debate is underway as to whether the Greek-speaking population of Southern Albania is "autochthonous" or has migrated there relatively recently. Unfortunately, while the most recent general works on the history, language, and culture of individual microregions such as Himara[2] (Nasi et al. 2004) or Dropull (Lítsios 2009) display a wealth of factual material, their analyses betray the well-known ethnic and national-political preferences of their authors, be they Albanian or Hellenic. In particular, there is a widely-held view among Albanian experts that "Being in an area of Greek influence, in the immediate proximity of the island of Corfu, the Orthodox residents of Himara were subject to Graecization. Residents of the town of Himarë and villages of Dhërmi and Palasë speak Greek but nonetheless consider themselves to be Albanian. Furthermore, the population of the coastal villages still recognizes their genetic ties as coming from inner Labëria, from where their ancestors came" (Desnitskaya (1968: 353) with reference to Kola (1939)). Perhaps in future we shall be obliged to reexamine the historical evidence presented in such sources as the 1722 description of 14 villages of Himarë by the Catholic missionary and Italo-Albanian Joseph Schirò (Borgia 1942: 132–139; Malltezi 2006; Giakoumis 2016), but, in the absence of a sufficient number of reliable historical sources and written texts, the validity of linguistic, cultural and anthropological research conducted in the field remains, for us, indisputable. It should be noted that, to date, a sufficient number of such works from the standpoint of Albanian studies have been published (e.g., Totoni (1964); Memushaj (2006); Sotiri (2006); Tirta (2006); Memushaj & Grillo (2009), among many others). These pay special attention to the Albanian population and toward demonstrating the ethnic, cultural, linguistic – the anthropological – unity of Himara and Labëria.

---

[2] In Albania, the krajina Himara is a part of Labëria province (Desnitskaya 1968: 352), however the place name Labëria is sometimes used only for the region where the Muslim part of the population lives (Sotiri 2006: 264). Along with the Albanian name Himara, the names of component regions are also used: Bregu i Sipërm (alb.) = 'Upper Coastline, Coast' in the north, Bregu i Poshtëm (alb.) = 'Lower Coastline, Coast' in the south.

Recent general work on modern Greek dialects (Kisilier 2013), and on the Greek dialects of Albania in particular (Kyriazés & Spiro 2011; Spiro 2015), demonstrates the need to pinpoint efforts at description and analysis. Deep description of dialect groups such as that conducted by Bógkas (1966), Spiro (2008) and accounts of individual idioms such as those of Kyriazés (2012), Kisilier, Novik & Sobolev (2013) and Kisilier, Novik & Sobolev (2016) need to be extended to the Himara krajina (see Vagiakákos (1983), Kyriazés (2007), and Kokavésē (2010)), an area of research always in the public eye.³ As elsewhere in the Western Balkans, in Southern Albania and in Himara in particular, there is an urgent need, among other things, for toponomastic and microtoponomastic studies both in the field and on the basis of cartographic material (e.g., RPSSh 1977, 1978, 1983; RPSSh 1984). Such efforts should be aimed at establishing the historical and geographical distribution of the allogeneic names of individual localities and settlements. Furthermore, the region's sociolinguistic situation as a whole, its distribution of languages and issues related to its linguistic ecology, are no less important (see Brown & Joseph 2013).

The importance of linguistic, cultural and anthropological study of the Greeks in Southern Albania goes far beyond ethnically-centered Modern Greek philology. The linguistic stratifications formed over centuries and the panoplies of ethnic groups offer rich material for the *theory of language and cultural unions* which typify the Balkans (*Balkansprach-* and *Balkankulturbund*, see the discussion in Burkhart (1989) and Hinrichs et al. (2014)). In particular, one may raise the question as to whether this region is not and has not been the site of a genuine *ethnic symbiosis* of the Balkan peoples, Greeks and Albanians first of all?

2 How, then, shall we study the languages of such symbiotic communities?

Questions related to the *linguistic reconstruction* of ethnic symbioses among Balkan peoples, as well as criticism of the idea (usually from the standpoint of ethnically centered philology, as in Ismajli (2015)) have received ample coverage in both early and more recent literature and they do not require addressing here. Important studies have considered interactions between speakers of Romance languages and Albanian (Schutz 2009, with the literature), Romance speakers and Slavs along the Eastern Adriatic coast (Skok 1950; Holtus & Kramer

---

3 Cf. the discourse-oriented work of modern anthropologists (Gregorič Bon 2008; Zheltova 2016).

1987; Muljačić 2000, with literature; Vekarić 2011), Eastern Romance speakers and Slavs in Macedonia (Golomb 1959; 1979; 1982), Slavs and Albanians in the Western Balkans (Šufflay 1925; Desnitskaya 1976; Curtis 2012; Dombrowski 2013; Gashi 2015; Morozova 2017; Morozova & Rusakov 2019). It is essential, however, to address the fact that the word *symbiosis* has been used and continues to be used in this literature in an inconsistent and unsystematic fashion. Linguists usually do not take into account that, since the late 1960s, anthropologists consider that only those communities where groups of people enter into linguistic, cultural and anthropological relations of *complementary distribution* may properly be called symbiotic (see the recognized definitions in Barth (1969); for relatively recent individual publications, see Smith (2000) and Lehman (2001)).

Such groups in the Balkans in our time are rare and reliable scientific information about the small number of symbionts (members of symbiotic groups) open to *actual observation* of their languages and cultures is scant. Balkan studies has only now turned toward the material from Himara in Southern Albania with Novik & Sobolev (2018) and Kyriazés (2019). One of the central theoretical questions of such linguistic studies is whether such a community is characterized by a special type of *bilingualism*, and whether its languages observe a high degree of mutual *accommodation* and thus, consequently, a greater degree of manifestation of *alloglossia* in an area of closely related dialects. In the field of cultural anthropology such issues arise as the question of the role of *exogamy* in the formation of symbiotic communities in the Balkans, the question as to whether they can occur beyond actual linguistic and ethnic *borders*, as well as the question of the *cultural delimitation* of multilingual symbionts.

Russian research (see Sobolev 2013) has adopted an integrated approach that involves studying the history, structure and functioning of a language (at all levels) along with: a) traditional society and its culture, b) linguistic, social and cultural contacts, and c) bilingualism and multilingualism. For example, an important question arises as to whether symbiotic communities should be ascribed merely a marginal role in Balkan mixoglossia in the past, or whether they should be given a more important one. It should be emphasized that, according to the eloquent admission of a leading Dutch linguist-contactologist, most modern models of language interaction in contact are not able to describe or explain exactly those two types of processes which interest us, namely: 1) bilingualism occurring in a symmetrical situation without the dominance of one language over another, and 2) what leads to the emergence of convergent language groups, i.e. Sprachbünde (Muysken 2000: 726). The solution to these general questions allows us to, at once, test the whether the *creolization* hypothesis in the Balkans is at all applicable (Hinrichs 2004a; 2004b; Stern 2004) and whether language *hybridization* exists in Southern Albania in particular. Likewise, one of the specific objects for this research must be to determine the conditions under which proper hybridization might take place (Mufwene 2009; Brown & Joseph 2015; Joseph et al. 2019).

An important methodological question is whether examining the language, culture and social structure of one or several traditional symbiotic groups in the 21st century is able to provide a sufficient set of relevant parameters to *reconstruct* symbiotic relations between these and other such groups in the past. Is it indeed possible to reveal the mechanisms that bring symbiotic communities about and to determine what the regulating factors of such mechanisms are? Do these mechanisms include, in particular, the inclusion or exclusion of social groups to a core based around the idea of consanguinity and that is set alongside compulsory exogamy or, conversely, endogamy?

The symbiotic communities of the Balkans as they are known to us arose along linguistic and ethnic borderlands (see the classification of language boundaries in Furrer (2002: 135–153), see Joseph (2016)). The Albanian-Greek diatopic language *boundary* in southern Albania and, in particular, in Himara, as demonstrated by the toponymic material, may serve as the first important indicator for the verification of this hypothesis. According to Albanian military maps from the 1950s to the 1970s, at the northwestern edge of the Himara krajina in the area of the village *Palasë*,[4] microtoponyms are observed which betray a Greek influence: mali i *Thanasit*, faqja e *Pandaleos*, kurrizi i *Fajevos*, burimi i *Dhikules*, pylli i *Aljatheos*, malet e *Mesofijes*, kurrizi i *Skantavës*, prroi i *Parapotameos*, faqja e *Pjerivallos* (however, compare some ambiguous and some Albanian microtoponyms: faqja e *Abjenbrit*, faqja e *Qerashes*, prroi i *Qerashës*, përroi i *Thatë*). In contrast, Albanian microtoponyms dominate to the North of Palasë, in the Laberian villages of Dukati, Tërbaçi and Vranishti (sometimes with Romance, Slavic, Turkic, and other etymologies): faqja e *Pirit*, *Moçal*, faqja e *Gjipogës*, pylli i *Shalceve*, përroi *Radhimës*, mali i *Paliskës*, qafa e *Shën Gjergjit*, lumi i *Vreshtirës*, mali i *Plepit*, pylli i *Dushkut* (RPSSh 1978: K – 134 – 136 – A (Dukati)). It seems to us that the geographical distribution of Greek and Albanian names points toward a distinct *linguistic boundary* coinciding with the direction of the mountain range separating western Himara, inhabited by Orthodox Greeks, from the mountain hinterland inhabited by Albanians, both Muslims and, we must cautiously presume (Thomo 1998), Orthodox Christians to some extent. The historical character of this division between Greeks and Albanians is confirmed in an 18th century source which remarks: "…quattordici ville, le quali professano la

---

4 The official Albanian name of the village is Palasë. While known from antiquity, the village in 2005 registered 410 inhabitants according to the publicly available Albanian website Palasa Online (www.palasaonline.com) and local history (Koka 2008; 2011).

legge di Cristo nel rito greco: *Cimarra* capitale della provincia, *Drimades* e *Balasa* di natione greci..." (Borgia 1942: 133).

Further verification of the hypothesis of ethnic symbiosis in the krajina in general, and in the village of Palasë in particular, can be carried out based on Frederik Barth's definitions (Barth 1969: 9–38). One may thus pose a number of questions to guide future research in the microarea. Which of the possible models accounts for past and present linguistic, cultural, and anthropological interaction between the Greek and Albanian-speaking population (Orthodox and Muslim) along the physical-geographical and linguistic border in the west of Himara? To what extent have the factors of separation – a rugged mountain territory crosshatched by different religious faiths – contributed to the condition where particular areas are dominated by particular linguistic and ethnic groups? What is the model that regulates the interaction of "extensively relevant value differences" between Orthodox Christians and Sunni Muslims? Has there been any significant relocation in one or two directions (i.e., among the villages of Dukati, Tërbaçi and Vranishti to Palasë)?[5] Was there an Albanian dialect of Labëria in some families of Palasë as a language of daily communication? Did some sort of natural process as an "encompassing social system" lead to its development in the village of Palasë, or anywhere else in the region, owing to a complementarity of characteristic *cultural* features among Greeks and Albanians? Do the Greeks and Albanians of the region maintain differentially distinguished cultural traits that are standardized and stable within the ethnic group? Do they occupy different cultural and economic niches?[6] What social role do Greeks and Albanians and their languages play historically and at the present moment, what is their prestige and status? Finally, is it even possible to reconstruct the linguistic and ethnic origins of Palasë's inhabitants on the basis of linguistic, cultural and anthropological methods and, if so, how might it be done? Due to the preliminary character of our work here, only linguistic questions shall be addressed below.

---

[5] According to Albanian dialectologists, Palasë is home to clans of the *Gjin* from the village of Dukati, *Sinanaj* from Tepelenë, *Nikdedaj* of from the north Albanian krajina of Mirdita (Sotiri 2006: 265). According to our informants, the origin of the the clans *Babe, Gjinajt, Çaço, Paço, Xhelilaj*, which currently live in the village of Palasë, lies in the Albanian speaking village Dukati, along with the clan *Mëhilli*. At least one of the clans is from Kruja while the clans *Milaj* and *Papadhates* hale *from the Peloponnese*. In local historical publications about the village there are also Muslim surnames: *Liri Hasani* (Koka 2011: 62).

[6] According to our observations, Albanians, including Muslims, who are from the villages of Dukati, Vranishti and Kolorati, and who work in Palasë, are skilled workers in construction as well as herders in the livestock sector. The main occupation of the village dwellers, on the other hand, is olive cultivation, gardening and private tourism.

Map 1 *Republic of Albania, the village of Palasë (Himarë) and the villages of Dukati, Tërbaçi and Vranishti (Labëria)*

3 Greek and Albanian in Palasë, Himara

With the paucity of written sources that so typifies the Balkans, one may only answer most of the questions raised above on the basis of direct observation of the current situation and leave a large-scale collection of reliable testimony related to the village's history – that of individual families and individual biographies – as a subject of future research. At the moment it makes sense to turn to the data on the language collected by the author in 2015 over the course of a four-day research in Palasë. The effort was to demonstrate opportunities for establishing *similarities and differences in the competence of multilingual speakers* in each of the village's languages and cultures for the ethno-linguistic and lexical program of the *Minor Dialectological Atlas of the Balkan Languages* (Domosiletskaia (1997), MDABL 2003–2018).[7]

According to the very first observations taken, in modern times Albanian and Modern Greek have been equally present in the village, the first in at least its regional Tosk form and the latter in both standard and in dialectal use. All our informants speak both languages with no clear, so it seems, dominance of either. We have not examined in full the extent to which features of the Standard Albanian or Laberian dialect are represented in the Albanian of our informants.[8] According to their oral testimony, the first language they learn in childhood is Greek. Furthermore, there are elderly women in the village who do not speak Albanian. The following linguonyms were recorded: Alb. *ʃkip* and Gr. *alvanik'a* 'the Albanian language', Alb. *gərk'iʃtja* and Gr. *elenik'a* 'the Greek language', Gr. *palask'itika* and *palasik'a* 'the Greek idiom of the village of Palasë' (as opposed to both Modern Greek and the neighbouring Greek idiom of the town of Himara, henceforth "Pal."). The opposed terms: Gr. *alvanik'a ~ elenik'a ~ palask'itika* and *palasik'a* express linguistic sensibility, reflection and practice: Alb. *krah'or* 'breast' ~ Gr. *st'iθus* ~ Pal. *p'etu*; Alb. *paλasik'ot, paλasik'ote* 'dweller of Palasa, male and fem.', *ðərm'ies, ðərm'eʃa* 'dweller of Dhermi, male and fem.' ~ Pal.

---

[7] Materials have been taken from those collected during an expedition associated with the MDABL programme (MDABL 1997). Informants: Paraskevula Milu (P. M.), date of birth (DOB): 1935; Fevronia Milu, DOB: 1931; Maria Todoriani, DOB: 1934. Transcript: Andrey N. Sobolev (A. S.). Interviews conducted by the author with these informants on the subject of the folk calendar (Plotnikova 2009). Transcript: Aristotle Spiro, Maylinda Spiro). The survey and interviews were conducted by the author in Greek and Albanian.

[8] The fact that Albanian has been the state language and the only language of administration and school instruction over almost the entire second half of the 20th century has not led to its dominance over Greek – a language of thousands of years of high culture, the Orthodox community, and a more economically developed neighbouring country. It is very important to note, that the phonetics of the village's Albanian idiom is not Standard, but Laberian dialectal Albanian. These characteristics are: absence of /y/ (*di* 'two', *dizet* 'twelve', *si* 'eye', *ki* 'this', *frim* 'spirit', *krikʲ* 'cross', *gʲiʃa* 'grandmother', *ndr'iʃe* 'differently' (but *kʲymǝʃt* 'milk'); unstressed ǝ in Auslaut (*dr'ekǝ* 'dinner', *tǝ gr'uasǝ* 'wife.GenSg', *duɲ'anǝ* 'world.AccSg', *par'atǝ* 'money.Acc.Sg', *e v'ogǝλǝ* 'little', *v'ijnǝ* 'come.3Pl', *d'uanǝ* 'love.3Pl'); absence of /rr/ (*ruk* 'road', *rał* 'seldom', *ara* 'nut.Pl', *fur* 'oven', *ther* 'cut.3Sg', *θer* 'cut.3Sg', *mer* 'take.3Sg', *m'ara* 'take.Part'); absence of /h/, which is present in the Greek idiom of the village (*im'ara* 'Himarra', *(ɲǝ) 'erǝ* 'once', *'anǝ* 'eat.3Pl', *'ołat* 'money', *umb'asǝn* 'loose.3Pl', *b'ǝen* 'do.3PlPass', *ko'ǝ* 'time', *muab'et* 'talk'); presence of *yʲ* in borrowings from Greek (*yʲ'iton* 'neighbour'); presence of *t͡ʃ* and *d͡ʒ* (*t͡ʃart͡ʃ'af* 'bedsheet', *d͡ʒob'an* 'shepherd'); restricted distribution of diphthongs (*pag'ot͡ʃ* 'pay.2Sg.Conj', *pag'ojmǝ* 'pay.1Pl.Conj'; cf. also in the Greek idiom of the village: *θes* 'God'); instances of absent palatalization (*fuk'i* 'power', *ʃk'ip* 'albanian', *gǝrk'iʃt* 'greek', *ke* 'that'). Future research should indicate to what extent the speakers are sensitive to the opposition Standard Albanian ~ Laberian.

palaskin'os, palaskin'i 'dweller of Palasa, male and fem.', *δrom'aδis, δrom'iha* 'dweller of Dhermi, male and fem.'⁹

Primary data were obtained related to the following phenomena in the language competencies of Greek-Albanian bilinguals and their speech behaviour: 1) functional domains of the two languages, 2) code switching (see Muysken 2000; 2013; Adamou 2016), 3) the extent of heterogeneity in informants' speech, including their vocabulary, 4) the substantive results of language contacts as evidenced by the lexical system. It can be established that both languages observe three forms of contact both in the lexical system and at the level of spontaneous oral narrative: *complementary distribution, hybridization,* and *equal functional loading (equal fluent usage of two languages without any perceivable difference).*

3.1 Textual level

Oral texts reflecting the traditional religious culture of the village were recorded. Before presenting our material, one should take note of the Albanian ethnologist Mark Tirta's review article "Myths and beliefs on the Upper Coast of Himara" (Tirta 2006), which, despite the utter lack of information about the culture of the Greek-speaking population of the krajina, concludes that there is a *unity* of traditional religious culture among (Albanian-speaking) Muslims and (Albanian and Greek-speaking) Christians in Himara and Labëria. In this part of the chapter, we would like to draw attention to two cultural borrowings into Greek-speaking Himara from Albanian Labëria, the language code of which presumably points to symbiotic relations between the two groups of the population at least with respect to the historical past.

This is, first, the famous Balkan "Legend of the March Crone" (MDABL 2005: 92–93), which our informants had heard "from the old folks long ago" (Pal. "*Ap tes palj'es to ho k'usi. Na s p'ume hronj'a.*") and, in accordance with the interviewer's request, was told mostly in Greek.¹⁰ It relates that an old woman, thinking the

---

9 Although there is no monographic description of the village idiom, it is known that its vocalism is of "semi-northern type", showing full quantitative reduction of unstressed /i/, /u/ and partially qualitative reduction of unstressed /e/, /o/ to /i/, /u/ respectively (Qirjazi 2011: 43, 47). Kyriazés (2007) points to archaic Old Greek features of the idiom and difficulties with its classification.

10 In the course of her narration, an informant uttered an Albanian expression that makes contact with the listener by apologizing for the inappropriate fragments of a legend ("*Ki eft'i l'ei* (Pal.), *do mə f'aλni* (Alb.)" "And she says (Pal.).," "pardon me... (Alb.)"). She also, without any particular reason, translated into Albanian what she had just said in Greek ("*P'ern k'upa o... merr k'upən ai...*" (Gr.) "He takes the cup..." (Alb.) "He took up the cup..."). The interviewer imitated

winter has passed, went with her herd to summer mountain pasture (Gr.: *"vyʲ'ike so vun'i"* = "went to the mountains"). In the mountains, the shepherdess praised in Greek the new offspring of the herd. (Gr. *"Ta kats͡'ikja*[11] *mu yʲer'asan," l'ei. "Ta arnj'a mou k'ere pj'asan," l'ei. Plj'akan k'era.*[12] = "My goat kids have grown," she says. "And my lambs are putting on their horns," she says. (That is, their horns were tied.) She then mocked the month of March in Albanian (Alb. *"Δj'effa b'uzə m'arsit!"* (Gr.) l'ei = (Alb.) "I want to defecate on March" (Gr.) she says. This means that this month has gone and the crone and her herd have no more need of it. (Gr. *"'Efyjes t'ora, δe s 'ehume an'aŋgi"* = "Now you've gone, we have no need of you.") In answer to this, the month of March sent her foul weather (Gr. *"'evale ton ger'o"*), strong winds and hail, and her bucket of milk was carried off in the air. By the next day, the old woman and her animals were frozen in the mountains (Gr. *"Tn 'ali m'era tn 'epniks o θe'os. Ki eft'i pn'ike ke psof'isan 'ola*), where the old lady "hangs" to this day (Gr.: *"ki eft'i kremj'ete eδ'o"*).

At first glance, we are dealing with a Greek text where, in some sections, Greek and Albanian seem to carry an *equal functional load (are used without any perceivable difference)*; i.e., they alternate to the extent that they do not allow us to identify these fragments as belonging to one of the languages in isolation. However, close attention to both the narrative and the characters' statements reveals that, in other parts of the text, Greek and Albanian enter into a relationship of *complementary distribution*. First of all, while the main narrative and the absolute majority of the principal character's statements are spoken in Greek, one notes that the curse addressed to the month of March is spoken in Albanian: *Δj'effa b'uzə m'arsit!* "I want to defecate on March". It is possible that cursing is simply better put in a language with a lower status. However, as we discovered earlier for the town of Himara in Southern Albania, and the Mrkovići krajina in Montenegro (Novik & Sobolev 2018; Sobolev 2015), such code switching is an indication of Albanian as the first language of our informants' female ancestors[13] from whom this text – with its structure, formulas, and elementary language forms – was obtained as a cultural borrowing from Albanian to Greek.

---

this latter strategy by prompting segments in languages A and B by a sentence that is generally not identifiable as being either A or B (Muysken 2000: 712–713), for example: "*Ak'oma mnja for'a (Gr.), qə ŋga fil'imi.*" "One more time *(Gr.)*, from the beginning. *(Alb.)*"

11 A more archaic and authentic idiom for Palasë word derivation would be: (Pal.) *kats͡'iδa*.
12 The text is the narrative of a mythological character in rhymed verse with a metre of three unaccented and one accented syllable (- - - /).
13 The mother of another of our informants, Maria Todoriani, DOB 1934, was from an Orthodox family named Konomi from the Albanian-speaking village of Vuno. Her father was from Palasë.

The storytellers had heard this legend from the old folks long ago (Gr. "*Ap tes palj'es to ho k'usi. Na s p'ume hronj'a.*") According to the informants, the character of legend had a real prototype and she was some sort of old Albanian woman from some sort of village in the district (Gr. "*Kan'ena horj'o eδ'o y j'iro; Ap'eδo θa hi t'ihi. Ap'eδo 'itan, Alvan'iδa*"). Nonetheless, there is no particular reason why this phrase should be in Albanian (Alb. *Ku di 'unə? Kəʃt'u k'emi dəgjuar, kəʃt'u θ'emi.* = "How should I know? We tell it like we hear it.")

Secondly, as is well known in Albanian literature (Tirta 2006: 358), the ritual *mourning of the dead* has a special place in the linguistic code of Palasë. The women of Palasë, who themselves do not speak Albanian (including those now in their 80s) mourn for the dead in Albanian (Alb. "*Gj'iθə gr'atə e ʃʃ'atit pərp'ara nuk d'ininʃkʲip. Po kur kʲ'anin, kʲ'aninʃkʲip. Pər tə f'oλur, nuk d'inin.*" "None of the women in the village knew Albanian in the past. But when they mourned the dead in the grave, they did this in Albanian.") They did not hire mourners from outside, the ritual texts themselves were performed by the women of the family (Alb. "*Mə vdikʲ m'ua b'uri im, kʲ'aja 'unə ʃkʲip. M'otrat, kushər'irat, h'aɫatə.*" "When my husband died, I mourned (him) in Albanian. My sisters, my first cousins, aunts.") The words, as they relate, they knew "by heart" (Alb. "*Iʃin me tə dəgj'uar.*"). This previously uninvestigated phenomenon will be taken up in the next expedition.

3.2 The lexical level

At the lexical level, there is evidence of additional complementary distribution of Greek and Albanian in the folk (Orthodox) *calendar vocabulary*. According to the results of the lexical questionnaire, this lexical-semantic group does not emerge as two parallel collections of lexemes – Greek and Albanian – but as the consolidation of Greek as the main repository of knowledge about the Christian Orthodox calendar, its transmission and communication (see, for example., Gr. *hrist'uyʲena*). Conversely, Albanian retains its function of conveying traditional Balkan folk mythology (e.g., Alb. *ʃk'urtiʃ* = 'February', Alb. *njə m'arsi* = 'First March'), and the state calendar of Albania (and to a small extent the nomenclature of the Albanian Orthodox Church).

Table 1 Terms in the folk calendar

Date and translation	Names of festivals and their names in folk culture			Informant's commentary
	in standard formal Greek	in the Palasë dialect	in the Albanian Palasë dialect	
30.11 / 13.12. Feast of St. Andrew	i m'era tu ayʲ'iu andr'ea	ayʲandr'eos // tu ayʲandr'eos // yʲort'i tu ayʲandr'eos	dit fet'are tə ʃəndr'eut	(Gr.) ayʲandr'eas 'ehi m'ia apo ft'o: (Alb.) 'əʃtə shpət'us i d'etit. (Gr.) "St. Andrew can do this, (Alb.) he can save you at sea."
04.12 / 17.12. Feast of St. Barbara	i m'era tis ayʲ'as varv'aras	i yʲort'i tis ayʲio varv'aros	no Alb. equivalent	
20.12 / 2.1. Feast of St. Ignatius	tu ayʲ'iu iɣnat'iu	Passive	no Alb. equivalent	(Alb.) at'o i k'emi nə kaλand'ar. (Gr.) aft'o… 'ehome to kaland'ar so sp'iti ke ta… (Alb.) We have them in the calendar. (Gr.) "That is… we have a calendar at home and…"
24.12 / 6.1. Christmas Eve	paramon'i ton hris'uyʲenon	prin na rθi ta hris'uyʲena // i mkr'i p'asha	no Alb. equivalent	
25.12 / 7.1. Christmas	ta hris'uyʲena	ta hris'uyʲena // i mkr'i p'asha	dit e kr'iʃtit // hris'uyʲena // p'aʃka e v'ogəλə	(Alb.) n'eve aʃt'u i θ'emi hris'uyʲena ðe ʃqip ðe grekʲ'iʃt. "We call it 'hris'uyʲena' whether in Albanian or in Greek."
25.12–06.1 The 12 Days of Christmas.	ð'oðeka im'eres	does not exist	no Alb. equivalent	
Impure spirits are able to act during the holy days.	i kalik'andẑari	no data	no Alb. equivalent	
1.1 / 14.1. New Year	protohronʲ'a	protohronʲ'a	viti i r'i	
6.1 / 19.1 Theophany	ta f'ota	t ayʲio fot'on	'ujət e bek'uarə	

1–28/29.2. February	fevru'arios / flev'aris	ʃk'urtiʃ	ʃk'urti	ʃk'urti ɲə vit ka ɲəzetet'etə, ɲə ka ɲəzeten'əntə. ðe i θ'emi kəmbəʃk'urtər. se 'əʃtə… nuk 'əʃtə tam'əm m'uaj. i θ'emi t͡ʃaʎə, ʃkurt. "February (lit. Alb. 'short') some years has 28 and some years has 29 days. So we call it 'shorty'. Because it… is not a real month. So we call it gimpy, shorty."

The appearance of hybridization (or, rather, fusion) at the lexical level can be noted in traditional proper names: *Arqile Shishko, Elpiniqi Kosta Çaçi, Arianti Spiro Gjikuri, Pavllo Koka, Lluzur Marko Kulo, Dhimitrulla Kashta*, where Greek and Biblical personal names run up against Albanian surnames, several of which have within them an unadulterated sobriquet that means 'head' or 'straw'. And yet should one refuse to consider the name and surname as one unit, there is still in evidence the complementary distribution of Greek personal names and Albanian nicknames. There are undeniable hybrid examples in some tombstone inscriptions in the town cemetery, mixing letters of both Albanian and Greek alphabets (ex. *Σpiro Babe*). We find names of the months to be evidence of undeniable hybridization, consider the following: *yʲen'ariʃ* 'January', *ʃk'urtiʃ* 'February' (comp. Alb. *ʃkurt* 'short'; 'February'), *m'artiʃ* 'March', *apr'iliʃ* 'April', *m'aiʃ* 'May', *θer'itiʃ* 'June' (comp. Gr. *therízō* 'to reap, mow'), *alon'ariʃ* 'July' (comp. Gr. *alōnízō* 'to grind'), *'avyustoʃ* 'August', *tr'iyoʃ* 'September' (comp. Gr. *truyízō* 'to harvest grapes'), *'ayʲoʃ dim'itrioʃ* 'October', *tokʃ'arh'iʃ* 'November' (comp. Gr. *taksiárchēs* = 'archangel', *'ayʲoʃ andr'eaʃ* 'December'.

The fluent usage of Greek and Albanian with no perceivable difference, the ability to produce texts with segments that alternate between them, and general communicative competence, is also observed in certain sectors of the lexical system. Consider, for example, the completeness of the informants' knowledge of the names of human body parts in Greek and Albanian. A survey of lexical material was conducted as part of the MDABL "from meaning to form" programme (Sobolev et al. 1997); the total sample included 127 lexical units. A stimulus was offered to informants in the Albanian dialect of the Skrapar krajina, a version close to standard Tosk Albanian (Ylli & Sobolev 2002: 280–287), whereas a reaction was to be expected in the Greek dialect of Palasë (from Gr. *palask'ítika*) and, in the case of differences noted by the informant, in standard Greek (for Gr. *ellēniká*) as well. The following illustrative materials for the semantic microgroup 'the Human Body' give lexemes as they are used in the Greek subdialect of Palasë along with informants' actual responses, appropriate grammatical parsing[14] and etymology.

The semantic micro-group "The Human Body"

1. 'body' Alb. *trup* ~ Pal. *korm'i // kurm'i* N.SG (from AncGr. (Andriṓtēs 1995: 168));
2. 'trunk/torso' Alb. *truŋk* ~ Pal. no equivalent;
3. 'shoulder' Alb. *skep* ~ Pal. *s'upi* N.SG, *supj'a* N.PL (from Alb. *sup, supe* (Orel 1998: 405)) ~ Gr. *'omus*;
4. 'breast' *krah'or* ~ Pal. *p'eto // p'etu* N.SG (Gr. *péto* from Lat. *pectus* (Andriṓtēs 1995: 239) ~ Gr. *ʃt'iθus*;
5. 'female breast' Alb. *s'isa // dʑoks // krah'or* ~ Pal. *vʒ'i // viz'i s'upi* N.SG, *vʒ'ija // vizyʲ'a* N.PL (from AncGr. (Andriṓtēs 1995: 59));
6. 'nipple' Alb. *k'oka e s'isəs* ~ Pal. *r'ata* F.SG (unknown etymology);[15]
7. 'belly' Alb. *bark* ~ Pal. *kilʲ'a // t͡ɕilʲ'ia* F.SG (from AncGr. (Andriṓtēs 1995: 162));
8. 'navel' Alb. *kərθ'iza* ~ Pal. *afal'os* M.SG (from AncGr. (Andriṓtēs 1995: 44));
9. 'back' Alb. *kurr'is // ʃp'inə* ~ Pal. *pl'ati* F.SG // *pl'atis* M.SG (from AncGr. (Andriṓtēs 1995: 284));
10. 'lower back' Alb. *m'esi* ~ Pal. *m'esi* F.SG (from AncGr. (Andriṓtēs 1995: 206));
11. 'belt or waist' Alb. *m'esi // bejλ* ~ Pal. *m'esi* F.SG (from AncGr. (Andriṓtēs 1995: 206));
12. 'side' Alb. *'iɲə* ~ Pal. *prevl'o* N.SG (AncGr. (Andriṓtēs 1995: 285)) ~ Gr. *plevr'o*;
13. 'rear' Alb. *të ndəɲura* ~ Pal. *k'olus* M.SG (from AncGr. (Andriṓtēs 1995: 178));
14. 'buttock' Alb. *e nd'əɲur // moɫ'at͡ɕe* ~ Pal. *ambr'oskula* N.PL (from Alb. *broçkolla* Çabej (1976: 329, 276); comp. Gr. *brókolo* from It. *broccolo* (Andriṓtēs 1995: 224));
15. 'skin' Alb. *lək'urə* ~ Pal. *ð'erma* SG.PL (from AnGk. Andriṓtēs (1995: 77)).

From the etymological point of view, at least 10 of the 14 lexemes given date back to Ancient Greek etymons. This figure is lower than that of the southern Greek dialect of the village of Kastelli in the Peloponnese which had previously been surveyed by the same method (Leluda-Voss 2006: 403). Yet this does not make the lexical material of Palasë more allolexical than others of the modern Greek

---

14 // indicates doubled forms.
15 The lexeme *ráta* F.SG "vineyard", has been noted in an urban setting of the Ionian island of Lefkadia (Kontomíchēs 2005: 274).

dialectal continuum. This micro-group exhibits few contact lexemes (see Adamou 2016), i.e. borrowings from the contacting language, in our case Albanian – *s'upi* 'shoulder', *ambr'oskula* 'buttock'.

Moving on to other parts of the lexicon, we note that there is a strong tendency to integrate thematic parts of Albanian vocabulary (lexical groups) into the Greek language of our informants, and vice versa, to integrate parts of the Greek vocabulary into the Albanian language. As a result, there is only one set of colour terms for cattle in both Albanian and Greek, originating in Albanian. For instance, requesting local Greek words denoting goats of different colours, we received Albanian words as answers, such as *v'erδa* for a yellow goat. On the other hand, there is only one set of fish names (ichthyonyms) for both Greek and Albanian, originating in Greek; e.g., *tɕ'efalo* 'mullet' and *h'eλa* 'eel' (instead of Alb. *qefull* and *ngjal* respectively). Thus, one lexicon emerges, serving the two languages in contact.

4 Conclusion

The original materials on the Greek dialect of the bilingual village of Palasë presented in this chapter reflect the results and mechanisms of linguistic and cultural interaction between the Greek and Albanian-speaking populations in the south Albanian krajina of Himara. This data is considered in the context of ideas present in traditional ethnically-centred philology and ethnology as well as in modern cultural anthropology, contact linguistics, and Balkan linguistics as a whole.

The competence of Palasë's Greek and Albanian speakers should be recognized as complete and unlimited in both languages, exhibiting an *equal usage* both at the level of spontaneous oral narrative and in the parts of its lexical system. This is evidence of the existence of a special kind of non-dominant *bilingualism*, which is less studied by modern contact linguistics. Being in contact, the Greek and Albanian languages naturally enter into relations of *fusion* and *hybridization*, a circumstance which can be interpreted as an increased accommodation on the part of the Greek dialect to the Albanian language. The fact that levels of *alloglossia* in an area of closely related dialects is not very high should be further examined not just in lexicon but in other linguistic spheres from phonetics to grammar.

Without entering directly into the lively debate about the relative antiquity of the Greek and Albanian-speaking populations in Himara, it is possible to put forward a hypothesis about their possible partial *symbiosis* in the relatively recent past under the conditions of linguistic and confessional *borderlands*. This is evidenced by the traces of *complementary functional distribution* between Greek and

Albanian in legendary narratives, rites of passage, calendar terminology, and the like. This gives testament to the complementarity of *cultural* features typical to the region's two communities. It is indeed the language code that allows us to *delimit the traditional cultures* of multilingual symbionts and to reject the thesis of cultural uniformity in Southern Albania (Labëria), in general and in the Himara krajina in particular. We are dealing with two, traditional Greek and traditional Albanian cultures just as we are dealing with two Greek and Albanian languages. The study of their interrelationship is one of the most engaging and propitious tasks set before contemporary Balkan studies.

References

Adamou, Evangelia. 2016. *A Corpus-driven Approach to Language Contact: Endangered Languages in a Comparative Perspective*. Berlin & Boston: De Gruyter Mouton.

Andriṓtēs, N. P. 1995. *Etēmologikó leksikó tēs koinḗs neoellēnikḗs* [Etymological dictionary of modern Greek]. Thessaloniki: Institute of Modern Greek Studies.

Barth, Frederik. 1969. Introduction. In Barth, Frederik (ed.), *Ethnic Groups and Boundaries: the social organization of cultural difference*, 9–38. Bergen & Oslo: Universitetsforlaget.

Bógkas (Mpógkas), Euángelos Ath. 1966. *Tá glōssiká idiṓmata tḗs Ēpeírou (Voreíou, Kentrikḗs kaí Notíou)* [The dialects of Epirius (Voreius, Kentrike and Notius)]. Iōánnina: Etaireía Ēpeirōtikṓn Meletṓn.

Borgia, Nilo. 1942. *I monaci basiliani d'Italia in Albania. Appunti di storia missionaria (Secoli XVI–XVIII). Periodo secondo* [Italian Basilian monks in Albania. Notes on missionary history. The second period]. Roma: Istituto per l'Europa Orientale.

Brown, Christopher & Brian D. Joseph. 2013. The Texture of a Linguistic Environment: New Perspectives on the Greek of Southern Albania. *Albanohellenica* 14–15 (5). 145–152.

Brown, Christopher & Brian D. Joseph. 2015. On Hybrid Forms in Language Contact – Some evidence from the Greek of Southern Albania. *Albanohellenica* 16–17.6 (Proceedings of the 2nd International Conference of Greek-Albanian, Albanian-Greek Studies (Tirana, March 27th–28th, 2015)), https://albanohellenica.wixsite.com/greekalbanianstudies/conferences (accessed 15 March, 2021).

Burkhart, Dagmar. 1989. *Kulturraum Balkan: Studien Zur Volkskunde und Literatur Südosteuropas*. Berlin: Reimer.

Çabej, Eqrem (ed.). 1976–2014. *Studime etimologjike në fushë të shqipes* [Etymological studies in Albanian]. Vols. 1–7. Tirana: Akademia e shkencave e Shqipërisë.

Curtis, Matthew Cowan. 2012. *Slavic-Albanian Language Contact, Convergence, and Coexistence*. Ohio State University Doctoral Dissertation.

Desnitskaya, Agniya V. 1968. *Albanskii iazyk i ego dialekty* [Albanian and its dialects]. Leningrad: Nauka.

Desnitskaya, Agniya V. 1976. Evoliutsiia dialektnoi sistemy v usloviiakh etnicheskogo smesheniia (iz istorii slaviano-albanskikh iazykovykh kontaktov) [Evolution of a dialectical system under conditions ethnic mixing (from the history of Albanian-Slavic language contacts)]. *Voprosy etnogeneza i etnicheskoi istorii slavian i vostochnykh romantsev* [Issues of ethnogenesis and ethnic history of Slavs and Eastern Romance speakers], 186–197. Moscow: Nauka.

Desnitskaya, Agniya V. 1987 [1979]. O nachalakh sravnitel'nogo izucheniia balkanskikh iazykov [On the beginnings of the comparative research on Balkan languages]. In Agniya V. Desnitskaya (ed.), *Albanskaia literatura i albanskii iazyk* [Albanian literature and Albanian language], 276–293. Leningrad: Nauka.

Dombrowski, Andrew. 2013. *Phonological aspects of language contact along the Slavic periphery: an ecological approach.* University of Chicago Doctoral Dissertaton.

Domosiletskaia, Marina V., Anna A. Plotnikova & Andrey N. Sobolev. 1998. Malyi dialektologicheskii atlas balkanskikh iazykov [Minor Dialectological Atlas of Balkan Languages]. In *Slavianskoe iazykoznanie. XII mezhdunarodnyi s"ezd slavistov. Doklady rossiiskoi delegatsii*, 196–211. Moscow: Nauka.

Furrer, Norbert. 2002. *Die vierzigsprachige Schweiz. Sprachkontakte und Mehrsprachigkeit in der vorindustriellen Gesellschaft (15.–19. Jahrhundert)*, Vols 1–2. Zürich: Chronos.

Gashi, Skënder. 2015. *Kërkime onomastike-historike për minoritete të shuara e aktuale të Kosovës* [Onomastic-historical research on Kosovo's extinct and current minorities]. Prishtinë: AShAK.

Giakoumis, Konstantinos. 2016. Self-identifications by Himarriots, 16th to 19th Centuries. *Erytheia* 37. 205–246.

Golomb, Zbignjev. 1959. Genetički vrski meǵu karpatskata i balkanskata stočarska terminologija i ulogata na slovenskiot element vo ova področje [Genetic links between terms for animal husbandry and the role of the Slavic element in this field]. *Makedonski jazik* 10. 19–50.

Golomb, Zbignjev. 1979. Za "mehanizmot" na slovensko-romanskite odnosi na Balkanskiot poluostrov [On the "mechanism" of Slavic-Romance relations on the Balkan Peninsula]. *Makedonski jazik* 20. 5–18.

Golomb, Zbignjev. 1982. Makedonsko-vlaški leksički izednačuvanja kako primer na centralnobalkanskata kulturna zaednica [Macedonian-Vlach lexical homonyms as an example of central Balkan cultural convergence]. *Makedonski jazik* 32–33 (Festschrift Blaže Koneski). 137–146.

Gregorič Bon, Nataša. 2008. Storytelling as a spatial practice in Dhërmi (Drimades) of Southern Albania. *Anthropological notebooks* 14 (2). 7–29.

Hinrichs, Uwe. 2004a. Südosteuropa-Linguistik und Kreolisierung. *Zeitschrift für Balkanologie* 40 (1). 17–32.

Hinrichs, Uwe. 2004b. Orale Kultur, Mehrsprachigkeit, radikaler Analytismus: Zur Erklärung von Sprachstrukturen auf dem Balkan und im kreolischen Raum. Ein Beitrag zur Entmystifizierung der Balkanlinguistik. *Zeitschrift für Balkanologie* 40 (2). 141–174.

Hinrichs, Uwe et al. 2014. *Handbuch Balkan*. Wiesbaden: Harrassowitz.

Holtus, Günter & Johannes Kramer (eds.). 1987. *Romania et Slavia Adriatica: Festschrift für Žarko Muljačić*. Hamburg: Buske.

Ismajli, Rexhep. 2015. Über die slawischen Lehnwörter im Albanischen. In Demiraj Bardhyl (ed.), *Sprache und Kultur der Albaner. Zeitliche und räumliche Dimensionen.* Akten der 5. Deutschalbanischen kulturwissenschaftlichen Tagung (5–8 June 2014, Buçimas bei Pogradec, Albania), 557–590. Wiesbaden: Harrassowitz.

Joseph, Brian. 2016. Phonology and the Construction of Borders in the Balkans. In Tomasz Kamusella, Motoki Nomachi & Catherine Gibson (eds.), *The Palgrave Handbook of Slavic Languages, Identities and Borders*, 263–275. Basingstoke: Palgrave Macmillan.

Joseph, Brian, Rexhina Ndoci & Carly Dickerson. 2019. Language Mixing in Palasa. *Journal of Greek Linguistics* 19 (2): 227–243.

Kisilier, Maxim L. 2013. Novogrecheskaia dialektologiia: dostizheniia i problemy [Modern Greek dialectology: Achievements and problems]. *Voprosy Jazykoznaniia* 2. 83–98.

Kisilier, Maxim L., Aleksandr A. Novik & Andrey N. Sobolev. 2013. Studime etnolinguistike dhe dialektologjike në terren në Dropull, Shqipëri: Materialet e ekspeditës ruse të vitit 2009 [Ethnolinguistic and dialectological field studies in Dropull, Albania: Materials from the 2009 Russian Expedition]. *Albanohellenica* 5. 153–165.

Kisilier, Maxim L., Aleksandr A. Novik & Andrey N. Sobolev. 2016. Etnolingvisticheskie i dialektologicheskie nabliudeniia iz Dropula (Albaniia). Po materialam rossiiskoi ekspeditsii 2009 g. [Ethnolinguistic and dialectological observations from Dropula (Albania) based on materials from the Russian expedition of 2009]. *Acta Linguistica Petropolitana. Trudy Instituta lingvisticheskikh issledovanii* 12 (3). 111–134.

Koka, Pavllo. 2008. *Visare nga Palasa* [Treasures from Palasë]. Athens: Shën Dhimitri.

Koka, Pavllo. 2011. *Everjetë nga Palasa* [Everjetë from Palasë]. Athens: Shën Dhimitri.

Kokavésē, Eleonṓra-Elénē. 2010. Ē epivíōsē tēs chimaraías dialéktou ston 21o aiṓna. Voreioēpeirōtiká. [The survival of the dialect of Himara the 21st Century. Northern Epirus]. *Epistēmonikḗ epetērída Idrúmatos Boreioēpeirōtikṓn Ereunṓn*, Vol. 1, 95–130. Iōánnina.

Kola, Gjeto. 1939. Himara. *Hylli i drites* 15 (11–12). 574–585.

Kondis, Basil & Eleutheria Manta. 1994. *The Greek Minority in Albania: a Documentary Record (1921–1993)*. Thessaloniki: Institute of Balkan Studies.

Kontomíchēs, Pantazḗs. 2005. *Lexikó tou leukadítikou glōssikoú idiṓmatos. Idiōmatikó – Ermēneutikó – Laografikó* [Dictionary of the Lefkadian dialect. Dialectal – Interpretive – Folklore]. Athḗna: Grēgórēs.

Kyriazḗs, Dṓrēs K. 2007. Schésē tou ellēnikoú glōssikoú idiṓmatos tēs Chimáras me ta álla neoellēniká glōssiká idiṓmata [A comparison of the Greek dialect of Himara with other modern Greek dialects]. *Melétes gia tēn ellēnikḗ glṓssa* 27. (Praktiká tēs 27ēs Synántēsēs tou Toméa Glōssologías tou Tmḗmatos Filologías tēs Filosofikḗs Scholḗs A.P.Th., 6–7 Maḯou 2006), 198–209. Thessaloniki: Instioúto Neoellēnikṓn Spoudṓn.

Kyriazḗs, Dṓrēs K. 2012. To Ellēnikó glōssikó idíōma tēs Ártas Ablṓna [The Greek dialect of Artas, Ablona]. In Zoe Gavriilidou et al. (eds.), *Selected papers of the 10th International Conference on Greek Linguistics (Komotini, 1–4 September, 2011)*, 890–898. Komotini Greece: Democritus University of Thrace.

Kyriazḗs, Dṓrēs K. 2019. Ta neoellēniká idiṓmata tēs N. Albanías [The Greek idioms of South Albania]. In Tzitzilis, Christos & Georgios Papanastassiou (eds.), *Language contact in the Balkans and Asia Minor*, 156–175. Thessalonikē: Institute of Modern Greek Studies.

Kyriazḗs, Dṓrēs K. & Aristotélēs Ē. Spýrou. 2011. Ta ellēniká glōssiká idiṓmata tēs Albanías [The Greek dialects of Albania]. *Ellēnikḗ Dialektología* 6. 175–199. Athḗna: Akadēmía Athēnṓn. Kéntron Ereúnēs tōn Neoellēnikṓn Dialéktōn kai Idiōmátōn. I.L.N.E.S.

Leake, William M. 1814. *Researches in Greece*. London: Booth.

Leake, William M. 1835. *Travels in Northern Greece*, Vol. 1. London: Rodwell.

Lehman, Rosa. 2001. *Symbiosis and ambivalence: Poles and Jews in a small Galician town*. New York & Oxford: Berghahn Books.

Leluda-Voss, Christina. 2006. *Die südgriechische Mundart von Kastelli (Peloponnes)*. München: Biblion Verlag.

Lítsios, Fílippas. 2009. *To chronikó tēs Drópolēs* [The history of Dropull]. Tirana: Neraida.

Malltezi, Luan. 2006. Rreth karakterit shqiptar të popullsisë së krahinës së Himarës (shek. XV–XVIII) [On the Albanian character of the population of Himara province (15–18th centuries)]. In Nasi, Lefter et al. (eds.), *Himara në shekuj* [Himara over the centuries], 113–123. Tirana: Akademia e Shkencave e Shqipërisë.

MDABL – Andrey N. Sobolev (ed.). 2003–2018. *Malyi dialektologicheskii atlas balkanskikh iazykov. Probnyi vypusk (2003). Seriia leksicheskaia. Tom I. Leksika dukhovnoi kul'tury (2005). Tom II. Chelovek. Sem'ia (2006). Tom III. Zhivotnovodstvo (2009). Tom IV. (Avtor: M. V. Domosiletskaia). Landshaftnaia leksika (2010). Tom V. (Avtor: M. V. Domosiletskaia). Meteorologiia (2012). Tom VI. Polevodstvo. Ogorodnichestvo (2013). Tom VII. (Avtor: M. V. Domosiletskaia). Pčelovodstvo (2018). Seriia grammaticheskaia. Tom I. Kategorii imeni sushchestvitel'nogo (2005)* [Minor dialect atlas of the Balkan languages. Test launch (2003). Lexical series. Vol. 1. Cultural vocabulary (2005). Vol. 2. The person and human relations (2006). Vol. 3. Animal husbandry (2009). Vol. 4. (M. V. Domosiletskaia, author). Landscape (2010). Vol. 5 (M. V. Domosiletskaia, author). Meteorology (2012). Vol. 6. Field-tending and Gardening (2013). Vol. 7. (M. V. Domosiletskaia, author). Apiculture (2018). Grammatical series. Vol. 1. Noun categories (2005)]. St. Petersburg, München: Nauka, Verlag Otto Sagner.
Memushaj, Rami. 2004. Patronimia e Himarës [The Patronymics of Himara]. In Nasi, Lefter et al. (eds.), *Himara në shekuj* [Himara over the centuries], 293–319. Tirana: Akademia e Shkencave e Shqipërisë.
Memushaj, Rami & Helena Grillo. 2009. Vendi i së folmes së Himarës në dialektin jugor të shqipes [The place of the Himara idiom in the southern Albanian dialect]. *Studime filologjike* 1–2. 29–62.
Morozova, Maria S. 2017. Albanskii govor ili govory Gorany? Genezis i funktsionirovanie [Albanian subdialect(s) of Gorana? Genesis and functioning]. *Vestnik Sankt-Peterburgskogo gosudarstvennogo universiteta. Iazyk i literatura* 14 (2), 222–237.
Morozova, Maria S. & Alexander Yu. Rusakov. 2019. Montenegrin-Albanian Linguistic Border: In Search of "Balanced Language Contact". *Slověne* 2. 258–302.
Mufwene, Salikoko S. 2009. Restructuring, hybridization, and complexity in language evolution. In Enoch O. Aboh & Norval Smith (eds.), *Complex Processes in New Languages*, 367–400. Amsterdam: John Benjamins.
Muljačić, Žarko. 2000. *Das Dalmatische. Studien zu einer untergegangenen Sprache*. Köln: Böhlau.
Muysken, Pieter. 2000. *Bilingual Speech. A Typology of Code-mixing*. Cambridge: Cambridge University Press.
Muysken, Pieter. 2013. Language contact as the result of bilingual optimization strategies. *Bilingualism: Language and Cognition* 16 (4). 709–730.
Nasi, Lefter et al. (eds.). 2004. *Himara në shekuj* [Himara over the centuries]. Tirana: Akademia e Shkencave e Shqipërisë.
Novik, Aleksandr A. & Andrey N. Sobolev. 2018. Studime etnolinguistike në Himarë dhe në zonën e Vurgut (Materialet e ekspeditës 2014) [Ethnolinguistic Studies in Himara and the Vurgu Area (Materials of the 2014 Expedition)]. *Albanohellenica* 16–17 (6). (Proceedings of the 2nd International Conference of Greek-Albanian / Albanian-Greek Studies (Tirana, 27–28 March 2015)). http://albanohellenica.wixsite.com/greekalbanianstudies/albanohellenica-6-contents (accessed 15 March, 2021).
Novik, Aleksandr & Andrey N. Sobolev. 2016. Traditional wedding costume of the Mrkovići in Montenegro: between real heritage and folk construction (materials of the Russian expeditions in 2012–2014). *Folklore* 66. 15–36.
Orel, Vladimir. 1998. *Albanian etymological dictionary*. Leiden, Boston, Köln: Brill.
Plotnikova, Anna. 2009. *Materialy dlya etnolingvisticheskogo izucheniya balkanoslavyanskogo areala* [Materials for the ethnolinguistic study of the Balkan-Slavic area]. Moscow. http://inslav.ru/images/stories/pdf/2009_Plotnikova.pdf (accessed 15 March, 2021).

Qirjazi, Dhori. 2011. Rreth marrëdhënieve të së folmes greke të Himarës me të folmet e tjera të greqishtes së re [On the relations between Greek dialects in Himara and other New Greek dialects]. *Albanohellenica* 4. 39–52.

RPSSh. 1977, 1978, 1983 – *Republika popullore socialiste e Shqipërisë 1 : 50.000* [The People's Socialist Republic of Albania 1 : 50.000]. Tirana, 1977, 1978, 1983. K – 134 – 136 – A (Dukat i) – B (Kuçi) – C (Himara) – D (Qeparoi).

RPSSh. 1984 – *Republika popullore socialiste e Shqipërisë 1 : 200.000* [The People's Socialist Republic of Albania 1 : 200.000]. K – 34 – XXXII – Vlora. Tirana, 1984.

Schutz (Shütz), Ishtvan. 2009. Albano-valashskii simbioz i slavianskie zaimstvovaniia v rumynskom i albanskom iazykakh [Albanian-Vlach symbiosis and Slavic borrowing the Romanian and Albanian languages]. *Acta Linguistica Petropolitana. Trudy instituta lingvisticheskikh issledovanii* 5 (1). 305–321.

Skok, Petar. 1950. *Slavenstvo i romanstvo na jadranskim otocima: Toponomastička ispitivanja* [Slavic and Romance languages on the Adriatic islands. A toponymic examination]. Zagreb: JAZU.

Smith, Norval. 2000. Symbiotic mixed languages: A question of terminology. *Bilingualism: Language and Cognition* 3.122–23.

Sobolev, Andrey N. 2013. *Osnovy lingvokul'turnoi antropogeografii Balkanskogo poluostrova. Tom I. Homo balcanicus i ego prostranstvo* [Foundations of linguocultural anthropogeography on the Balkan peninsula. Vol. 1. Homo balcanicus and his space]. St. Petersburg: Nauka, Munich: Otto Sagner Verlag.

Sobolev, Andrey N. 2015. Mrkovichi (i Gorana): iazyki i dialekty chernogorskogo Primor'ia v kontekste noveishikh balkanisticheskikh issledovanii [Mrkovići (and Gorana): Languages and dialects of the Montenegro coast in the context of recent Balkan research]. In Demiraj Bardhyl (ed.), *Sprache und Kultur der Albaner: Zeitliche und raumliche Dimensionen. Akten der 5. Deutsch-albanischen kulturwissenschaftlichen Tagung (Albanien, Buçimas bei Pogradec, 5.–8. Juni 2014)*, 533–556. Wiesbaden: Harrassowitz.

Sobolev, Andrey N. 2017. Iazyki simbioticheskikh soobschestv Zapadnykh Balkan: grecheskii i albanskii iazyki v sele Paliasa v kraine Himara, Albaniia [Languages in the Western Balkan Symbiotic Societies: Greek and Albanian in Palasa, Himara, Albania]. *Vestnik Sankt-Peterburgskogo gosudarstvennogo universiteta. Iazyk i literatura* 14 (3). 421–442.

Sobolev, Andrey N. & Aleksandr A. Novik. 2016. Aktual'nye tendentsii v izuchenii iazyka i kul'tury grekov Albanii [Important trends in the study of the language and culture of Greeks in Albania]. In Ksenia A. Klimova (ed.), *Tezisy dokladov na mezhdunarodnoi konferentsii "Grecheskaia traditsionnaia kul'tura na evropeiskom fone" (Moscow, 5–8 April 2016)*, 72–79. Moscow: MGU.

Sobolev, Andrey N., Iurii A. Lopashov, Irina I. Voronina & Alexander Yu. Rusakov (eds.). 1997. *Malyi dialektologicheskii atlas balkanskikh iazykov. Sintaksicheskaia programma* [Minor dialectological atlas of Balkan languages. Syntactic program]. St. Petersburg: ILI RAN.

Sotiri, Natasha. 2006. E folmja e Himarës [The Himara dialect]. In Lefter Nasi et al. (eds.), *Himara në shekuj* [Himara over the centuries], 263–292. Tirana: Akademia e Shkencave e Shqipërisë.

Spiro (Spýrou), Aristotélēs H. 2008. *To Ellēnikó glōssikó idíōma tēs periochḗs Delvínou kai Agíōn Saránta* (Vibliothḗkē Sofías N. Saripólou. 109). Athḗna: Panepistḗmio Athēnṓn.

Spiro, Aristotle. 2015. The Modern Greek dialects of Albania – A general description and classification. In *43 Mezhdunarodnaia filologicheskaia konferentsiia* (11–16 March 2014) [43 International conference on philology], 396–417. St. Petersburg: St. Petersburg State University.

Stern, Dieter. 2004. Balkansprachen und Kreolsprachen: Versuch einer kontakttypologischen Grenzziehung. *Zeitschrift für Balkanologie* 42 (1–2). 206–225.
Šufflay, Milan. 1925. *Srbi i Arbanasi* [Serbs and Albanians]. Beograd: Izdanje seminara za arbanasku filologiju.
Thomo, Pirro. 1998. *Kishat Pasbizantine në Shqipërinë e Jugut* [Post-Byzantine churches in South Albania]. Tirana: Botim i Kishës orthodokse autoqefale të Shqipërisë.
Tirta, Mark. 2006. Mite e besime në Bregdetin e Sipërm të Himarës [Myths and Beliefs on the Upper Himara Coast]. In Lefter Nasi et al. (ed.), *Himara në shekuj* [Himara over the centuries], 353–372. Tirana: Akademia e Shkencave e Shqipërisë.
Totoni, Minella. 1964. E Folmja e Bregdetit të Poshtëm [The Lower Costal Dialects]. *Studime filologjike* 1 (4). 121–139.
Vagiakákos, Dikaíos V. 1983. Glōssiká kaí laografiká Chimáras, B. Ēpeírou kaí Mánēs. [Linguistic and ethnographic data from Himara, N. Epirus and Mani]. In *Praktiká B' Symposíou glōssologías voreioelladikoú chṓrou*, 9–26. Thessaloníkē: IMChA.
Vekarić, Nenad. 2011. *Vlastela grada Dubrovnika. Knj. 1. Korijeni, struktura i razvoj dubrovačkog plemstva* [The aristocracy of Dubrovnik. Vol. 1. Roots, structure and development of the Dubrovnik nobility]. Zagreb: HAZU, Zavod za povijesne znanosti u Dubrovniku.
Ylli [Iully], Xhelal [Dzhelial'] & Andrey N. Sobolev. 2002. *Albanskii tosksii govor sela Leshnia (Kraina Skrapar). Sintaksis. Leksika. Etnolingvistika. Teksty* [The Albanian-Tosk subdialect of the town of Leshnia (Skrapar Krajina). Syntax. Lexicon. Ethnolinguistics. Texts]. Marburg: Biblion Verlag.
Zheltova, Ekaterina A. 2016. Konstruiruia "grecheskii" i "albanskii": lingvisticheskie ideologii v grekogovoriashchikh soobshchestvakh Iuzhnoi Albanii (Severnogo Epira) [The construction of "Greek" and "Albanain" linguistic ideology in the Greek-speaking communities of Southern Albania (South Epirius)]. *Antropologicheskii forum* 28. 246–259.

Daria V. Konior
Minority within a Minority: Iabalcea and Carașova in Romania

Abstract: One of the few remaining groups that could have represented **a symbiotic Slavic-Romance community in the past** is the Krashovani, a mostly Slavic-speaking Catholic people, who presumably came to the territory of the Romanian Banat over several waves of migration. In one of the Krashovani villages called Iabalcea we observe a rather atypical collection of cultural features. Members of a small community identify themselves as Croats or Krashovani and share a Catholic culture along with some features taken from Orthodox folk tradition while speaking Romanian in everyday communication. The lexical subsystem of traditional wedding rituals in Carașova and Iabalcea seems to be a single cultural code presented in two separate, but closely related, linguistic iterations. It is argued that such diffusion becomes possible in areas where migration flows are large and the population is put under a special type of state and church authority.[1]

1 Introduction

Krashovani (Rom *C(a)rașoveni*, BCMS *K(a)rašovani*) are a mainly Slavic-speaking Catholic ethnic minority from Romania whose ethnic and linguistic origins, history, identity, and linguistic affiliation[2] have been subject to intense scientific and political discussion. Members of this community live in seven villages located in the historical region of Banat: Carașova,[3] Lupac, Vodnic, Rafnic, Nermed, Clocotici and Iabalcea.[4]

---

[1] This research was made possible by a grant from the Russian Science Foundation (the projects "From Separation to Symbiosis: South Eastern European languages and cultures in contact", No. 14-18-01405 and "Balkan bilingualism in dominant and equilibrium contact situations in diatopy, diachrony and diastraty", No. 19-18-00244).
[2] This involves attributing their dialect to Serbian, Croatian, Bulgarian, or even to a reconstructed "Daco-Slavic".
[3] Henceforth, the following proper names are used: Karashevo, a toponym naming the whole Slavic-speaking microregion (7 villages); Carașova, the name of the largest village and economic and cultural centre of the microregion; and Krashovani, which has the meaning of affiliation to the Karashevo microregion.
[4] A small number of Krashovani also live in the village of Tirol (Rom *Tirol*, BCMS *Tilori*) in Reșița, Timișoara, Arad, Anina, as well as in other settlements in the area of these towns. In the beginning of 20th century, Krashovani used to live in the villages of the Serbian (Yugoslav) Banat (Radan 2015: 25–31).

https://doi.org/10.1515/9781501509254-006

Against the background of Serbs and the other ethnic or subethnic groups of Banat, Krashovani are recognisable by the archaic Slavic variety they speak, a particular traditional costume, and the customs and traditions preserved down (in a reduced form) to the present day – customs that at least partially descended from their hypothetical ancestral homeland (Radan 2000: 28). The group of Krashovani dialects is one of the most interesting and original elements in the linguistic mosaic of the multi-ethnic and multi-confessional Banat region, now divided by the border between Romania, Serbia and Hungary.

In recent decades, interest in the Krashovani microregion has increased significantly. There have been some new publications of a linguistic nature (Radan 2000; Sikimić [1999–]2017; Lațchici 2012), folklore (Radan Uscatu 2014; Vlahović 1999/2000) and works considering Krashovani history and identity (Manea-Grgin 2012; Crețan et al. 2014). Such an increase in interest has been triggered by a whole range of research questions related to the Krashovani, which, among other things, concern the ethnogenesis of the Slavic and Romanic populations of the Balkan Peninsula, Slavic and Romance dialectology, as well as the genesis and functioning of bilingual communities in Southeastern Europe.

Krashovani are one of the few remaining groups of people who might have been involved in Slavic-non-Slavic symbiosis[5] in the Balkans. Their linguistic variety (more precisely, their group of dialects, one of which is of Romance and not Slavic origin) has not been previously studied from the point of view of sociolinguistics and the theory of language contact.

By all appearances, the Romano-Slavic symbiosis began in the 5th or 6th centuries, when Slavic tribes came to the Balkans moving through the Carpathian region to the territories south of the Danube (Herrity 2014: 1427; Niederle 1956: 7). This is confirmed by mutual borrowings (some of them estimated to be very old) found in Romanian and in South Slavic languages (Hinrichs, Büttner 1999; Paliga 2003: 102–105; Klepikova 2005: 156). Emil Petrovici writes that this contact resulted in the formation of some kind of a mixed language – "Daco-Slavic" (*daco-slava*) – presuming that it had been spoken by the Slavs of Dacia before they assimilated into the Romanian (or proto-Romanian) population (Petrovici 1943: 1–5). Conclusions regarding this language can be made on the basis of Romanian toponyms: *Glâmboaca* (Sibiu county), *Glâmboca* (Severin county) < proto-Slavic *glǫbokŭ* 'deep', *Indol* (Turda country) <*jǫdolŭ* 'valley' (Petrovici 1943: 1–5, 23; Leschber 1999; Konior 2019). We do not know much about how the processes of

---

5 Since the end of the 1960s, anthropologists have been using the term "symbiotic" for the communities in which ethnic and linguistic groups of people enter into additional distribution relationships (see Barth 1969; Lehman 2001). In recent linguistic research the concept of "symbiosis" is used in a less strict and non-terminological fashion (Sobolev 2017: 423).

convergent development of the Slavic and Romance idioms in the Balkans took place, whether it led to the formation of a particular type of symbiotic community, and, if so, how the relics of such communities function at present.

Krashovani are worth examining also from the point of view of synchronic linguistics. Most of these people are bilingual with Slavic dialect as L1 and Romanian as L2. The ethno-linguistic situation that has developed in the village of Iabalcea is quite unique. There locals claim to have the same ethnicity with the inhabitants of other Krashovani villages, and they share cultural markers with them, but yet they use the Romanian language in everyday communication.

This chapter analyzes the data I collected during several expeditions to the villages of Carașova and Iabalcea in the years between 2013 and 2017. My goals were to trace the development of the Krashovani dialect group[6] (henceforth KDG) starting from the most archaic layers and ending with the present, and to draw possible parallels between the social and linguistic realia of the community in past and present.

Drawing from the data on Balkan history and ethnogenesis, using the methods of Slavic and Romance dialectology, ethnolinguistics, Balkan studies, and theory of language contact, while also paying attention to the phenomena of bilingualism observed in this community, I shall try to determine which intralinguistic, social and political factors contributed to the formation of KDG in the villages of Carașova and Iabalcea.

2 Krashovani as a Banat people: history and identity

The historical region of Banat is a territory bounded by the Tisa, Mureș and Danube rivers, by the mountains Chicera Comărli, Poiana Rusca, and Morarul, which separate Banat from Transylvania. The area of the region is 28,526 km^2: 18,966 km^2 belong to Romania, one third belongs to Serbia (9,276 km^2), and a small area (284 km^2) in the north-west, at the confluence of the rivers Mureș and Tisa, is now a part of Hungary (Buzarnescu & Pribac 2002). Banat is the place where the Krashovani have been formed as a (sub)ethnos and their history, culture, and language must be considered in its context.

In all probability, the population of Banat consisted of Slavs (Serbs) and Romanians (Romanized Dacians) between, approximately, the fifth and sixth centuries and the Hungarian conquests of the eleventh century (Vinogradov 1987:

---

6 See note 15 for more information on this term.

16–20; Barnea et al. 2001: 725–739). The Ottoman period (1552–1718) left significant traces in the idioms of these peoples (Radan & Bošnjaković 2010). The Slavic presence in the plains of Banat has been demonstrated by some archaeological findings and by the local toponymic terminology, mostly noted in areas near the Tisa and Danube rivers.[7]

In the later Middle Ages, Banat became a battle ground in Europe's war against the Ottoman Empire, which was gaining more and more in force. Frequent attacks of Turks and devastation of the villages between Timișoara and Lugoj ended in 1503 with the signing of a peace treaty that became the first agreement establishing the Turkish-Hungarian border. From that moment, traders were able to cross the border and trade under the laws of the host state (Engel 2001: 360). However, in the 1520s, with the Ottoman Empire in its heyday and the Kingdom of Hungary in a serious crisis, the latter had to give away most of the strategically important fortresses to the Turks. In 1552 Timișoara, which later gained unofficial status as Banat's capital, was also occupied. The Timișoara eyalet existed until 1716 when Eugene of Savoy conquered the city and, in 1718, the Treaty of Požarevac (Passarowitz) was signed (Bromley et al. 1963: 262–263; Krstić 2010: 86). Some historians believe this to be the beginning of a new era for Banat and that it has since been undertaking its own course of development as a separate region (Buzarnescu & Pribac 2002).

In the second half of the 18th century, on the left bank of the Danube, the formation of the Military Frontier begins (Rom *Granița militară bănățeană*, BCMS *Banatska vojna granica*, Germ *Banater Militärgrenze*). Superiors of the Military Frontier were subordinate directly to the court military council. In peacetime, men were engaged in agriculture, in wartime they served as soldiers, "a human fence against the Ottomans" (Clewing & Schmidt 2011: 316–317, 320; Pavković 2009: 58–61).

Of all the parts of present Vojvodina (the regions of Srem, Banat and Bačka in Serbia), Banat stood particularly well with the authorities of the Habsburg monarchy. They expected it to become an economically prosperous region; people of different confessions and nationalities were sent there with the main criterion of choice being their professional skills. A special role was assigned to German colonists as loyal subjects and good workers, builders and soldiers (Mitrović 2004:

---

[7] G. Weigand considered the Banat toponymy to be more of a Bulgarian than a Serbo-Croatian type, however, later researchers either used the neutral term "Slavic" (K. Scheiner), or spoke about "features of East-Bulgarian and West-Serbian dialects" (J. Melich). I. Kniesza does not find "undoubtedly Bulgarian toponyms" in Banat at all (Petrovici 1943: 6–7). E. Petrovici proposes to distinguish two layers of Slavic toponyms in Banat: the first and older one of Bulgarian type and the second and newer one of a Serbo-Croatian type resulting from migrations from the Balkan Peninsula in the 15th century (*Dubova, Belareca, Cutina*) (Petrovici 1943: 18, 37, 38). A. Loma is also known for his contributions to the study of Slavic toponymy in Banat (Loma 2010).

125–126, 130; Clewing & Schmitt 2011: 320). Thus, a series of measures undertaken by the authorities formed the basis for a multi-ethnic and multi-lingual social development.[8] According to the 1770 census, Banat hosted 181,639 Romanians, 78,780 Serbs, 8,683 Bulgarians, 5,272 Romani, 42,201 Swabians, Italians and French, 353 Jews; in total 317,928 people. However, all these neighbouring ethnic and linguistic groups were to some extent isolated from one another. In 1992, in Romania in the county (Rom *judeţ*) of Timiş alone there were, among others, Romanians, Hungarians, Germans, Serbs, Romani, Ukrainians, Bulgarians, Slovaks, Jews, Czechs, Croats, Lipovans, Poles, Greeks, Turks, Armenians, and Tatars (Buzarnescu & Pribac 2002; Jordan 1995). Historians believe that the territory has never witnessed any serious or protracted interethnic conflicts. This situation has been due to the presence of a strong government that organized and supported colonization, and favoured the unity of the various Christian denominations in the region (Hurezan & Colta 2002: 91). For our study, the following fact is important: in order to consolidate the peoples living in this territory and to strengthen religious institutionalization, terms such as the "Illyrian nation" were put back into usage. The "Illyrians" were Orthodox Romanians and Serbs of Banat, who in 1690 were granted "Illyrian privileges"; i. e., the right to work in economic and political spheres, or the system of secondary and higher education, so that the Illyrian nation might have the same rights as Hungarians throughout the territory of the empire. Nikola Pavković reports on the creation of the "Illyrian" and "Vlacho-Illyrian" infantry regiments on the "old Illyrian border". After a century, however, the Serbian-Romanian "union" disintegrated (Boldureanu 2004: 30; Pavković 2009: 59; Konior 2020).

So, what role do the Krashovani people play in linguistic and cultural mosaic of Banat? As in many other cases, this (sub)ethnic group does not fit in with the simple opposition of "autochthonous ~ alien" people. Not all the researchers share the same opinion concerning ancestral homeland of the Krashovani.[9] Ivan Popović, Jovan Erdeljanović, and Mihai Radan consider them to be descendants

---

[8] Thus, the Germans, along with their native language, spoke Romanian and Hungarian; Serbs and Bulgarians were almost always bilingual, as Romanian was learned as a second language in their families; Jews spoke different languages. Along with Slovak, most residents of the town of Nădlac spoke Romanian and Hungarian (Buzarnescu & Pribac 2002). These data should be verified by the linguistic study of multilingualism in Banat. At the moment, the literature on this issue is scarce.

[9] According to different popular etymologies, the ethnonym "Krashovani" arose from the Bosnian toponym *Kruševo* or Serbian *Kruševac*. However, there are more than twenty similar toponyms on the map of the Balkan Peninsula, for example, the Macedonian town of *Kruševo*, an important center of Vlach (Aromanian) culture. The fact that priests were sent to the microregion from the province of Srebrena Bosna, is also believed to be an argument for the Bosnian origin of the Krashovani, but among the missionaries there were also Croatian, German and local priests

of the first Slavs who came to the Balkans in the 7th century, settled north of the Danube and mixed subsequently with several waves of migrants from different regions of the Balkan Peninsula. This theory is partially supported by linguistic data (Radan 2015; Belić & Erdeljanović 1925; Popović 1955).

The second colonization, apparently, occurred in the 15th–16th centuries from the area of Kruševac, Niš, Vranje, Skopje, Prizren and Priština (the upper course of the Morava river). As a result, a compactly living Slavic speaking community was formed in the Karashevo microregion.

The third colonization is attributed to the middle of the 18th century. Bulgarian Catholics (Rom *chiproviceni*) came to Banat. Albanian Clementines (Rom *clementini*), who came in 1740, are also mentioned in chronicles. These migrations may be associated with the later attribution of the Krashovani to the Bulgarian nation and with the hypothesis of their Albanian origin (Simu 1939: 43–44).[10]

Carașova is the largest Krashovani village and the most important cultural and economic centre of the microregion. It is also one of the oldest settlements in Banat: the local fortress (Rom *Cetatea Turcului*, BCMS *Turski grad*) is mentioned for the first time in 1247 under the name of *Castrum Crassou* (Radan 2015: 32). The oldest surviving records of births, deaths and marriages (dated 1726) contain data on the deceased at the age of 100 years. This allows us to conclude that the Krashovani had already lived in Banat in the middle of the 16th century. Until the end of the 1740s, which coincides with the first half of the "Illyrian nation" century of existence, a large number of Romanian surnames, such as *Beul*[11] and *Lackul*, are found in the records. These records also prove that a direct contact between Krashovani and Romanian speakers was taking place in the microregion at that time and resulted in mixed marriages. In most such cases, brides had a Romanian surname, and grooms had a Slavic one. Subsequently, the wives who had come to Karashevo, did not interrupt their relations with neighbouring Romanian-speaking villages (Doman, Cuptoare, Ričica [present Reșița]), where their relatives lived. Traian Simu compares this feature of the Krashovani ethnogenesis to a specific process of diffusion he calls "osmosis", and believes that it was facilitated by the ecclesiastical authority of that time in the microregion, consisting of Franciscans, Jesuits, and secular priests who welcomed assimilation of the Romanian population in order to spread their religion (Simu 1939: 80–83). So, in this case we

---

(Deleanu 1999: 46; Simu 1939: 43–44). For more information, see (Manea-Grgin 2004; Radan 2015: 46–47).

10 Frequently used in KDG the verb *banim* 'to stand' supposedly came to there from Alb *banoj* (id.) and may be an evidence of the direct contact between the KDG and the Albanian language in the past, although no other Albanisms have been found in the KDG (Petrovici 1935: 223–224).

11 This surname is still common in the microregion, especially in the village of Iabalcea.

are not dealing with community migration from one region to another, but with a stage-by-stage formation of the Krashovani (sub)ethnos on the territory of Banat. As will be shown later, the same is also true for the linguistic variety.

In the 20th century, the modern history of the Krashovani people begins. No collectivization was carried out in the microregion. Local men were forced to find jobs in the nearby industrial towns of Reșița and Anina while women took on the burden of house and field work. This difficult situation contributed to their integration in widespread processes of urbanization and technological development, as well as strengthening contacts with the "outside world". Yet the community continued to be fairly closed and conservative until the 1990s, when, due to the economic and political crisis in Romania, most local enterprises in the area were closed. Krashovani men were forced to go to work to Serbia and Croatia, and later to Western European countries (Austria, Germany, Italy, and others). Since then, mainly elderly people and children have resided permanently in the microregion. Radan believes that it was the economic factor (along with centuries of the Catholic Church's work on the modification of Orthodox and pagan customs) that led to a partial loss of the traditional way of life (Radan 2004b: 210–214; Konior 2018).

Also associated with these events is a change of paradigms related to ethnic identity that arose among Krashovani during the second half of the 20th century. Until that time, they had called themselves, mainly, *Karaševci / Crașovenii*, and claimed to speak *karaševski / crașovenęśće* (Crețan, Kun & Vesalon 2014; Radan 2004a). This state of affairs was not affected by such historical circumstances as the centuries-old coexistence with Orthodox Romanians and Serbs, the emergence of Balkan nation states, or military conflicts in the region. However, in the context of a serious economic crisis in Romania after the collapse of the Ceaușescu regime, the Croatization of the Krashovani (especially of the younger generation) that already begun in the 19th century, was successfully completed. It is noted that, having received Croatian citizenship, most of the youth went to work in Croatia, at that time a more stable state. Their commitment to the Croatian nation was also influenced by centuries-old confessional links with other Croatians from Croatia, Bosnia and Herzegovina, Dalmatia, Bačka (Bunjevci and Šokci) and Banat (the Turopolje communities: Kajkavci, Šokci and descendants of settlers from Lika and Dalmatia, mainly Ikavian Štokavci) (Bara 2011: 62; Crețan, Kun & Vesalon 2014). Of the two options, one of which was largely indicated by the linguistic factor and territorial proximity (Serbs), and the other by confessional affiliation (Croats), the Krashovani chose the one whose representatives were more open to dialogue.[12] In 1930s, Petrovici wrote: "It is at school and in

---

12 There are some indirect evidence that the Krashovani (or a part of them) could have professed Orthodox Christianity in the remote past (Radan 2015: 47–57).

church that the Krashovani learned they were Croats". This linguist also considered religion the main reason why they were not assimilated by Romanians (Petrovici 1935, in Deleanu 1999: 42). Simu considered that the Krashovani managed to preserve their idiom with the help of Catholic missionary priests of Slavic origin[13] who quickly mastered the local variety (Simu 1939: 43).

Currently, local priests are sent directly from Croatia or, being of Krashovani origin, are trained and ordained in Zagreb. Services are conducted mainly in the Croatian language, both in the Slavic-speaking villages and in the Romanian-speaking village of Iabalcea (Konior & Makarova 2015: 85). The official position of the Krashovani clergy is that *karaševski* is a regional form of the Croatian language, and the ethnonym *Krašovani* is nothing but a given nickname ("*nadimak samo za selo*") (Konior & Makarova 2015: 89).

3 KDG in a language contact perspective

The Krashovani dialect group, together with the Svinița dialect,[14] is the most archaic Serbo-Croatian variety on the territory of the Romanian Banat. All varieties,[15] apart from the Romanian dialect of Iabalcea discussed further in this text, are Štokavian and Ekavian Serbo-Croat dialects with a certain number of Ikavisms that appeared quite late (Radan 2015: 102). Let us review some of the main features of the KDG that distinguish them against the background of other Serbo-Croatian dialects. At the phonetic level: the phonologically independent status of the jat reflex in a stressed position: *d'efka*[16] 'young woman', *t'ęlo* 'body', *d'ęca* 'children' (which allows us to attribute the KDG to so-called "peripheral dialects with unreplaced jat" (Ivanov 1988)); preservation of the initial consonant

---

13 According to the Vatican archives, Croatian priests have served in the Romanian Banat since the 16th century (Vlahović 1999 [2000]: 76).
14 For more information regarding the Svinița dialect, see (Tomić 1984; Sobolev 1995).
15 Until the 20th century, attention of the scientific community was concentrated mainly on the village of Carașova, while the remaining six Krashovani villages remained poorly researched. As a consequence, instead of "the Krashovani dialect" spoken in all seven villages, now we are talking about seven different dialects (or "the Krashovani dialect group" (Radan 2000: 5), for the reason that these dialects have some differences among them, especially at the phonetic and lexical levels. Depending on the reflexes of reduced vowels *ь and *ъ, the Krashovani Slavic dialects are divided into three groups: in Carașova (and Iabalcea) ə > a, in Clocotici, Lupac, Nermed and Vodnic ə was preserved, while in Rafnic mainly ə > ę.
16 All data gathered by the author of this text are given in IPA transcription, while the linguistic examples found in literature are presented as in the source (i. e., with the use of the standard BSCM and Romanian letters).

group č'r-, which is one of the most important arguments for the KDG centuries-old isolation from the rest of the Serbo-Croatian space (Radan 2015: 92–100, 195): č'ərn 'black', č'r'ešńe 'sweet cherry', č'ęręvo 'hose; bowels'. In morphology archaic inflections in the noun declension are observed: -ove/-eve and -e in nominative plural: satove 'clocks', cigańe 'Gypsies', kotlovę 'cooking pots', vragovę 'devils' (in Štokavian dialects, the -ovi/-evi endings have been noted since the 16th century (Petrovici 1935: 136)); auxiliary verb forms in the future tense lam, laš, la, lamo, latę, laju[17] (< proto-Slavic *vĭlamĭ (Petrovici 1935: 190–191)): laš da si 'you want to be', lam da popęvam 'I will sing'. In lexicon: some very archaic words, such as: p'ita 'bread', per'ina 'pillow', g'orun 'oak', v'eligdan 'Easter', več'era 'evening', m'ajka 'grandmother', n'əna 'father', sv'etak 'holiday', prosvet 'fire, bonfire', brnja / bljudo 'dish', slap 'weak', indi 'somewhere else', lud'e 'people', ozli 'near', sliva 'plum', and others (Radan 2000: 216).

Other speakers of Serbo-Croatian dialects in Romanian Banat[18] live at the distance of at least 60 km from the Karashevo microregion, so the contact between them and the Krashovani has been of moderate intensity (Radan 2004a: 178–179). However, in their article "On the common origin of the archaic Serbian dialects from the Romanian Banat (Banat Montenegrin, Krashovani and Svinița dialects)", Radan and Milin made an important conclusion about the unity of these most archaic Serbian dialects of the Romanian Banat. Despite the fact that these varieties belong to different subdialects of the Serbo-Croatian dialect continuum (the Svinița one is of Prizren-Timok type, "Banat Montenegrin" are of the Smederevo-Vršac type, and the Krashovani dialects are of the Kosovo-Resava origin),[19] it is

---

[17] Petrovici believes these relics from Common Slavic could indicate the Krashovani connection to the Bosnian territory (Petrovici 1935: 190–191).

[18] The Serbian and Croatian dialects of the Romanian Banat are divided into several groups: the Serbian Banat dialects (northern, central and southern subtypes are distinguished); Klisura dialect; Svinița dialect; the Krashovani dialects; the Serbian dialect from Recaș; Banat Montenegrin dialects; the Croatian dialect from Checea (Radan 2004a: 178–179).

[19] Among the features that unite all these dialects, there are: preservation of final -l at the end of a word or a syllable (petal 'rooster', debel 'large, fat', si oral 'you plowed'); softer pronunciation of affricates compared to the majority of Štokavian dialects; comparative formation with the po particle and initial adjectival form; the archaic ending -omu in the dative singular in case of the masculine form of the adjectives babinomu 'to a granny's [e.g. house]', dobromu 'to a good [e.g. man]'); the predominance of the ending -o after soft stems in the nominative and accusative cases of adjectives of the neuter gender (sinjo more 'blue sea', goveđo meso 'beef meat', svo selo 'the whole village'); forms niki 'somebody', ničiji 'somebody's' of indefinite pronouns; the contraction dn > n in neutral jeno 'one (it)' and feminine jena 'one (she)' of the numeral jedan; frequency of genitive constructions with the preposition od: čorba od paradajsa 'tomato soup', mleko od krave 'cow's milk', meso od kokoške 'chicken meat'; use of the dative-possessive constructions typical for the Romanian language nena slugi mojemu 'my servant's father (lit.

supposed that they might have arisen from an extinct Banat Slavic idiom whose speakers have mixed with the Serbs migrating into Banat from the 14th to the 18th centuries (Milin & Radan 2002: 64–65).

Along with the archaisms, in KDG there are some innovations that appeared at different points of history in situations of language contact, or in interaction with neighbouring or similar cultures. Although the microregion was a part of the Austro-Hungarian Empire for a long time, both Hungarian and German influence on KDG is limited to some lexical borrowings: *šajtóv* 'barrel valve' probably, from Hung *sajtol* 'to plug', or *sajtó* 'mechanical press', *Nermit'* the name of one of the Krashovani villages, *galer* 'collar' from Hung *gallér*, *poprika* 'bell pepper', 'paint' from Hung *paprika*[20] (Petrovici 1935: 46; Radan 2000: 93). Undoubtedly, the Krashovani dialects have been in the most intensive contact with the Romanian language, which is especially evident from archaic and newer borrowings from this language: *palarija* 'hat' < Rom *pălărie*; *kofetarija* 'confectionary' < Rom *cofetărie*; *cinta* 'aim'< Rom *țintă*, *skrum(j)era* 'ashtray' < Rom *scrumieră*; *dor* < Rom *dor* 'longing for smth. / smb.'; *kukurudz* < Rom *cucurudz* 'maize'; *cuknuti* < Rom *a țuca* 'to kiss'; *mrkonj* < Rom dial. *morcoń* 'carrot'; *pironj* < Rom dial. *piroń* 'nail'; *guša* < Rom *gușă* 'craw' (Petrovici 1935: 46; Radan 2000: 93, 204–210; Milin & Radan 2002: 60). In phonetics, the main contact phenomena include: simplification of the accent system; loss of intonation and of qualitative and quantitative characteristics of stress. In grammar, we observe mixing of the case endings of locative/instrumental of place and accusative of direction: *sedim u Rekaš* 'I'm in Recaș', *bio pred mene* '[he] was in front of me', *lonac je pod trpezu* 'the saucepan is under the table', the analytical comparative and superlative of adjectives, and others. Syntactic innovations include: reduplication of personal pronouns in the accusative and dative: *njemu mu dal imanje* 'he gave him the property', *vam vi povedal* 'I've said to you', and frequent postposition of the attribute: *idem sestrom mojom* 'I go with my sister', *idem človekam tem* 'I go with this man'. As for the lexical level, it seems to be the most permeable to the Romanian influence, which is responsible for greater dynamics of changes here. Numerous old and newer borrowings from the standard Romanian and from the Banat dialect are now present in all possible lexical-semantic groups of KDG: *mašina* 'car', *programiraju* 'they arrange', *distrakcija* 'distraction', *porta* 'door', *pikature* 'drops', *cast* 'covered fire-pan'(Radan 2009: 193–201).

"father to my servant")', *lajanje psetu* 'dog's barking (lit. "barking to a dog"); lexical archaisms *vrag* 'devil', *smetana* 'sour cream', *krstine* 'lower part of the back', *grdina* 'garden', among others (Milin & Radan 2002: 56–65).

[20] Radan thinks that German borrowings in KDG are quite numerous. They continued to penetrate into the KGD up to 1918 (Radan 2015: 170–171).

The Romanian influence on the Krashovani dialects must be considered both in a diachronic perspective (centuries-old coexistence with the Romanian Banat dialect, a Romanian component in the Krashovani ethnogenesis) and in synchronic perspective (as the language of the national majority, as a result of increasing number of mixed marriages in recent decades, through Romanian television, Internet and other media). The combination of these factors is gradually leading to a decrease of the lexical competence of the Krashovani in comparison with their grammatical competence (Radan & Bošnjaković 2010: 151), and to the formation of a special type of bilingualism in the microregion. Most adult and young Krashovani are bilinguals, for whom the first language is Slavic, and the second language is Romanian, in its almost standard variety. Only elderly women who have never worked outside their native village and do not have close relatives among local Romanians, or people from Iabalcea in general, are not fluent in Romanian.

Representatives of all generations of speakers frequently use Romanian discourse markers, such as: *bun* 'well', *haide* 'come on', *pe părerea mea* 'in my opinion', *deci* 'so', *cum se zice* 'as they say', *salut* 'hi'. "Hybrid constructions" are also quite interesting: *vade ši teško < vai și amar* 'woe unto me!'(Radan 2000: 158); *budi ozbiljan, pe kuvănt* 'be serious, honestly' (Lațchici 2012: 17).

Also, modern Krashovani speech tolerates a large number of the Romanian insertions:[21]

Table 1 Insertions

On drʒi ruke, i ona ga poʎe, ili on utʃini ovako si prstne na kuʃulju, gaʨe, **port natsional**, *nije bil* **kostum ʃi to**.	'He holds his hands, and she pours, or he will do so, and the water splashes on his shirt, pants, traditional clothes, back then there were no costumes.'
Sad je ʃlajer, rokʎa za **mireasu**.	'Now they have costumes, and dresses for brides.'
To je neka dr̩ʒava **de dinkolo**.	'This is some foreign country.'

---

[21] Differentiation of borrowing from the code-switching phenomena is often a problematic issue. The following criteria are normally applied: frequency (borrowing affects the lexicon of the recipient language, while code switching can appear in the individual speech), as well as phonology (Poplack & Sankoff 1988). The first criterion cannot always be applied in the case of idioms that do not have a standard (and in our opinion, no modern South Slavic language is related to the KDG as a literary norm, neither can it be applied in the case of small corpora). Neither can we rely on the phonological criterion in the case of contact between the KDG and the Romanian Banat dialect, since these idioms are phonologically relatively close.

*Da im dam **in ʒur** 8 kilo mesa.*	'I'll give them around 8 kg of meat.'
*Nije bilo kako sad, nije bilo **bogacije**.*	'It wasn't as it is now, there was no wealth.'
*Bili smo petog augusta ili, **mə rog**, kad.*	'We were there on the fifth of August, or, for all I know, when.'
*Da imaʃ **amintire t͡ʃe** bil Sveti Ilija.*	'For you to have a memory of Saint Elijah.'
*Ne dod͡ʒu dok ne znaju malko **aprobare**.*	'They won't come until they know there is a kind of approval.'
*Sad je **dezastru**!*	'Now it's a catastrophe!'
*Nesu **kapabil** da vesele prijateʎi.*	'They are not capable of having fun, the groom's and bride's parents.'

For such insertions, I find it convenient to use the term nonce loans that first appeared in (Poplack & Sankoff 1988: 47–104). Nonce, or occasional loans are not necessarily repeatable and widely distributed, but just like borrowings they have a high degree of integration into L1. In a later article, Shana Poplack and Nathalie Dion, based on their observations of English-origin items in Quebecois French over a period of 61 years, claim that, contrary to a common belief, code-switches are not normally converted to borrowings and, moreover, that the processes underlying these phenomena are not the same. Borrowings (words that occur more frequently) and nonce (occasional) loans are already established (i. e., adapted) in the recipient language in the moment of speech. But they do not involve a process of mixing itself, as they do not even necessarily come along with good access and knowledge of the donor language. Real switches do, and they are usually multiword (Poplack & Dion 2012: 307–312). It seems that our case argues for that explanation as well. Even now, when the access to Romanian is much wider than it used to be a hundred years ago, multiword code-switches are relatively rare even in the narratives of the middle generation of Krashovani. Moreover, these code-switches seem to be basically grounded in the informants' wish to explain everything I ask in the most understandable way, as they practically repeat in L2 the information given me previously in L1.[22]

---

[22] Similar pragamtics behind code-switching in the village of Palasa in Himara, Albania is mentioned in (Joseph, Ndoci & Dickerson 2019: 230).

Table 2 Multiword switching or self-translations?

U t͡ʃetvrtak, opet je sva famila kod devojke (…), poprave rizant͡se, ja znam, t͡ʃupaju ʒivinu, kolat͡ʃe (…)… **Perit͡ʃore, sarmale ʃi praʒiturʲ**.	'On Thursday, the whole family gathers again at the bride's, they make noodles, I don't know, pluck poultry, (make) pies (…) … **Cabbage rolls and cakes**.'
A kapara… **programiraju** kad t͡su kaparu. Onda se vikne kum, kuma, tetka, baba, **un nepot, un veriʃor, un… ʃi ɛa tot aʃa. ʃi se adunə maj mult͡sʲ**.	'And engagement… They arrange when it will be. Then kum is called, kuma, aunt, godmother, **nephew, cousin… And she as well. And many people come together**.'
I onda kad je gotova svadba, tu notʲ, u vtornik uvet͡ʃe, **mart͡s sarə kind e nunta, ej abja aʃtept** kad ukradu, kad ukradu.	'And when the wedding is over, that night, on Tuesday evening, **on Tuesday evening, when the wedding is, they cannot wait** to be stolen (brides' accessories), to be stolen.'
ʃi kind ij pun kununə la mireasə, fiekare se duɡe ʂi pun akolo un ban, o sutə de lej, ʃi spune aʃa – Jo- t͡sʲ dau put͡sin, Dumnezeu sə-t͡sʲ de mult – norok ʃi sənatate. **Ja ti malko, Bog da ti da mnogo – sret͡ɕu, ʒivot i zdravʎe**.	'And when they put the nuptial crown on the bride, everyone goes and puts a penny in, one hundred lei, and says – I'll give to you little, let God give you a lot – luck and health. **I'll give to you little, let God give you a lot – luck and health**.'

Thus, the Romanian (or Eastern Romance) influence on the Krashovani dialects can be divided into two periods: an ancient one, seen, among other things, in the grammatical structure of dialects; and a second, modern one. Until the 20th century, all contacts with the Romanian population were of moderate intensity and consisted of relatively rare mixed marriages and trade with neighbouring Romanian villages. In the 20th century, Romanian became the state language in this part of Banat. In the 1950s, the Krashovani went to work in factories in neighbouring industrial towns on a massive scale, and, finally, from the 1970s and the 80s, public and church condemnation of exogamy has gradually weakened. All these factors are reflected in the Krashovani group of dialects, which have managed to preserve their grammatical structure as a whole but are losing integrity at the lexical level (Radan & Bošnjaković 2010: 151).

4 The Iabalcea phenomenon

The ethno-linguistic situation that has developed in the smallest[23] Krashovani village of Iabalcea is less typical. In general, it can be described as follows: having Romanian as the dominant Language 1 (spoken at home), the local people passively know the Slavic idiom as Language 2.

The first linguists working in the microregion had already mentioned that people in Iabalcea spoke mostly Romanian, so the shift to that language must have happened no later than at the beginning of the 19th century (Syrku 1899: 641; Petrovici 1935: 4). The moment of the shift was not documented, nor present in the memory of older people. In our informants' versions, the story that workers from different parts of Romania had come to Iabalcea and married local girls, resulting in the village began to speak Romanian, is often repeated.

| *Dziċe kə o fost vreunu slugə, nu stɕu tʃe a fost, de undeva, unu dən, də la romini. ʃi aşa o rəmas ələ akolo, ʃi o rəmas Iabaltʃea ku romin^j, sə vorbɛascə romineʃtɕe.* | 'They say that there was a servant, I do not know who he was, from where [he came], a Romanian. And he stayed there, and Iabalcea remained with Romanians, to speak Romanian.' |

Representatives of the middle and younger generations know the local Slavic dialect only passively, while among elderly people the degree of proficiency can vary from the ability to translate some of the lexemes from Romanian to Krashovani Slavic to the ability to produce coherent texts, in which the interference of their first language can be traced. Nevertheless, they all refer to themselves as Krashovani (or, over the last few decades, as Croat) people, profess a Catholic faith, and are included in the historical, social, cultural and economic contexts of this community:

| *Eu ʃtɕiu krɔata, da. Detʃ, kraʃoveneʃtɕe, kum nisəm noj. Na... natsionalitatɕe nisəm krɔats^j. Numa' kə vorbim romaneʃtɕe, satu əsta. Da noj tot krɔats^j səntem, natsionalitatɛa noᵃstre.* | 'I know Croatian, yes. That is, Krashovani, as we say. Our ethnicity is Croat. But we speak Romanian in this village. But we are also Croats, our ethnicity.' |

On the one hand, the residents of Iabalcea have a full competence in Romanian; it is undoubtedly their L1, learned at home since childhood and used in communication in the village and in the country. My informants can freely generate phonetically, grammatically and semantically correct utterances and texts of any duration

---

[23] At the moment there are about 70 houses (according to Nicușor Ifca, one of our informants from Iabalcea).

or subject (Konior & Sobolev 2017). The following dialectisms noted in Iabalcea allow us to correlate their variety to the Romanian Banat dialect, but most of them alternate with literary forms: epenthetic *v* in diphthongs with *u* (*a* AUX.3SG *luvat* PP 'he took'), preservation of the affricate *d̂z* at the beginning of a word (*d̂zik*-ø PRES-1SG 'I am saying' ~ *zitʃ-e* PRES-3SG 'he is saying'); preservation of the archaic sonant *ɲ* (*ɲe* PRO -*am* AUX.1PL *dus* PP 'we went' ~ *spun-e* PRES-3SG 'he tells'); appearance of the affricate *d̂ʑ* and fricative *ɕ* in the position *d, c + e, i* (*aiɕea* ADV 'here' ~ *aitʃea* ADV 'here', *und̂ʑe* WH.Q 'where' ~ *dimineatsa* ADV '(in the) morning'); archaic preposition *prən* (***prən*** PREP 'on' ~ *pe* PREP 'on'); the analytic perfect auxiliary verb 'to have' in the form *o, or* (*o* AUX.3SG *spəlat* PP 'she washed' ~ *a* AUX.3SG *lovit* PP 'he hit') (Coteanu 1961: 90–94; Konior & Sobolev 2017).

On the other hand, local people's competence in the Slavic Krashovani idiom is limited. They know it as L2, at least passively, gaining familiarity with it from childhood in church[24] and in conversations with Slavic-speaking neighbours (including women from other Krashovani villages who came to Iabalcea after marriage). A number of experiments conducted by Andrey N. Sobolev showed significantly uneven distribution of language competence among the Romanian-speaking inhabitants of Iabalcea in the Slavic Krashovani dialect on different language levels.

Competence in integral utterance and coherent text generation is incomplete. A considerable portion of the informants resolutely refuses to generate narratives or to conduct a dialogue in the Krashovani dialect, asserting their inability to do so (*Nu ʃtiu!* 'I don't know! I can't!'). Some informants are able to produce complete utterances and even small cohesive texts in Slavic,[25] but most of these contain spontaneous shifts into Romanian, hesitation and equivalent recalling (Konior & Sobolev 2017).

*Su jeli rizantsi, periʃore, krompiri, kolaĉi, i… toliko. Kat se t͡ʃinilo neʃto da kaʑemo u! slatko za **vard̂ʑe** te alte krude, kum se spune … kum **d̂ʑiku** in **krǫate**? Salate! Salate od in, od slatko, slatka kapusta! Kapusta, kapusta **se spune in krǫate**.*	'We used to eat noodles, meatballs, potatoes, pies, and… everything. When they made something, how to say, eh! sweet for cabbage, these other raw, as it's called… how will it be in Croatian? Salads! Salads [made] of, of sweet cabbage! Cabbage, cabbage in Croatian.'

---

[24] The church service in Iabalcea is currently held in two languages: liturgical texts are sung in Croatian, and the sermon is read in Romanian.
[25] Only one of our informants born in Iabalcea, but living for fifty years in Carașova, seems to speak very fluent Slavic. Her speech analysis can be found in (Konior 2019a).

However, the Iabalcea inhabitants do have the following competences in L2:
1) full listener's competence;
2) a likely full phonetic and phonological competence (for example, distinguishing the Krashovani /ę/ and /ẹ/, distinguishing /t͡ʃ/ and /t͡ɕ/);
3) apparently, sufficient morphonological competence (for example, the implementation of the rule 'orę SG, or'ẹsi PL 'walnut');
4) full competence in morphology, as evidenced by: substantive, pronominal and adjective inflexion (quantitative: *dva* NUM *t͡ʃlovẹka* GEN/PAUC 'two men'; case: *na* PREP *taɲiru* LOC 'on the plate'; *polije* PRES.3SG *mladoʒeɲu* ACC 'He/she will water the bridesman'; *pore* PREP *mlade* GEN 'near the bride', *uvate* 3PL *vodu* ACC 'They will grab the water', *taɲir* NOM/ACC *s tortom* INSTR 'plate with the cake'; *u* PREP *Austriji* LOC 'in Austria'; *malomu* ADJ.DAT *detetu* DAT 'to a small child', *idu* PRES.3PL *vedram* COM/INSTR 'They go with the bucket'; *svakomu* DAT 'to the every person'; adjective feminine plural: *babe* NOM/ACC *stare* NOM/ACC 'old women'; *ret͡ʃi* NOM/ACC *drugat͡ʃke* NOM/ACC 'other words'); verb inflexion (*kaʒ-em*.PRES-1SG 'I say'; *odi-ʃ*.PRES-2SG 'you go' ~ *razume-ʃ*. PRES-2SG 'you understand'; *se* PRO *id-e*.PRES-3SG 'they go (impersonal)' ~ *se* PRO *pip-a*.PRES-3SG 'they touch (impersonal)' ~ *vel-i*.PRES-3SG 'he says'; *zna-mo*.PRES-1PL 'we know'; *govori-te*.PRES-2PL 'you tell'; *ima-ju*.PRES-3PL 'they have', *id-u*.PRES-3PL 'they go' ~ *govor-e*.PRES-3PL 'they tell', *uvat-e*.PRES-3PL 'they grab'). It is interesting that in the Krashovani speech of the Iabalcea inhabitants, despite the dominant position of Romanian, the full nominal word inflexion, including the form of the locative as a case of location, is preserved (*na* PREP *taɲiru* LOC 'on the plate'; *u* PREP *Austriji* LOC 'in Austria');
5) partially sufficient lexical competence of the following lexical-semantic groups ("Agriculture (common terms)", "House utensils", "Agricultural inventory", "Animals", "Cultivated plants");
6) full competence in generating etiquette speech formulas in dialogues: – *Da ste zdravi! – I vi ste zdravi! – Fala!* 'Be healthy!' – 'And you!' – 'Thank you'. Between Romanian and Krashovani formulas equivalency relations are established: *Da te Bog ʒivi!* ~ *Sə te binekuvînteze d͡zeu!* 'May the Lord protect you' (Konior & Sobolev 2017).

Possible contact-induced phenomena in morphosyntax and syntax include the following categories: the case of the direct object (*Su*.AUX *jel-i*.PST-3PL *rizant͡s-i* NOM, *periʃore* NOM, *krompiri* NOM, *kolat͡ʃi* NOM 'They ate noodles, vegetables, potatoes, cakes'. *Oni* PRO *govor-e*.PRES-3PL *malo* ADV *druga* ADJ.NOM *forma* NOM 'They speak in a slightly different way'); neutralization of the opposition comitative ~ instrumental (*id-u*.PRES-3PL *vedram* COM/DAT 'They go with the bucket'); irregularities in the case forms use in prepositional constructions (*salate*... ACC *od* PREP *slatko* ADJ, *slatka* NOM *kapusta* NOM 'sweet cabbage salads'); attribute's postposition (*glava* SUBST *tvoja* POSS 'your head', *babe* SUBST *stare* ADJ 'old women', *retʃi* SUBST *drugatʃke* ADJ 'different words' ~ *druga* ADJ *forma* SUBST 'different form', *slatka* ADJ *kapusta* SUBST 'sweet cabbage', *malomu* ADJ *detetu* SUBST 'to a little child'); preposition of verbal clitics (*su*.AUX *jel-i*.PST-3PL 'they ate', *su*.AUX *nosil-i*.PST-3PL 'they brought', *se*.REFL *tʃinil-o*.PST-3SG 'was done', *se*.REFL *poprav-i*.PRES-3SG 'repair, fix'); avoiding *pro drop* (*mi* PRO *zna-mo*.PRES-1PL 'you know', *vi* PRO *govori-te*.PRES-2PL 'you speak', *oni* PRO *uvat-e*.PRES-3PL 'they catch') (Konior & Sobolev 2017).

All of the above says that the case of the Krashovani dialect used by Iabalcea's residents gives evidence to an increased degree of accommodation to Romanian. Nevertheless, for most phenomena (postposition of the attribute, nominative of theme, etc.), for the moment it would be more accurate to speak of an increased frequency of constructions isomorphic to Romanian, in comparison with some "typically Slavic constructions", rather than of a much greater degree of alloglossia in comparison with the Krashovani dialects in Slavic-speaking villages.

Thus, in Iabalcea we are dealing with a nonequilibrium bilingualism phenomenon, manifested in a whole spectrum from the lack of ability to generate utterances to systemic lexical lacunae in a number of lexical-semantic groups, and other limitations in L2 for a number of speakers (Konior & Sobolev 2017).

In this regard, Krashovani onomastics are worth examining. Mile Tomici writes that the share of Romanian names in the Krashovani onomastics is more than 51% with 60% of bearers (Tomić 1972: 221). If we speak specifically about the Iabalcea onomasticon, the following surnames were found on the gravestones of the local cemetery in September, 2017: *Beul, Ursul, Ifca, Rebegila, Kokora, Baciuna, Padineanț, Ghițoi, Filka, Toma*. Apparently, only one of them (*Ifca*) is of Slavic origin. Also, one of my informants gave the examples of typical nicknames in Iabalcea. They are as follows: *Ceapă, Gâscă, Straică, Chioru, Pușcă*. Such data make us think of Iabalcea's particular marriage geography. Generally in the Karashovani villages, endogamy within a single locality was considered to be the most convenient and profitable from the point of view of property and economics (Konior 2018). Of course, Iabalcea's small size did not always allow locals to adopt this strategy. According to our informants, many of the villagers have one of their parents from Nermed (the closest neighbouring village, alongside with Carașova) or other villages of the microregion; most of the elderly women moved there from Carașova after marriage. As for the much more significant Romanian component in Iabalcea compared to other Krashovani villages, we can only build more or less plausible assumptions. Perhaps before the 19th century, the male population had been decreasing as a result of constant conflicts with the Turks, which forced this part of the community to violate the principle of endogamy and accept foreigners. However, Iabalcea remained in the Krashovani sphere of influence due to a special geographical situation: on one side the village is surrounded by forests and mountains, on the other – by the Krashovani settlements. Let us not forget that the Catholic Church, once having strengthened its position in the micro-region, did not want to weaken it. One of our informants reported that "there could not be many Romanians here, the priest would not have even let you marry them!" which is probably true – but the 19th and 20th century situation is all we know (Konior 2018). To have a deeper look into cultural and linguistic components, one should examine the strata which are likely to preserve archaic elements, as well as reflect the dynamics of change. In the next section, I shall analyse the spiritual heritage and cultural vocabulary of Carașova and Iabalcea through the example of wedding rituals and kinship terminology.

5 Analysis of vocabulary: wedding rites and terms of kinship

This section analyses lexemes recorded in the expeditions of 2013 to 2017 to the villages of Carașova and Iabalcea. They all are connected to the traditional Krashovani wedding both in a narrow terminological way and through a secondary sign function acquired already as an element of a rite.[26] In order to understand whether or not a symbiotic interaction between Slavic and Romance languages and cultures took place in Iabalcea, and, if so, what its nature was, we analysed traditional wedding vocabulary. This included terminology of the Krashovani wedding rituals and, in a broader sense, elements of the lexical-semantic group of a traditional wedding: terms of kinship, the names of dishes served, the names of parts of the traditional costume, and the like. As we know, in this field there is a discernible connection between language and culture. The following methods were used to obtain the Iabalcea Romanian correspondences of previously collected Krashovani Slavic words: 1. semi-structured interviews conducted in the

---

26 "Actions that are included into the ritual text are usually not specifically of a ceremonial nature, rather being quite practical, like running, going round something, ejecting, bouncing, burning, dousing with water, etc. They acquire a sign function secondarily, as a part of ritual, in the language of culture. "Primary" signs, i. e., not having utilitarian use, but created specifically for cultural purposes are significantly less common in the language of culture. These are, for example, so-called ritual objects: wedding trees, round loaves, the bride's crown, sheaves of hay, dolls, stuffed animals, etc." (Tolstaya 2013).

Romanian language (based on the questionnaire developed by Anna Plotnikova for the MDABL (Plotnikova 2009)); 2. translation of the Krashovani words into Romanian made by our informants (by elicitation method). Subsequently, the words obtained were combined into bilingual tables with an indication as to their etymology for each case.

It turned out that a significant portion of the lexemes recorded in Carașova are of Slavic origin: *zorŋatʃa* 'kind of a wedding dance', *veseʎe* 'wedding', *kobasitsa* 'sausage', *jabuka* 'apple', *rodbina* 'family', *nastojnik* 'wedding cook', *dar* 'gift', *posteʎina* 'bedclothes', *sukŋa* 'dress', *zlatni novats* 'gold coins', *venats* 'bride's crown', etc. Other notable groups: Romanian borrowings (including many Banat regionalisms and archaisms): *kuskri* 'in-law relatives', *moʃuli* 'guisers', *tsast* 'chafting pan', *tɕutura* 'a vessel for rakia' etc.; Turkisms: *haʎina* 'dress', *marama* 'shawl', *ketsa* 'gore', *kafa* 'coffee' etc.; borrowings from European languages: *misa* 'church service', *ʃtap* 'crabstick', *akordeon* 'accordion', *klarinet* 'clarinet', *kotɕija* 'two-seat carriage', etc. (Skok 1971–1988; Trubachev 1974–2005).

As for the lexical-semantic group of wedding terms in Iabalcea, it seemed necessary to consider the strategies of their formation in relation to the Krashovani set of lexemes. In the tables below, some examples of these strategies are shown.

Table 3 Transfer of a Krashovani Slavic lexeme / cultureme into Romanian

№	Carașova	Etymology	Iabalcea	Etymology
1.	*pogoditi se* 'to make wedding arrangements'	PSl and OChSl *godъ* (HJP)	*se pogodʒi (de nuntə)*	reg. pop. *a se pogodi* 'think, arrange' (from BCMS *pogoditi*) (DLRLC 1955–1957)
2.	*krizmaŋe* 'first communion'	Lat *chrisma* < MGr *chrísma* (HJP)	*krizməit*	from KrSl *krizmanje* (see Rom *hrizmă*) (Scriban 1939)
3.	*nameŋati* 'say wishes to newlyweds'	PSl and OChSl *měna* (HJP)	*a numeni*	in Rom has the meaning 'name, baptize' (Scriban 1939)
4.	*starisvat* 'master of wedding ceremonies'	reg. word, from PSl and OChSl *starъ* and PSl *svatъ (HJP)	*tərisvat / naʃu mik*	reg. 'master of wedding ceremonies' (from BCMS *stari svat*) (DEX 2009); from Lat *nonnus* (DEX 2009); Rom *mic* with the meaning 'small' (most likely, from Lat *miccus*) (Cioránescu 2001)

№ Caraşova	Etymology	Iabalcea	Etymology
5. *dever* 'bridesman'	from PSl *děverъ (HJP)	*dzever*	see Bulg *děver*, BCMS *djever* 'master of wedding ceremonies; bridesman' (Trubachev & Zhuravlev 1974–2005)
6. *sukɲa / rokʎa* 'skirt'	Rom *rochie*; PSl, Balt root (see Rus. *sukno*) (HJP)	*sukɲa / rokija*	reg. word (from BCMS *suknja*)
7. *gaʨiʦe* 'underwear'	dim. from *gaće* 'pants, trousers' (Skok 1971–1988)	*gaʧe / pantaloɲ*	reg. word (from Serb *gače*)
8. *ogrʎak* 'collar'	reg., PSl *gъrdlo* 'throat' (Trubachev & Zhuravlev 1974–2005) > *ogrljak* '(dog-)collar' (Skok 1971–1988)	*ogrlęak*	from KrSl *ogrljak*

Of all the analysed tokens (190 pairs of words and word combinations), the transfer of a Krashovani Slavic lexeme/cultureme into Romanian is used in less than 32 cases. The words 7. *gaʧe*, 6. *sukɲa*, 8. *ogrʎak* and 2. *krizməit* are not present in Romanian dictionaries as regionalisms (although for the first two cases, Romanian analogues are also recorded). Other lexemes, namely: wedding party's names 5. *dzever*, 4. *tərisvat* and verbs 3. *a numeni*, 1. *a se pogodzi* are borrowed from the Slavic languages, present in the dictionaries, but perceived as regional and archaic words (sometimes with different meanings). Probably, the names of wedding dances also belong here. In general, I recorded the following ones: *ʃetajka, zorɲaʧa, portaɲe, slnʧa, zdupatura, dansu bətrinesk, dansu sirbesk*. However, almost all these lexemes appear in the informants' speech in both villages; at the same time, people find it difficult to find a translated equivalent.

Table 4 A Krashovani lexeme / cultureme translation into Romanian

№	Caraşova	Etymology	Iabalcea	Etymology
9.	proʎevaɲe vode 'water-spilling'	PSl and OChSl liti (HJP); PSl and OChSl voda (HJP)	vərsatul apej	from Lat versare 'to spoil'; from Lat aqua (Ciorănescu 2001)
10.	most 'bridge'	OChSl mostъ (Trubachev & Zhuravlev 1974–2005)	podu	from OChSl podъ (DEX 2009)
11.	kut͡slit͡ɕi/uprvit͡ʃe 'lunch at the bride's parents one week after wedding'	prob., from PSl *kucati (Trubachev & Zhuravlev 1974–2005); PSl *pьrvъ (Skok 1971–1988)	kət͡sej	from Lat catellus (Ciorănescu 2001)
12.	proʃba/proʃeɲe 'proposal of marriage'	PSl and OChSl prositi (HJP)	pet͡sit/t͡ʃerut	from Lat petere (pop. form *petire) (Ciorănescu 2001); from Lat quaerere (DEX 2009)
13.	igra/igranka 'horo'	PSl *jьgra, OChSl igrь (HJP)	ʒok/horə	from Lat jocus (DEX 2009); into Rom via Bulg horo (Ciorănescu 2001)
14.	ureku mladu 'to jinx the bride'	PSl *rokъ; PSl *moldъ, OChSl mladъ (HJP)	a ind͡ziokjea pe fatə	Ban variant of Rom a deochea < Lat oc(u)lus; from Lat feta (DEX 2009)
15.	primeɲu mladu 'to dress up bride'	PSl and OChSl měna (HJP); PSl *moldъ OChSl mladъ (HJP)	se imbreɕe mirɛasa	from Lat *imbracare (< braca 'trousers'); mireasă < mire 'groom' – prob., from MGr μύρον (Ciorănescu 2001)
16.	(joj) met͡ɕu krpu 'they put (her) in a shawl'	OChSl mesti (Trubachev & Zhuravlev 1974–2005)	(ij) pun kirpa	from Lat ponere; from Serb krpa (DEX 2009)
17.	ʃiju stek 'they make wedding banner'	PSl *šiti (HJP); PSl *stęgъ, *stěgъ or via Rom steag < Rus стяг (Skok 1971–1988)	impodobitul stęaguluj	from OChSl podobati; OChSl stěgъ (DEX 2009)
18.	kum 'kum'	PSl *kumъ (Trubachev & Zhuravlev 1974–2005)	naʃu	from Lat nonnus (DEX 2009)

№	Carașova	Etymology	Iabalcea	Etymology
19.	svadbaʃ 'wedding guest'	PSl *svatьba > svat (Skok 1971–1988)	nuntaʃ	reg. word, from Lat *nunptiae, or nuntiare (DEX 2009)
20.	nastojnik 'wedding cook'	PSl and OChSl stati, see Bulg and Serb words with adjacent meaning (Trubachev & Zhuravlev 1974–2005)	gətətor	local derivate from Rom a găti < gata < cf. Alb gat (Ciorănescu 2001)
21.	rodbina / rodove / famila 'newlyweds families'	PSl and OChSl rodъ (HJP); famila < Rom familie 'family' (DEX 2009)	ɲɛamurj	most likely, from OChSl němъ (Ciorănescu 2001)
22.	taʃta 'mother-in-law'	PSl and OChSl tьstь (Skok 1971–1988)	sǫakrə	from Lat socrus (= socer) (DEX 2009)
23.	svet / narot 'local people, guests'	PSl and OChSl světъ (HJP); PSl and OChSl rodъ (Skok 1971–1988)	lume	from Lat lumen (DEX 2009)
24.	venats͡ 'bride's crown'	PSl, OChSl věnьcь 'crown' (Skok 1971–1988)	kununə	from Lat corona (DEX 2009)

This group represents the most common strategy. Here, the item 20. gətətor is worth mentioning. It is formed with the widespread Romanian stem găt-, though it cannot be found in the dictionaries, being, apparently, an exclusively local Romanian derivative. The item 11. kat͡sej is a literal translation of the Krashovani lexeme, although the custom to visit the bride's parents during the first week after the wedding is also common among the Romanians (Pop 1999; Marianu 1890).

It should be noted that the strategy of translating Krashovani words into Romanian is also observed in Iabalcea toponyms, i. e. names of the hills: *Faca Mikula, Kičer, Krajište, Muke, Sumbrak*; names of the valleys: **Čoka (Șoacă)**[27], *Dolina*, **Kobilina Gropa (Groapa Iepii), Kameno polje (Poiana Stâncoasă)**, *Krno polje*; names of the pastures: *Dos, Kod studenci, Krno polje, Pašak*; arable lands: *Borkeš, Dealu Lipondij, Komarnik,* **Polje (Câmp)**, *Ravnište, Studenac*; names of the rivers: *Sumrak, Toplica*; and finally, names of the groves: *Gabrova*,

---

27 In this case, apparently, the Krashovani word *Čoka* < Rom *Șoacă*.

Korlan, Krstin hrt, Krъguja, Padina saka, Șoacă cu apă, **Velika čoka (Șoacă mare)** (Birta 1993: 439–440).

In addition to the "translated toponyms" (those listed above with their translations in brackets), there are other elements of the Romance origin (*Dos, Dealu Lipondij, Korlan, Șoacă cu apă*), whose proportion in Iabalcea seems to be larger than in other Krashovani villages (for data on them, see (Birta 1993: 440–447)).

Table 5 Transfer of a Romanian lexeme / cultureme into the Krashovani code

№	Carașova	Etymology	Iabalcea	Etymology
25.	feʎin 'godchild'	from Lat *filianus (DEX 2009)	fin	from Lat *filianus (DEX 2009)
26.	moʃuli 'guisers'	Rom moșuli	moʃuli / maskat͡s	prob., moș 'old man' < Lat annosus or local word (DEX 2009)
27.	veriʃora 'cousin'	Rom verișoară	veriʃoara	from Lat (consobrinus) verus (DEX 2009)
28.	t͡soʎe 'clothes'	Rom țoale	t͡soale	prob. from Tr çul via MGr tsóli/tsoúli (Ciorănescu 2001)
29.	malaj 'pie made of corn flour'	Rom mălai	malaj	Rom mălai of unknown etymology, prob., from Dacian (Ciorănescu 2001)
30.	t͡sast 'covered fire-pan'	Rom reg. (DEX 2009)	t͡səst	from Lat testum 'pottery vessel' (DEX 2009)
31.	t͡ɕuble / ɕuble 'dinnerware'	Rom reg. archaic ciublă 'vessel', prob. from Germ Kübel, but phonetically inexplicable (Ciorănescu 2001)	farfurij / vesela	MGr farfuri (DEX 2009); Fr vaisselle (DEX 2009)
32.	palarija 'hat'	from Rom pălărie	palərije	prob., from It cappelleria (Ciorănescu 2001)

In this category, there are many lexemes referring to wedding participants, objects used in rituals and other actions (although most of them are formed by translating the Krashovani lexemes into Romanian). In the "actional code" of the wedding[28], translation is the most common strategy.

We should mention one more strategy of mutual borrowing between Krashovani Slavic and Iabalcea Romanian codes, – calquing, or pattern borrowing. This strategy works in both ways – "from Slavic to Romanian", and "from Romanian to Slavic". One of the examples could be *stave most* > *fak podu*. The inner form of this expression is "they make bridge", which refers to one of the wedding rites known in Karashevo microregion and also in the Romanian Banat. We can make conclusions about the direction of borrowing based on the fact that Banat Romanians do not use this term, so linguistically it is clearly a calque from the Slavic expression. The other example of pattern borrowing is *ide zet* < *se duc̆e d͡ʒiɲere* (inner form "[he] goes son-in-law"). This expression describes the quite rare situation when a young man went to live to his wife's house after the wedding. The direction of borrowing is "from Romanian to Slavic", as the morphological structure concords much more naturally in the Iabalcea variant.

Thus, the Iabalcea Romanian terms represent a rather heterogeneous layer of vocabulary. In addition to standard Romanian (*pələrie* 'hat', *kimeʃə* 'shirt, robe', *patu* 'bedclothes', *aur* 'gold coin', *galben* 'gold coin' and others), its two main components are Banat regionalisms and archaisms (*malaj* 'pie made of corn flour', *t͡sǫale* 'clothes', *ɕuturə* 'one litre vessel for rakia', *kauk* 'soup ladle'), as well as words of a Slavic origin. In part these Slavisms are borrowed from the Krashovani dialect (*ogrlȩak* 'collar', *gat͡ʃe* 'pants', *sukɲa* 'dress') and in part from other Slavic varieties, commonly used in much wider areas not limited to the Banat region (*dar* 'gift', *opreg* 'gore', *krȩangu* 'fir branch', *lant͡siʃor* 'chainlet').

Some etymologies (*kotarit͡sa/kotarit͡sə* 'basket', *lajber/lajber* 'sleeveless jacket', *bronka/brǫankə* 'contabass', *opregu* 'gore', *krʒa* 'stick', *kot͡ɕija/koʃia* 'two-seat carriage', etc.), and how these items made their way into the Slavic or Romanian code of the Krashovani wedding, do not lend themselves to an unambiguous interpretation. For instance, the word *steg* 'wedding banner' could have appeared in the KDG as borrowed from Romanian, or come directly from **stĕgŭ*. Similarly, *krʒa/kɨrʒə* 'stick' could have come from Vlachs to Slavs, or vice versa, in

---

[28] "Objective" code relates to all objects used in the ceremony and celebration, "personal" code consists of all characters who participate in a wedding, while "actional" code refers to the rituals themselves. A variant of such division was originally proposed by N. I. Tolstoy (1981). Consequently, this form has been widely used by other members of the Moscow ethnolinguistic school (Gura 2012: 80–382; Uzenyova 2010: 30–190). This triad is quite helpful for researchers in their endeavour to comprehend and interpret complex cultural and linguistic phenomena related to the traditional wedding, but obviously, neither it is visible in practise, where all three codes are strongly intertwined, nor does it exist in traditional community members' perception.

the Middle Ages (Skok 1971–1988). In the case of t͡ʃep od brada 'fir branch', we are also dealing with an unclear etymology and difficulties in establishing the source of borrowing.[29] In general, the presence of its own lexeme in each of the two codes is quite visible. These lexical correspondences are used by informants in translating a message into a second language (Konior 2016).

Analysing sets of lexemes associated with the traditional Krashovani wedding recorded in Caraşova and Iabalcea, we have come to the conclusion that there are one-to-one correspondences between the elements of these sets. In this case, the Slavic code seems to have preserved its inherited core despite numerous influences and can be called – to a certain extent – an "autochthonous" one. The second seems to be a "symbiotic code" that has arisen as a result of the close interaction of the Romanian Banat dialect with the KDG. The sequence of their traditional wedding ceremony, as well as both Slavic (Krashovani) and Romanian (Iabalcea) wedding vocabulary show us how – in a deep contact situation – a common cultural code presented in the form of two different, but closely related language manifestations can result from intimate language contact (Konior 2016).

6 Conclusion

A centuries-old proximity to Romanians could not but exert an influence upon the Krashovani dialects. Penetration of contact innovations was facilitated by bilingualism, a peripheral position and the isolation of these dialects, as well as, not least, by a Romance substratum (Radan 2009: 191). The main sociopolitical factors that could have influenced the development of the Krashovani dialect group are as follows. Firstly, it is the will to preserve the Catholic religion, language and identity in the conditions of living on Austro-Hungarian territory, an idea that was effected with the active participation of Catholic missionary priests of Slavic origin (Simu 1939: 43–44). Secondly, the factor of family language and language attitude is crucial to this matter. And finally, it is economic globalization which, metaphorically speaking, leaves "no door closed" and forces even the most closed communities to integrate.

---

[29] Most names of musical instruments that were used during the wedding are of Italian or Western European origin. Against their background, the word *bronka / brǫankə* seems worth mentioning. It could have appeared in KDG under the influence of the Romanian Banat dialect, but since the etymology of this word is also unclear in the Romanian language, it is possible that it was preserved from a hypothetical Slavic substratum spread on the territory of the present Banat. As for the rest, the names of musical instruments recorded in Iabalcea are almost identical to those used in Caraşova (Konior 2016).

Frequently, language contacts occurred under conditions of social inequality, wars, colonialism and forced migrations (Chambers et al. 2004). This is partly true for the historical region of Banat, but with regard to the Romanian-Slavic contact on this territory, the linguistic data confirm the historians' thesis about a special type of Banat multiculturalism (see Buzarnescu & Pribac 2002; Hurezan & Colta 2002, 91): in conditions of relative equality in Carașova, Iabalcea and other Krashovani villages, a bilingual community that shares religion, major cultural markers, and patterns of labour has been formed.

However, with almost identical social conditions in Carașova and Iabalcea, the outcomes of language contact in these two villages are rather different. In the first case, it is language maintenance, in the second a shift to Romanian. Now some lexical-semantic groups mainly related to family and local culture (including onomastica) still contain many references to the Krashovani Slavic vocabulary. At the same time, in their Romanian grammar (as well as in the Slavic one in the case of those informants who can produce utterances) we scarcely see such mixture.

It is not without interest to theorize on the possibility of existence of a mixed language at some stage of the shift from Krashovani Slavic to Romanian in Iabalcea. Hypothetically, there could be some favouring conditions, such as "a process of identity crystalisation", "migration or acculturation", or "wide-scale intermarriage and the emergence of mixed households" (Matras 2009: 290). On the other hand, despite the fact that the very notion of mixed languages is a rather disputable matter, there seems to be a consensus on dependency between its emergence and a rise to new ethno-cultural identities (Matras 2000: 80; O'Shannessy 2020: 326). In this case, there was no social need to create a new identity. In fact, there must have been a restriction in this practise on the part of the Catholic church which, undoubtedly, had (and continues to have) a rather strong influence in the microregion. It is acknowledged that deliberate decisions of community members are important for the contact outcome (Golovko 2003). Lack of identity shift accompanying the language shift makes the existence of mixed language in the Karashevo microregion rather unplausible. As for the social factors of language contact, the Iabalcea onomasticon suggests that it was demography that played crucial role in the formation of local dialect and culture.

Thus the case of Iabalcea shows us a quite rare example of "a minority within minority", but only in terms of language, not traditional culture. In that regard the Iabalcea people are undoubtedly a part of the Krashovani community.

To make more far-reaching conclusions about the interrelationships of social and intralinguistic factors in situations of language contact in the Balkans, it is necessary to explore other communities of the peninsula where the interaction of the Eastern Romance and South Slavic forms of speech occurs. These would include the Serbian dialects of the Romanian Banat, Vlach dialects of Eastern Serbia, or the Romanian idiom in the Serbian Banat. Some of these "isocontacting" communities might exhibit a similarly high level of interpenetration of cultures as that which is observed in the Krashovani dialects and which allows us to call this community a symbiotic one (Konior 2019).

References

Bara, Mario. 2011. Prešućeni karaševski Hrvati: Karaševci u vojvođanskom dijelu Banata [The forgotten Croats of Karashevo: Krashovani in the Vojvodina part of Banat]. *Godišnjak za znanstvena istraživanja* ZKVH-a 3. 57–84.
Barnea, Alexandru, Mihai Bărbulescu, Dumitru Protase & Alexandru Suceveanu. 2010. *Istoria românilor* [History of the Romanian people]. Vol. 2, Daco-romani, romanici, alogeni. București: Editura Enciclopedică 2.
Barth, Frederik. 1969. Introduction. In Barth, Frederik (ed.), *Ethnic Groups and Boundaries: the social organization of cultural difference*, 9–38. Bergen & Oslo: Universitetsforlaget.
Belić, Aleksandar & Jovan Erdeljanović. 1925. Tragovi najstarijeg slavenskog sloja u Banatu [Traces of the oldest Slavic layer in Banat]. In Josef Schránil & Lubor Niederle (eds.), *Obzor praehistorický 4. Niederlův sbornik*, 275–305. Praha: Společnost československých praehistoriků.
Birta, Ivan. 1993. *Karaševci (Narodne umotvorine sa etnološkim osvrtom)* [Krashovani (Folklore in the light of ethnology)]. București: Romcart.
Boldureanu, Ioan Viorel. 2004. *Cultura populară bănățeană* [The folk culture of Banat]. Timișoara: Mirton.
Bromley, Yulian, Irina Dostyan, Sergey Nikitin & Viktor Karasev. 1963. *Istoriya Yougoslavii* [History of Yugoslavia], vol. 1. Moscow: Izdatel'stvo Akademii Nauk SSSR.
Buzărnescu, Ștefan & Sorin Pribac. 2002. Sursele istorico-antropologice ale interculturalității interactive din Banat [The historical and anthropological sources of interactive interculturality in Banat]. In Rudolf Poledna, François Ruegg & Rus Călin (eds.), *Interculturalitate: cercetări și perspective românești*. Cluj: Presa Universitară Clujeană.
Chambers, Jack K., Peter Trudgill & Natalie Schilling-Estes (eds.). 2004. *The Handbook of Language Variation and Change*. Malden, MA: Blackwell.
Ciorănescu, Alexandru I. 2001. *Dicționarul etimologic al limbii române* [Etymological dictionary of Romanian]. Șandru Mehedinți Tudora & Magdalena Popescu Marin (trans.). București: Saeculum I. O.
Clewing, Konrad & Oliver Jens Schmitt (eds.). 2011. *Geschichte Südosteuropas: Vom frühen Mittelalter bis zur Gegenwart*. Regensburg: Pustet.
Coteanu, Ion. 1961. *Elemente de dialectologie a limbii romîne* [Elements of Romanian dialectology]. București: Editura Științifică.
Crețan, Remus, Paul Kun & Lucian Vesalon. 2014. From Carașovan to Croat: The "ethnic enigma" of a (re)invented identity in Romania. *Journal of Balkan and Near Eastern Studies* 16 (4). 437–458.
Deleanu, Marcu Mihai. 1999. *Însemnări despre Carașoveni* [Notes about Krashovani]. Reșița: Editura Banatica.

DEX. 2009. *Dicționarul explicativ al limbii române* [Explanatory dictionary of the Romanian language]. București: Academia Română, Institutul de Lingvistică "Iorgu Iordan – Alexandru Rossetti", Editura Univers Enciclopedic.
Engel, Pál. 2001. *The Realm of St Stephen: A History of Medieval Hungary*. London & New York: I. B. Tauris.
Golovko, Evgeniy. 2003. Language contact and group identity: the role of "folk" linguistic engineering. In Yaron Matras & Peter Bakker (eds.), *The Mixed Language Debate: Theoretical and Empirical Advances*, 177–208. Berlin & New York: Mouton de Gruyter.
Gura, Alexandr. 2012. *Brak i svad'ba v slavyanskoi narodnoi kulture: semantika i simvolika* [Marriage and marriage rites in Slavic folk culture: semantics and symbolism]. Moscow: Indrik.
Herrity, Peter. 2014. Herausbildung der Standardspache: Slovenisch. History of the Standard Language: Slovenian. In Karl Gutschmidt, Sebastian Kempgen, Tilman Berger & Peter Kosta (eds.), *Die slavischen Sprachen. The Slavic Languages. Ein internationales Handbuch zu ihrer Struktur, ihrer Geschichte und ihrer Erforschung* (Handbücher zur Sprach- und Kommunikationswissenschaft. 32), vol. 2, 1427–1446. Berlin & Boston: De Gruyter Mouton.
Hinrichs, Uwe & Uwe Büttner (eds.). 1999. *Handbuch der Südosteuropa-Linguistik* (Slavistische Studienbücher). Vol. 10. Wiesbaden: Harrassowitz.
HJP. *Hrvatski jezični portal*. 2018. http://hjp.znanje.hr (accessed 15 March, 2021).
Hurezan, Pascu & Elena Rodica Colta (eds.). 2002. *Interetnicitate în Europa Centrală și de Est. Lucrările Simpozionului Internațional Interdisciplinar 26 mai 2002* [Interethnicity in Central and Eastern Europe. Works of the International Interdisciplinary Symposium 26 May 2002]. Arad: Complexul Muzeal Arad.
Ivanov, Valeriy V. (ed.). 1988. *Obscheslavyanskiy lingvisticheskiy atlas (Seria fonetiko-grammaticheskaya). Vypusk 1* [Common Slavic linguistic atlas (Phonetics and Grammar). Vol. 1]. Beograd: SANU.
Jordan, Peter. 1995. *Atlas Ost- und Südosteuropa = aktuelle Karten zu Ökologie, Bevölkerung und Wirtschaft / 2.7-S1 Ethnische Struktur Südosteuropas um 1992*. Stuttgart: Borntraeger.
Klepikova, Galina. 2005. Stratifikaciya slavyanskih zaimstvovaniy v rumynskih dialektah [Stratification of Slavic loans in Romanian dialects]. *Issledovaniya po slavyanskoy dialektologii* 6. 157–172.
Konior (Koner), Daria V. 2016. Leksicheskaya realizatsiya predmetnogo koda karashevskoi svad'by ["Objective code" of the Krashovani wedding vocabulary and its lexical manifestation]. *Acta linguistica Petropolitana. Trudy Instituta lingvisticheskih issledovaniy* 12. 629–649.
Konior (Koner), Daria V. 2018. Krashovani gender specific language in the middle of 20th century: (discourse analysis of) an atypical female narrative. *Zeitschrift für Balkanologie* 54 (2). 189–199.
Konior (Koner), Daria V. 2019. Text of the Krashovani traditional wedding in the light of Romano-Slavic contact in the Balkans. *Romanoslavica* (in print).
Konior (Koner), Daria V. 2015. Mezhdunarodnaya konferenciya "Grammaticheskaya gibridizaciya i socialnyye usloviya" [Grammatical hybridization and social conditions. Workshop in Leipzig]. *Voprosy yazykoznaniya* 3. 149–153.
Konior (Koner), Daria V. & Anastasia L. Makarova. 2015. Osobennosti etnoyazykovoy situacii v regione Karashevo (Rumyniya) [On the ethnolinguistic situation in the community of Karashevo (Romania)]. *Poznańskie studia slawistyczne* 8. 83–91.
Konior (Koner), Daria V. & Andrey N. Sobolev. 2017. Osobennosti neravnovesnogo bilingvizma u rumynoyazychnyh karashevtsev v sele Yabaltcha [On some aspects of nonequilibrium Romanian-Slavic bilingualism in the village of Iabalcea]. *Indoevropeyskoye yazykoznaniye i klassicheskaya filologiya* 21. 985–1001.

Krstić, Aleksandar. 2010. Banat u Srednjem veku [Banat in the Middle Ages]. In Miograg Maticki & Vidojko Jović (eds.), *Banat kroz vekove: slojevi kultura Banata*. Beograd: Vukova Zadužbina.
Lațchici, Maria. 2012. *Graiul croaţilor din Lupac în contextul raporturilor lingvistice sud(slavo)-române (rezumat al tezei de doctorat)* [Croat dialect from Lupac in the context of South-Slavic Romanian language contact]. Universitatea București Doctoral Dissertation summary.
Lehman, Rosa. 2001. *Symbiosis and ambivalence: Poles and Jews in a small Galician town*. New York & Oxford: Berghahn Books.
Leschber, Corinna. 1999. Das slavische Substrat in Rumänien untersucht anhand des Flächenstärken-Diagramms. *Wiener Slavistisches Jahrbuch* 45. 281–302.
Loma, Aleksandar. 2010. Slovenski imenski slojevi u Banatu: pregled dosadašnjih nalaza i preostala pitanja [Slavic names in Banat: an overview of current findings and other questions]. In Miograg Maticki & Vidojko Jović (eds.), *Banat kroz vekove: slojevi kultura Banata*. Beograd: Vukova zadužbina.
Macrea, Dimitrie, Emil Petrovici & Alexandru Rossetti (eds.). 1955–1957. *Dicționarul limbii romîne literare contemporane* [Dictionary of the Romanian modern literary language]. București: Editura Academiei Republicii Populare Romîne.
Manea-Grgin, Castilia. 2004. Prilog poznavanju vjerske povijesti karaševskih Hrvata u ranom novom vijeku [A contribution to the religious history of the Krashovani Croats in the early modern age]. *Povijesni prilozi* 27. 57–69.
Manea-Grgin, Castilia. 2012. *Povijest karaševskih Hrvata u rumunjskom Banatu (16.–18. stoljeće)* [History of the Krashovani Croats in the Romanian Banat (16th–18th centuries)]. Zagreb: FF press.
Marianu, Simeonu Florea. 1890. *Nunta la Români: studiu istorico-etnograficu comparativu* [The Romanian wedding: historical and ethnographic comparative study]. București: Tipografia Carol Göbl.
Matras, Yaron. 2000. Mixed languages: a functional-communicative approach. *Bilingualism: Language and Cognition* 3 (2). 79–99.
Matras, Yaron. 2009. *Language contact*. New York: Cambridge University press.
Milin, Jiva & Mihai Radan. 2002. O zajedničkom poreklu arhaičnih srpskih govora sa područja rumunskog Banata ("Banatsko-crnogorski", karaševski i sviniċki govori) [On the common origin of the archaic Serbian subdialects from the Romanian Banat ("Banat Montenegro", Karashevo and Svinița dialects)]. *Romanoslavica* 38. 41–67.
Mitrović, Mirko. 2004. Etnička slika Banata krajem 18. i početkom 19. veka [Ethnicity in Banat in 18th–19th century]. *Istraživanja* 15. 125–134.
Niederle, Lubomir. 1956. *Slavyanskie drevnosti* [Slavic antiquities]. Moscow: Izdatel'stvo inostrannoy literatury.
O'Shannessy, Carmel. 2020. Mixed languages. In Evangelia Adamou & Yaron Matras (eds.), *The Routledge Handbook of Language Contact*. London; New York: Routledge.
Paliga, Sorin. 2003. *Influențe romane și preromane în limbile slave de sud* [The influence of Romanian and proto-Romanian in south Slavic languages]. București. https://www.researchgate.net/profile/Sorin_Paliga/publication/242644290_Influente_romane_si_preromane_in_limbile_slave_de_sud/links/54a594880cf267bdb9082776/Influente-romane-si-preromane-in-limbile-slave-de-sud.pdf (accessed 15 March, 2021).
Pavković, Nikola. 2009. *Banatsko selo. Društvene i kulturne promene* [Banat village. Social and cultural changes]. Novi Sad: Matica Srpska.
Petrovici, Emil. 1935. *Graiul Carașovenilor. Studiu de dialectologie slavă meridională* [The Krashovani dialect. A Southern Slavic dialectology study]. București: Imprimeria Națională.
Petrovici, Emil. 1943. Daco-slava [The Daco-Slavic language]. *Dacoromania* 10 (2). 1–45.

Plotnikova, Anna. 2009. *Materialy dlya etnolingvisticheskogo izucheniya balkanoslavyanskogo areala* [Materials for the ethnolinguistic study of the Balkan-Slavic area]. Moscow. http://inslav.ru/images/stories/pdf/2009_Plotnikova.pdf (accessed 15 March, 2021).

Pop, Mihai & Rodica Zane. 1999. *Obiceiuri tradiționale românești* [Traditional Romanian customs]. București: Univers.

Poplack, Shana & Nathalie Dion. 2012. Myths and facts about loanword development. *Language Variation and Change* 24 (3). 279–315.

Poplack, Shana & David Sankoff. 1988. The social correlates and linguistic process of lexical borrowing and assimilation. *Linguistics* 26. 47–104.

Popović, Ivan. 1955. *Istorija srskohrvatskog jezika* [History of the Serbo-Croatian language]. Novi Sad: Matica Srpska.

Radan, Mihai. 2000. *Graiurile carașovene azi. Fonetica și fonologia* [The Krashovani dialect group now. Phonetics and phonology]. Timișoara: Anthropos.

Radan, Mihai. 2004a. *U pohode tajnovitom Karašu* [Visiting the mysterious Karaš]. Temišvar: Savez Srba u Rumuniji.

Radan, Mihai. 2004b. Uzroci kolebanja Karaševaka pri etničkom opredeljivanju. In Biljana Sikimić (ed.), *Skrivene manjine na Balkanu*. Beograd: Balkanološki institut SANU.

Radan, Mihai. 2009. Influența limbii române asupra graiurilor sârbești din Banatul românesc [The Romanian influence on the Serbian dialects in the Romanian Banat]. In Thede Kahl (ed.), *Das Rumänische und seine Nachbarn*, 187–205. Berlin: Frank & Timme.

Radan, Mihaj N. 2015. *Fonetika i fonologija karaševskih govora danas. Prilog proučavanju srpskih govora u Rumuniji* [Phonetics and phonology of the Krashovani dialect group now. A contribution to the Serbian dialects in Romania study]. Novi Sad: Matica Srpska.

Radan, Mihai & Žarko Bošnjaković. 2010. Dosadašnja istraživanja o uticaju rumunskog jezika na leksiku srpskih govora rumunskog dela Banata [Previous research of Romanian influence on the vocabulary of Serbian subdialects in the Romanian Banat]. *Južnoslovenski filolog* 66. 135–161.

Radan Uscatu, Miljana-Radmila. 2014. *Botezul, nunta și funeraliile la carașoveni* [Baptism, wedding and funerals among the Krashovani people]. Timișoara: Editura Universității de Vest.

Scriban, August. 1939. *Dicționaru limbii românești (etimologii, înțelesuri, exemple, citațiuni, arhaizme, neologizme, provincialisme)* [Dictionary of Romanian language (etymologies, meanings, examples, citations, archaisms, neologisms, provincialisms)]. Iași: Presa Bună.

Sikimić, Biljana (ed.). 2017. *Digitalna arhiva Balkanološkog instituta*. Beograd: SANU. http://balksrv2012.sanu.ac.rs/webdict/dabi/odabiju (accessed 15 March, 2021).

Simu, Traian. 1939. *Originea crașovenilor. Studiu istoric și etnografic* [The origin of the Krashovani people. A historical and ethnographic study]. Lugoj: Tipografia Corvin.

Skok, Petar. 1971–1988. *Etimologijski rječnik hrvatskoga ili srpskoga jezika, knj. I–III* [Etymological dictionary of Croatian or Serbian language, Vols I–III]. Zagreb: Jugoslavenska akademija znanosti i umjetnosti.

Sobolev, Andrey N. 1995. O nekim južnoslovenskim govornim oazama u istočnoj Srbiji, zapadnoj Bugarskoj i Rumuniji (Vratarnica, Novo Selo, Svinica) [About some South Slavic subdialect oases in Eastern Serbia, West Bulgaria and Romania (Vratarnica, Novo Selo, Svinița)]. *Zbornik Matice srpske za filologiju i lingvistiku* 38 (2). 183–207.

Sobolev, Andrey N. 2017. Iazyki simbioticheskikh soobschestv Zapadnykh Balkan: grecheskii i albanskii iazyki v sele Paliasa v kraine Himara, Albaniia [Languages in the Western Balkan Symbiotic Societies: Greek and Albanian in Palasa, Himara, Albania]. *Vestnik Sankt-Peterburgskogo gosudarstvennogo universiteta. Iazyk i literatura* 14 (3). 421–442.

Syrku, Polikhroniy A. 1899. Narechie karashevcev [The Krashovani dialect]. *Izvestiya* ORYAS *Imperatorskoy AN* 2. 641–660.
Tolstaya, Svetlana M. 2013. Postulaty moskovskoy etnolingvistiki [Postulates of ethnolinguistics in the Moscow School]. In Svetlana Tolstaya & Nikita Il'ich Tolstoi (eds.), *Slavyanskaya etnolingvistika: voprosy teorii*. Moscow: InSlav RAN.
Tolstoy, Nikita I. 1981. Verbalnyi tekst kak kluch k semantike obryada [Verbal text as a key to the semantics of a rite]. In Vyacheslav V. Ivanov, Tamara M. Sudnik & Tatiana V. Civ'yan (eds.), *Struktura teksta-81. Tezisy simpoziuma*, 46–47. Moscow: Institut slavyanovedeniya I balkanistiki AN SSSR.
Tomić, Mile. 1972. Antroponimija Kraševaca [The Krashovani anthroponymy]. *Zbornik za filologiju i lingvistiku* 15 (2). 213–226.
Tomić, Mile. 1984. Govor Sviničana [The Siniţa dialect]. *Srspski dijalektološki zbornik* 30. 7–265.
Trubachev, Oleg N. & Anatoliy V. Zhuravlev. 1974–2005. *Etimologicheskii slovar' slavianskikh iazykov. Praslavianskii leksicheskii fond* [Etymological dictionary of Slavic languages. Proto-Slavic lexical stock], 40 vols. Moscow: Nauka.
Vinogradov, Vladlen. 1987. *Kratkaya istoriya Rumynii (s drevneyshih vremen do nashih dney)* [A brief history of Romania (from ancient times to our days)]. Moscow: Nauka.
Vlahović, Petar. 1999. Karaševci. Prilog etničkoj istoriji [Krashovani. A contribution to the ethnic history]. *Rad Muzeja Vojvodine* 41–42. 75–84.
Uzenyova, Elena S. 2010. *Bolgarskaya svad'ba: etnolingvisticheskoye issledovaniye* [The Bulgarian wedding: an ethnolinguistic study]. Moscow: Indrik.

Vyacheslav V. Kozak
Evidence for Past Coexistence: Romance Stratum in Croatian Glagolitic Sources from Krk, Croatia

Abstract. The chapter[1] discusses the application of the **semantic and formal analysis of lexical loans** for the reconstruction of social, cultural, ethnic, and linguistic interaction between the Slavic and the Romance population in the island of Krk during the Late Middle Ages and Early Modern period. As a source of linguistic material, two types of texts were selected: 1) the Old Croatian (Čakavian) portions of the Vrbnik Statute, a Glagolitic manuscript from the 16th century, containing different legal acts ranging from between the 14th and the 16th centuries, and 2) Old Croatian Glagolitic inscriptions from the 10th to 11th centuries and 14th to the 18th centuries. Semantic analysis guided by the conceptual system of Hallig and von Wartburg and formal analysis, including etymology, historical phonetics, grammar, and onomastics permits us to determine two main replication patterns for Romance linguistic phenomena: cultural borrowings and onomastic borrowings. The high number of borrowed Romance terms related to legal proceedings (e.g., *apelaciûnь, denunciê, fruštati, kaštigati*), administrative acts (*kuntentati, termenivati*), economics (*intrada, libra, soldinь, bagatinь, vьrnizь*), and clerical organization (*plovanь, prьvьdь*) shows the key role the Romance (mainly Venetian) stratum played in legal, administrative, economic and religious discourse. The linguistic influence of Dalmatian can be found in fishing terminology (*sipa, oliga, menula*). In the domain of onomastics there are Slavic surnames derived from Romance proper names (*Fugošicь < Fulgo, Malateštinicь < Malateste*). In contrast to the usually postulated thesis of the Slavic-Romance cultural and linguistic separation in the island of Krk, the replication of Romance linguistic phenomena in the Glagolitic sources demonstrates a certain level of linguistic and ethnic convergence. However, a small relative share of loans, a low level of grammatical interference and the predominance of the addition mechanism of borrowing indicate that the depth of this convergence (within the written Glagolic culture) is rather small.

---

1 This research was made possible by a grant from the Russian Science Foundation (the projects "From Separation to Symbiosis: South Eastern European languages and cultures in contact", No. 14-18-01405 and "Balkan bilingualism in dominant and equilibrium contact situations in diatopy, diachrony and diastraty", No. 19-18-00244).

https://doi.org/10.1515/9781501509254-007

1 Introduction

1.1 The case description

The island of Krk is located in the north of the Adriatic Sea together with the islands of Cres, Lošinj, Rab and Pag (as well as a number of smaller ones), making up the Kvarner archipelago. The term "Kvarner" in the broad sense refers to a geographic region bounded on the west by the Istrian peninsula and the east by the ridges of Velika Kapela and Velebit (Kalmeta 1970: 19) and located in an area of contact between three macrogeographical regions: the Dinaric, Alpine and Pannonian (Kalmeta 1970: 29). More generally speaking, this area is the northern part of the historical and geographical region of Dalmatia (Sobolev 2013: 144).

Its remarkable geographical position, favourable climate and the vast amount of natural resources it has provided throughout its history have made the island of Krk attractive both strategically and economically (Kalmeta 1970: 34). Its residents in different periods have been speakers of Illyrian, Greek, Latin, Romance (primarily Vegliot Dalmatian and Venetian) and Slavic (especially Čakavian) dialects. The language of the Romanic population of the island (speakers of the Vegliot dialect of the Dalmatian language) dates back to the colloquial Latin of the Roman colonists that settled there in the first centuries CE. Later, in the era of Venetian rule over Dalmatia (15th to 18th centuries), the Vegliot dialect experienced significant influence from the Venetian and Italian literary languages (Repina & Narumov 2001: 681). The last speaker of the Vegliot dialect died in 1898. Slavic speakers appeared on the island, probably from the end of the 6th through the 9th centuries, during the migration of the groups of the trans-Danubian population to the Balkans as they passed through Dalmatia (Shuvalov 1998: 18; Dzino 2010: 211–212). Thus from the 7th till the 19th century, Krk has been a site of direct contact of Slavic speakers with the Romanic substratum and adstratum (see Breu 2014: 1176). In addition to the spoken languages of the Middle Ages, there were high literary languages: medieval Latin, Italian, Church Slavonic and written Čakavian.

This linguistic and sociohistorical context has prompted some researchers to posit a theory of linguistic, ethnic, and cultural opposition between the Romance town of Krk, with its surrounding territory dominated by Latin and Venetian written culture and a Romanic language of communication, with the Slavic remainder of the island dominated by Church Slavonic, Čakavian writing, and a colloquial Čakavian language of communication (see Bolonić 1966: 122; Doria 1989: 534–536).

At the same time, to denote the interaction that has arisen between the Slavic and Romance populations, the term "Slavic-Romance symbiosis" is used in the Croatian scientific tradition. As noted by Ž. Muljačić (1967), the first to use this term was P. Skok, and under the word "Romance" he meant the Dalmatian language. Muljačić expanded his understanding of the "Slavic-Romance symbiosis" by including in the content of the "Romance" the Venetian, Istro-Romance, Istro-Rumanian, and also some other dialects, that is, all Romanic idioms of the region. By "symbiosis" Skok and Muljačić understood the direct coexistence of multilingual groups of the population, accompanied by bilingualism and the phenomena resulting from it (phonetic, grammatical and lexical interference and corresponding borrowings). However, the correctness of the term "symbiosis" as applied to the situation of Slavic-Romance coexistence is controversial because the humanities maintain another understanding of it, going back to the work of Frederik Barth, that defines symbiosis as a situation in which various ethnic groups, while preserving their identity, are in an additional distribution relationship (Barth 1998: 19). The question of the existence of such relations between the Slavs and the Romance of Dalmatia remains open.

Thus, the two approaches mentioned above put Slavic-Romance coexistence in Dalmatia between two different possible models of contact: separation and symbiosis. Still, the grounding of these notions and the description of the processes and mechanisms they refer to need a complex study of all the languages involved in contact spanning more than a thousand years. The greatest hindrance to the study is the dearth of attested Dalmatian texts (Repina & Narumov 2001: 682–683). This issue has resulted in a whole tradition of research dealing with the linguistic stratification of Eastern Adriatic Romance and the reconstruction of Dalmatian and Slavic-Romance linguistic relations on the basis of etymological research. The main leaders in this line of research are P. Skok (1933, 1950, 1971), M. Deanović (1938, 1966), Ž. Muljačić (1967, 2000), P. Tekavčić (1970, 1976), V. Vinja (1986, 1998–2004), M. Županović (1994, 1995a, 1995b, 1997, 1998), N. Vuletić (2006, 2010) and O. Ligorio (Ligorio & Vuletić 2013; Ligorio 2014), among others. Their studies are especially important for understanding the significant role of the Romance stratum in the development of the Slavic onomastics and terminology of navigation, fishing, flora and fauna (see Ligorio 2014: 21).

The work of Slavists (primarily dialectologists) usually describes Romance borrowing in modern dialects of Croatian (Gačić 1979a, 1979b, 2003; Galović 2013, 2014; Galović & Papić 2016; Marasović-Alujević 1984; Miočić 2011a, 2011b, 2012, 2014; Nigoević 2007; Nigoević & Lasić 2012; Pliško 2009, 2016; Spicijarić 2009; Spicijarić Paškvan 2014). These researchers note the significant influence of Romance languages on the Slavic dialects of Dalmatia in the semantic fields of administration, church, city life, professional activities (viticulture and construction in particular), leisure, gastronomy, housing and clothing. The Dubrovnik sources from the 16th to the 19th centuries demonstrate a huge number of lexical borrowings for terms of thinking, feelings, attitudes, characteristics, household things, home, garden, furniture, family relationships, body parts, time, and others (Sočanac 2005, 2007).

Another type of a linguistic source which has a unique importance for the Dalmatian culture is the corpus of Glagolitic texts. The Glagolitic script was likely brought to Dalmatia by the disciples of Cyril and Methodius after the death of the latter in 885 (Bolonić 1980: 97; Aničić 2012: 115). The centres of the Glagolitic tradition were Istria, the islands of Kvarner (the oldest sources from the 11th to 12th centuries), Vinodol, Lika, Zadar and the adjacent islands (Reinhart 2014: 1295). Finds of recent years, in particular the inscription from Župa Dubrovačka from the 11th century, allow us to significantly expand our understanding of Glagolitic's geographical distribution in the past (Čunčić & Perkić 2009).

One of the most important centres for the distribution of Glagolitic literacy is the island of Krk, as evidenced by the numerous monuments, including such ancient ones as the Old Church Slavonic Glagolita Clozianus from the 11th century (Aničić 2012: 116; Miklas & Sadovski 2014). Krk's particular sociohistorical features allow us to take the culture of this island as representative of that of the whole Kvarner region or Northern Dalmatia as concentrated in a small area. These features include: a long (until the 19th century) subsistence of a Dalmatian substratum; the richest written (primarily Glagolitic) tradition; long-term Venetian political influence; diversity of the local economy; cultural, political and social opposition between the Romance city and Slavic villages; the key economic role of the church; community organization and the existence of numerous parochial brotherhoods. Thus its examination can become key to understanding the processes and consequences of Slavic-Romance language contacts throughout the whole region.

1.2 Data and methods

This research for the first time attempts to investigate the interaction between the Latin-Romanic and Slavic cultures in the northwest of the Balkan Peninsula by a systematic study of the Glagolitic sources. In particular, I analyse Glagolitic texts mainly from the 14th to the 18th centuries that originate from the island of Krk. These sources are assorted Glagolitic inscriptions (hereafter GI) and the Statute of Vrbnik (Croatian *Vrbnički* (*Krčki, Vrbanski*) *statut*, hereafter VS).

The oldest portion of the VS text dates back to the 1388. The text contains information on the regulation of many different aspects of social life: the mining of natural resources, grazing of cattle, punishments for crime, the procedure for electing officials, and so on. The text was preserved in a single manuscript dating to the 16th century, kept in the Collection of manuscripts and old books of the

National and University Library in Zagreb (R 4003), and has been published on numerous occasions (Kukuljević Sakcinski 1852: 277–307; Evreinova 1880; Rački, Jagić & Črnčić 1890: 145–177; Margetić & Strčić 1988; Margetić 2012: 506–571). The Slavic part of the VS contains about 5,265 words, its vocabulary consists of approximately 682 lexemes.

Secondly, I analysed 88 Glagolitic inscriptions from from the 10th to 11th and 14th to the 18th centuries, all which can be found in B. Fučić's edition (1982). The length of the inscriptions varies from just a few letters to extensive texts, which all together total about 1000 words (ca. 161 lexemes). The majority of the inscriptions can be divided on the basis of where they were located: on buildings and burial monuments (tombstones, etc.). For more details about the composition, genres, and content of the Glagolitic inscriptions from the island of Krk (see Aničić 2012).

The central goal of this study is to determine, based on the etymological, semantic, grammatical and quantitative analysis of Latin and Romance loans in the appellative lexicon of Glagolitic monuments from the island of Krk, the exact nature of the interaction between the Latin-Romance and Slavic cultures in the northwest of the Balkan Peninsula. A study of the scope of lexical borrowing is of particular importance as it allows one to draw conclusions as to the nature and degree of interaction between coexisting linguistic communities (see Asenova 2002: 43) and reconstruct the history of linguistic interaction in the region (see Desnitskaya 1988: 134–135; Sobolev 2001). In general the analysis of Latin and Romance loans contributes to the reconstruction and description of the processes of linguistic (as well as cultural, social, ethnic) divergence, convergence, and symbiosis of the Romanic and Slavic population at all stages and in all areas of their coexistence.

2 Lexical interference

2.1 The Vrbnik Statute

Among the approximately 682 lexemes of the VS 105 are loanwords that make up about 15.4 % of the whole vocabulary.

2.1.1 Semantic analysis of borrowed vocabulary

Borrowings were observed in the semantic fields of property management, fishing, farming, clothing, work, (government) power, law, community, office, leisure, finances, town, navigation, religion & clergy, quantity, time and situation.

Loanwords absolutely dominate in the semantic field of **power (legislative, executive and judicial)**. Since the VS is a legislative document, this fact is very often exhibited and demonstrates an influence of the non-Slavic languages in the power discourse.

- Legislative terms: *busoviĉь* 'herald', *civilь* 'civil', *kuntentati* 'to decree', *liganca* 'obligation', *mandatь* 'order', *obligati* 'to oblige', *štatutь* 'statute', *termenivati/terminati* 'to decree', *urdinь* 'order'.
- Executive terms: *licenciê* 'permission', *kasati* 'to debar', *kaštelь* 'municipality', *komunьski* 'municipal', *oficiê/oficii* 'service, office', *oficiêlь* 'official', *providurь* 'provveditore'.
- Judicial terms: *apelaciûnь* 'appeal', *apelati* 'to file an appeal', *banžati* 'to chase' (*banžani* 'outlaw'), *berlina* 'stocks', *denunciê* 'denunciation', *denunciêti* 'to dinounce', *falь* 'fraud', *fruštati* 'to scourge', *karmenalь* 'crime', *kaštigati* 'to castigate', *pena* 'fine', *permanь* 'court official', *provati* 'to prove', *prьžunь* 'prison', *sentenciê* 'verdict', *sentenciêvati* 'to bring in verdict', *zaminati* 'to examine'.

Only a few Slavic words occur in this field: *dvorь* 'court', *dvorьnikь* 'court official', *kupь/vьkupь* 'meeting', *kьnezь* 'prince, count', *podьkьnežinь*, *prisežьnikь*, *sьtьnik* (administrative positions), *opьĉina* 'municipality', *podьložьnikь* 'subject', *službɑ* 'office', *sudьcь* 'judge', *vêĉe* 'popular assembly', *vêĉьnikь* 'popular assembly's member', etc.

As a collection of legislative acts, the VS contains a large number of verbs used to report on the adoption of a legislative decision. Due to their diversity, these lexemes deserve a separate study. Most of the verbs used belong to the native vocabulary: *dogovoriti se* 'to reach an agreement', *hotêti* 'to want', *lagoditi se* 'to decree', *načiniti* 'to decree', *naložiti* 'to assign', *napraviti se* 'to decide', *narediti* 'to command', *odlučiti* 'to decide', *učiniti* 'to decree', *ulagoditi se* 'to decree', *vidêti* 'to provide' and *zapovêdati* 'to command', among others. The same group includes borrowings mentioned above: *kuntentati*, *obligati*, *senticiêvati*, *termenivati/terminati* 'to decide'.

Full synonymy between native and borrowed words is demonstrated by the lexemes *denunciêti – kazati* 'to inform about a crime, to denounce' in the field of judicial terminology. The usual term is *kazati*, while *denunciêti* is used only in 1 example.

In the judicial context synonyms are the words *osuditi* 'to condemn' and *senticiêvati* 'to make a verdict'.

These synonymic pairs between native and borrowed lexemes allow us to draw an important conclusion. In the process of lexical borrowing, not only is there a mechanism of additional acts (that is, bringing into the linguistic system both the designated and denoting elements), but there is also a substitution mechanism (the introduction of a signifier if there is a corresponding one designated in the recipient language). The latter is shown by synonymous pairs, consisting of native and borrowed lexemes. *The action of the substitution mechanism is important evidence for the prestige of the Romance languages in the judicial and legislative discourse on the island of Krk.*

Close to the semantic field of governing power and legislative documents lies the terminology of the official functions which consists almost completely of loanwords: *bergamina* 'parchment', *bumbažinъ* 'paper', *harta* 'paper', *kancilarъ* 'clerc', *kapitulъ* 'chapter (in a book)', *notarъ* 'clerk', *škuriti* 'to expire'. As in the previous fields there are only a few Slavic terms here: *listъ* 'document', *pisьcь* 'clerk'.

Once again special attention should be paid to lexical doublets (complete synonyms) that are infrequently encountered: *notarъ* and *pisьcь* 'clerk' as well as *oficiê* and *služьba* 'service'. The term *služьba* is used several times only in the statement from the 1477 *K(a)p(i)t(u)l' od' s'lužbi k'met'* '*chapter about the service of peasants*'.

The terms for property management have different origins. The majority are of Slavic origin (*blago* 'property', *dobitъkъ* 'property', *gibuĉi* 'movable', *stanovuĉi* 'immovable'). Among the rest there are words borrowed from Greek (*drъmunъ* 'forest'), German (*škoda* 'injury') and Italian languages (*tištamentъ* 'testament', *štimati* 'estimate').

The lexemes *lêsъ* and *drъmunъ* have the base meaning of 'forest', but if the first (Slavic) denotes 'forest' in general, then the second (borrowed) one is a 'forest' that is privately owned.

The semantic field of commerce and finance attracts attention by its large number of names of monetary units, both borrowed (*bagatinъ, bečъ, dukatъ, libra, soldinъ, vъrnizъ*), and native (*cъlezъ, pênezъ, zlati*). At the same time, other terminology related to financial operations is Slavic (*plaĉa* 'payment', *prodaê* 'sale', etc.), excepting the word *intrada* 'income'.

Slavic terminology dominates the farming domain. There are only few old loanwords here: *komarda* 'granary, storehouse', *mošunъ* 'animal pen', *onukle* 'yearling, one year old animal', *ulьe* 'oil', along with the more ancient borrowing *kъmetъ* 'peasant'. These words can be compared with the huge number of Slavic terms: *drobъ* 'animal entrails', *ênьcь* 'lamb', *hlêbъ* 'bread', *hrana* 'food', *kobila* 'mare', *kokošь* 'hen', *konь* 'horse', *koza* 'goat', *kozъliĉь* 'kid', *krava* 'cow', *mekota* 'ploughed land', *meso* 'meat', *mlisti* 'to milk', *nerêzъ* 'abandoned field', *osьlica* 'female donkey', *osьlъ* 'donkey', *ovьca* 'sheep', *ovьnъ* 'ram', *ozimъkъ/ozimъče* 'spring lamb', *pasti* 'to graze', *pêtehъ* 'cock', *prazъ* 'pig', *pьsъ* 'dog', *sêêti* 'to seed', *sirь* 'cheese', *skopьčevinь* 'castrated sheep, wether', *ûnьcь* 'calf', *vino*[2] 'wine', *volь* 'ox', *žirь* 'fat', *žito* 'grain', *živina* 'animal', *žrêbьcь* 'foal'.

The field of farming is related with the terminology of work (in the social aspect), which is presented by three loanwords *fatiga* 'work', *ingariê* 'corvee' and *komunь* 'communal duty'.

Loanwords in the field of fishing do not dominate either, except in the types of fish: the Romance (especially of the Dalmatian origin) words *gara* 'Smaris vulgaris', *ligьnь* 'Loligo vulgaris', *menula* 'Smaris vulgaris', *oliga* 'Atherina hepsetus, Smaris vulgaris or another small sea fish', *sipa* 'Sepia officinalis' and Slavic *hobotьnica* 'Octopus vulgaris', *kamenica* 'Ostrea edulis', *volovina* 'Myliobatis aquila (?)' and the general notion *riba* 'fish'. The word denoting the fisherman (*ribarь*) is Slavic. There are two lexemes for a fishing net: the Slavic *mrêža* and the Italian *trata*. The opposition of partial synonyms *mrêža* and *trata* is analogous to the opposition *lêsь* and *drьmunь*. The native word denotes the general term 'fishing net', whereas the borrowing a particular type of net.

Borrowed words can be found also in other semantic fields of different social activities, such as navigation (*goliê* 'galley', *navkirь* 'sailor') and leisure (*harta* 'playing card', *zarь* 'gambling').

Terms for religion are native Slavic (*blaženi* 'blessed', *bogь* 'God', *svetь* 'saint'), or belong to ancient borrowings of the Proto-Slavic period (*amenь* 'amen', *crêki* 'church', *mьša/misa* 'mass'). The terminology for clergy is almost entirely constituted of borrowings (*opatь* 'abbot'[3], *plovanь* 'priest', *prьvьdь* 'priest, deacon', *žakanь* 'deacon'), with the only exception of the Proto-Slavic borrowing from the Germanic *popь* 'priest'.

In the semantic field "Clothing" there are two terms denoting different types of headgear: native *klobukь* and borrowing *berita*.

The field "Town" contains the loanwords *placa* 'square', *polača* 'palatial urban building, palazzo' and *toverna* 'tavern'. To express the meaning 'house, building', the native words *domь*, *hiša*, *hramь*, *kuća* are usually used.

The borrowed terms occur not only in the semantic fields of concrete objects or terminology of social institutions, but also denote more abstract matter such as quantity, time or social relations. The borrowed quantity terminology consists of the words *duplo* 'double quantity', *librica* 'unit of weight', *minutь* 'less', *suma* 'sum'. Within the field of time, Latin names of the months (*decembьrь* 'December', *envarь* 'January', *iûnь* 'June', *mai* 'May', *marьčь* 'March', *novembьrь* 'November', *oktebьrь* 'October', *pervarь* 'February', *sektebьrь* 'September') correspond to the native Slavic concepts of time: *dьnь* 'day', *mêsecь* 'month' (generic concept),

---

[2] A Proto-Slavic borrowing.
[3] See also *opatiê* 'abbey'.

godъ 'year', *lêto* 'year', *vêkъ* 'century' and actually *vrême* 'time'. Along with the names of the months this field has one more borrowing – the term *durati* 'to last'.

The last field we will point to relates to a more abstract and vague field of notions for some aspects of human relations ("situations"). Borrowings occurring there are *kuštiûnъ* 'conflict, situation', *mankati/pomankati* 'to lack', *prezentati* 'to present, or introduce, something or someone to somebody', *računъ* 'the cause',[4] *skuža* 'excuse, cause' and *vižitanie* 'visitation'.

As the semantic analysis has shown, the borrowed lexemes occur in different types of semantic groups: as names of concrete notions, institutional and occupational terms and abstract categories. Thus the cultural impact on the Slavic vocabulary of the Glagolitic monuments is rather strong. The next stage of research is to stratify the loanwords according to their donor-languages.

2.1.2 Etymological stratification of the semantic fields

The lack of written sources usually does not allow us to decisively attribute a borrowing to the donor language. Multiple attempts to stratify borrowings within the Croatian language continuum have met with serious difficulties (see Ligorio 2014). For this reason Glagolitic borrowings will be divided into groups not according to the donor language, but to the donor languoid (= donor languages or donor families) (Haspelmath 2009: 45). To denote borrowings from Latin and Romance languages, in the scientific tradition the term "Romanism" is usually used (Galović 2013: 159). Romanisms include elements of Latin and Romance origin proper, and elements that have entered the Slavic language through the Latin-Romance medium (Gačić 1979: 4). The central problem of studying Romanisms is the method of their stratification. In general, they are divided into two main groups: older Romanisms (going back to Latin, Dalmatian and Dalmatian-Venetian languages / dialects) and younger ones (going back to Venetian, Trieste and Italian literary languages / dialects) (Galović 2013: 160; see Tekavčić 1976: 37). Since it can be hard to distinguish direct borrowings from Greek from words of Greek origin, but borrowed through Latin (see Slavic *ingariê*, Latin *angaria* and Greek ἀγγαρεία or Slavic *komarda*, Latin *camarda* and Greek καμάρδα, etc.), we will go further by distinguishing two etymological groups of loanwords: an older substratum (Greek, Vulgar Latin, Dalmatian and early Romance) and a younger adstratum (written official Latin and Italian including Venetian) borrowings.

---

[4] The word *računъ* is functioning within the construction *koga kolê računa* 'any', that has a Slavic synonym in the text of VS *ke kolê vrъsti* 'any'.

The majority of borrowings within the vocabulary of the VS (64 lexemes = 61%) belong to the younger adstratum. These lexemes can be found almost in all semantic fields (except "Farming", "Navigation" and "Religion"), especially in the field of power: *apelaciûnъ* 'appeal', *denunciêti* 'to dinounce', *fruštati* 'to scourge', *kuntentati* 'to decree', *provati* 'to prove', etc. Single words can be found in the fields of property management (*tištamentъ* 'testament', *štimati* 'estimate'), fishing (*trata* 'fishing net'), work (*fatiga* 'work', *komunъ* 'communal duty'), situation (*kuštiûnъ* 'conflict, situation', *mankati* 'to lack', etc.), office (*bergamina* 'parchment', *kancilarъ* 'clerc', *notarъ* 'clerk', etc.), leisure (*zarъ* 'gambling'), clothes (*berita* 'headgear'), monetary units, town (*toverna* 'tavern'), quantity (*duplo* 'double quantity', *librica* 'unit of weight', etc.) and time (*durati* 'to last').

Being mostly connected with the terminology of state, borrowings from the younger adstratum reflect *the political and administrative domination of Venice on the island of Krk and in Dalmatia.*

As was mentioned above, there are three semantic fields, in which only loanwords from the older substratum are present: "Farming" (*komarda* 'granary, storehouse', *kъmetъ* 'peasant', *mošunъ* 'animal pen', *onukle* 'yearling, one year old animal', *ulьe* 'oil'), "Navigation" (*goliê* 'galley', *navъkirъ* 'sailor') and "Religion" (*amenъ* 'amen', *mъša/misa* 'mass', *opatiê* 'abbey', *opatъ* 'abbot', *plovanъ* 'priest', *prъvъdъ* 'priest, deacon', *žakanъ* 'deacon'). The older loanwords dominate also in the fields of fishing (types of fish) and time (names of the months). They also constitute their part within the fields of property management (*drъmunъ* 'forest'), work (*ingariê* 'corvée'), situation (*računъ* 'the cause'), office (*harta* 'paper'), leisure (*harta* 'playing card'), town (*placa* 'square', *polača* 'palatial urban building, palazzo'). The older substratum associated with Balkan Latin or the older Romance languages makes up 33.5 % of all borrowings and refers to the process of *integrating the Slavic-speaking population into the Mediterranean culture of Dalmatia* (in the spheres of social organization, economic activity, calendar and religious life).

Only a few Germanic (*crêki* 'church', *permanъ* 'court official', *popъ* 'priest', *škoda* 'injury') and, possibly, Hungarian (*birъ* 'tax paid to a priest') borrowings were noticed. Thus, *the influence of Greek, Hungarian and Germanic languages on the language of the Glagolitic monuments is minimal.*

2.1.3 Frequency

The appellative lexicon of the VS includes 358 usages of borrowed tokens, which makes up about 7 % of all tokens of the monument (according to approximate calculations ca. 5265). Most of the lexical borrowing (62 units, or 61 %) is used in the text of the Statute for 1 time, 14 borrowings occur 2 times, 9 occur 3 times and 19 lexemes occur more than 3 times.

Table 1 Loanword frequency in the VS

Number of usages	Number of lexemes
4	*kuntentati* 'to decree', *žakanь* 'deacon'
5	*duplo* 'double quantity'
6	*obligati* 'to oblige', *popь* 'priest', *štatutь* 'statute'
7	*urdinь* 'order'
8	*drьmunь* 'forest', *librica* 'unit of weight')
9	*kaštelь* 'municipality', *kьmetь* 'peasant'
10	*oficiê* 'service, office', *provati* 'to prove'
15	*providurь* 'provveditore'
17	*škoda* 'injury'
23	*soldinь* 'monetary unit'
29	*libra* 'monetary unit'
35	*pena* 'fine'
47	*kapitulь* 'chapter (in a book)'

The majority of these frequent borrowings belong to the younger adstratum (*kuntentati* 'to decree', *provati* 'to prove', *providurь* 'provveditore', etc.). Also included in this list are several words going back to the older substratum (*drьmunь* 'forest', *kьmetь* 'peasant', *žakanь* 'deacon') and to the Germanic adstratum (*škoda* 'injury').

The frequency of these lexemes is determined by the genre features of the monument: dividing into chapters (*kapitulь* 'chapter (in a book)'), determining the amount of damage and monetary fine (*libra* 'monetary unit', *pena* 'fine', *soldinь* 'monetary unit', *škoda* 'injury'), reference to the sanction of the supervisor (*providurь* 'provveditore'), and so on.

2.1.4 Typological approach

The most elaborate hierarchy of permeability for borrowings in different semantic fields can be found in (Haspelmath & Tadmor 2009: 64). Since the questionnaire method applied there (even for the dead languages) is not suitable for the language of a single text (or even group of texts), but for an entire language, direct parallels cannot be drawn here. However, results can be compared within the semantic field "Law" (since the legal terminology is sufficiently presented) and the total amount of borrowings found.

16 of the 26 meanings of the semantic field "Law" (see Haspelmath & Tadmor (2009: 33)) have correspondences in the VS).

Table 2 The semantic field "Law" (see Haspelmath & Tadmor (2009: 33))

Meaning	Word	Meaning	Word
law	zakonь 'law'	to acquit	—
court	sudь / dvorь / pitanьe 'court'	guilty	—
to adjudicate	**sentenciivati / osuditi** 'to condemn'	innocent	prostь 'innocent'
judgment	**sentenciê / osudь** 'verdict'	penalty or punishment	—
judge	sudьcь 'judge'	fine	**pena 'fine'**
plaintiff	—	prison	**prьžunь 'prison'**
defendant	—	murder	—
witness	sьvêdokь 'witness'	adultery	—
to swear	otьprisêci, prisêci, rotiti 'to swear'	rape	sila 'rape'
oath	rota 'oath'	arson	—
to accuse	ovaditi, obrêci 'to accuse'	perjury	—
to condemn	—	to steal	krasti, ueti, ukrasti 'to steal'
to convict	osuditi 'to convict'	thief	tatь 'thief'

12–14[5] of the 16 words are native = 75–87.5 %. Thus borrowings make up only 12.5–25 % of the semantic field "Law", which can be compared with the cross-linguistic average of 34.3 % from Haspelmath & Tadmor (2009: 64).

The overall rate of the loanwords within the appellative vocabulary of the VS is 15.4 %, that is rather low against the cross-linguistic average of 24.2 %.

On the basis of these observations, we can conclude that the language of the VS, despite the prestigious status of the Romance stratum, demonstrates *a relatively low share of lexical borrowing.*

---

[5] Because of "*sentenciivati / osuditi*" and "*sentenciê / osudь*" pairs.

2.1.5 Evidence from the Latin and Romance parts

Although the detailed analysis of the Latin and Romance parts of the VS was not the primary task of the study, it is important to mention here that there are no loanwords from Slavic except the Romanized forms of Slavic names of different origin (*Nicolaus Bosanich/Bosanig, Gerga Drusinich, Mattheus Fugossich, Ghersanus, Jurchus Valcich, Nicolaus Valkouich, Jacobus de Zutinis*, etc.). This fact characterizes the Slavic language in that situation of contact as completely recipient with respect to the Latin-Romance stratum. However, this thesis needs a separate study.

2.2 The Glagolitic inscriptions

Among the approximately 161 appellative lexemes of the Krk Glagolitic inscriptions there are 46 loanwords, which make up about 28.5 % of the vocabulary.

2.2.1 Semantic analysis of borrowed vocabulary

Having analysed the vocabulary of the GI, I grouped the borrowed lexemes into 6 semantic fields: "Building & architecture", "Property management", "Religion", "Power" and "Time". Also, since there are 15 different words denoting clergymen, there is a separate group "Clergy".

The groups of the religious and clerical terminology are some of the biggest and contain together about a half of all loanwords. The reason for this is in the purpose of the majority of the inscriptions. Most of them are official building inscriptions related to the new cult objects (churches, chapels, etc.). The borrowed religious terminology includes 6 words: *amenъ* 'amen', *ankuniê* 'altar painting', *apustolь* 'apostle', *krizma* 'chrism', *olei* 'chrism', *oltarъ* 'altar'. At the same time about three quarters of the religious terminology is native Slavic: *blaženъ* 'blessed', *bogъ* (*božii*) 'God', *dêva* '(Holy) Virgin', *duša* 'soul', *gospodь* (*gospodenъ, gospodinъ*) 'Lord', *grêhъ* 'sin', *mazъ* another word for 'chrism, holy anointing oil', *moĉi* 'relic', *otьcь* '(God) the Father', *prêkrъstiti* 'to sanctify again', *roistvo* 'Christmas', *stъlpъnikъ* 'stylite', *svetъ* 'saint', *ukropiti* 'to sparge', *žъrtva* 'offering'.

All 15 words denoting clergymen are loanwords, borrowed by the Slavic language across different periods: *biskupъ* 'bishop', *dominъ* 'priest' (usually before a name), *fra* 'brother' (usually before a name), *gvardiênъ* 'guardian in the Order of St. Francis', *kapelanъ* 'chaplain', *kapitulъ* 'chapter (assembly), council of clergymen', *klerъ* 'clergy', *kurato* 'priest responsible for a certain church', *ministrъ* 'minister in the Order of St. Francis', *opatъ* 'abbot', *plovanъ* 'priest', *popъ* 'priest', *pre* 'priest' (usually before a name), *prъvъdъ* 'priest, deacon', *žakanъ* 'deacon'.

Building inscriptions may contain information about the property rights for a built object. The terminology of property law is mostly borrowed: *dotati* 'to subsidize', *eredъ/redъ* 'heir', *guvernati* 'to rule, to govern', *ištrumentъ* 'document', *jereditadъ* 'inheritance', *kaštaldъ/gastaldъ* 'oikonomos in a chapter or a brotherhood', *madrigula* 'charter, regulations', *prokuraturъ/prokuradurъ* 'official', *urdinъ* 'order', *ûspaternatusъ* 'right of patronage'. There is also a remarkable example of the Romance-Slavic synonymic pairs: *urdinъ* and *naredъba* 'order'. The term *urdinъ* refers to the order more as a written document, while *naredъba* has a more common sense: *ka bi činena učiniti u bnec(i)h' od menie(!) marina cvitoviĉa kotoranina po naredbi* (...) *g(ospodi)na popa bariĉa bozaniĉa* (Vrbnik, 1599, 'It was ordered to be made in Venice by me, Marin Cvitović, on an errand of his lordship the priest Barić Božanić'). The terminology of property management is closely connected with the semantic field of power, but, since the pragmatics of the inscriptions is more close per se to the property right discourse rather than to the legislative or executive discourse, I put lexemes like *guvernati* or *urdinъ* in that field rather than in the field of power terminology. That's why I put only one borrowed word in the field of power – *guvernъnъ* 'rule, government', which is used directly in the political meaning.

The genre of a building inscription conveys the usage of building terminology. There are 7 borrowed terms of this type, including types of buildings (*crêki* 'church', *kapela* 'chapel', *kaštelъ* 'fort'), architectural details (*fondamentъ* 'foundation', *ponestra* 'window'), actors (*meštarъ* 'master, builder') and general terms (*fabrika* 'building or constriction as a process and its result/product'). The term *kaštelъ* is used here in its original meaning 'fort' (comp. the word *kaštelъ* 'municipality' in the VS). In its second meaning 'result/product of a process of building or constriction' the lexeme *fabrika* seems to have a Slavic synonym *načinъba*. The latter however features in the only phraseoligical example *načinba od' ankunij* 'altarpiece'. Another curious fact about this field is that all verbs with a (contextual) meaning 'to build' used in the inscriptions are native Slavic: *činiti, dêlati, postaviti, sazidati, svrъšiti, učiniti, uzidati, zidati*.

The last semantic field containing borrowings is that of time terminology. The situation here is close to the same field in the VS: there are names of the months, borrowed from the older substratum (*aprilъ* 'April', *decembъrъ* 'December', *envarъ* 'January', *iûnъ* 'June', *mai* 'May', *marъčъ* 'March', *oktebъrъ/ohtobъrъ* 'October', *pervarъ* 'February', *sektebъrъ* 'September'), and the Slavic general terms for time (*dъnъ* 'day', *godъ* 'year', *lêto* 'year', *mêsecъ* 'month', *vêkъ* 'century', *vrême* 'time').

2.2.2 Etymological stratification of the semantic fields

Compared with the data of the VS, only half of the loanwords in the GI belong to the younger adstratum (26, or 56 %). These words are in each field except "Time": "Building & architecture" (*fabrika* 'building', *fondamentъ* 'foundation', *meštarъ* 'master, builder', among others), "Property management" (*dotati* 'to subsidize', *eredъ* 'heir', *ûspaternatusъ* 'right of patronage', among others), "Religion" (*ankuniê* 'altar painting', *gvardiênъ* 'guardian in the Order of St. Francis', *kurato* 'priest responsible for a certain church', etc.) and "Power" (*guverъnъ* 'rule, government').

The loanwords from the older substratum make up 43 % of all borrowings (20 lexemes) and are presented in the fields of building (*ponestra* 'window') and religion (*krizma* 'chrism', *olei* 'chrism', *plovanъ* 'priest', etc.). They dominate within the borrowed terms of time (the names of the months).

As in the previous case there are some ancient borrowings from the Germanic adstratum: *crêki* 'church' and *popъ* 'priest'.

The different correlation between the older substratum and younger adstratum against the VS data reflects inclusion of the inscriptions in a different, older discourse of religious building and tombstone inscriptions whose basic elements (dates, religious terms, architectural details and others) were borrowed from the Latin-Romance stratum during the earlier period of contact.

Both the VS and the GI were created during the period of migration to the island and further migrations of Dalmatian Vlachs who spoke Balkan Romance dialects. Nevertheless, no traces of their idiom in the text investigated were found. The absence of traces of contact with Balkan Romance dialects in the language of the Glagolitic texts is the evidence *of the separation* of this population group.

2.2.3 Frequency

The appellative lexicon of the GI numbers 135 usages of loanwords against the total amount of the approximately 1000 tokens, which makes up 14 % of the total.

The majority of the loanwords occur once (22 units, or 48 %), 11 occur 2 times and 15 lexemes more than twice.

Among the frequent borrowings there are from the older substratum (*iûnъ* 'June', *plovanъ* 'priest', *žakanъ* 'deacon', and others), the old Germanic adstratum (*crêki* 'church', *popъ* 'priest') and the younger adstratum (*kaštaldъ* 'oikonomos in a chapter or a brotherhood', *meštarъ* 'master, builder', *pre* 'priest', and others). The frequency of borrowings relies on the generic features of the inscriptions, which mostly reflect building practices. They usually contain information about a master (*meštarъ* 'master, builder'), an employer (often 'priest', *plovanъ* or *popъ*), responsible persons (*eredъ* 'heir', *kaštaldъ* 'oikonomos in a chapter or a brotherhood'), building types (*kapela* 'chapel'), time (names of the months) and an introduction prayer (*amenъ* 'amen').

Table 3 Loanword frequency in the GI

Number of usages	Number of lexemes
3	*fra* 'brother', *kapitulъ* 'chapter (assembly), council of clergymen'
4	*oktebrъ* 'October', *pre* 'priest', *žakanъ* 'deacon'
5	*iûnъ* 'June', *mai* 'May'
6	*eredъ* 'heir', *gastaldъ*/*kaštaldъ* 'oikonomos in a chapter or a brotherhood'
8	*kapela* 'chapel'
10	*plovanъ* 'priest'
11	*crêki* 'church'
15	*amenъ* 'amen'
19	*meštarъ* 'master, builder'
23	*popъ* 'priest'

2.2.4 Typological approach

Because of the limited vocabulary of the Glagolitic inscriptions it is hard to draw any parallels between its semantic fields and the list in Haspelmath and Tadmor (2009). Yet the average amount of loanwords can be compared with the typological results. From this point of view, the language of the inscriptions demonstrates the level of borrowing, relatively comparable to the average or even higher (28.5 % against 24.2 %), that obviously differs from the VS data (15.4 %). This difference can be explained by the laconicism the inscriptions and the genre constraints. The latter determine the text structure of the majority of the inscriptions that supposes the usage of the borrowed terms in the topics mentioned above.

In general, we can conclude that the language of the Glagolitic monuments of the island of Krk, despite the prestigious status of the Romance stratum, demonstrates a relatively average share of lexical borrowings within all sources together (20.5 %). This observation characterizes the Slavic-Romance language contact of the island of Krk *more as a separation, than as a symbiosis of any kind.*

3 Structural interference

Having understood the degree of the lexical interference between the Slavic language of the Glagolitic monuments and the Latin-Romance continuum, we should now test our sources for interference in grammar.

3.1 Morphological interference

Among the 136 borrowings from both the VS and GI there is, of course, an overwhelming majority of nouns (113 = 83 %). There are also 20 verbs (*apelati* 'to file an appeal', *banžati* 'to chase', *denunciêti* 'to dinounce', *dotati* 'to subsidize', *durati* 'to last', etc.), 2 adverbs (*amenь* 'amen', *minutь* 'less') and 1 adjective (*komunьski* 'municipal').

The borrowed nouns usually keep the gender of a source lexeme. As it was already discussed (see Gabrić-Bagarić 1993), the -a final of the feminine nouns is interpreted as the flexion of the Slavic feminine nouns. The final vowel of the Italian masculine nouns is discarded, so the borrowed word receives the zero flexion in the nominative singular form.

There are only few cases when a loanword changes its gender. The Slavic *onukle* (n) 'yearling, one year old animal' from the Latin *annuclus* 'one-year-old' could change its gender under the influence of other words denoting young animals (e.g., *ozimьče* 'young animal'). The Latin feminine nouns on -io, -onis usually receive the masculine form on -unь/-iûnь: *kuštiûnь* (m) 'conflict, situation', *prьžunь* (m) 'prison' from *questione* 'question, issue, argument', *prigione* 'prison' (f). The Latin feminine nouns on -tas, -tatis undergo the similar process: *jereditadь* (m) 'inheritance', Latin *hereditas* or Italian *eredità* (f) 'heritage, legacy, inheritance'. The Latin neutral nouns receive the masculine gender losing the ending -um: e.g., *kapitulь* (m) 'chapter' from *capitulum* (n), though perhaps under the influence of Italian *capitolo* (m) 'chapter'.

All borrowings of the feminine gender change in type, going back to the Proto-Slavic declination of the stems on *-(')ā. In the forms GEN.SG (-e/-i), NOM. PL (-e/-i) and ACC.PL (-e/-i), there is a morphological dimorphism, caused by the process of generalizing the Proto-Slavic declination of the stems on *-(')ā on the soft or hard type in West-South-Slavonic dialects.

Table 4 Feminine nouns

Feminine nouns	SG	PL
NOM	a (*pena* 'fine', *sentenciê* [-ja] 'verdict')	-i (*libri* 'monetary unit', *librici* 'unit of weight') -e (*librice* 'unit of weight')
GEN	-e (*fatige* 'work', *sen'ten'cie* 'verdict')	-ø (*menul* 'Spicara smaris') -i (*harti* 'paper')
DAT		
ACC	-u (*beritu* 'headgear', *ligan'cu* 'obligation')	-e (*trate* 'fishing net') -i (*harti* 'paper')
INSTR	-u (*licen'ciû* 'permission')	
LOC	-ê = -i (*komar'dê* 'granary, storehouse', *š'kodi* 'injury', *d[en]unciji* 'denunciation')	

Most of the borrowings of the masculine gender change in type, going back to the Proto-Slavic declination of the stems on * -(')ŏ. In the forms of the locative singular and genitive plural, some lexemes use inflections, ascending to the Proto-Slavic declination of the stems on *-ŭ and *-ĭ. These forms, however, are used inconsistently: *vrnizi*, but *vrniz* 'monetary unit'; *kaštelov*, but *kaš'tel'* 'municipality'. Similar fluctuations are noted both in the Čakavian Glagolitic texts and in modern dialects.

Table 5 Masculine nouns

Masculine nouns	SG	PL
NOM	-ø (*apelaciûn* 'appeal', *beč* 'monetary unit')	-i (*bagatini* 'monetary unit')
GEN	-a (*karmenala* 'crime', *oficiê* 'service, office')	-ø (*dukat'* 'monetary unit', *ligan* 'Loligo vulgaris') -i (*vrnizi* 'monetary units') -ovь (*kaštelov* 'municipality')
DAT	-u (*providuru* 'provveditore')	
ACC	-ø (*apelaciûn* 'appeal', *uficii* 'service, office')	-i (*d'r'muni* 'forest') -e (*oficje* 'service, office')
INSTR	-omь (*providurom'* 'provveditore')	
LOC	-ê = -i (*mošuni* 'animal pen', *oficiji* 'service, office')	-ihь (*dr'munih'* 'forest')

A few borrowed nouns of the neutral genus show the same fluctuation in the LOC. SG (-i/-u) forms as the masculine lexemes.

Table 6 Neutral nouns

Neutral nouns	SG	PL
NOM	-e (*onuk'le* 'yearling')	
GEN		
DAT		
ACC	-e (*ul'e* 'oil')	-a (*on[u]k[l]a* 'yearling')
INSTR		
LOC	-u (*duplu* 'double quantity') -i (*vižitani* 'visitation')	

Thus, the borrowed nouns demonstrate not only the grammatical adaptation to the Slavic system of nominal inflection, but also the same morphological variability as the original lexemes.

The alteration of borrowed verbs in the language of the Vrbnik Statute depends on the type of conjugation of the source lexeme in the donor language. In most cases, historically this is the first conjugation of the Latin language (-āre). Accordingly, borrowed verbs vary in type, ascending to the Proto-Slavic verbal stems of the infinitive in *-a- and of the present in *-aje-. The suffix of the infinitive appears in two forms: -ti (*denunciêti* 'to dinounce', *provati* 'to prove', *štimati* 'to estimate', *zaminati* 'to examine') and -t (*apelat* 'to file an appeal', *durat* 'to last', *prezen'tat*' 'to present'). Variationality in verbal forms is observed in the third person singular of the present tense, as in the form with the inflection -t (*kuntentat* 'to decree') and forms without it (*pom[a]n'ka* 'to lack', *š'tima* 'to estimate'). The only borrowed verb belonging to a different type of conjugation is the verb *škuriti* 'to expire', the lexeme whose source (Italian *scurire* 'to darken') is characterized by the type of inflection, which goes back to the Latin fourth conjugation (-īre): *škuri*$_{PRS/IMP.3SG}$.

Some borrowed lexemes are characterized by the presence of Slavic derivational affixes: the prefix po- (*pomankati* 'to lack'), the suffix of the nouns -ic- (*librica* 'unit of weight') and the suffix of the verb imperfective -(i)va- (*senticiêvati* 'to bring in verdict', *termenivati* 'to decree').

3.2 Syntactic interference

The Latin and Romance influence on the Old Croatian legal texts in the domain of syntactical constructions was summarized by B. Kuzmić (2009). Since he gives no examples from either the VS or the GI, we will partially fill that gap here.

One of the most common syntactical phenomena that has arisen under Romance influence is the usage of the preposition *odъ* in accordance with the Latin/Romance preposition *de*: *ničinba odъ ankunij* 'alterpiece', *ivan od' ture* (proper name), *prokuraturi od crikve* 'procurators of the church' (GI Vrbnik 1599), *raki od fugošiĉ* 'reliquaries of Fugošiĉ' (GI, Vrbnik, 1685), *k(a)p(i)t(ul') od ênca* 'chapter about a lamb' (VS 6), *k(a)p(i)t(ul') od tad'bi kuĉ'ne* 'chapter about a theft inside a house' (VS 10), *urdini od rib'* 'laws about fish' (VS 26), *stvari od karmenala* 'crimes' (29), and others.

Another case of prepositional interference is the construction *za* + INF instead of a dependent clause or a purpose construction: *imite biti obligani priseĉi pred milostivim' providurom' za učiniti uficii nih' pravednim' zakonom'* 'You must swear before a merciful governor (It. *provveditore*) that you will fulfill their will according to the law' (VS 27), *da dod'u pomoĉ' za êti rečenih' tati* '(They) must help to seize those thieves' (VS 28).

The last phenomenon to be mentioned here is the usage of the verb *činiti* 'to do, to make' in accordance with the Latin/Romance *facere*, for example: *kapela ku čini učinit pop matij vlčijiĉ* 'chapel which the priest Matij Vlčijiĉ ordered built' (GI Omišalj 1525), *tu criki s(ve)te marie čini uzidati* '(Someone who was) made to build that church of Holy Mary' (GI Dobrinj 1576), *ka bi činena učiniti u bnec(i)h'* '(An altarpiece) that was ordered to be made in Venice' (GI Vrbnik 1599), *učiniš' k'licati i naves'titi v'sêm' tim' lûdem'* 'You will order (someone) to call and to announce (this) to all these people' (VS 19), *obligani êti ili činiti êti rečenoga tata* '(You are) obliged to arrest or to order (someone) to arrest this thief' (VS 28).

Collecting our observations we can now conclude that the lexical interference discussed in the Section 2 correlates with a slight grammatical interference – the copying of Latin/Romance written constructions.

4 Conclusion

As this analysis has shown, vocabulary serves as the main field of Slavic-Romance interference in the Glagolitic monuments. Earlier borrowings from the (Greek-)Latin-Romance substratum dominate in fields of farming, navigation, religion, fishing and time and refer to the process of *integrating the Slavic-speaking population into the Mediterranean culture of Dalmatia* (in the spheres of social organization, economic activity, calendar and religious life).

Later borrowings from the younger adstratum occupy mainly domains of governmental power and property management and reflect *the political and administrative domination of Venice on the island of Krk and in Dalmatia*.

The language of Krk's Glagolitic monuments, despite the prestigious status of the Romance stratum, demonstrates a relatively average share of lexical borrowings (20.5 %).

The rather rich inventory of the lexical borrowings contrasts with the low level of grammatical interference. While the syntax of the texts demonstrates examples of the replication of some syntactical constructions, almost all loanwords are fully adapted morphologically. There are no traces of a possible language shift among the autochthonic Romance population.

All this argues for a situation of language maintenance with lexical and slight structural borrowing in accordance with the system of Thomason and Kaufman (1988: 78–83), which implies an average level of cultural pressure. This observation characterizes the Slavic-Romance language contact of the island of Krk *more as a separation, than as a symbiosis of any kind* and thus distinguishes this situation from other examples of Slavic-Romance language contact on the Balkan Peninsula.

References

Aničić, Luka. 2012. Glagoljski natpisi otoka Krka kao povijesni izvor [Glagolitic inscriptions of Krk island as a historical source]. *Vjesnik istarskog arhiva* 19. 115–126.

Asenova, Petia. 2002. *Balkansko ezikoznanie* [Balkan linguistics]. Sofia: Faber.

Barth, Frederik. 1998. *Ethnic Groups and Boundaries: The Social Organization of Cultural Difference*. Long Grove: Waveland Press, Inc.

Bolonić, Mihovil. 1966. Seoski kaptoli u krčkoj biskupiji [County seats in the Krk Diocese]. *Bogoslovska smotra* 36 (1). 122–145.

Bolonić, Mihovil. 1980. Profil krčkog glagoljaša u prošlosti [The profile of Krk Glagolithic priests in the past]. *Christiana Periodica* 1980 (4). 96–115.

Breu, Walter. 2014. Substrate auf slavischem Sprachgebiet (Südslavisch). In Karl Gutschmidt, Sebastian Kempgen, Tilman Berger & Peter Kosta (eds.), *Die slavischen Sprachen* [The Slavic Languages]. *Ein internationales Handbuch zu ihrer Struktur, ihrer Geschichte und ihrer Erforschung* (Handbücher zur Sprach- und Kommunikationswissenschaft. 32), Vol. 2, 1175–1181. Berlin & Boston: De Gruyter Mouton.

Čunčić, Marica & Marta Perkić. 2009. Hrvatski glagoljski natpis Župe Dubrovačke iz 11. stoljeća [The Croatian Glagolitic inscription of Župa Dubrovačka from the 11th century]. *Slovo* 59. 77–122.

Deanović, Mirko. 1938. Divergences entre les emprunts latinoromans en Dalmatie. *Bulletin de la société de linguistique de Paris* 39 (1). 25–48.

Deanović, Mirko. 1966. Stratifikacija naših pomorskih i ribarskih naziva po njihovu porijeklu [Stratification of our maritime and fisheries terminology on the basis of their origins]. *Pomorski zbornik* 4(1). 735–744.

Desnitskaya, Agniya V. 1988. Tipy leksicheskikh vzaimosviazei i voprosy obrazovaniia balkanskogo iazykovogo soiuza [Types of lexical relations and questions related to the establishment of the Balkan Sprachbund]. *Slavianskoe iazykoznanie. X Mezhdunarodnyi s"ezd slavistov. Doklady sovetskoi delegatsii*, conference publication, 131–50. Moscow: Nauka.

Doria, Mario. 1989. Dalmatisch = Dalmatico. In Günter Holtus (ed.), *Lexikon der Romanistischen Linguistik, Bd. 3. Die einzelnen romanischen Sprachen und Sprachgebiete von der Renaissance bis zur Gegenwart: Rumänisch, Dalmatisch/Istroromanisch, Friaulisch, Ladinisch, Bündnerromanisch*, vol. 3, 522–536. Tübingen: Max Niemeyer Verlag.

Dzino, Danijel. 2010. *Becoming Slav, Becoming Croat: Identity Transformations in Post-Roman and Early Medieval Dalmatia*. Leiden; Boston: Brill.

Evreinova, Anna M. 1880. *Statut ostrova Kŭrka 1388* [The statute of Krk Island 1388]. 2 Vols. St. Petersburg.

Fučić, Branko. 1982. *Glagoljski natpisi* [Glagolitic inscriptions]. Zagreb: JAZU.

Gabrić-Bagarić, D. 1993. Morfološka prilagodba posuđenica u "Dijalozima Grgura Velikoga" iz 1513. godine [The morphological adaptation of loan words in the "Dialogues of Grgur the Great"]. *Rasprave: Časopis Instituta za hrvatski jezik i jezikoslovlje* 19 (1). 93–111.

Gačić, Jasna. 1979a. Romanski elementi u splitskom čakavskom govoru [Romance elements in the Chakavian subdialect of Split]. *Čakavska rič* 1979 (1). 3–54.

Gačić, Jasna. 1979b. Romanski elementi u splitskom čakavskom govoru (nastavak) [Romance elements in the Chakavian subdialect of Split (continued)]. *Čakavska rič* 1979 (2). 107–155.

Gačić, Jasna. 2003. Jezična slojevitost na istočnoj obali Jadrana i dalmatinskomletački dijalekt [Linguistic stratification on the east coast of the Adriatic and Dalmatian-Venetian dialect]. *Filologija* 41. 21–32.

Galović, Filip. 2013. Romanski elementi u nazivlju odjevnih predmeta, obuće i modnih dodataka u milnarskome idiomu [Roman loanwords in the terminology of garments, footwear, and accessories in Milna's idiom]. *Čakavska rič* 2013 (1–2). 159–188.

Galović, Filip. 2014. Nazivi za zanimanja, zvanja i počasne službe romanskoga podrijetla u govoru Ložišća na otoku Braču [The Romance origin lexis related to professions, occupations and honorary positions in the local dialect of Ložišća on the island of Brač]. *Čakavska rič* 2014 (1–2). 87–112.

Galović, Filip & Keti Papić. 2016. Imenice romanskoga podrijetla u semantičkoj sferi odjevnih predmeta, obuće te modnih i drugih dodataka u ložiškome govoru [Nouns of Romance origin within the semantic sphere of garments, footwear, fashion and other accessories in the speech of Ložišće]. *Čakavska rič* 2016 (1–2). 79–129.

Haspelmath, Martin. 2009. Lexical borrowing: Concepts and issues. In Haspelmath, Martin & Uri Tadmor (eds.), *Loanwords in the world's languages: A comparative handbook*, 35–54. Berlin & Boston: De Gruyter Mouton.

Haspelmath, Martin & Uri Tadmor (eds.). 2009. *Loanwords in the world's languages: A comparative handbook*. Berlin & Boston: De Gruyter Mouton.

Kalmeta, Ratimir. 1970. Geografski položaj otoka Krka [The geographical location of Krk island]. *Krčki zbornik* 1. 19–58.

Kukuljević Sakcinski, Ivan. 1852. *Arkiv za pověstnicu jugoslavensku* [South Slavic historical archive]. Vol. 2. Zagreb.

Kuzmić, Boris. 2009. Jezik hrvatskih srednjovjekovnih pravnih spomenika [The language of Croatian medieval legal documents]. In Stjepan Damjanović (ed.), *Povijest hrvatskoga jezika, 1. knjiga: srednji vijek*, Vol. 1, 405–455. Zagreb: Društvo za promicanje hrvatske kulture i znanosti CROATICA.

Ligorio, Orsat. 2014. *Problem leksičke stratifikacije u Adriatistici* [The problem of lexical stratification in the Adriatic studies], doctoral dissertation. Zadar: Sveučilište u Zadru.

Ligorio, Orsat & Nikola Vuletić. 2013. Dopune Jadranskim etimologijama Vojmira Vinje: Treći prilog. [Additions to Vojmir Vinja's Adriatic etymologies. Part 3]. *Croatica et Slavica Iadertina* 9 (1). 51–62.

Marasović-Alujević, Marina. 1984. Romanizmi u graditeljskoj terminologiji u Dalmaciji [Romance elements in Dalmatian architectural terminology]. *Čakavska rič* 1–2. 55–103.

Margetić, Lujo. (ed.). 2012. *Srednjovjekovni zakoni i opći akti na Kvarneru* [Medieval laws and general acts in Kvarner]. Zagreb: Rijeka.

Margetić, Lujo & Petar Strčić (eds.). 1988. *Krčki (Vrbanski) statut iz 1388.* [The Krk (Vrban) statute of 1388]. Krk: Povijesno društvo otoka Krka.

Miklas, Heinz & Velizar Sadovski. 2014. Die Struktur des Altkirchenslavischen. In Karl Gutschmidt, Sebastian Kempgen, Tilman Berger & Peter Kosta (eds.), *Die slavischen Sprachen* [The Slavic Languages]. *Ein internationales Handbuch zu ihrer Struktur, ihrer Geschichte und ihrer Erforschung* (Handbücher zur Sprach- und Kommunikationswissenschaft. 32), Vol. 2, 1175–1181. Berlin & Boston: De Gruyter Mouton.

Miočić, Kristina. 2011a. Romanizmi u govoru Baških Oštarija [Romance loanwords in the dialect of Baške Oštarije]. *Jezikoslovlje* 12. 51–74.

Miočić, Kristina. 2011b. Romanizmi u kuhinjskom i kulinarskom leksiku ražanačkog kraja [Romance loanwords in the cuisine and culinary lexicon of the Ražanac area]. *Čakavska rič* 39 (1–2). 31–65.

Miočić, Kristina. 2012. Romanski elementi u nazivlju predmeta vezanih za tekstil, odjeću i obuću u govoru ražanačkoga kraja [Romance elements in the names of items having to do with textile, clothes and footwear in the dialect of Ražanac area]. *Čakavska rič* 40 (1–2). 47–70.

Miočić, Kristina. 2014. Romanski leksički elementi u govoru Baških Oštarija [Romance lexical elements in the dialect of Baške Oštarije]. *Jezikoslovlje* 15. 91–108.

Muljačić, Žarko. 1967. Die slavisch-romanische Symbiose in Dalmatien in struktureller Sicht. *Zeitschrift für Balkanologie* 5 (1). 51–70.

Muljačić, Žarko. 2000. *Das Dalmatische: Studien zu einer untergegangenen Sprache.* Köln: Böhlau.

Nigoević, Magdalena & Josip Lasić. 2007. Adaptacija glagola romanskog podrijetla u splitskom govoru [Adaptation of verbs of Romance origin in the Split dialect]. In Jagoda Granić (ed.), *Jezik i identiteti*, 365–375. Zagreb, Split: Hrvatsko društvo za primijenjenu lingvistiku.

Nigoević, Magdalena & Josip Lasić. 2012. Adaptacije romanskih pridjevskih posuđenica u govorima Zabiokovlja [Adjectives of Romance origin in the speech of the Biokovo Mountain hinterland]. *Rasprave: Časopis Instituta za hrvatski jezik i jezikoslovlje* 38 (2), 401–431.

Pliško, Lina. 2009. Romanizmi u leksemima za dom i posjed u jugozapadnome istarskome ili štakavsko-čakavskome dijalektu [Romanisms in lexical items related to home and house lot in SW Istrian or stokavian-chakavian dialect]. *Čakavska rič* 1–2. 147–158.

Pliško, Lina. 2016. Romanizmi u hreljićkoj spavaćoj sobi [Romance loan words in Hreljić bedroom]. *Fluminensia* 2016 (28). 27–38.

Rački, Franjo, Vatroslav Jagić & Ivan Črnčić. 1890. Statuta lingua croatica conscripta = Hrvatski pisani zakoni: Vinodolski, Poljički, Vrbanski a donekle i svega Krčkog otoka, Kastavski, Veprinački i Trsatski [Statuta lingua croatica conscripta = Croatian written laws: of Vinodol, Poljica, Vrbnik and the whole island of Krk, Kastav, Veprinac and Trsat]. *Monumenta historico-juridica slavorum meridionalium* 4 (1). Zagreb: Dionička tiskara.

Reinhart, Johannes. 2014. Das Kroatisch-Kirchenslavische. In Karl Gutschmidt, Sebastian Kempgen, Tilman Berger & Peter Kosta (eds.), *Die slavischen Sprachen* [The Slavic Languages]. *Ein internationales Handbuch zu ihrer Struktur, ihrer Geschichte und ihrer Erforschung*, vol. 2, 1294–1308. Berlin & Boston: De Gruyter Mouton.

Repina, Tamara A. & Boris P. Narumov. 2001. Dalmatinskii iazyk [The Dalmatian language]. In Irina I. Chelysheva, Boris P. Narumov & Ol'ga I. Romanova (eds.), *Iazyki mira: Romanskie iazyki*, 681–694. Moscow: Academia.

Shuvalov, Petr V. 1998. Proniknovenie slavian na Balkany [Penetration of the Slavs into the Balkans]. In Agniya V. Desnitskaya & Nikita I. Tolstoi (eds.), *Osnovy balkanskogo iazykoznaniia. Iazyki balkanskogo regiona, Ch. 2 (slavianskie iazyki)* [Foundations of Balkan linguistics. The languages of the Balkan region. Pt. 2 (Slavic languages)], vol. 2, 5–28. St. Petersburg: Nauka.

Skok, Petar. 1933. *Naša pomorska i ribarska terminologija na Jadranu: Od koga naučiše jadranski Jugosloveni pomorstvo i ribarstvo?* [Our maritime and fishing terminology on the Adriatic: From whom did the Adriatic South Slavs learn seafaring and fishing?]. Split: Jadranska straža.

Skok, Petar. 1950. *Slavenstvo i romanstvo na jadranskim otocima: Toponomastička ispitivanja* [Slavonic and Romance population on the Adriatic islands: A toponymic examination]. Zagreb: JAZU.

Skok, Petar. 1971. *Etimologijski rječnik hrvatskoga ili srpskoga jezika*, kn. I–III [Etymological dictionary of Croatian or Serbian language, vol. I–III]. Zagreb: Jugoslavenska akademija znanosti i umjetnosti.

Sobolev, Andrey N. 2001. Balkanskaia leksika v areal'nom i areal'no-tipologicheskom osveshchenii [Balkan lexicon in the the light of areal and areal-typological study]. *Voprosy iazykoznaniia* 2. 59–93.

Sobolev, Andrey N. 2013. *Osnovy lingvokul'turnoi antropogeografii Balkanskogo poluostrova. Tom I. Homo balcanicus i ego prostranstvo* [Foundations of linguocultural anthropogeography on the Balkan peninsula. Vol. 1. Homo balcanicus and his space]. St. Petersburg: Nauka, München: Otto Sagner Verlag.

Sočanac, Lelija. 2005. Language contacts in the Ragusan Republic. In P. Sture Urland (ed.), *Studies in Eurolinguistics. Vol. 2. Integration of European Language Research*, 585–604. Berlin: Logos.

Sočanac, Lelija. 2007. The Ragusan Republic and Western Europe: The Sea as a Medium of Language Contact. In P. Sture Ureland, A. Lodge & S. Pugh (eds.), *Studies in Eurolinguistics. Vol. 5. Language Contact and Minority Languages on the Littorals of Europe*, 225–246. Berlin: Logos.

Spicijarić, Nina. 2009. Romanizmi u nazivlju kuhinjskih predmeta u govoru Dubašnice na otoku Krku — etimološka i leksikološka obradba [Romanisms in the names of kitchen items in the speech of Dubašnica on the island of Krk – etymological and lexicological analysis]. *Fluminensia* 21. 7–24.

Spicijarić Paškvan, Nina. 2014. Dalmatski (veljotski) i mletački utjecaji u govorima otoka Krka [Dalmatian (Vegliot) and Venetian influences in the dialects of the island of Krk]. *Krčki zbornik* 70. 71–88.

Tekavčić, Pavao. 1970. *Uvod u vulgarni latinitet (s izborom tekstova)* [An introduction to Vulgar Latin (with a collection of texts)]. Zagreb: Kućna tiskara Sveučilišta u Zagrebu.

Tekavčić, Pavao. 1976. O kriterijima stratifikacije i regionalne diferencijacije jugoslavenskog romanstva u svjetlu toponomastike [On the criteria for stratification and regional differentiation of Yugoslav romance languages in the light of toponyms]. *Onomastica Jugoslavica* 6. 35–56.

Thomason, Sarah Grey & Terrence Kaufman. 1988. *Language Contact, Creolization, and Genetic Linguistics*. Berkeley: University of California Press.
Vinja, Vojmir. 1986. *Jadranska fauna: Etimologija i struktura naziva* [Adriatic fauna: Etymology and structure of terms]. Split: Logos.
Vinja, Vojmir. 1998–2004. *Jadranske etimologije: Jadranske dopune Skokovu etimologijskom rječniku* [Adriatic etymologies: Adriatic additions to the P. Skok's etymological dictionary]. Vols. 1–3. Zagreb: HAZU.
Vuletić, Nikola. 2006. Dopune "Jadranskim etimologijama" Vojmira Vinje: Prvi prilog [Additions to Vojmira Vinja's "Adriatic Etymologies": Part one]. *Croatica et Slavica Iadertina* 2 (2). 135–144.
Vuletić, Nikola. 2010. Etimološke bilješke s hrvatskih otoka i obale (uz Vinjine "Jadranske etimologije") [Etymological notes from the Croatian islands and coasts (after Vinjina's "Adriatic etymologies"]. *Croatica et Slavica Iadertina* 6 (6). 9–19.
Županović, Šime. 1994. Ribarstvo i ribarska terminologija zadarskog područja [Fisheries and fishing terminology in the Zadar region]. *Čakavska rič* 22 (2). 3–63.
Županović, Šime. 1995a. *Hrvati i more* [Croats and the Sea]. Vol. 1–2. Zagreb: AGM.
Županović, Šime. 1995b. Osnovne značajke postanja i strukture nazivlja zadarsko-kvarnerske (ZD-KV) i šibensko-hvarske (ŠB-HV) talasofaune [Basic characteristics of the origin and structure of the Zadar – Kvarner (ZD–KV) and Šibenik – Hvar (ŠB-HV) thalassofauna terminology]. *Čakavska rič* 23 (1–2). 19–68.
Županović, Šime. 1997. Podrijetlo hrvatske ribarske terminologije [The origin of the Croatian fishery terminology]. *Čakavska rič* 25 (1–2). 97–138.
Županović, Šime. 1998. *Hrvati i more* [Croats and the Sea]. Vol. 3–4. Zagreb: AGM.

Maxim L. Kisilier
Reconstructing Past Coexistence: Problems and Mysteries in the Multilingual History of Tsakonia, Greece

Abstract: This chapter[1] is about the historical development of Tsakonian and the unique aspects of its current situation. Tsakonian is one of the **most mysterious Modern Greek dialects** that is generally considered to be a direct descendant of Ancient Greek Doric Laconian which developed in separation and isolation. It has a number of rare features that can scarcely be explained from the point of view of Greek dialectology and historical grammar. These involve phonetics (such as (/ʒ/ or /ʃ/ < /ri/ or /nd/ < /z/) and morphosyntax (e. g., absence of a synthetic present and imperfect, and special regulations in the placement of pronominal clitics). Such features cannot be found elsewhere in Modern Greek dialects. Linguistic descriptions of Tsakonian are almost always accompanied with the statement that Tsakonian is the only (sic!) Modern Greek dialect which does not originate from the Hellenistic Koiné. But it is not clear how that fact, even if true, would explain the "strange" features of Tsakonian as their connection with Ancient Laconian are still to be demonstrated. A logical explanation would be interaction with other languages during the Byzantine and Post-Byzantine periods since toponymic and lexical data suggest that Greeks were not the only residents of the region. Still the possibilities for reconstructing any details are very limited. Unlike previous studies, this chapter demonstrates that Tsakonian in its evolution was not entirely independent of the influence of other languages and dialects. At least during the last two centuries Tsakonian had constant contact only with Standard Modern Greek. The study of earlier stages of Tsakonian demands that the researcher hypothesize some past contact situation but not to be content just with a pure description of the contemporary state of the art. While presenting the rare and amazing interplay of archaisms and innovations that make Tsakonian what it is, the goal of this paper is somewhat challenging. On one hand, I intend to discuss the limits and possibilities of reconstructing past contact and, on the other hand, to show why the contact-oriented approach may be important for

---

[1] This research was made possible by a grant from the Russian Science Foundation (the projects "From separation to symbiosis: South Eastern European languages and cultures in contact", No. 14-18-01405 and "Balkan bilingualism in dominant and equilibrium contact situations in diatopy, diachrony and diastraty", No. 19-18-00244). I would like to thank the anonymous reviewer, the editor of this volume, Alexander Yu. Rusakov and Daria V. Konior for their valuable remarks.

https://doi.org/10.1515/9781501509254-008

Tsakonian studies. This chapter is mostly based on data collected by the author between 2010 and 2019 in Tsakonian-speaking villages of Peloponnese (Greece).

1 Introduction

While describing multilingualism and multiculturalism, researchers are generally aware of the languages and cultures that are involved in contact. It is possible to trace which elements are borrowed and donated, and the direct observation and description of the language and cultural contact in synchrony may become a good basis for subsequent historical analysis.[2] Sometimes historical evidence supported by linguistic data and description of certain traditions enable the reconstruction of the past coexistence of various languages and cultures. For example, Azov Greeks until the end of the 20th century had contacts only with Russian, but in the Crimea where they lived before moving to the Azov steppe they had to communicate with the local Crimean Tatar majority.[3] There are thus a large number of lexical borrowings from Tatar in the dialect of Azov Greeks (Kisilier 2008: 157) and several traditions of Tatar origin in their culture (Novik 2009: 68–71).

Untill recently, the majority of Modern Greek dialects have been traditionally analysed without any reference to possible language contacts as if they had existed in a linguistic vacuum without any influence from the outside.[4] Moreover, scholars tried to reconstruct a hypothetical past state of affairs when the dialect, as they believed, must have been much purer. For instance, Peter Trudgill (2003: 48) suggests that "any classification of traditional Greek dialects that aims at portraying and summarising the full extent of our knowledge of the geographical configuration of these dialects should ideally be based on a description of the situation existing between, say, 1820 and 1920, when they were at their fullest extent, rather than on the situation today". However, it has become clear that the interaction of Modern Greek dialects with other languages is not a specific feature of the 20th century with its two World Wars, extensive migrations resulting

---

[2] This situation is both relevant for most cases described in this book and for many Modern Greek dialects outside Greece, for example, for the Greek dialect of Dropull in Albania (Kisilier, Novik & Sobolev 2016).
[3] Some Greeks in the Crimea (primarily the urban ones) even started speaking a dialect of Crimean Tatar instead of Greek though they remained Orthodox. Their language is now known as *Urum*.
[4] In the 19th and 20th centuries, Hellenic studies in general and Modern Greek dialectology in particular, mostly for political and ideological reasons (see, for example, a discussion on the highly controversial Fallmerayer's "Greek theory") did not pay much attention to language and inter-ethnic contacts by methods of contact linguistics.

from the Asia Minor Catastrophe of 1922, economic crises, and the processes of urbanization (cf. Pappas 2017), but started long before. Now it is almost a commonplace to study Grico and Grekaniko in South Italy (Ledgeway 2013), Greek dialects of Dropull (Kisilier, Novik & Sobolev 2016) and Himara (Joseph, Ndoci & Dickerson 2019) in Southern Albania, and Cappadocian (Janse 2019), Pontic (Sitaridou & Kaltsa 2014), and Propontis Tsakonian (Melissaropoulou 2018; 2019) in Asia Minor taking into account long and intensive contacts with local languages. Much less has been done in the field of language contacts within Greece itself (cf. Adamou 2008).

Unlike the aforementioned varieties of Greek, [Peloponnesian] Tsakonian, the Modern Greek dialect discussed in this chapter, has been always regarded as a separate "free-of-any-contact" language which even managed to escape the influence of Hellenistic Koiné (Kontosopoulos 2010: 191) and thereby to preserve multiple Ancient Doric features.[5] However, not all peculiarities of Tsakonian can be indisputably identified as Ancient Doric. Nor they are typical for Byzantine Greek, Standard Modern Greek or other Modern Greek varieties. Contemporary Tsakonian has no clear signs of intensive language contacts but this does not mean that it could not have interacted with other languages, non-dialect Greek inclusive, in the past. In the early 20th century, Dirk Christiaan Hesseling (1907: 153–168) suggested that Tsakonian should be treated as a creole language, which appeared as a result of contacts between the Dorians and the speakers of Ural-Altaic. His hypothesis was angrily rejected by the most famous specialist in Tsakonian Michael Deffner, who even called a meeting of the local community "to condemn the anthellenic outrage" (Nicholas 2009).

The goal of this chapter is not to prove Hesseling's point of view – the data we have at our disposal makes that hardly possible. Rather, I intend to demonstrate that:

(a) Tsakonians were not separated from other nations and other Greeks and Tsakonian was not isolated over the scope of its history;
(b) it could have had contacts with different languages and with non-dialect Greek[6] (by means of education and folklore);
(c) a contact-oriented approach may help to explain some linguistic peculiarities of Tsakonian.

---

[5] According to widespread opinion, the Tsakonian-speaking region (so called Tsakonia) was separated from the rest of Greece until the 1950s (Charalampopoulos 1980a: 19).
[6] I intentionally avoid the term 'Standard Modern Greek' here, because these contacts, as it will be shown later, started long before the 20th century.

Taking into account that some readers may have only vague ideas about Tsakonian, in Section 4 I shall provide general information on the dialect and make a brief overview of the state of Tsakonian studies. Besides, along with analysis of possible borrowings and impact of Standard Greek in Section 5, I am going to highlight historical, geographical and cultural evidence in Sections 2 and 3 in order to demonstrate that speakers of Tsakonian had contacts with other languages and cultures in the past. The data for this chapter was collected from 2010 to 2019 over the course of expeditions to the Tsakonian speaking region in Peloponnese organized by the Hellenic Institute of Saint Petersburg University with a support of the Institute for Linguistic Studies of the Russian Academy of Sciences.[7]

2 Tsakonia: geography and population

2.1 Geography

Tsakonian is a Modern Greek dialect currently distributed in Arkadia (Eastern Peloponnese) in the municipality of South Kynouria[8] and in two villages[9] on the southern slope of mount Parnon in the municipality of North Kynouria. Previously it was also spoken in the Tsakonian colonies Vatika and Havoutsi on the Sea of Marmara near Gönen.[10] Due to population exchanges in 1923–1924, speakers of Propontis Tsakonian moved to West Macedonia in northern Greece. This variety of Tsakonian disappeared around 1970[11] and is not described in this chapter.

The Tsakonian-speaking area, or *Tsakonia*, as it will be termed henceforth, is surrounded by mountains (except in two villages in North Kynouria) and is not easily accessed from the mainland. There is no railway and a road was built only in 1960. Unlike many other regions in Peloponnese, for example the neighboring Laconia, there are just a few flat areas close to the sea or far up in the highlands. Several decades ago, there was more rain in winter and the summer heat was not

---

[7] Some information about these expeditions and the results may be found in (Kisilier 2014a; 2014c).
[8] The towns of Leonidio, Agios Andreas/Prastos and Tyros, the villages of Sapounakeika, Melana, Pragmateftis and Vaskina.
[9] Kastanitsa and Sitena.
[10] The life, traditions, and culture of these colonies are described in (Costakis 1979).
[11] Evidently, Propontis Tsakonian was influenced by other Greek dialects of Asia Minor (Costakis 1956b; 1969; Melissaropoulou 2018; 2019), and the change of linguistic environment led to language death.

so extreme,[12] but water was still insufficient for successful agriculture. Only in the milder climate and with the spring water of the highland could potatoes and chestnuts be cultivated in the villages of Kastanitsa and Sitena. This does not mean that other parts of Tsakonia had no agriculture at all: residents of Vaskina planted peas and lentils;[13] almost everywhere there were olives and grapes, but the quality of these goods was inferior to that of other regions. Thus the two main occupations in Tsakonia were cattle-breeding in the mountains (e. g., around the village of Vaskina) and seamanship/fishing in the coastal settlement of Tyros.

In winter, shepherds from Vaskina with their families and cattle migrated to adjacent Laconia. They rented fields and stayed in Laconia until March or April. The same field was usually rented by different generations of the same family. It was not easy to find an appropriate spare field, and shepherds from Vaskina were unable to rent fields close to one another. Therefore, their neighbors in Laconia were Laconians, but not Tsakonians.[14]

2.2 Toponyms

Unfortunately, I have not found detailed maps of Tsakonia from the Venetian or Ottoman periods, and it is difficult even to imagine what toponyms would have looked like before the late 19th century. One can only guess how many of them were renamed after Greece became independent.[15] Toponymics can be extremely helpful in revealing who lived in Tsakonia in the past since Tsakonians are no longer in contact with other languages than Standard Modern Greek. Even contemporary toponyms may give some interesting evidence.

As could be expected, most toponyms are Greek (Amantos 1964: 339–340). The capital of Tsakonia Leonidio (*áje líði* in Tsakonian) has multiple etymologies. It is generally derived either from Leonidas the king of Sparta (Sarris 1956: 26–27; Vagenas 1969b: 34), or Saint Leonidas (Vagenas 1969b: 33–34). Probably, the town was not called directly after the Saint but after the church devoted to him (Zarbanos 1956: 63; Sarris 1984). The Tsakonian name of the town consists of two words: *áje* – most probably 'saint' and *líði* which could be interpreted as either Leonidas,

---

[12] According to my informant, he used to sail the river Dafnon with his father from the Myrtoon Sea to the center of Leonidio. Now the river has water only once in several years.
[13] They bore them to Kastanitsa and exchanged them for potatoes and chestnuts.
[14] The situation changed in the 1970s. It became possible to buy cattle pens close to Leonidio or a car and to keep cattle far from home. Still, even now some residents of Vaskina migrate to Lakonia in winter.
[15] For example, Agios Andreas primarily had the name *jalé* 'shore'.

or Elias, or Lydis. It is noteworthy that there are churches dedicated to each of these saints not far away (Vagenas 1969b: 35, 38).[16]

Nevertheless, some toponyms are definitely not Greek, but Slavic: Sitena < *Sitъno or *Sitъna 'rush, marsh weed' (Vasmer 1941: 158), Zaggoli < za golim 'behind the place that has no trees or bushes' (Antonakatou & Mauros 1980: 47), Zaritse 'the place behind the river'. Probably, Prastos is also a Slavic toponym. Max Vasmer (1941: 157) proposes to derive it from *prostъ 'simple, rude', although he admits that it could also have an Ancient Greek etymology: προάστειον /proáste:on/ 'outskirts'.[17] Prastos could also originate from πρᾶος τόπος /práos tópos/ 'a calm/nice place' (Romaios 1956: 8).

Near Melana there is a microtoponym fráŋgo that evidently refers to French invaders of Medieval Peloponnese (see Section 3.1) generally called Φράγκοι /fráŋgi/ 'Francs'. It is likely they had salt mines there (Lysikatos 1980: 180) during the Principality of Achaea in the 13th century. The name of mountain range Malevos – Malevé in Tsakonian – seems to have at least one Albanian constituent: mal, -i 'mountain'.[18] A number of microtoponyms sound non-Greek as well, but it is not possible yet to arrive at any appropriate etymology: e. g., múzya, serbetsía, serniáli, soxá, tʃárko (Lysikatos 1980: 182–184).

The analysis of toponymics, despite the lack of data, definitely shows that in some periods in the past, the region of Tsakonia had Slavs, Francs and, perhaps, Albanians.

---

[16] There is also a witty suggestion that áje líði or ajelíði could originate from αιγιαλός /ejalós/ 'coast' (Vagenas 1969b: 35–36). Detailed analysis of various etymologies is available in (Vagenas 1971: 88–95). For other toponyms of Greek origin see (Romaios 1956). The most famous are: Tyros, mentioned in a 6th century BC inscription and the names Poulithra and the mountain Oriontas that can be found in Pausanias, 2nd century AD.

[17] In this chapter, all Ancient Greek and Modern Greek examples are followed with a transription. This happens not only because Greek has its special font but in order to avoid any potential ambiguity. During its long history, Greek phonetics and phonology have undergone multiple crucial changes while orthography has remained unchanged. Vowels and diphthongs: αι – AncGr /ai/ vs. MGr /e/, ει – AncGr /ɛ:/ vs. MGr /i/, η – AncGr /e:/ vs. MGr /i/, οι – AncGr /oi/ vs. MGr /i/, ου – AncGr /o:/ vs. MGr /u/, υ – AncGr /y/ vs. MGr /i/, ω – AncGr /ɔ:/ vs. MGr /o/. Consonants: β – AncGr /b/ vs. MGr /v/, γ – AncGr /g/ vs. MGr /ɣ/, δ – AncGr /d/ vs. MGr /ð/, θ – AncGr /tʰ/ vs. MGr /θ/, φ – AncGr /pʰ/ vs. MGr /f/, etc.

[18] Probably, the second constituent -ve also has an Albanian origin and comes from the word vezë, -a 'egg' (Pitsinos 1951: 4).

2.3 Population

According to Theodoros Pitsios (1986: 224), residents of Tsakonia, or Tsakonians, as they are usually called, are a representative group for the population of the Peloponnese. Most of them believe that their ancestors were ancient Spartans, and this belief is not just the basis of Tsakonian identity[19] but it deeply influences Tsakonian studies all over the world, see Sections 3.2 and 4.1 below. Regardless of their ability to speak the dialect, Tsakonians are very proud of their identity.[20]

In 2017, the Tsakonian Archive in Leonidio started a new project aimed at creating genealogical trees of major Tsakonian families. Though the process of collecting the data has taken much longer than expected, during my interviews I had the good fortune to learn some interesting facts about the parents and grandparents of some of my informants. One of them had a mother from North Macedonia who was probably Serbian, while the father of another informant spent all his childhood in Romania. When he came to Leonidio at the age of 16, he could speak neither Tsakonian, nor Greek. Another informant told me about his relatives in Geraki, a village in Lakonia 39 km southeast of Sparta. He had never seen these relatives, but he knows from his grandparents that they have/had the same surname as he does.[21] There is also some evidence that residents of the village Kastanitsa could have come from Ouranoupoli in the northwest of the peninsula of Athos (Siakotos 2011: 347).

Tsakonian surnames/family names may also be helpful in the search for former contacts. Most have Greek etymology and should be connected with some local realities (Merikakis 1969: 10). One of them – *Tsakonas* – is expectedly widely used outside Tsakonia (Vagenas 1980: 97). However, I could find at least three surnames/family names that either refer to other nationalities: Βλάχος /vláxos/[22]

---

19 Tsakonians were aware of their Spartan origin even in the first decades of the 19th century. The famous British traveler Martin Leake (1830: 505) wondered who told Tsakonians about their ancestors, as he, evidently, did not support this hypothesis.
20 During the expedition to Tsakonia in January 2010, I came across the following proverb: "a Greek brain is equal to a thousand European brains, while a Tsakonian brain is equal to thousand Greek brains". These proverbs may lead to erroneous assumptions that (a) Tsakonians are violent nationalists and (b) Tsakonian think that they are not Greeks. However, the both are false: Tsakonians are very tolerant and hospitable, and they are sure that they have preserved more original Greek features than those found elsewhere in Greece.
21 This story in a way supports the information provided by the "Chronicle of Morea" (14th century) that Geraki was a part of Tsakonia (Egea Sanchez 1996: 98).
22 From MGr Βλάχος /vláxos/ 'Aromanian'.

and family name Αρβανιταίοι /arvanitéi/[23] (Costakis 1958–1959: 232), or have non-Greek etymology: Βλάμης /vlámis/ < Alb vëllam, -i 'sworn brother'.

3 Tsakonia: history, ethnography and culture

3.1 History

The area of modern Tsakonia was already inhabited in Mycenaean times.[24] Some settlements of the region, for example *Prasíai* or *Brasíai* (Pritchett 1991: 142–143), were mentioned by Thucydides, Strabo and Pausanias. The word 'Tsakonians' was first used in the 10th century AD by Constantine Porphyrogenitus (Reiske 1829: 696), as he wrote that Tsakonians were soldiers in frontier fortresses, although it is not clear whom exactly the emperor referred to with this term.

After the Conquest of Constantinople in 1204, French crusaders founded the Principality of Achaea in Peloponnese. According to the "Chronicle of the Morea",[25] Tsakonians did not want to acknowledge foreign power and strongly opposed it. They assisted Byzantine troops in 1261 and became part of the Despotate of the Morea (Vagenas 1971: 104–106). The population of the Despotate was multiethnic. Along with Greeks, it included Slavs and Albanians. In 1460, Mehmet the Conqueror destroyed the Despotate of the Morea, but the war did not end before 1476 when Leonidio was ruined (Balta 2009: 178).[26] For a short period (from 1685 to 1715), Tsakonia was under Venetian rule (Dernikos 1956: 17; Vagenas 1969a; 1971: 138; Balta 2009: 182–187).

Under Ottoman rule, Tsakonians began to trade in Nafplio and Constantinople. It is not known what goods they sold. Agricultural production varied from village to village. Most merchants were from Prastos and hired sailors in coastal villages like Tyros. The commerce, especially the butter trade (Pouqueville 1820: 174),[27] made Tsakonian merchants very rich. Prastos became one of the most prosperous trading towns of the region with two- or three-story stone buildings. Its residents frequently went to work in Constantinople (Balta 2009: 181) and then

---

23 From Αρβανίτης /arvanítis/, a term used for a bilingual group in Greece who speaks Modern Greek and an Albanian dialect known as αρβανίτικα /arvanitika/.
24 In 2011, heavy rains revealed Mycenaean tombs near Vaskina (Archaeology 2011).
25 The "Chronicle of the Morea" is an anonymous Greek romance of the 14th century, about the Principality of Achaea. It is still unknown if its author was pro-Frankish Greek, or Greek-speaking Frank, but definitely a supporter of the Franks.
26 Leonidio did not have permanent population until 1613.
27 Tsakonian merchants bought butter in the Crimea (Papageorgiou 1984).

spent a lot of money decorating their houses, building churches and marble fountains (Merikakis 1974: 86).[28] Letters of one of the most successful merchants Costas Chatzipanagiotis (Kremmydas 1974; 1980) demonstrate that the geography of trade connections on the part of Tsakonian merchants included various countries: Russia, Italy, France and Egypt (Tsakonas 1980: 123).[29] The richest families from Prastos sent their children to study in Italy and Russia where they usually got medical degrees (Vagenas 1984).

In the early 19th century, Peloponnese became the center of a liberation movement, and as can be seen from some folk songs (Petakos 2003: 36), Tsakonians participated in the Greek War of Independence which started in 1821. During the war with the Ottoman empire, Ibrahim Pasha of Egypt attacked the Peloponnese and destroyed Prastos and Kastanitsa.[30] Before he arrived, the population of Prastos abandoned their homes. Some of them already had houses in Leonidio, closer to the coast, others left for Constantinople, Romania and Italy. However, Prastos did not remain empty for long. Soon after Ibrahim's attack, shepherds came from the other villages, rebuilt some of the houses, and settled there with their cattle. Prastos ceased to be the center of Tsakonia, while Leonidio took its place as the most powerful town in the area.

In 1833, the capital of Greece moved from Nafplio (Peloponnese) to Athens, and the economy of Tsakonia started to decline. With no road to other regions, there was no transport other than by foot or sea. Despite poverty, from the 1820s, there were several schools in Tsakonia (Tsakonas 1974; Petris 2014). Teachers were not from Tsakonia, they did not understand the dialect, and it was strictly forbidden to speak the local language at school.

In the beginning of the 20th century, Tsakonia was one of the poorest regions in Greece. Tsakonians tried to find a work abroad, especially in the USA. Many residents of Tyros worked as sailors and spent most time away from Tsakonia.

During World War II, Tsakonia was occupied by Italians and Germans, and several years after the war were a period of starvation. There was no money at all, so the settlements in Tsakonia exchanged the goods they produced. The only way to earn money was emigration to Germany, the USA and Australia. The emigrants sent money to their families and preferred not to return. In 1960, a road to Leonidio was built and, since 1969, Tsakonia has electricity. The road improved the economic situation of the region. Prastos was abandoned for the second time,

---

28 In the 18th century, there even appeared a proverb: "Constantinople earns money and Prastos spends it" (Merikakis 1956: 53).
29 Tsakonian merchants had trade offices in many Greek cities and in Italy where they sent younger family members (Tsakonas 1980: 123) and, perhaps, in Germany (Beis 1961: 8).
30 For details of Ibrahim's military operation in Peloponnese see (Kotsonis 1977).

because it was far from the road, and its population moved to Agios Andreas. They return to Prastos only in summer.

3.2 Etymology of Tsakonia/Tsakonian

The etymology of the terms 'Tsakonian' and 'Tsakonia' is one of the main topics of Tsakonian studies (Pagoulatos 1947: 41–72; Vagiakakos 1963–1964: 245–248; Constantinopoulos 1969; Famerie 2007: 235–237). The most popular hypothesis connects Tsakonians with Laconians (Vyzantios 1874: 484; Deffner 1875: 18; Thumb 1894; Amantos 1921; Pagoulatos 1947: 52f; Sarris 1956: 25–26; Vagenas 1971: 253; Sjuzjumov 1974: 211; Papageorgiou 1984) and confirms their ethnic identity. However, it faces certain phonetic difficulties which each of its supporters tries to overcome in his own way.[31]

Another theory derives ethnonym Tsakonians from the name of Pelasgian tribe Caucones (Korais 1805: 289; Oikonomos o ex Oikonomon 1830: 767; Mullach 1856: 104; Spratt 1865: 357; Mantouvalou 2014), though it cannot explain, how could /káfkones/ transform into either /t͡sákones/, or /d͡zákones/, or /t͡sékones/, /d͡zékones/. Nor can it explain why one should refer to the Caucones, who disappeared by the 1st century, BC if the opinion of Strabo (*Geographica* 7.7.2) is to be believed, while the ethnonym *Tsakonians* emerged for the first time only in the 10th century AD, see Section 3.1.

For the present study, it is also worth mentioning several less popular versions that directly or indirectly connect Tsakonians with other nations: (a) Tsakonians are Saxons (Vagenas 1971: 256), (b) Tsakonians are identified either with a hypothetical Slavic tribe of Chakonians that could have lived in the Peloponnese in the Middle Ages (Symeonidis 1972: 25, Sjuzjumov 1974: 211) or with Macedonian *zakón* 'custom, habit' (Vagenas 1971: 254), (c) the ethnonym is derived from Sanskrit t͡sáko 'robber, pirate' (Lekos 1920: 88).

Hardly any of the etymologies mentioned in this section may be accepted without serious dispute.[32] However, they demonstrate that, along with the dominating idea of Tsakonian "integrity" and "uniqueness", there have always existed assumptions that Tsakonians must have had cultural and language contacts in the past.

---

[31] Even the best attempts like (Witczak 2015) do not seem persuasive enough to accept this hypothesis.
[32] The etymology of Tsakonia/Tsakonian is thoroughly discussed in (Kisilier 2014b: 286–301) with a relevant bibliography.

3.3 Ethnography, culture and folklore

Tsakonian society is a very traditional one. Customs here are maintained and remembered not only by elderly women, but also by men aged 45 to 50. This does not mean, certainly, that modern Tsakonian culture consists only of archaic elements, but some of them, like Tsakonian dance[33] are definitely important attributes of local identity (Merikakis 1969: 7–8). Many ancient traditions are not exclusively Tsakonian and have parallels elsewhere in Greece or Balkans, e. g., the construction sacrifice,[34] swearing an oath upon one's ancestors[35] and bathing of a weak newborn child in wine.

The most famous Tsakonian ethnographical event is the celebration of Easter in Leonidio. As soon as the liturgy is over, the sky becomes full of homemade paper lamps that symbolize the Resurrection of Christ. This tradition is generally regarded as a purely Tsakonian one, however I managed to find similar events in different regions of Greece, in particular, in some other parts of Peloponnese (cf. Gomosto 2017; Kalamata 2020) and in Thessaly (cf. Tachydromos 2015). The Tsakonian tradition of Easter lamps is relatively new: Tsakonians themselves believe that it was brought by Tsakonian sailors from China in the 19th century. The existence of the similar traditions elsewhere in Greece likely indicates that they could have a common source much nearer than in China, for example in Asia Minor where Tsakonian merchants had their business interests. One cannot also exclude an alternative explanation: the Tsakonian tradition could have spread to other regions of Peloponnese and Greece. Both possibilities suppose that Tsakonia should have had many more cultural contacts with the "external" world than is generally believed. Other cultural events that support contemporary Tsakonian identity, such as reciting in Tsakonian a part of the Gospel of John during the Easter service in Leonidio (Kisilier & Fedchenko 2010), a liturgy in Tsakonian for the Dormition of Virgin Mary in Prastos, and the Melitzazz festival in Leonidio have appeared only several decades ago.

A very important part of the cultural tradition is folklore, and Tsakonia is no exception here. It seems that the majority of old Tsakonian songs, with the exception

---

[33] Tsakonian dance is generally described as one of the most ancient dances in Greece. It descends from the Ancient Greek ritual "crane dance" Γερανός /yeranós/ and associated with the route of Theseus inside the Labyrinth (Vagena 1984; Petakos 2003).

[34] This tradition is well represented in Balkan and Greek folklore (Megas 1976; Taloş 1997; Ivanov 2004; Golant 2009). In Tsakonia in this case the cock is slaughtered, and its best part is given to the chief builder.

[35] This oath is the most severe one and may not be broken. The person who swears should spill some drops of wine over the ground. I have heard about this oath in Prastos when an old shepherd related how he swore to his future father-in-law when he invited his fiancé to go for a walk.

of laments, were not originally in Tsakonian (Kisilier 2016c). Even the words of the famous Tsakonian dance are in Standard Modern Greek. Most songs in Tsakonian (Petakos 2003: 35–40) refer to Tsakonian identity and could not have appeared earlier than the 19th century, as they are related to the Greek War of Independence. It is also difficult to find a fairy tale in Tsakonian, because they are usually not published. The German classical philologist Michael Deffner prepared an edition of seven fairy tales in Tsakonian (Deffner 1926), but he evidently translated them into Tsakonian himself (Holzmann 2010: 173). The fact that few folklore texts appear in Tsakonian is not something extraordinary. Folklore in general is superdialectal (Desnitskaya 1970: 11–42), especially in its poetic form. Greek folklore in dialect exists only on some islands, for example, on Cyprus, or in Greek enclaves, such as Azov Sea (Kisilier 2017a) or Pontic regions. It does not mean that there is no Tsakonian folklore at all,[36] but it definitely proves that Tsakonians were less separated from the "Greek world" than their Cypriot, Pontic or Azov compatriots.

4 The Tsakonian dialect: general information

4.1 Primary sources and previous research[37]

The Tsakonian dialect was first mentioned by famous Turkish traveler Evliya Çelebi in 1668. In his times Tsakonian was probably distributed throughout the Peloponnese together with Maniot and Albanian (Costakis 1969: 45). However, it is hard to believe that Çelebi dared to go deep into Tsakonian-speaking region. More likely he came across Tsakonians in Nafplio, the biggest city of Peloponnese,[38] where they could have been his porters (Costakis 1986d: 65). According to Çelebi, Tsakonians spoke neither Greek, nor Italian, and it was impossible to understand them without an interpreter (Vagenas 1971: 274). He did not try to find out the origin of the dialect and just wrote down several words.[39] About a century later, in 1788, some Tsakonian words were mentioned by Villoison (Famerie 2007, cf. Manolessou 2019: 298–306), though with many mistakes (Costakis 1956a: 34).

---

[36] On the contrary, most narratives in Tsakonain I collected from my best informants should be regarded as modern folklore.
[37] For those who are interested in the history of Tsakonian studies I also recommend (Liosis 2016; Kisilier 2019b).
[38] Possible route of Çelebi in Peloponnese is described in (Costakis 1980–1981).
[39] This wordlist is available in (Costakis 1969: 45–46) or transcribed into the Latin alphabet with Ottoman and English translations in (Dankoff 1991: 133). For the analysis of these words see (Manolessou 2019: 293–298).

The first serious attempts to describe Tsakonian were made only in the 19th century. Tsakonian became interesting from the point of view of Classical philology as it was regarded as the only surviving Ancient Greek dialect. The first grammars even attempted to find a dative that was already absent in spoken Greek (Thiersch 1832: 520–521).[40] The best descriptions of Tsakonian (such as Scutt 1912–1913; 1913–1914; Pernot 1914; 1934; Anagnostopoulos 1926; Pernot & Costakis 1933; Costakis 1951; 1999), are usually free of such shortcomings,[41] but their goal is not just to describe the dialect, but to underline archaic features in vocabulary (Hatzidakis 1926; Costakis 1986a; Blažek 2010), phonetics (Deffner 1881; Mirambel 1960–1961: 258; Charalampopoulos 1980b), nominal forms (Deffner 1874; Schwyzer 1921) and verb morphology (Pernot 1910), etc.

4.2 Ancient Greek features

As has already been mentioned in Section 1, most scholars believe that Tsakonian originates directly from Ancient Doric Laconian and has escaped any influence of the Hellenistic Koiné. This widespread opinion is supported by linguistic evidence thoroughly described in Tzitzilis (2013) so a brief overview will be enough:

(a) Many words in Tsakonian vocabulary have an Ancient Greek origin (cf. Kassian 2018; Nicholas 2019), but they are no longer in use either in Standard Modern Greek[42] or in other Modern Greek dialects:

- [e]psilé 'eye' < AncGr, Lac ὀπτίλος /optílos/;[43]
- ío 'water' < AncGr ὕδωρ /ʰýdɔːr/;

---

40 Sometimes first grammars treated articles /tʰo/ and /tʰa/ in singular and /tʰon/ in plural as dative (Oikonomos 1870: 17, 20; Costakis 1986d: 68). This mistake demonstrates misunderstanding of Tsakonian morphonology: /tʰ/ generally results from /s/ + /t/, e. g.: /tʰúma/ 'mouth', see MGr στόμα /stóma/. Thus, the forms /tʰo/, /tʰa/, and /tʰon/ are just fusions of a preposition σε /se/ 'in' and article in accusative. It may seem strange, but the same mistake also appears in some Tsakonian grammars of the 20th century (Lekos 1920: 28–32).
41 In these papers some forms or constructions are usually mentioned that cannot be found in modern Tsakonian (see Kisilier & Mertyris 2018, where several peculiar genitives are described). In all likelihood, Tsakonian could have undergone significant changes over the last fifty years, or these peculiar forms just reflect some personal ideas of the authors about the dialect.
42 Still, almost all these words are known to most speakers of the Standard Modern Greek either because of some set phrases, or thanks to school education.
43 Hereafter in this chapter, I translate a Tsakonian word only if its meaning differs from its Ancient/Modern Greek or foreign counterpart. All Tsakonian examples are from the expeditions' archive unless indicated otherwise.

- *kúe* 'dog' < AncGr κύων /kýɔ:n/;
- *vu* 'bull' < AncGr βοῦς /bõ:s/;
- *kuváne* 'black' < κυανοῦς AncGr /kyanõ:s/ 'dark blue, dark, black';
- [*énʲi*] *orú* '[I] see' (lit. '[I am] seeing)')⁴⁴ < AncGr ὁράω /ʸoráɔ:/;
- *píu* 'do' < AncGr ποιέω /pojéɔ:/;
- *ekáne* '[he] arrived' <AOR> < AncGr ἱκάνω /ʸikánɔ:/ 'come';
- *o* 'not' <NEG> < AncGr οὐκ /o:k/.⁴⁵

(b) Tsakonian preserves several Ancient Greek phonetic features:

- preservation of AncGr /u/ which transformed into /i/ in Standard Modern Greek: Tsak *psuxré* 'cool' < ψ**u**χρός AncGr /ps**u**xrós/ vs. MGr /ps**i**xrós/, Tsak *grʲúfu* 'hide' < AncGr κρ**ύ**πτω /kr**ý**ptɔ:/ vs. MGr κρύβω /krívo/, Tsak *t͡ʃuraká* 'Sunday' < AncGr κ**ύ**ριος /k**ý**rios/ 'master' vs. MGr Κυριακή /kirʲakí/;
- vowel /e/ that originates from AncGr /e:/:⁴⁶ Tsak *pselé* 'high' < AncGr ὑψ**η**λός /ʸyps**e**:lós/ vs. MGr ψ**η**λός /ps**i**lós/, Tsak *néma* 'thread' < AncGr ν**ῆ**μα /n**ẽ**:ma/ vs. MGr ν**ή**μα /n**í**ma/;
- Ancient Greek F /v/⁴⁷ now absent in Standard Modern Greek and its dialects: Tsak *ván[n]e* 'ram (sheep)' < AncGr F**α**ρνός /**v**arnós/, *kúvane* 'blue' < AncGr *κύFανος /kývanos/ (Deffner 1881: 13–14).

Some phonetic peculiarities of Tsakonian demonstrate its relations with Ancient Doric Laconian:

- Tsakonian still has Doric /a:/:⁴⁸ Tsak *máti* 'mother' < AncDor μ**ά**τηρ /m**á**te:r/ vs. MGr μητέρα /mitéra/, Tsakonian feminine article *a* < AncDor ἀ /ʸa/ vs. MGr η /i/;
- there are separate traces of rhotacism in Tsakonian when /r/ appears in intervocalic position at a junction of words: Tsak *tar ayáki* <DEF.F.SG.GEN love> vs. MGr τη**ς** αγάπης /ti**s** ayápis/, Tsak *pʰur ési* <how be.PRS.2SG> like in Lac πάσο**ρ** /páso**r**/ 'ardency' vs. AncGr πάθο**ς** /pátʰo**s**/ (Boisacq 1904: 31);

---

44 Tsakonian has only the analytical present and imperfect (Liosis 2011; Kisilier 2016a). In this chapter, Tsakonian verbs in the wordlists are given without their auxiliary.
45 There is also a group of Tsakonian words such as *apoú* 'let go', *áde* 'bread', *sáti* 'daughter' that also exist in Standard Modern Greek (ἀπολύω /apolío/, ἄρτος /ártos/, θυγάτηρ /θiyátir/), but they are not used in everyday speech.
46 AncGr /e:/ has become /i/ in Modern Greek.
47 F was preserved longer in Western Ancient Greek dialects (Méndez Dosuna 2001: 331), for example in Doric, which is generally regarded as the direct ancestor of Tsakonian.
48 Doric /a:/ corresponds to /e:/ in other Ancient Greek dialects which later became /i/.

- in Laconian, Ancient Greek /tʰ/ became /s/ (Bourguet 1927: 75–78),⁴⁹ the results of this transformation can be seen in Tsakonian: *seríndu* 'reap' < Lac σεριδδω /seríddɔ:/ vs. θερίζω MGr /θerízo/ < AttGr /tʰerídzɔ:/, Tsak *sáti* 'daughter' vs. MGr θυγατέρα /θiyatéra/ < AttGr θυγάτηρ /tʰygáte:r/.

These peculiarities generally are not productive patterns, but just traces of a previous situation, probably a rather distant one. Some of them are also found in other Modern Greek dialects. Again, they are thoroughly analysed in (Tzitzilis 2013) and so it will be enough to provide just a few illustrations here:

- Doric /a/ is also met in the dialects of Karpathos, Symi and Mani (Rylik 2012: 735–736);
- along with Tsakonian, Ancient Greek /u/ is preserved in Old Athenian, especially in the variants of Megara (Kisilier 2013: 85), Mani and Kimi (Trudgill 2003: 54), and in Griko, though the latter demonstrates certain differences with Tsakonian (Liosis & Papadamou 2011);
- AncGr /e:/ has not become /i/ not only in Tsakonian, but in Pontic (Eloeva 2004: 104) and some other Greek dialects of the Asia Minor (Kapsomenos 1985: 55) as well;
- except Tsakonian, AncGr digamma (F /v/) still exists in Cretan, in the dialect of Agrafa (Pindus) and in North Macedonia (Tzitzilis 2013).

(c) Multiple morphological forms in Tsakonian can be traced back to Ancient Doric:

- the pronominal system is full of Doric elements, e. g.: Tsak *eníu* <1SG.OBL> < Lac ἐμίω /emíɔ:/, Tsak *nʲi* <3PL.OBL> < AncDor νιν /nin/, Tsak *etíne* 'that' < Lac τῆνος /tē:nos/, etc. (Tzitzilis 2013);
- present and past forms of the verb 'to be' in Tsakonian resemble very much those of Ancient Doric, like Tsak *éni* '[he] is', cf. AncDor ἔνι /éni/, Tsak *étʰe* '[you] <PL> are' cf. AncDor ἔστε /éste/, etc.;
- the active aorist of labial, dental and velar stems originates from "Doric" perfect: Tsak *ékreva* '[I] stole', cf. Messenian perfect participle κεκλεβώς /keklebɔ́:s/, Tsak *égrava* '[I] wrote' < AncDor γέγραβα /gégraba/ (Tzitzilis 2013);
- in singular, for most Tsakonian nouns with *a*-flexion, with few exceptions, genitive has the same ending as the nominative and accusative. Edward Schwyzer (1921: 85–86) believes that it is a logical internal development of the Laconian nominal system.

---

49 In Modern Greek, /tʰ/ has transformed into /θ/.

Sometimes an Ancient Doric origin is not the only possible explanation of Tsakonian morphological peculiarities. For instance, the forms of the verb 'to be' in Tsakonian could be connected not with Ancient Laconian but with Byzantine Greek (Pernot 1910), and the loss of special flexion in the genitive may merely result from a general unification/simplification of the nominal declension which can be traced in many Modern Greek dialects as well as Tsakonian (see Kisilier & Mertyris 2018: 237–238).

4.3 Subdialectal diversity in Tsakonian

Due to its geography and history, the Tsakonian dialect is not uniform but has local varieties. One of these – Propontis Tsakonian – has already been mentioned in Section 2.1. This subdialect is highly divergent from Peloponnesian Tsakonian because of its contacts with Asia Minor Greek and Turkish (cf. Melissaropoulou 2018; 2019) and it will not be described here. Peloponnesian Tsakonian can also be divided in some groups. Most descriptions acknowledge two varieties (see Pernot 1934: 15; Kontosopoulos 2010: 191): Southern (Leonidio, Vaskina, Melana, Pragmateftis, Sapounakeika, Tyros and Agios Andreas/Prastos) and Northern (Kastanitsa and Sitena). The latter has been much more poorly described,[50] and it is generally believed that Northern Tsakonian has been influenced by Standard Modern Greek (Kontosopoulos 2001: 3–4). And there are indeed some examples where Northern Tsakonian uses "more modern" vocabulary than the Southern, such as Northern *malía* 'hair' vs. Southern *t͡ʃíxe* or *t͡síxe* though these words also exist in the local variety of Kastanitsa. The principal difference between Southern and Northern Tsakonian is of the loss of intervocalic /-l-/:

- Northern *t͡séla* 'house' < Lat *cella* 'small room' vs. Southern *t͡séa/d͡zéa*;
- Northern *t͡sufála* 'head' < AncGr /kefalé:/ vs. Southern *t͡sufá/t͡ʃufá*;
- Northern *lalú* 'speak' < AncGr /lalɔ́:/ 'talk' vs. Southern *aú*.

These examples, especially the comparison with Latin and Ancient Greek, cast doubt on the idea that /-l-/ in Northern Tsakonian is an innovation influenced by Standard Modern Greek. It seems more likely that it is not Northern but Southern Tsakonian that has changed.

There is another problem as well: Prastos and Kastanitsa are situated on different slopes of the same mountain. Still they belong to different subdialects – Northern

---

50 The most recent data on this variety is available in (Liosis 2007).

in Kastanitsa and Southern in Prastos – despite the fact that Prastos is rather far from other Tsakonian-speaking settlements (a possible explanation will be offered in fn. 56).

The division of Peloponnesian Tsakonian into two subdialects is an oversimplification. In 1956, Thanassis Costakis (1956c) published his emendations to Deffner (1922). It is known that Michael Deffner conducted his research in Prastos, while Costakis himself was from Melana. According to Valentina Fedchenko (2013: 78–79), there are two types of emendations by Costakis:

(a) instead of a non-palatalized /r/ (Deffner 1922) a palatalized /ʃ/ is used in (Costakis 1956c): *afría* 'bay laurel (*Laurus nobilis*)' vs. *aʃʃia*;
(b) a palatalized /rᶾ/ in (Deffner 1922) is substituted by /ʒ/ in (Costakis 1956c): *ayrᶾokúmare* 'wild strawberry' vs. *ayʒokúmare*.

A more thorough analysis shows that these emendations are not corrections of Deffner's "mistakes", but are replacements of the Prastos phonetic variant by one from Melana. Later, in his "Dictionary", Costakis (1986b, 1986c, 1987) does not try to unify varieties from different villages and even distinguishes subdialects of Melana/Pragmateftis, Tyros/Sapounakeika and Prastos/Agios Andreas along with Northern Tsakonian and Propontis Tsakonian. This subdialectal diversity (with addition of the variety of Vaskina[51]) is supported on all linguistic levels. Although the subject still requires complex and thorough research,[52] it is possible to formulate some options for local isoglosses. In phonetics, these are:

– representation of /ri/ – while in Vaskina and Kastanitsa it preserves its initial form, in Tyros and Sapounakeika, /ri/ turns into /ʃ/ or /ʒ/, in Prastos, it transforms into /ʃ/ or /rᶾ/ and in Melana and Pragmateftis both variants are possible – either /ri/ or /ʃ/: Vaskina, Kastanitsa *kriáða* 'cold, frost' vs. Melana, Tyros, Prastos *kʃáða*; Vaskina *mári* 'mule', Kastanitsa *mulári*, Melana *muári/mári* vs. Tyros *muáʒi*, Prastos *muárˢi/márˢi*;
– representation of /tr/ – it becomes /t͡ʃ/ in Vaskina, Tyros, Sapounakeika, Prastos and Kastanitsa and /t͡s/ or /t͡sʲ/ in Melana and Pragmateftis: Vaskina, Tyros, Prastos, Kastanitsa *at͡ʃé* 'big' vs. Melana *at͡sé*; Vaskina, Tyros, Prastos, Kastanitsa *t͡ʃíxe* 'hair' vs. Melana *t͡síxe/t͡sʲíxa*;

---

[51] See Vaskina *olpíða* 'hope' vs. Melana *elpíða*, Vaskina *skorpíe* 'rustyback (*Asplenium ceterach*)' vs. Melana *skorkíði* vs. Kastanitsa *skurkʲó*, Vaskina *lulújði* 'flower' vs. Prastos *lalúði*.
[52] For example, the creation of the Electronic online corpus of Tsakonian could be very helpful (Arkhangelskiy, Kisilier & Plungian 2018).

- tsitakism vs. palatalization – in Tyros and Sapounakeia, /kʲ/ changes into /t͡s/, while in all other villages it may become both /t͡s/ and /t͡ʃ/: Vaskina, Melana, Prastos, Kastanitsa *t͡sufá* 'head' vs. Tyros *t͡sʲufá/t͡ʃʲufá*; Vaskina, Melana *yunét͡se* 'women' <PL> vs. Tyros *yunét͡se/yunét͡ʃe*;
- diphthongization of /a/ may happen in Vaskina, Tyros, Sapounakeika and Prastos: Vaskina, Prastos *kiyáði/kiyájði* 'spring', Tyros *tiyáði/kiyájði* vs. Melana *kiyáði*; Vaskina *ajθá* 'sister', Tyros *aθé/ajθé*, Prastos *aθʲá/ajθé* vs. Melana *aθé*;
- insertion of /u/ is found in Vaskina, Melana, Tyros and Sapounakeika: Vaskina, Melana, Tyros *avuyó* 'egg' vs. Prastos/Kastanits *avyó*.

In Tsakonian vocabulary there is also subdialectal distribution: seamanship and fishing terminology is better known in Tyros, while cattle-breeding and agricultural terminology are more used in the mountain villages, like Vaskina. Melana belongs to the mixed type. This distribution also results in the distribution of lexical borrowings (see Section 5.4): borrowings from Venetian dialect are generally connected with seamanship and terms of cattle-breeding and agriculture often have Slavic, Albanian or Aromanian origin. Some words may vary in their meaning in different localities:

- *ajázi* — Melana 'cold' (noun), Tyros 'draught';
- *eresári* — Melana 'extremely thin', Tyros 'piteous'.

As was already mentioned in Section 4.2, Tsakonian tends to lose the genitive. According to Thanassis Costakis (1999: 52, 55, 60), there are several types of declension where genitives still exist in Tsakonian. During my expeditions to Tsakonia, I checked his examples in Vaskina, Melana and Tyros:

- feminine nouns with flexion /-a/: *xúra* 'village' – Vaskina *ta*[53] *xur-é* <DEF.F.SG.OBL village-SG.GEN> vs. Melana, Tyros *ta xúr-a* <DEF.F.SG.OBL village-SG.NGEN>; *kʰára* 'fire, fireplace' – Vaskina *ta kʰar-é* <DEF.F.SG.OBL fireplace-SG.GEN>/*ta kʰár-a* <DEF.F.SG.OBL village-SG.NGEN> vs. Melana, Tyros no form for genitive;
- neuter nouns with flexion /-o/: *ylikó* 'sweet, dessert' – Vaskina *tu ylik-ó* <DEF.NF.SG.GEN sweet-SG.NGEN>/*tu ylik-ú* <DEF.NF.SG.GEN sweet-SG.GEN>, Melana

---

[53] In Tsakonian, if a feminine noun has an initial consonant, the article in the genitive coincides with the one in the accusative: GEN *ta xuré* 'field' (Lekos 1920: 29; Costakis 1999: 55, 60) and ACC *ta xúra* vs. GEN *tar ayáki* 'love' and ACC *tan ayáki*, for more details see (Kisilier & Fedchenko 2013: 421–422; Kisilier & Mertyris 2018: 228).

tu ylik-ó <DEF.NF.SG.GEN sweet-SG.NGEN> vs. Tyros *tu ylik-ú* <DEF.NF.SG.GEN sweet-SG.GEN>; *sák^{h}o* 'sack' — Vaskina, Tyros *tu sák^h-u* <DEF.NF.SG.GEN sack-SG.GEN> vs. Melana no form for the genitive;
- *ya* 'milk' – Vaskina *ap ta ya* <from DEF.N.PL.NGEN milk>/*tu ya* <DEF.NF.SG.GEN milk> vs. Melana *apó ya* <from milk> vs. Tyros *tu yálatu* <DEF.NF.SG.GEN milk.SG.GEN>.

In morphosyntax, the subdialectal diversity can be seen in distribution of irrealis constructions. These constructions will be described in Section 4.4, because they also highly depend on the gender of the speaker.

4.4 The sociolinguistic situation

Modern Tsakonian is sometimes described as a critically endangered language with only a few hundred elderly fluent speakers left. Thus, according to Tapani Salminen (2007: 271–272), just about 200 inhabitants of Tsakonia can speak the dialect. On the contrary, the famous Greek dialectologist Nikolaos Kontosopoulos (2001: 3) believes that the number of speakers reaches 8000.[54] It is difficult to assess now without any special research how many people in Tsakonia really speak Tsakonian (see Charalampopoulos 1980a: 23), but this number is definitely more than just a few hundred. For example, most inhabitants of Melana, Pragmateftis and Sapounakeika have some basic competence in the dialect. Official statistics demonstrate that Melana has 260 inhabitants (with another 66 in adjacent Livadi), Pragmateftis – 269 and Sapounakeika – 157. So these three villages alone have more than 500 potential speakers. Objective calculations are difficult because Tsakonian society is very reserved and the dialect is rarely spoken in the presence of a stranger.[55] Besides, it seems that many attempts to assess the number of speakers were undertaken mostly in Leonidio where even 60 years ago Tsakonian was not so much in use in contrast to Vaskina, Melana, Pragmateftis and Sapounakeika (see Lysikatos 1961). Those who can speak Tsakonian in Leonidio were born and spent their childhood in some nearby village. It is also noteworthy that the descendants of the first inhabitants of Prastos who left the town

---

54 Other calculations are 300 (provided by UNESCO), 1200 (Multitree 2018) and 2000–4000 speakers (ELP 2020).
55 During my expeditions, I usually interview my informants in Tsakonian. When I took my students with me, most informants would immediately switch to Standard Modern Greek although I was asking my questions in Tsakonian.

before 1821 and moved to Leonidio (see Section 3.1)[56] can neither speak Tsakonian nor remember that their parents or grandparents could speak it. This most probably means that Tsakonian was hardly ever spoken in Prastos at least by its richest and more educated residents[57] who became the core of population of Leonidio. That is why, in my opinion, it is so difficult to hear any Tsakonian in Leonidio.

In general, the younger generation does not speak Tsakonian though many of them have a good passive knowledge of the dialect.[58] Most speakers are older than 45. However, in Sapounakeika and in Agios Andreas/Prastos I came across multiple young men aged 20 and even younger who could fluently speak Tsakonian. The lack of young speakers is definitely connected with the low prestige of the dialect although recently the situation has started to change mostly due to the interest on the part of the Russian scholars who have been visiting Tsakonian villages at least twice a year since 2010 and are able to speak fluent Tsakonian.[59]

Besides geographical variants (see Section 4.3), Tsakonian demonstrates gender-dependent variation. This phenomenon is not unique. William Labov (1966) was one of the first to describe it and then differences between male and female speech became a key subject of sociolinguistics (see Lakoff 1973; Crawford 1995; Simpson 2009) for many languages. Although gender dependent variation is encountered not only in Tsakonian but in other Modern Greek dialects as well (Vergis 2012), this phenomenon still remains almost undescribed in Modern Greek dialectology as if men and women everywhere in Greece spoke the same way. The most obvious characteristic of female speech in several villages of Tsakonia is a palatalized /ʃ/ or /ʒ/ instead of /rʲ/:

---

[56] As has already been mentioned, Prastos did not stay empty for very long. Soon after the emigration of its first inhabitants, it was populated by shepherds and peasants from elsewhere who moved into the empty houses. Many residents of Leonidio even now can show which houses in Prastos once belonged to their families. It is not clear where the "new residents" came from. They spoke Tsakonian but their subdialect was and is much closer to the subdialect of faraway Tyros than that of Kastanitsa and Sitena (see section 4.3), which are quite near to Prastos, on the other side of the same mountain. So, perhaps, they came not from nearby mountains but from the coast.
[57] One of my informants from Prastos (aged 93) told me that she learned Tsakonian only after her marriage in order to communicate with her husband's family who were much poorer than her own parents.
[58] In 2016, I was invited to the Elementary School of Leonidio to advocate for elective classes in Tsakonian. As a part of the presentation, we discussed various subjects with an old woman from Vaskina in Tsakonian. Two classes were present, and unexpectedly, the children had no problem in translating and retelling our conversation.
[59] Another important contributing factor has been the appearance of the webpage of the Tsakonian Archive: http://www.tsakonianarchives.gr/ (accessed 15 March, 2021), see (Kisilier & Christodoulou 2018).

— Melana and Tyros: *kʃáða* 'cold, frost' (female) vs. *kriáða* (male);
— Tyros and Prastos: *éʒifo* 'goat kid' (female) vs. *érifo* (male).[60]

Sometimes during the interviews, informants preferred the "female" pronunciation, because their mothers used to speak this way. However, they admitted that they would have never used "female" pronunciation in public because "it would be shameful for a man". Women younger than 60 occasionally prefer "male" variant with /ri/. Agathokles Charalampopoulos (1980b: 38–39) believes that this has happened due to the influence of the "male" pronunciation, but more likely it is just a result of more increased close contact with Standard Modern Greek (see Section 5.2).

There are also several examples from Tyros when diphthongization depends on gender:[61]

— *ajθé* 'sister' (female) vs. *aθé* (male);
— *kiyájði* 'spring (= natural fountain)' (female) vs. *kiyáði* (male);
— *t͡ʃajθía* 'needle' (female) vs. *t͡ʃaθía* (male);
— *θa=najθí* '[it] will happen' (female) vs. *θa=naθí* (male).

The speaker's gender does not influence only phonetics but morphosyntax as well. Tsakonian has multiple forms of irrealis. Typological overview of Tsakonian irrealis was presented by Nikos Liosis (2010) but his study could not encompass sociolinguistic factors. Recent field research demonstrated that this approach is not less important here than the typological one (see Fedchenko 2013: 83–85). Some Tsakonian subdialects[62] have their own way to express irrealis both in female and male speech.

(1) Melana:
    a. *θa=éma*   *parí-u*   *an*
       FUT=AUX.PST.1SG   come.IPFV-PTCP.M.SG   if
       m=ésa   *aú-ø*   *éa*
       1SG.OBL=AUX.PST.2SG say.IPFV-PTCP-M.SG come
       'I would have come if you had told me: "Come"' (male)

---

[60] This tendency is more optional in Melana. For example, female speakers born in Melana pronounce *érʲa* 'wool' <PL> instead of *éʒa* in Sapounakeika and Tyros.
[61] In other villages this kind diphthongization may also exist but it has no gender distribution.
[62] Unfortunately, there is still no data for Kastanitsa and Sitena.

b. **θa=kʲa=**nd=al-íu   éa
   FUT=SBJV=2SG.OBL=say.IPFV.SBJV-1SG.SBJV   come
   o=θa=mól-ere   mazí=mi
   NEG=FUT=come.PFV.SBJV-2SG   with=1SG.OBL
   'I would have told you: "Come" [but] you would not come with me' (female)

(2) Tyros/Sapounakeika:
   a. **θa=éma**   parí-u   ton   diré
      FUT=AUX.PST.1SG   come.IPFV-PTCP.M.SG   DEF.M.SG.ACC   Tyros
      áma   ó-nʲi   bor-ú-ø
      but   NEG-AUX.PRS.1SG   can-IPFV.PTCP-M.SG
      'I would come to Tyros but I cannot' (male)
   b. θa=éma   paʒi-a   t͡se   ezú
      FUT=AUX.PST.1SG   come.IPFV-PTCP.F.SG   and   1SG.NOM
      ta   xór-a   nʲúmu
      DEF.F.SG.OBL   country-SG.NGEN   2PL.POSS
      θa=m=éki   arés-a
      FUT=1SG.OBL=AUX.PST.3SG   like-PTCP.F.SG
      a   xór-a   nʲúmu
      DEF.F.SG.NOM   country-SG.NGEN   2PL.POSS
      '[If] I came to your country, I would like your country' (female)

(3) Prastos/Agios Andreas:
   a. áma   éma   bor-ú-ø
      if   AUX.PST.1SG   can-IPFV.PTCP-M.SG
      θa=nʲ=éma   pí-u
      FUT=3SG.OBL=AUX.PST.1SG   do.IPFV-PTCP.M.SG
      'If I could, I would do it' (male)
   b. **éki**   **θa=**nd=al-íu   tan
      SBJV   FUT=2SG.ACC=say.IPFV.SBJV-1SG.SBJV   DEF.F.SG.ACC
      alíθʲ-a   alá   ó-nʲi   bor-ú-a
      truth-SG   but   NEG-AUX.PRS.1SG   can-IPFV.PTCP-F.SG
      'I would tell you the truth but I cannot' (female)

(4) Vaskina:
   a. **éki**   **θ=**al-íu   tan   alíθʲ-a
      SBJV   FUT=say.IPFV.SBJV-1SG.SBJV   DEF.F.SG.ACC   truth-SG
      alá   ó-nʲi   bor-ú-ø
      but   NEG-AUX.PRS.1SG   can-IPFV.PTCP-M.SG
      'I would tell the truth but I cannot' (male)

b. *e*   *θé-a*   *na*=nd=al-íu
   AUX.PRS.1SG   want.IPFV-F.SG   SBJV=2SG.OBL-say.IPFV.SBJV-1SG.SBJV
   tan   *alíθʲ-a*   *alá*   *ó-j*   *bor-ú-ə*
   DEF.F.SG.ACC   truth-SG   but   NEG-AUX.PRS.1SG   can-IPFV.PTCP-F.SG
   'I would tell you the truth but I cannot' (female)

The most widely spread pattern (1a, 2, 3a) – the combination of *θa* with imperfective past – is a recent innovation which has been influenced by Standard Modern Greek. Thus, in Tyros and Sapounakeika (2) there is no specific gender variation (but endings of the participle), because original forms of irrealis have already disappeared. Forms *kʲa* (1b) and *éki* (3b, 4a) are not clear although *éki* coincides with auxiliary in the past. The construction *e θéa na* + subjunctive in (4b), in my opinion, is not grammaticalized. Probably, after grammaticalization it might transform into *éki θa* + subjunctive (3b, 4a). If this hypothesis is correct, in Vaskina irrealis is grammaticalized in male speech, but not grammaticalized in female speech.

5 Language contacts in Tsakonia

5.1 Preliminary remarks

Usually it is not difficult to recognize a language contact situation: either the speakers of the dialect live in a "foreign" environment and are bilingual (Grico and Grekaniko in South Italy or Asia Minor Greek in Turkey) or it is well known that multiple speakers of some other language enjoyed dominance in the region (like Venetians in Renaissance Crete), or at least were present there. Besides, the fact of contact is often evident from various linguistic innovations if their origins can be traced. Thus, in the dialect of Eratyra (Northern Greece), a clitic pronoun is incorporated inside the verb (5a) and this pattern is clearly borrowed from Albanian (5b):

(5) a. *lisí-**me**-ti*
       untie.PFV-1SG.ACC-IMP.2PL
       'untie **me**' (Lopashov 2006: 162; cf. Joseph 1990: 176)
   b. *ndihmo-**na**-ni*
       help-1PL.ACC-IMP.2PL
       'help **us**' (Buchholz & Fiedler 1987: 452)

Another example is a remarkable periphrastic construction in Azov Greek which consists of the auxiliary *kámu* 'do' and infinitive of a Russian verb. It is often used instead of the traditional finite verb form:

(6) kám-u   ʒár-itʲ
    do-PRS.1SG   roast-INF
    '[I] roast' (Kisilier 2019a: 36)

The Tsakonian situation is much more complex. While there is little doubt that Tsakonian and Modern Greek have been in contact (see Section 5.2), irrespective of age, all speakers of Tsakonian are bilingual and Tsakonian is always L2. However, except for some indirect information in Byzantine historiography (see Section 3.1), non-Greek toponyms (Section 2.2) and a few foreign family names (Section 2.3), no documented evidence is available that Tsakonia was once a site of massive immigration or was on the route of cross-regional shepherd migrations.

Nevertheless, the study of lexical borrowings (Section 5.4) may help to find out which languages could have been involved in Tsakonian language contacts. Even a brief typological comparison of Tsakonian with other Modern Greek dialects (section 5.3), along with some historical and cultural data mentioned in Sections 3.1 and 3.3, shows that Tsakonia was not so "closed" or separated as it is generally believed.

5.2 Tsakonian and Hellenistic and Modern Greek Koinés

In this section, I am going to examine possible contacts of Tsakonian with Hellenistic Koiné and with Modern Greek. Since the history of Tsakonian is still unknown, it is not possible to determine the chronolology of interactions. That is why it would be more logical not to separate Hellenistic influence from the Modern Greek one.

According to the traditional point of view, Tsakonian is the only contemporary Greek dialect which descends directly from Ancient Greek (Doric Laconian) and not from Hellenistic Koiné. Not everyone supports this theory (see Kapsomenos 1985: 64–67) and, as Christos Tzitzilis (2013) has brilliantly demonstrated, many Modern Greek dialects have numerous Ancient Greek and even Doric peculiarities at least in their vocabulary and phonetics. This means that the "encounter" with Hellenistic Koiné could provoke a serious transformation of an Ancient Greek dialect but did not inevitably lead to language death. Two characteristics of Tsakonian highly likely indicate the influence of Hellenistic Koiné:

(a) The main speech verb in Tsakonian – Southern *aú* or Northern *lalú* 'say' (cf. Section 4.3) originates from Ancient Greek λαλῶ /lalɔ̃:/ (< λαλέω /laléɔ:/) 'talk, chat', but not from /légɔ:/ 'say', as it is in most dialects. In the first centuries AD, the verb λαλῶ /lalɔ̃:/ frequently replaced λέγω /légɔ:/ in the sense of 'say' (Lampe 1961: 790–791). Apart from Tsakonian, λαλώ /laló/ remained the main verb of speech in Cypriot.

(b) In Tsakonian, synthetic forms of the present and imperfect are found only in the subjunctive (Haspelmath 1998). In the indicative they have been replaced by analytical forms with the auxiliary 'to be' and a participle in the appropriate number and gender:

(7) a. *énʲi*   *a-ú-ø*
    AUX.PRS.1SG say.IPFV-PTCP-M.SG
  b. *énʲi*   *a-ú-a*
    AUX.PRS.1SG say.IPFV-PTCP-F.SG
    'I say'
  c. *íni*   *a-ú-nde*
    AUX.PRS.3PL say.IPFV-PTCP-NN.PL
    'They say'

Christos Tzitzilis (2013) and Nikos Liosis (2014: 449) believe that these analytical forms are inherited from Ancient Laconian, because there are two Laconian glosses in Hesychius: ἐξηλημβώρ /ekse:le:mbɔ́:r/ '[s/he] saw' (where the perfect participle expresses the imperfect) and ἀπεσουτήρ /apeso:té:r/ '[s/he] was saved' (participle of the passive aorist). Liosis points out that in the Tsakonian analytical form one can find the traces of the use of perfect participle – *émi* **apostakú** '[I] open my legs' (Northern Tsakonian), cf. AncGr εἰμι **ἀφεστεκώς** /ɛ:mi **apʰestekɔ́:s**/. But in the most cases, Tsakonian analytical forms have present participles as in (7): Tsak. *aú* < AncGr λαλῶν /lalɔ̃:n/, Tsak. *aúa* < AncGr λαλοῦσα /lalɔ̃:sa/, Tsak. *aúnde* < AncGr λαλοῦντες /lalɔ̃:ntes/. Similar periphrastic constructions can be encountered in the classical Attic dialect of Ancient Greek (Björck 1940; Caragounis 2004: 177); yet their use peaked in New Testament Greek (Kisilier 2016a: 101–102). They are met in many popular Early Byzantine hagiographic texts that are based on popular, and not high literary tradition, for example in the *"Pratum Spirituale"* by John Moschos (Kisilier 2011: 61–62). However, this approach does not propose a complete solution: it explains the analytical forms of imperfect and leaves aside the present forms. One could certainly suppose that they are constructed by analogy according to the imperfect pattern, but this suggestion is not persuasive enough.

Some Tsakonian lexemes from basic vocabulary are more similar to Medieval or Modern Greek words than to Ancient Greek ones:

- *éna* 'one' vs. MGr ένα /éna/ and AncGr εἷς /ʰɛ̃:s/;
- *fri* 'brow' vs. MGr φρύδι /frídi/ and AncGr ὀφρῦς /opʰrŷs/;
- *kséru* 'know' vs. MGr ξέρω /kséro/ and AncGr οἶδα /õjda/;
- *níxi* 'nail' vs. MGr νύχι /níxi/ and AncGr ὄνυξ /ónyks/;
- *pʲe* 'who' vs. MGr ποιος /pʲos/ 'who' and AncGr ποῖος /põjos/ 'what, which';
- *psári* 'fish' vs. MGr ψάρι /psári/ and AncGr ἰχθύς /ixtʰýs/ or NTGr ὀψάριον /opsárion/;
- *psíra* 'louse' vs. MGr ψείρα /psíra/ and AncGr φθείρ /pʰtʰɛ:r/;
- *pulí* 'bird' vs. MGr πουλί /pulí/ and AncGr ὄρνις /órnis/;
- *sínefo* 'cloud' vs. MGr σύννεφο /sínefo/ and AncGr νέφος /népʰos/;
- *tsaprúkʰu* 'to lie' (position) vs. MGr ξαπλώνω /ksaplóno/ and AncGr κεῖμαι /kɛ̃:maj/;
- *tsítrine* 'yellow' vs. MGr κίτρινος /kítrinos/ and AncGr χλωρός /xlɔ:rós/, etc.[63]

These examples demonstrate that certain phonetical changes in Tsakonian coincide with Modern Greek ones. For instance, Ancient Greek /y/ in most cases has transformed into /i/ even in Ancient Greek lexemes themselves: Tsak. *ío* 'water' < AncGr ὕδωρ /ʰýdɔ:r/, Tsak. *ípre* 'dream' < AncGr ὕπνος /ʰýpnos/. There are also some stems in Tsakonian that have forms with both /u/ and /i/: Tsak. *psuxré* 'cold, cool' (adjective) < AncGr ψυχρός /psyxrós/, but Tsak. *psíxra* 'cold' (noun).

Tsakonian morphology in general resembles that of Modern Greek, despite some ancient features and analytical present and imperfect forms.[64] Most probably, Tsakonian perfect (8a) and past perfect (8b) are not original but were borrowed from Modern Greek. These forms could be roughly called a "second derivative analytic form" as they are constructed by means of an analytical form of the auxiliary verb 'to have' and a passive participle:

(8) a. *énʲi*   *éx-u*   *za-tʰé*
    AUX.PRS.1SG have(AUX)-PTCP-M.SG go.PFV-PTCP.INACT.M.SG
    '[I] have gone'
  b. *éma*   *éx-u*   *za-tʰé*
    AUX.PST.1SG have(AUX)-PTCP-M.SG go.PFV-PTCP.INACT.M.SG
    '[I] had gone'

It seems that Medieval Greek had no perfect forms (Janssen 2013; Kisilier 2016b). This explains why Modern Greek and its dialects, unlike other Balkan languages, have no evidentialis which requires perfect forms. Tsakonian is no exception

---

[63] More examples are available in (Kisilier 2017b: 125–133).
[64] Note the discussion of the Tsakonian genitive in section 4.3 and Kisilier & Fedchenko (2013).

here. It has no evidentialis, probably because perfect forms appeared in Tsakonian only after possible intensive contact with other Balkan languages.

Like Modern Greek, Tsakonian is a pro-drop language. It also has proleptic and resumptive object pronouns:

(9) o=ni=**m**=e-ðúts-ere   s   **eníu**
     NEG=3SG.OBL=1SG.OBL=PST-give.PFV-2SG in 1SG.OBL
     '[You] did not give it to me'[65]

Unexpectedly, when the object is a 1st or 2nd person plural pronoun, the proleptic or resumptive pronoun in the singular is used (cf. Joseph 1990: 177):

(10) a. **m**=or-ákate   **námu**
        1SG.OBL=see-AOR.2PL   1PL.OBL
        'You saw us'
     b. ét^{h}e   θé-nde   na=**ndi**=ð̃-u   **n^{j}úmu**
        AUX.PRS.2PL want-PTCP.NN.PL   SBJV=2SG.OBL-give.PFV-SBJV.1SG   1PL.OBL
        'Do you want me to give it to you?'

Nikos Liosis (2017: 63–64) believes that such examples result from the reanalysis of the 1st or 2nd person plural pronouns. My explanation of this phenomenon is more simple. Clitic doubling evidently appeared in Medieval Greek and did not spread into all Modern Greek dialects. For example, it is absent from Pontic. In some dialects, like in Azov Greek, it has not developed to the full extent that it has in Modern Greek and actually is a set of various competing patterns. This is also likely to be the case with Tsakonian where in clitic doubling two clitics but not a stressed pronoun and a clitic may be involved (11a), comp. with Azov Greek (11b):

---

[65] In (9), Tsakonian violates the Modern Greek pattern where a direct object should follow an indirect one: μου το έ-δωσ-ες /mu=to=é-ðos-es/ <1SG.GEN=3.N.SG.NGEN=PST-give.PFV-PST.2SG> 'you gave it to me'. The same "violation" as in Tsakonian is also found in Azov Greek (Kisilier 2009: 390), Cappadocian (Janse 1998: 268), Grekanico and Lesbian (Ralli 2006: 147). In all these dialects, both orders are possible: (a) "violated" (a direct object clitic pronoun precedes an indirect object clitic pronoun) and (b) "standard" (a direct object clitic pronoun follows an indirect object clitic pronoun). This phenomenon is not mentioned in section 5.3 because, as I believe, it has nothing to do either with interactions between Tsakonian and other Modern Greek dialects or linguistic typology. In Tsakonian, Azov Greek, Cappadocian, Grekaniko and Lesbian, for different reasons pronominal clitics are used in the same form for the direct object as well as the indirect one. Loss of morphological difference, probably, led to dissapearance of the syntactic constraint.

(11) a. **nʲ=e-pék-a=ni**   nʲúmu
       3SG.OBL=PST-tell.AOR-AOR.1SG=3SG.OBL   2PL.OBL
       'How many times I have told you **that**'
   b. **mas**=fórʲas-an=**mas**
       1SG.OBL=dress.PFV-PST.3PL=1SG.OBL
       '[They] dressed **us**' (Borisova 2009: 400)

Evidently, in Tsakonian this construction was borrowed from Modern Greek. Tsakonian has no clear opposition between stressed, orthotonic (strong) and unstressed, clitic (weak) pronouns in plural, so they are replicated with a clitic pronoun in singular. However, examples of clitic doubling with the 1st or 2nd person plural pronouns (10) are to be found much more rarely than those with singular (9). Phrases such as (10) seem very artificial. Most speakers try to avoid them in their speech and prefer another pattern which is much closer to Standard Modern Greek:

(12) éngi t͡s   éngi **nam**=e-ᵐbík-ai   **námu**
     this and   this 1PL.OBL=PST-do.AOR-AOR.3PL 1PL.OBL
     '...and that and that [they] did to **us**' (Costakis 1987: 394)[66]

In (12), the speakers of Tsakonian try to create a clitic form *nam* from the stressed pronoun *námu* on the pattern of the clitic *nʲum* from *nʲúmu* in (15b).

Personal clitic pronouns in singular are generally placed according to the same rules as in Standard Modern Greek. Therefore, they precede the finite verb (13a) and follow the imperative (13b):

(13) a. **ndʲ**=epé-ka
       2SG.OBL=say.PFV-AOR.1SG
       'I told it to **you**' [= "How many times do I have to tell you"]
   b. ð-i=**mi**
       give.PFV-IMP.2SG=1SG.OBL
       'Give **me**'

A personal object pronoun in plural may also precede the finite verb (14a), but, more frequently, it is used in postposition (14b):

(14) a. **nʲum**=or-ákame
       2PL.OBL=see-AOR.1PL

---

[66] I have transformed the example into IPA. Liosis (2017: 63) gives another interpretation of this sentence.

b. *or-ákame* **nʲúmu**
   see-AOR.1PL 2PL.OBL
   '[We] saw **you**'

It seems that contemporary Tsakonian sets the phonological status of the personal object pronouns in plural somewhere between a stressed form and a clitic. On the one hand, the postposition generally is a position of a nonclitic pronoun, see (10, 12, 17a). On the other hand, the personal object pronoun in plural (*námu* or *nʲúmu*) either affects the position of a clitic pronoun and obviously creates a cluster with it as in (15a), or appears in front of the verb because of the particle *na* (15b) where the consequence *na nʲúmu* resembles a cluster of clitics.

(15) a. *e-ðú-ka=ni*   *nʲúmu*
        PST-give.PFV-AOR.1SG=3SG.OBL 2SG.OBL
        '[I] gave it to you'
     b. *na=nʲum=al-îu*
        SBJV–1PL.OBL–say.IPFV.SBJV-1SG.SBJV
        '[I] would like to tell you'

Still, the pronouns *námu* or *nʲúmu* are "less clitic" than "real" clitic pronouns. In singular, a proclitic pronoun *mi* in (16) "attracts" another clitic proniun *ni* to the position in front of the verb and creates a cluster with it, though *námu* stays behind the verb:

(16) **mi=nʲ**=*e-ðúts-ere*   *námu*
     1SG.OBL=3SG.OBL=PST-give.PFV-2SG 1PL.OBL
     'You gave it to us'

A similar situation was relevant for Late Koiné Greek when all disyllabic personal object pronouns could function both as strong and weak forms (Kisilier 2011: 163–178). Probably, the peculiarities of Tsakonian pronominal syntax actually are just isolated traces of previous, more archaic, patterns that followed Wackernagel's law. They affect not only disyllabic personal object pronouns in plural, but personal clitic pronouns in singular as well. As it was mentioned before, clitic pronouns in general in Tsakonian (13) are placed according to the same regulations as in Standard Modern Greek. However, there is at least one exception. Modern Tsakonian has two negations: *o* which originates from Ancient Greek /o:k/ and almost always leads to postposition of pronominal clitic (17a) and *ðe[n]* which coincides with a Modern Greek negation and does not provoke any change in the constituent order within VP (17b):

(17) a. *o=ðúts-ere=ni*   s   eníu
       NEG=give.PFV-2SG=3SG.OBL in 1SG.OBL
       '[You] did not give it to me'
    b. *ðe=mʲ=e-péts-ere*
       NEG=1SG.OBL=PST-say.PFV-2SG
       '[You] did not tell me'

Apparently, a postposition after *o* is a remnant of some more archaic situation. This word order pattern is less productive, than the pattern with *ðe*[*n*], and sooner or later will be replaced by the latter. From the point of view of pronominal syntax Tsakonian is closer to the Modern Greek one than, for example, Pontic with its obligatory postposition of pronominal clitics (Condoravdi & Kiparsky 2001: 17), or in Azov Greek where the position of clitic pronouns rather depends on prosody than the form of the verb (Kisilier 2009: 388–390).

Tsakonian is evidently not an Ancient Greek dialect. Archaic elements coexist with modern ones on almost all linguistic levels. The emergence of non-archaic forms is owing to long-term contact with Greek Koinés and, perhaps, with other varieties of Greek.

5.3 Tsakonian and Modern Greek dialects

Tsakonian is rarely compared to other Modern Greek dialects. Brian Newton (1972) simply decided to exclude it from his classification, along with all Modern Greek dialects outside Greece. Nikolaos Kontosopoulos (2001: xxiii), Peter Trudgill (2003: 54–56), and Angela Ralli (2006) tried to bring Tsakonian closer to other Modern Greek dialects, but pointed out only isolated similarities. Hubert Pernot (1905) and Anastasios Karanastasis (1986) specified certain archaic peculiarities of Tsakonian which exist in some other Modern Greek dialects as well (see Section 4.2). In this section, I shall demonstrate that some phonetic and morphological features relevant for current classifications of Modern Greek dialects are present in Tsakonian as well.

Vocalism:
- /o/ > /u/: Tsak *kistíu* 'believe', Azov *pistévu* vs. MGr πιστεύω /pistévo/, see NGr *kutóplu* 'hen' vs. MGr κοτόπουλο /kotópulo/;
- /i/ > /j/ can be found in most dialects, e. g. MGr παιδιά /peðiá/ 'children, guys', but it does not happen in Old Athenian and Pontic (*peðia*), Azov Greek (*peðíja*) and Tsakonian (*kabzía*).

Consonantism:
- palatalization (i. e. /k/ > /t͡ʃ/, /x/ > /ʃ/, /γ/ > /ʒ/ in front of /e/, /i/ or /j/) is found in many dialects such as Cypr, Cret t͡ʃerós 'time, weather', Azov t͡ʃirós or tʲirós vs. MGr καιρός /kerós/, Tsak t͡ʃufá 'head' vs. MGr κεφάλη /kefáli/;
- tsitakism, further fronting of /k/ before /i/, /e/ and /j/ to /t͡s/: Rhode tserós 'time, weather', Tsak t͡seré vs. MGr καιρός /kerós/. According to Trudgill (2003: 56), the area where this phenomenon occurs includes most of the Cyclades and some varieties of Old Athenian. In Tsakonian tsitakism is so widely spread that, on the one hand, it often replaces palatalization (t͡sufá 'head' instead of t͡ʃufá), and on the other hand, it involves both /t/ (Tsak t͡sípta 'nothing' vs. MGr τίποτα /típota/) and /k/ (Tsak t͡se 'and' vs. MGr και /ke/);
- loss of /-ð-/ is encountered in Southeastern dialects and in Tsakonian: Cypr láin 'oil', Tsak ái vs. MGr λάδι /láði/;
- like most Modern Greek dialects, Tsakonian has no final /-n/ retention and no geminates.

Table 1 Tsakonian and other dialects: phonetics

Feature		Northern	Old Athenian	Cretan	Southeastern	Tsakonian	Cappadocian	Griko	Pontic	Azov Greek
1.	/e/ > /i/, /o/ > /u/	+	–	–	–	+/–	+/–	+/–	–?	+
1.	palatalization	+	+	+	+	+	+	+	+	+
2.	tsitakism	–/+	+	+	+	+	–	+	+/–	–/+?
3.	geminates	–/+	–/+	–	+	–	–	+	–	–
4.	/i/ > /j/	+	–	+/–	+	+/–	–	–	–	–
5.	/y/ > /u/	–	+	–	–	+	–	+/–	+	–
6.	loss of /-ð-/	–	+/–	–	+	+	–	+/–	–	–/+
7.	retention of /-n/	–	–	–	+	–	+/–	+	+/–	–
8.	/vγ/ > /vg/	–	–?	–?	+	–	?	?	–	–
9.	epenthesis of /-γ-/	+/–	–/+	+	+	–	+/–	–	+	–

Morphology:
- as in Griko, Northern dialects and Cretan, Tsakonian makes wide use of the perfect, though in all these dialects this is most likely a relatively recent borrowing from Modern Greek (cf. Section 5.2);
- In Tsakonian, periphrastic constructions with the accusative, or the accusative form itself tend to replace the genitive (see Section 4.3). The same occurs in Azov Greek, in Northern Greek and in Pontic.

Table 2 Tsakonian and other dialects: morphology

Feature	Northern	Old Athenian	Cretan	Southeastern	Tsakonian	Cappadocian	Griko	Pontic	Azov Greek
1. sigmatic aorist	+	+	+	+	−	+	−/+	+	+
2. analytical present	−	−	−	−	+	−	−	−	−
3. perfect	+	−	+	−	+	−	+	−	−

One could also propose lexical and syntactic parameters. For example, Tsakonian belongs to those dialects where 'what' is /ti/ but not /ínta/ or its variants, and it is a pro-drop dialect, unlike Azov Greek, etc. Even those features that seem to be particularly Tsakonian can be better approached from the typological point of view, such as verb morphology (Pernot 1933; Aerts 1965: 125–127), or phonetics. Thus palatalization of /ri/ is typical for Tsakonian, see (Kisilier & Fedchenko 2011: 263–264): Tsak *tʃía* 'three' vs. MGr τρία /tría/, Tsak *ðakʒízu* 'weep' vs. MGr δακρίζω /ðakrízo/. This phenomenon cannot be easily explained merely from "inside" Tsakonian, so it is important that mutations of /ri/ are met in other dialects as well, for example in Skyros (Kontosopoulos 2001: 112).

However, the question is inevitably raised as to whether these similarities are just a typological coincidence or whether they result from language contacts between dialects that remain unknown to us. If we accept this latter possibility, we may also hypothesize that some of the so-called "Modern Greek" features of Tsakonian (described in Section 5.2) may not have come from Standard Modern Greek but from the Peloponnesian-Ionian dialect group which actually was the basis for Standard Modern Greek. Unfortunately, there is not enough evidence either to prove or reject these ideas and their destiny is to remain purely hypothetical.

5.4 Possible contacts with other languages

Tsakonian studies in the 20th century could not escape the problem of the Tsakonian past. Although the official version has always insisted on the integrity of Tsakonian and linked it directly to Ancient Laconian, it is evident that the situation is more complex than has been presented. It could not be denied that Tsakonian had multiple similar features with other Modern Greek dialects (see Section 5.3). If these dialects were far away, one could claim that similarities were the result of parallel development and try to explain them by means of typology alone, taking into account that it is almost impossible to verify direct contact. Nevertheless, in case of Maniot that has multiple peculiarities which resemble Tsakonian (Vagiakakos 1986) and is only about 120 km away from the Tsakonian speaking area, it is difficult to be content with just a typological explanation, and an account that includes dialect or language contact seems more and more convincing. Most local researchers have not wanted to accept the idea of possible contacts with other dialects and languages, especially with Slavic (see Sarris 1956: 27; Vagenas 1974: 155). Still, an analysis of Tsakonian vocabulary (see Kisilier 2017b) demonstrates that such point of view is purely ideological.

Tsakonian has many loan words from Slavic, Albanian, Aromanian, Romanian and Italian,[67] all languages which at certain periods were spoken in Peloponnese (see Sections 2.2 and 3.1). Balkan and Italian borrowings have both geographic (Section 4.3) and semantic restrictions in distribution. The borrowings from Balkan languages generally refer to agriculture and animal husbandry (cf. MDABL 2009):

- *bártʃe* 'whitish kid with ash-grey marks' < Alb (*i, e*) *bardh* 'white';
- *drén^jje* 'a kid with white head and black front or black body' < Alb *dren|e, -ia* 'longicorn goat';
- *kórbe* 'black goat or mule' < Alb *korb, -i* 'any black animal' or 'crow, raven';
- *kúk^je* 'white kid with coffee-colored or reddish spots' < Alb (*i*) *kuq*, (*e*) *kuqe* 'red';
- *mútʃkure* 'a kid with white spots on black head' < Alb (*i, e*) *mushkër* 'grey' or 'grey goat' (Domosiletskaya 2002: 160, 163);
- *palivó* 'whitish (about a kid)' < Alb (*i, e*) *balë* 'white (frequently met in derivatives used for cattle color designation)'.

---

[67] Most borrowings are from the Venetian dialect. Venetian words were checked in (Vocobolario 2020).

Tsakonian words with Italian origin are usually connected with seamanship and trade. However many of them have parallels in Modern Greek:

- *álbure* 'mast' < Ven *alboro*, comp. MGr άλμπουρο /álburo/;
- *yánd͡ʒo* 'iron anchor' < Ven *gànzo* 'hook' < AncGr γαμψός /gampsós/ 'crooked', comp. MGr γάντζος /yáⁿdzos/ 'metal hook';
- *timóni* 'rudder' < Ven *timón*, comp. MGr τιμόνι /timóni/;
- *vapóri/papóri* 'steamer' < It *vapore*, comp. MGr βαπόρι /vapóri/;
- *fanéla* 'jersey, sailor shirt' < Ven *fanèla* 'knitted clothes', comp. It *flanella* 'flannel' < Eng *flannel*, comp. MGr φανέλα /fanéla/ 'cotton or wool jersey';
- *punéndis* 'west wind' < It *ponente*, comp. MGr πονέντες /ponéndes/ or πουνέντες /punéndes/;
- *barbúni* 'red goatfish (*mullus surmuletus*)' < Ven *barbón* 'black bullhead (*ameiurus melas*)', comp. MGr μπαρμπούνι /barbúni/ 'red goatfish';
- *rénga* 'salted herring' < Ven *rénga* 'herring', comp. MGr ρέγγα /rénga/;
- *bót͡sa* 'wooden vessel for wine ≈ 3 litres' or '3 litres' volume', or '9 litres' volume' < Ven *bòza* 'large bottle', comp. Medieval Greek μπότσα /ᵐbót͡sa/ 'barrel for wine or oil' (Kriaras 1990: 129);
- *mastélo* 'iron vessel for liquids' < Ven *mastèlo/mastèla* 'bucket' < It *mastello* < AncGr /mastós/ 'nipple, breast, udder', comp. MGr μαστέλο /mastélo/ 'barrel';
- *móstra* 'a small part of a cloth, sample' < It *mostra* 'demonstration', comp. MGr μόστρα /móstra/ 'sample';
- *niterét͡ʃe* 'interest, profit' < It *interesse*, comp. MGr νιτερέσο /niteréso/ (Triantafyllidis 2009: 913);
- *próka* 'nail' < Ven *bròca*, comp. MGr πρόκα /próka/;
- *vʲolí* 'violin' < Ven *violin*, comp. It *violino* and MGr βιολί /vʲolí/.

Though some of these terms could have appeared in Tsakonian through Modern Greek, it does not mean that no direct contacts between Tsakonian and Italian/Venetian took place.[68] There are also Tsakonian borrowings from Italian and Venetian with no evident parallels in Standard Modern Greek:

- *álture* 'otherwise' < It *altro* 'another';
- *aléyro* 'agile' < It *allegro* 'vivacious';
- *alésta* 'ready' < It *alla lesta* 'rapidly';
- *brávo* 'excellent' <adverb> < It *bravo*;

---

[68] Thus, Tsak *varéla* 'barrel' is feminine like MGr βαρέλα /varéla/, unlike It *barile* which is masculine, or the meaning of Tsakonian *paróla* 'frivolous talk' is closer to MGr παρόλα /paróla/ 'stilted but senseless words' (Triantafyllidis 2009: 1036) than to original It *parola* 'word'.

- *frésko* 'fresh' < It *fresco*;
- *kapátso* 'capable' < It *capace*;
- *máni* 'rapidly' < It *in mano* 'at hand';
- *skúre* 'dark' < It *oscuro*;
- *várða* 'look out' < Ven *vàrda*.

Many loanwords in Tsakonian are also met in other Modern Greek dialects:

- *bélo/béla* 'white sheep', comp. OChSlav *bělъ(jь)* 'white' (Trubachev 1975: 79–81), the same word is also encountered in Thessalian (Chantziaras 1995: 277);[69]
- *férmeli* 'elegant male waistcoat worn together with fustanella' < Alb *fermel|e, -ja* 'female overcoat without sleeves decorated with gold or silver', comp. Thess *fermílʲ* 'waistcoat with embroidery worn together with fustanella';
- *karíta/karúta* 'cattle trough', comp. Bulg *korito* (Trubachev 1984: 121–126; MDABL 2009: 206), and in Modern Greek dialects: Kastelli (Peloponnese) *koríta* (MDABL 2009: 206), Thess *karúta* 'wooden tube for dirty clothes';
- *láje* 'black sheep', comp. Arom (Krania or Turia) *lajᵘ/laj* 'black (about ram)' (< Lat *lābēs* 'vice, shame') and in Modern Greek dialects: NGr (Eratyra) *láju* 'black (about ram)', Kastelli *lájo/lája* 'black (about sheep)' (MDABL 2009: 148–149)', Thess *lájus* 'black ram';
- *lʲjare* 'black-and-white (about any animal)' < Alb *lar|ë, -a* 'colored spot' or 'an animal with colored spot', comp. Thess *lʲára* 'white goat (also a name)' and *lʲárus* 'a bull with black-and-white spots';
- *xuméli* 'something very sweet', comp. Bulg *хмел* /xmel/ 'hop' and Cret *xúmeli* 'a kind of a plant' or 'sweet' <adjective> (Idomeneos 2006: 569);
- *zakóni* 'custom, habit', comp. Maced *закон* /zakón/ and Thess, Lesb *zakónʲ*.

The analysis of vocabulary borrowed from Balkan languages demonstrates that quite often it is impossible to decide which Balkan language the word could have been taken from:

- *bútʃiko* 'a kid with ash-grey spots on white, goldish or black wool' < Arom *bučiu* or *bučicu* (Papahagi 1974: 290; see MDABL 2009: 42, 138, 160, 439); according to (Domosiletskaya 2002: 420), *buç- / buş-* is simultaneously an Albanian and Aromanian isogloss with an unclear etymology;
- *katʃúla* 'shepherd's hood in the form of a cone', comp. Rom *căciúlă* 'sheepskin cap or a fur cap', Arom, MeglRom *căţiulă* (Coteanu, Seche & Seche 1998: 147;

---

69 Dimitrios Chantziaras erroneously connects the Thessalian word with It *bello* 'beautiful'.

Ciorănescu 2007: 131), Alb *kaçul|e, -ja* 'hood of a shepherds (fur or woolen) cloak' or 'hood of a raincoat', or 'children's woolen bonnet';
- *kolástra* 'beestings' or 'hot drink from boiled colostrum', comp. Rom *coráslă/ colástră/culástra/colástru/corast(r)ă*, Arom *curastă/culastă* and MeglRom *gulastră* 'colostrum' (Coteanu, Seche & Seche 1998: 195–225);
- *rogátʃ[i?]* 'entire goat or ram', comp. Bulg *рогач* /rogátʃ/ and Arom (Krania/ Turia) *rungátʃku* 'not entirely castrated ram' (MDABL 2009: 46);
- *sívo* 'bright animal with black strands', comp. Serb, Bulg *сив* /siv/ 'grey' and multiple Albanian, Aromanian and Megleno-Romanian parallels (Domosiletskaya 2002: 449).

Most probably this means that language contacts in the Tsakonian speaking area were complex and multilateral and Tsakonian shepherds were involved in seasonal migrations together with shepherds of Greek and non-Greek origins. These contacts primarily affected vocabulary but one cannot exclude that they could have influenced other linguistic levels as well (see Katsanis 1989; Liosis 2007), though the latter is not so evident and is much more difficult to investigate.

6 Conclusions

In spite of the widespread opinion that Tsakonians lived separately in a kind of "reservation" and had little or no connections with speakers of other dialects and languages, it is known that they undertook seasonal migrations to other parts of the Peloponnese and travelled to various regions and countries. Some facts (primarily lexical borrowings) allow for the supposition that, in Tsakonia and on nearby islands, they had contacts with Venetians (and, perhaps, other Italians), Slavs, Aromanians and Albanians. Along with lexical borrowings from these languages in Tsakonian and the fact that speakers of these languages were present in the Peloponnese at least for several centuries, there is clear indirect evidence in favour of this assumption:

(a) toponyms: Slavic – Sitena, Zaggoli, Zaritse and, perhaps, Prastos; Albanian – Malevos; French *frángo*, etc.;
(b) family names which refer to other nationalities: Βλάχος /vláxos/, Αρβανιταίοι /arvanitéi/, Βλάμης /vlámis/;
(c) common Balkan traditions such as the construction sacrifice, oath on one's ancestors, bathing of a weak newborn child in wine.

Each fact alone is by no means convincing, but together they begin to carry the weight of evidence. Probably some of the results of these contacts are still to be discovered. It is at present not possible to say to what extent the population of Tsakonia was multilingual and, if so, which language was L1, L2, or L3.

In the largest and richest Tsakonian towns, Prastos and, later, Leonidio, the dialect was hardly ever spoken, and Tsakonian was long in contact with some kind of Modern Greek Koiné. In my opinion, this experience has helped Tsakonian survive to the present day. It is evident that Standard Greek–Tsakonian bilingualism has existed for several centuries. Tsakonian has borrowed many words from Standard Greek and transformed them according to its own phonetics and morphology and, probably, has adopted a number of morphological and morphosyntactic patterns (e. g. perfect forms and the combination of a particle θα with imperfective past which used to express irrealis). Recent "rollback" in the female speech from /ʃi/, /ʒi/ or /rʲi/ to /ri/ is obviously also the affect from the part of the Standard Modern Greek.

Meanwhile Tsakonian managed to keep a number of its original (or previously adopted) features such as palatalization of /ri/ and its transformation into /ʃi/, /ʒi/ or /rʲi/ and some peculiarities of pronominal syntax. Evidently, most phonetic and morphological variants in Tsakonian, unlike some lexical ones, are not affected by other languages or dialects. Nevertheless, it is almost impossible to decide now whether a particular feature or pattern was borrowed and adopted or whether it just has typological parallels to Standard Modern Greek and other Modern Greek dialects.

Certain Tsakonian phonetic and morphological peculiarities cannot be easily analysed using the data we possess today. We are almost completely unaware of either the actual origin of Tsakonian or its history before the 19th century. Tsakonian has multiple Ancient Doric traces but they do not help us to explain why Tsakonian phonetics and morphology are sometimes so unusual. It is very tempting to suppose that Tsakonian is a result of interaction between Greek and non-Greek speakers and, at the very beginning, played the role of a local *lingua franca among various ethnic groups*. Although it is not clear which groups and languages were interacting (presumably some local Greek dialect, some Slavic language and Albanian, along with unknown others), and their contacts can scarcely be demonstrated, a contact-oriented approach opens new perspectives and may become another framework for Tsakonian studies. Thus, palatalization of /ri/ and its transformation into /ʃi/, /ʒi/ or /rʲi/ could be easily regarded as a contact-induced change: it is registered not only in other Modern Greek dialects (cf. Section 5.3) but also in other languages, for example, Sicilian /t͡ʃi/ 'three' vs. It *tré*. Tsakonian morphological and morphosyntactic phenomena that require reinvestigation in light of language contact are, certainly, the analytical forms of the present and imperfect and the means of expressing the irrealis apart from combinations of θα and imperfect. Even if this approach fails to reveal direct connections with other languages and dialects, it will still provide invaluable typological evidence which will make possible the creation of, at last, a consistent description of the Tsakonian dialect.

References

Adamou, Evangelia. 2008. *Le patrimoine plurilingue de la Grèce*. Louvain-la-Neuve: Peeters.
Aerts, Willem J. 1965. *Perphrastica. An investigation into the use of eînai and échein as auxiliaries or pseudo-auxiliaries in Greek from Homer up to the present day*. Amsterdam: Adolf M. Hakkert.
Amantos, Constantinos I. 1921. Tsakōnía – Sclavonia [Tsakonia – Sclavonia]. In *Aphiérōma eis G. Chatzidákin. Diatribaí phílōn kaí mathētôn epí tê triakostê pémptē epéteiō tês en tô panepistēmíō kathēgesías autoû* [Festsschrift in honor of G. Hatzidakis. Articles by his friends and students dedicated to the 35th anniversary of his professorship at the University], 130–134. Athens: P. D. Sakellarios.
Amantos, Constantinos I. 1964. *Glōssiká meletḗmata* [Linguistic studies]. Athens: Typographeion Adelphon Myrtidi.
Anagnostopoulos, Georgios P. 1926. *Tsakonische Grammatik*. Berlin; Athens: Urania Buchhandlung; Verlag P. D. Sakellarios.
Antonakatou, Ntiana & Takis Mauros. 1980. Éna askētério tês Arkadías. Hē Panagía stḗ Zaggólē tês Tsakṓnikēs Sítainas [A hermitage in Arcadia. Virgin Mary of Zaggoli in Tsakonian Sitena]. *Tsakonian Chronicles* 5. 45–47.
Archaeology 2011: Mycenaean cemetery revealed after heavy rains. *Archaelogy News Network*. 18 September: https://archaeologynewsnetwork.blogspot.ru/2011/09/mycenean-cemetery-revealed-after-heavy.html#5mO8TJQs6AlbUVzf.97 (accessed 15 March, 2021).
Arkhangelskiy, Timofey, Maxim Kisilier & Vladimir Plungian. 2018. Ēlektronikó sṓma keiménōn tēs Tsakōnikḗs dialéktou: Ti eínai kai giatí chreiázetai [Electronic corpus of the Tsakonian dialect: what it is and how it can be used]. *Tsakonian Chronicles* 23 (1). 89–93.
Balta, Evangelia. 2009. Venetians and Ottomans in the Southeast Peloponnese (15th–18th century). In Taşkın Takış & Sunay Aksoy (eds.), *Halil İnalcık armağanı: Tarih araştırmaları. Vol. 1: Adlı çalışmada yer alan konular ve makaleler şöyledir*, 168–204. Ancara: Doğu Batı Yayınları.
Beis, Nikos A. 1961. Hoi Tsákōnes kaí hē Tsakṓnikē diálektos [The Tsakonians and the Tsakonian dialect]. *Tsakonian Chronicles* 2. 7–11.
Björck, Gudmund. 1940. HN ΔΙΔΑΣΚΩΝ: *Die periphrastischen Konstruktionen im Griechischen* (Skrifter utgivna av K. Humanistiska Vetenskaps-Samfundet i Uppsala. Vol. 32 (2). Uppsala: Almqvist Wiksells Boktryckeri-A.-B.; Leipzig: O. Harrassowitz.
Blažek, Václav. 2010. Glottochronological analysis of the Greek lexicon: Modern, Tsakonian, Old and Mycenaean Greek. *Graeco-Latina Brunensia* 15 (1). 17–35.
Boisacq, Émile. 1904. Sur le traitement du sigma intervocalique en laconien. In Maurits Basse (ed.), *Mélanges Paul Frédéricq: hommage de la Société pour le progrès des études philologiques et historiques*, 29–32. Bruxelles: Henri Lamertin.
Borisova, Anna B. 2009. Mestoimennyĭ povtor dopolneniia [Clitic doubling]. Ch. 13. In Maxim L. Kisilier (ed.), *Iazyk i kil'tura mariupol'skikh grekov* [Language and culture of Mariupolis

Greeks]. Vol. 1: *Lingvisticheskaiã i ėtnokul'turnaiã situatsiiã v grecheskikh selakh Priazov'iã. Po materĩalam ėkspeditsii 2001–2004 godov* [Language and ethno-cultural situation in Greek villages of Azov region], 394–402. Saint Petersburg: Aleteia.

Bourguet, Émile. 1927. *Le dialecte laconien* (Collection linguistique publiée par la Société de linguistique de Paris. Vol. 23). Paris: Librairie ancienne honoré champion [Libraire de la Société de linguistique de Paris].

Buchholz, Oda & Wilfried Fiedler. 1987. *Albanische Grammatik.* Leipzig: VEB Verlag Enzyklopädie.

Caragounis, Chrys C. 2004. *The development of Greek and the New Testament: morphology, syntax, and textual transmission* (Untersuchungen zum Neuen Testament. Vol. 167). Tübingen: Mohr Siebeck.

Chantziaras, Dimitrios P. 1995. *To thessalikó glōssikó idíōma. Glōssari – lexikó* [The Thessalian dialect. Glossary – Dictionary]. Athens: Dimiourgia.

Charalampopoulos, Agathokles L. 1980a. Anánkē apographês tês sēmerinês Tsakōnikês (Prótasē giá miá koinōnioglōssikḗ melétē) [The need to describe the Tsakonian dialect in its current state (Proposal for a sociolinguistic study)]. *Tsakonian Chronicles* 5. 17–25.

Charalampopoulos, Agathokles L. 1980b. *Phōnologikḗ análysē tēs Tsakōnikḗs dialéktou* [A phonological analysis of the Tsakonian dialect]. Thessaloniki: Aristotle University of Thessaloniki, Doctoral thesis.

Ciorănescu, Alexandru. 2007. *Dicționarul etimologic al limbii române* [Etymological dictionary of Romanian]. Trans. by Tudora Șandru Mehedinți și Magdalena Popescu Marin. București: Saeculum I. O.

Condoravdi, Cleo & Paul Kiparsky. 2001. Clitics and clause structure. *Journal of Greek Linguistics* 2. 1–40.

Constantinopoulos, Christos G. 1969. Gýrō stḗ sēmasía tôn léxeōn "Tsakōnía" kaí "Tsákōnas" [On the names "Tsakonia" and "Tsakonas"]. *Tsakonian Chronicles* 3. 67–76.

Costakis, Thanasis P. 1951. *Sýntomē grammatikḗ tês Tsakōnikês dialéktou* [A brief grammar of the Tsakonian dialect] (Collection de l'Institut Français d'Athènes. Vol. 35). Athens: Institut Français d'Athènes.

Costakis, Thanasis P. 1956a. Apó tḗn istoría tês glṓssas mâs [On the history of our language]. *Tsakonian Chronicles* 1. 33–35. Reprinted 2006.

Costakis, Thanasis P. 1956b. Paratērḗseis stá Tsakōniká tēs Propontídas [Observations on Propontis Tsakonian]. *Peloponnēsiaká* [Peloponnesian Studies] 1. 108–126.

Costakis, Thanasis P. 1956c. Prosthḗkes kaí diorthṓseis stē "Chlōrída tês Tsakōniâs" toû Michaḗl Déphner [Additions and corrections to Michael Deffner's "Flora of Tsakonia"]. In *Mélanges offerts à Octave et Melpo Merlier: à l'occasion du 25e anniversaire de leur arrivée en Grèce.* Vol. 1, 133–156. Athens: Institut Français d'Athènes.

Costakis, Thanasis P. 1958–1959. Tsakṓnika kýria onómata [Tsakonian proper names]. *Pleoponnēsiaká* [Peloponnesian Studies] 3–4. 230–240.

Costakis, Thanasis P. 1969. Tá Tsakṓnika tês Propontídas [Propontis Tsakonian]. *Tsakonian Chronicles* 3. 41–47.

Costakis, Thanasis P. 1979. *Vátika kai Chavoutsí: Ta tsakōnochṓria tēs Propontídas* [Vatika and Havoutzi: the Tsakonian settlements of Propontis]. Athens: Centre for Asia Minor Studies.

Costakis, Thanasis P. 1980–1981. O Evliyâ Çelebi stḗn Peloponnḗso [Evliyâ Çelebi in Peloponnese]. *Peloponnēsiaká* [Peloponnesian Studies] 14. 238–306.

Costakis, Thanasis P. 1986a. Archaía glōssḗmata sta sēmeriná Tsakṓnika [Ancient words in modern Tsakonian]. *Tsakonian Chronicles* 7. 56–63.

Costakis, Thanasis P. 1986b. *Lexikó tēs Tsakṓnikēs dialéktou* [Dictionary of the Tsakonian dialect]. Vol. 1 (A–I). Athens: Academy of Athens.

Costakis, Thanasis P. 1986c. *Lexikó tēs Tsakṓnikēs dialéktou* [Dictionary of the Tsakonian dialect]. Vol. 2 (K–O). Athens: Academy of Athens.

Costakis, Thanasis P. 1986d. O Kōnstantínos Oikonómos o ex Oikonómōn kai ta Tsakṓnika [Constantine Oikonomos ex Oikonomon and the Tsakonian dialect]. *Tsakonian Chronicles* 7. 64–69.

Costakis, Thanasis P. 1987. *Lexikó tēs Tsakṓnikēs dialéktou* [Dictionary of the Tsakonian dialect]. Vol. 3 (P–Ō). Athens: Academy of Athens.

Costakis, Thanasis P. 1999. Grammatikḗ tēs Tsakōnikḗs dialéktou (periphéreia Leōnidíou – Prastoú) [Grammar of the Tsakonian dialect (the regions of Leonidio and Prastos)]. *Tsakonian Chronicles* 15.

Coteanu, Ion, Luiza Seche & Mircea Seche. 1998. *Dicţionarul explicativ al limbii române.* [Explanatory dictionary of Romanian]. 2nd edn. Bucureşti: Univers enciclopedic.

Crawford, Mary. 1995. *Talking difference. On gender and language.* London: SAGE publications.

Dankoff, Robert. 1991. A*n Evliya Çelebi glossary. Unusual, dialectal and foreign words in the Seyahat-name* (Şinasi Tekin & Gönül Alpay Tekin (eds.), Sources of oriental languages and literatures 14 (Turkish sources XII)). Cambridge, MA: The Department of Near Eastern Languages and Civilizations, Harvard University.

Deffner, Michael. 1874. Reste älterer Casusbildung im Zakonischen. *Nea Ellas* 34. 19 October.

Deffner, Michael. 1875. Zakonisches. *Monatsbericht der Königlich Preußischen Akademie der Wissenschaften zu Berlin* 18. 15–30.

Deffner, Michael. 1881. *Zakonische Grammatik.* Vol. 1. Lautlehre. Berlin: Weidmannsche Buchhandlung.

Deffner, Michael. 1922. *Chlōrís tês Tsakōniâs* (Geōponikḗ bibliothḗkē 2) [The Flora of Tsakonia (Library of Agriculture. Vol. 2)]. Athens: Stauros Christos & Sia.

Deffner, Michael. 1926. *Hephtá ōraîa paramýthia eis tḗn dēmṓdē neoellēnikḗn kai tsakōnikḗn diálekton* [Seven beautiful fairy tales in Modern Greek and Tsakonian]. Athens: (n. p.).

Dernikos, Dimitris. 1956. Hē Tsakōniá epí tourkokratías [Tsakonia under Turkish rule]. *Tsakonian Chronicles* 1. 17–23. Reprinted 2006.

Desnitskaya, Agniya V. 1970. *Naddialektnye formy ustnoĭ rechi i ikh rol' v istorii ĭazyka* [Superdialectal forms of spoken language and their role in historical linguistics]. Leningrad: Nauka.

Domosiletskaya, Marina V. 2002. *Albansko-vostochnoromanskiĭ sopostavitel'nyĭ poniatiinyĭ slovar'. Skotovodcheskaĭa leksika* [Albanian-Eastern Romance comparative conceptual dictionary: the pastoral vocabulary]. Saint Petersburg: Nauka.

Egea Sanchez, José M. 1996. *La Crónica de Morea* (Nueva Roma: Biblioteca Graeca et Latina Aevi Posterioris. Vol. 2). Madrid: Consejo superior de investigaciones científicas.

Eloeva, Fatima A. 2004. *Pontiĭskiĭ dialekt v sinkhronii i diakhronii* [The Pontic dialect in synchrony and diachrony]. St. Petersburg: Saint Petersburg State University.

ELP 2020: *Endangered languages project*: http://www.endangeredlanguages.com/lang/3499 (accessed 15 March, 2021).

Famerie, Étienne. 2007. Villoison et la redécouverte du dialecte tsakonien. *Anabase* 6. 235–242.

Fedchenko, Valentina. 2013. Subdialectal diversity in the Tsakonian speaking area of Arkadia. In Mark Janse, Brian D. Joseph, Angela, Ralli & Metin Bagriacik (eds.), *Proceedings of the 5th international conference of Modern Greek dialects and linguistic theory (*MGDLT 5*). Ghent, Belgium. 20–22 September 2012*, 76–88. Patras: University of Patras.

Golant, Natalia G. 2009. Obraz zhenshchiny v balladakh o stroitel'noĭ zhertve (po materialam iz karpato-balkanskogo regiona) [Images of women in ballads related to the building sacrifice (materials from the Carpatho-Russian area)]. In Yuri K. Chistov & Maria A. Rubtsova (eds.),

Radlovskiĭ sbornik: Nauchnye issledovaniia i muzeĭnye proekty MAĖ RAN v 2008 [Radlov collection: Research and museum studies in the Peter the Great Museum of Anthropology and Ethnography (the Kunstkamera) ras], 135–139. Saint Petersburg: Peter the Great Museum of Anthropology and Ethnography (the Kunstkamera) RAS.

Gomosto 2017: *Sýllogos Gomostoú. Pétaxan chártina aerósata tēn ṓra tēs Anástasēs! Éna ómorfo théama... pou «taxídepse» to mḗnyma tēs agápēs! Binteo kai phṓto* [Society of Gomosto. Paper lamps were launched while celebrating the Resurraction! Beautiful view... when the message of love "travelled"! Video and photo]. *Dytika nea.gr.* 16 April. http://dytikanea.gr/?p=69604 (accessed 15 March, 2021).

Haspelmath, Martin. 1998. The semantic development of old presents: new futures and subjunctives without grammaticalization. *Diachronica* 15. 29–62.

Hatzidakis, Georgios N. 1926. Athí, athía, athoíne, aphoútsi im Zakonischen. *Indogermanische Forschungen* 43 (1). 65–68.

Hesseling, Dirk Christiaan. 1907. De Koine en de oude dialekten van Griekenland. *Verslagen en mededeelingen der Koninklijke Akademie van wetenschappen. Afdeeling Letterkunde* 4 (8). 133–169.

Holzmann, Heidi (ed.). 2010. *Tsakonische Volksmärchen.* Simmern: Pandion Verlag.

Idomeneos, Marinos I. 2006. *Krētikó glōssário. Lémmata. Mantinádes. Paroimíes* [A Cretan glossary. Vocabulary. Mantinades. Proverbs]. Irakleio: Vikelaia Demotic Library.

Ivanov, Vyacheslav Vs. 2004. Proiskhozhdenie i transformatsii fabuly ballady o mastere Manole [The origins and transformations of the plot of the ballad about the master builder Manolas]. *Trudy russkoĭ antropologicheskoĭ shkoly* [Studies of the Russian school of anthropology] 1, 9–23.

Janse, Mark. 1998. Cappadocian clitics and the syntax-morphology interface. In Brian D. Joseph, Geoffrey C. Horrocks & Irene Philippaki-Warburton (eds.), *Themes in Greek linguistics.* Vol. 2, 257–282. Amsterdam & Philadelphia: John Benjamins.

Janse, Mark. 2019. Agglutinative noun inflection in Cappadocian. Ch. 2. In Angela Ralli (ed.), *The morphology of Asia Minor Greek. Selected topics* (Empirical Approaches to Linguistic Theory. Vol. 13), 66–115. Leiden; Boston: Brill.

Janssen, Marjolijne. 2013. Perfectly absent: the emergence of the Modern Greek perfect in Early Modern Greek. *Byzantine and Modern Greek Studies* 37. 245–260.

Joseph, Brian D. 1990. The benefits of morphological classification: On some apparently problematic clitics in Modern Greek. In Wolfgang U. Dressler, Hans C. Luschützky, Oscar E. Pfeifer & John Rennison (eds.), *Contemporary morphology,* 171–181. Berlin & New York: Mouton de Gruyter.

Joseph, Brian D., Rexhina Ndoci & Carly Dickerson. 2019. Language mixing in Palasa. *Journal of Greek Linguistics* 19. 227–243.

Kalamata 2020: *Pétagma aerostátou stēn Kalamáta* [Launching a balloon in Kalamata]. https://www.youtube.com/watch?v=AVD9PiDq5LU (accessed April 2, 2021).

Kapsomenos, Stylianos G. 1985. *Apó tḗn istoría tês Hellēnikês glṓssas. Hē Hellēnikē glṓssa apó tá Hellēnistiká hōs tá neṓtera chrónia. Hē Hellēnikē glṓssa stēn Aígypto* [From the history of the Greek language. The Greek language from the Hellenistic period up to the present. The Greek language in Egypt]. Thessaloniki: Institute of Modern Greek Studies. Manolis Triandafyllidis Foundation.

Karanastasis, Anastasios. 1986. Ē syngéneia tēs Tsakōnikḗs me ta Ellēniká Katōïtalliká idiṓmata [Relations of Tsakonian and Modern Greek idioms of South Italy]. *Tsakonian Chronicles* 7. 70–75.

Kassian, Alexei. 2018. Annotated Swadesh wordlists for the Greek group (Indo-European family). http://starling.rinet.ru/new100/grk.pdf (accessed 15 March, 2021).

Katsanis, Níkos. 1989. Koutsobláchika kai Tsakónika [Aromanian and Tsakonian]. *Ellēnikḗ dialektología* [Greek dialectology] 1. 41–54.

Kisilier, Maxim L. 2008. Éna ellēnikó idíōma stēn Anatolikḗ Oukranía (periochḗ Marioúpolēs) [A Greek dialect in the Eastern Ukraine (Mariupol region)]. *Acta Linguistica Petropolitana* 4 (1). 156–166.

Kisilier, Maxim L. 2009. Poriadok slov [Word order]. Ch. 12. In Maxim L. Kisilier (ed.), *Iazyk i kil'tura mariupol'skikh grekov* [Language and culture of Mariupolis Greeks]. Vol. 1: *Lingvisticheskaia i ėtnokul'turnaia situatsiia v grecheskikh selakh Priazov'ia. Po materialam ėkspeditsii 2001–2004 godov* [Language and ethno-cultural situation in Greek villages of Azov region], 374–393. Saint-Petersburg: Aleteia.

Kisilier, Maxim L. 2011. *Mestoimennye klitiki v "Luge Dukhovnom" Ioanna Moskha* [Pronominal clitics in the "Pratum" by John Moschos]. Saint Petersburg: Nestor-Istoria.

Kisilier, Maxim L. 2013. Novogrecheskaia dialektologiia: dostizheniia i problemy [Studies in Modern Greek dialects: Achievements and problems]. *Voprosy Jazykoznanija* [Topics in the study of language] 2. 83–98.

Kisilier, Maxim L. 2014a. Apostolés apó tēn Agía Petroúpolē: o skopós tous kai ta prṓta symperásmata [The expeditions from Saint Petersburg: Their aims and preliminary results]. *Tsakonian Chronicles* 22 (1). 119–125.

Kisilier, Maxim L. 2014b. O Tsakonii i tsakontsakh: na styke istorii i filologii [Tsakonia and Tsakonians: Historical and philological approach]. *Acta Linguistica Petropolitana* 10 (1). 283–306.

Kisilier, Maxim L. 2014c. Tsakonskiĭ dialekt: novyĭ vzgliad [Tsakonian: new approach]. In Valentin F. Vydrin & Natalia V. Kuznetsova (eds.), *Ot Bikina do Bambaliumy, iz variag v greki. Ėkkspeditsionnye ėtiudy v chest' Eleny Vsevolodovny Perekhval'skoi* [From Bikin to Banbaluma, from the Varangians to the Greeks. Field-inspired essays in honour of Elena V. Perekhvalskaya], 330–348. Saint Petersburg: Nestor-Istoria.

Kisilier, Maxim L. 2016a. Analiticheskie formy nastoiashchego vremeni i imperfekta v tsakonskom dialekte novogrecheskogo iazyka [Tsakonian analytic forms of present and imperfect]. *Acta Linguistica Petropolitana* 12 (3). 93–109.

Kisilier, Maxim L. 2016b. Iz istorii novogrecheskogo perfekta [About the perfect forms in Early Modern Greek]. *Indoevropeiskoe iazykoznanie i klassicheskaia filologia* [Indo-European Linguistics and Classical Philology] 20 (1). 426–439.

Kisilier, Maxim L. 2016c. O tsakonskom fol'klore [About Tsakonian folklore]. In Mikhail V. Bibikov, Ksenia A. Klimova, Dmitri E. Afinogenov, K. V. Norkin, Dionisis Maroulis, Irina V. Tryasorukova & Dmitri A. Yalamas (eds.), *Grecheskaia traditsionnaia kultura na evropeĭskom fone* [Greek traditional culture against the European background]. *Abstracts of the conference. Moscow, April 5–8, 2016*, 28–33. Moscow, Moscow State University, Faculty of Philology.

Kisilier, Maxim L. 2017a. Folklore, literature and identity, or once more about Azov Greeks. *Judaica Petropolitana* 8. 83–97.

Kisilier, Maxim L. 2017b. Leksicheskie osobennosti tsakonskogo dialekta novogrecheskogo iazyka: Predvaritel'nye nabliudeniia i perspektivy issledovaniia [Lexical peculiarities of the Tsakonian dialect of Modern Greek: Preliminary observations and perspectives of study]. *Voprosy Jazykoznanija* [Topics in the study of language] 1. 105–136.

Kisilier, Maxim. 2019a. Azov Greek in a typological perspective. In Andreea Madalina Balas, Sophia Giannopoulou & Angeliki Zagoura (eds.), *Proceedings of the 5th Patras international conference of graduate students in linguistics (PICGL5). Patras, Greece. 27–29 May 2018*, 34–47. Patras: University of Patras.

Kisilier, Maxim L. 2019b. Ob odnoĭ nauchnoĭ polemike, ili iz istorii izucheniia tsakonskogo dialekta [About one scholarly polemic or from the history of Tsakonian studies]. *Indoevropeiskoe iazykoznanie i klassicheskaia filologia* [Indo-European Linguistics and Classical Philology] 23 (1). 493–511.

Kisilier, Maxim L. & Giannis Christodoulou. 2018. Tsakṓnikes spoudés stēn Agía Petroúpolē kai Archeío tēs Tsakōniás [Tsakonian studies in St. Petersburg and the Tsakonian Archives]. *Tsakonian Chronicles* 23 (1). 233–238

Kisilier, Maxim L. & Valentina V. Fedchenko. 2010. Evangelie Liubvi (Ioann 20: 19–25): tsakonskiĭ variant ["The Love Gospel" (John 20: 19–25): Tsakonian version]. *Indoevropeiskoe iazykoznanie i klassicheskaia filologia* [Indo-European Linguistics and Classical Philology] 14 (2). 47–57.

Kisilier, Maxim L. & Valentina V. Fedchenko. 2011. K voprosu o miagkikh soglasnykh v tsakonskom dialekte novogrecheskogo iazyka [Palatal sonants in Tsakonian. Discussing the problem]. *Indoevropeiskoe iazykoznanie i klassicheskaia filologia* [Indo-European Linguistics and Classical Philology] 15. 259–266.

Kisilier, Maxim L. & Valentina V. Fedchenko. 2013. Formy genitiva i zameshchaiushchie ikh konstruktsii v tsakonskom dialekte novogrecheskogo iazyka [Genitive forms and correspondent periphrastic constructions in Tsakonian]. *Indoevropeiskoe iazykoznanie i klassicheskaia filologia* [Indo-European Linguistics and Classical Philology] 17. 418–428.

Kisilier, Maxim L. & Dionysios Mertyris. 2018. Perí tēs genikḗs sta Tsakṓnika ousiastiká [About the genitive in Tsakonian]. *Tsakonian Chronicles* 23 (2). 219–242.

Kisilier, Maxim L., Aleksandr A. Novik & Andrey N. Sobolev. 2016. Ėtnolingvisticheskie i dialektologicheskie nabliudeniia iz Dropula (Albaniia). Po materialam rossiiskoĭ ekspeditsii 2009 g. [Ethnolinguistic and dialectological observations from Dropull, Albania. Some data of the Russian expedition in 2009]. *Acta Linguistica Petropolitana* 12 (3). 111–134.

Kontosopoulos, Nikolaos G. 2001. *Diálektoi kai idiṓmata tēs néas ellēnikḗs* [Dialects and idioms of Modern Greek]. Athens: Grigoris Publishers.

Kontosopoulos, Nikolaos G. 2010. Katōitalikḗ kai Tsakṓnikē [Greek of South Italy and Tsakonian]. In Michalis Kopidakis Z. (ed.), *Istoría tēs Ellēnikḗs glṓssas* [History of the Greek language], 190–192. Athens: National Bank of Greece Cultural Foundation.

Korais, Adamantios. 1805. *Pródromos Hellēnikês Bibliothḗkēs: periéchōn Klaudíou Ailianoû tḗn Poikílēn Istorían, Hērakleídou toû Pontikoû, Nikoláou toû Damaskēnoû tá Sōzómena. Hoîs prosetéthēsan kaí bracheîai sēmeiṓseis, kaí Stochasmoí autoschédioi perí tês Hellēnikês paideías kaí glṓssēs* [Herald of the Hellenic library: with the Varia Historia by Claudius Ailianus, extant texts by Heraklides Ponticus, Nicholas Damascenus. To these were added and brief notes, as well as essays on the education of the Greek language]. Paris: Phirminou Didotou.

Kotsonis, Konstantinos L. 1977. Prṓtē eisbolḗ toû Impraḗm eis Lakōnían [Ibrahim's first incursion into Lakonia]. *Lakōnikaí Spoudaí* [Laconian Studies] 3. 111–184.

Kremmydas, Vasilis. 1974. Hē emporikḗ allēlographía toû Kṓsta Chatzipanagiṓtē A (1821–1831) [The commercial correspondence of Costas Chatzipanagiotis, pt. 1 (1821–1831)]. *Tsakonian Chronicles* 4. 33–67.

Kremmydas, Vasilis. 1980. Hē emporikḗ allēlographía toû Kṓsta Chatzipanagiṓtē B (1831–1836) [The commercial correspondence of Costas Chatzipanagiotis, pt. 2 (1831–1836)]. *Tsakonian Chronicles* 5. 33–43.

Kriaras, Emmanouil. 1990. *Lexikó tēs mesaiōnikḗs ellēnikḗs dēmṓdous grammateías (1100–1669)* [A lexicon of Medieval Greek vernacular literature]. Vol. 11. Thessaloniki: Centre for the Greek Language.

Labov, William. 1966. Hypercorrection by the lower middle class as a factor in sound change. In William Bright (ed.), *Sociolinguistics*, 88–101. The Hague: Mouton.

Lakoff, Robin. 1973. Language and woman's place. *Language in Society* 2 (1). 45–80.

Lampe, Geoffrey Wilhelm Hugo. 1961. *A Patristic Greek lexicon*. Oxford: Clarendon.

Leake, William M. 1830. *Travels in Morea*. Vol. 2. London: Cambridge University Press.

Ledgeway, Adam. 2013. Greek disguised as Romance? The case of Southern Italy. In Mark Janse, Brian D. Joseph, Angela Ralli & Metin Bagriacik (eds.), *Proceedings of the 5th international conference of Modern Greek dialects and linguistic theory (MGDLT 5). Ghent, Belgium. 20–22 September 2012*, 184–227. Patras: University of Patras.

Lekos, Michail A. 1920. *Perí Tsakṓnōn kaí tês Tsakōnikḗs dialéktou* [On Tsakonians and the Tsakonian dialect]. Athens: Papapaulou.

Liosis, Nikos. 2007. *Glōssikés epaphés stē Notioanatoliké Pelopónnēso* [Language contact in southeastern Peloponnese]. Thessaloniki: Aristotle University of Thessaloniki, Doctoral thesis.

Liosis, Nikos. 2010. Counterfactuality in the Tsakonian dialect: a contribution to the history of éthela and émoun. In Angella Ralli, Brian D. Joseph, Mark Janse & Athanasios Karasimos (eds.), *Online proceedings of the fourth international conference of Modern Greek dialects and linguistic theory (MGDLT 4). Chios, 11–14 June 2009*, 105–117. Patras: University of Patras.

Liosis, Nikos. 2011. Auxiliary verbs and the participle in the Tsakonian dialect: towards a periphrastic verbal system. In Katerina Chatzopoulou, Alexandra Ioannidou & Suwon Yoon (eds.), *Proceedings of the 9th international conference on Greek linguistics (ICGL 9), University of Chicago. Chicago. Illinois. 29–31 October 2009*, 469–479. Ohio: Ohio State University.

Liosis, Nikos. 2014. Tsakonian. In Georgios K. Giannakis, Vit Bubenik, Emilio Crespo, Chris Golston, Alexandra Lianeri, Silvia Luraghi & Stephanos Matthaios (eds.), *Encyclopedia of Ancient Greek language and linguistics*. Vol. 3 (P-Z, Index), 446–450. Leiden; Boston: Brill.

Liosis, Nikos. 2016. Tsakonian studies: The state of the art. *Studies in Greek linguistics* 36. 205–218.

Liosis, Nikos. 2017. Auxiliary verb constructions and clitic placement. Evidence from Tsakonian. *Journal of Greek Linguistics* 17. 37–72.

Liosis, Nikos & Eleni Papadamou 2011. Ē exélixē tou y stis Neoellēnikés dialéktous: ē Katōitaliké se sýnkrēsē me tēn Tsakṓnikē [Evolution of y in Modern Greek dialects: Greek of South Italy in comparison with Tsakonian]. *Neoellēnikḗ dialektología* [Modern Greek dialectology] 6. 201–223.

Lopashov, Yuri A. 2006. Ob odnom albanizme v severnogrecheskom govore [About an Albanian feature in a Northern Greek dialect]. In Rusakov, Alexander Yu. (ed.), *Problemy balanskoĭ fililogii* [Problems of Balkan philology]. *Selected articles*, 161–163. Saint Petersburg: Nauka.

Lysikatos, Dimitris M. 1961. Hē Tsakṓnikē diálektos kindyneúei. Prépei ná gínē agṓn diá ná diasōthḗ [The Tsakonian dialect is at risk. It's time to take up the effort to preserve it]. *Tsakonian Chronicles* 2. 29–32.

Lysikatos, Sotiris. 1980. Melaniṓtika topōnýmia [The toponyms of Melana]. *Tsakonian Chronicles* 5. 177–184.

Manolessou, Io. 2019. Néa dedoména gia tēn istoría tēs tsakōnikḗs dialéktou [New data on the history of the Tsakonian dialect]. In Argiris Archakis, Nikos Koutsoukos, George J.

Xydopoulos, Dimitris Papazachariou (eds.), *Glōssikḗ poikilía. Melétes afierōménes stēn Aggelikḗ Rállē* [Linguistic variation. Studies devoted to Angela Ralli], 289–311. Athens: Kapa Ekdotiki.
Mantouvalou, Maria. 2014. Tsákōnes, to thrakikó phýlo Kaúkōnes [Tsakonians, the Thracian tribe Caucones]. *Tsakonian Chronicles* 22 (1). 43–55.
MDABL 2009: Sobolev, Andrey N. (ed.). 2009. *Malyĭ dialektologicheskiĭ atlas balkanskikh i͡azykov*. [Minor dialectological atlas of Balkan languages] (Serii͡a leksicheskai͡a. T. 3: Zhivotnovodstvo [Lexical series. Vol. 3: Animal husbandry]). Saint Petersburg: Nauka, München: Otto Sagner Verlag.
Megas, Georgios A. 1976. *Die Ballade von der Arta-Brücke. Eine vergleichende Untersuchung*. Thessaloniki: Institute for Balkan Studies.
Melissaropoulou, Dimitra. 2018. Morphologiká charaktēristiká tēs Tsakṓnikēs tēs Propontídas [The morphological characteristics of Propontis Tsakonian]. *Tsakonian Chronicles* 23 (1). 177–201.
Melissaropoulou, Dimitra. 2019. Morphological innovations in Propontis Tsakonian. Ch. 9. In Angela Ralli (ed.), *Morphology in Asia Minor dialects* (Empirical Approaches to Linguistic Theory. Vol. 13), 284–314. Leiden; Boston: Brill.
Méndez Dosuna, Julián. 2001. Dōrikés diálektoi [Doric dialects]. In Anastasios Christidis (ed.), *Istoría tēs Ellēnikḗs glṓssas. Apó tēs archḗs éōs tēn ýsterē archaiótēta* [A history of Ancient Greek. From the beginnings to late Antiquity], 326–338. Thessaloniki: Center of the Modern Greek Language; Institute of Modern Greek Studies. Manolis Triandafyllidis Foundation.
Merikakis, Stylianos S. 1956. Tó empório tôn Tsakṓnōn stá chrónia tês tourkokratías [The Tsakonian trade during Turkish rule]. *Tsakonian Chronicles* 1. 52–57. Reprinted 2006.
Merikakis, Stylianos S. 1969. Tsakṓnika charaktēristiká gnōrísmata [The characteristic features of Tsakonian]. *Tsakonian Chronicles* 3. 7–12.
Merikakis, Stylianos S. 1974. Prosphorá kaí drásis tôn Tsakṓnōn katá tḗn epanástasi toû eikosiéna [Donations and deeds of Tsakonians in the period of the Greek war of Independence]. *Tsakonian Chronicles* 4, 81–99.
Mirambel, André. 1960–1961. Histoire et structure à propos des dialectes Néo-Helléniques. *Glotta* 39 (3–4). 238–265.
Mullach, Friedrich Wilhelm. 1856. *Grammatik der Griechischen Vulgärsprache in historischer Entwicklung*. Berlin: Ferd. Dümmlers Verlagsbuchhandlung.
Multitree 2018: *A digital library of language relationships*: http://multitree.org/codes/tsd (accessed 15 March, 2021).
Newton, Brian. 1972. *The generative interpretation of the dialect. A study of Modern Greek phonology*. Cambridge: Cambridge University Press.
Nicholas, Nick. 2009. Michael Deffner, scoundrel: http://hellenisteukontos.blogspot.ru/2009/04/michael-deffner-scoundrel.html (accessed 15 March, 2021).
Nicholas, Nick. 2019. A critical lexicostatistical examination of Ancient and Modern Greek and Tsakonian. *Journal of Applied Linguistics and Lexicography* 1 (1). 18–68.
Novik, Aleksandr A. 2009. Traditsionnai͡a kul'tura mariupol'skikh grekov [Traditional culture of the Mariupolitan Greeks]. Ch. 2. In Maxim L. Kisilier (ed.), *I͡azyk i kil'tura mariupol'skikh grekov* [The language and culture of Mariupolis Greeks]. Vol. 1: *Lingvisticheskai͡a i ėtnokul'turnai͡a situatsii͡a v grecheskikh selakh Priazov'i͡a. Po materi͡alam ėkspeditsii 2001–2004 godov* [Language and ethno-cultural situation in Greek villages of Azov region], 65–78. Saint Petersburg: Aleteia.

Oikonomos, Theodoros. 1870. *Grammatikḗ tês Tsakōnikês dialéktou en hḗ prosetéthēsan ásmata tiná, moirológia, diálogoi, paroimíai, kaí lexikón autês plḗres* [Grammar of the Tsakonian dialect with some songs, laments, proverbs and their complete glossaries]. Athens: L. Psylliakou & Sas.

Oikonomos o ex Oikonomon, Constantinos. 1830. *Perí tês gnēsías prophorâs tês Hellēnikês glṓssēs biblíon* [A book about the original pronunciation of the Greek language]. Petroupolos: Typography of the Ministry of Education.

Pagoulatos, Spyridon A. 1947. *Hoi Tsákōnes kaí tó perí tês Ktíseōs tês Monembasías Chronikón* [The Tsakonians and the Chronicle about the origin of Monemvasia]. Athens: (n. p.).

Papageorgiou, Georgios Th. 1984. Taxídi ston Prastó [A trip to Prastos]. *Tsakonian Chronicles* 6, 73–74.

Papahagi, Tache. 1974. *Dicţionarul dialectului aromân general şi etimologic. Dictionnaire Aroumain (Macédo-Roumain) général et étymologique.* 2nd edn. Bucureşti: Editura Academiei Republicii Socialiste România.

Pappas, Panayiotis A. 2017. Vowel raising and vowel deletion as sociolinguistic variables in Northern Greek. In Isabelle Buchstaller & Beat Siebenhaar (eds.), *Language variation – European perspectives VI. Selected papers from the 8th International Conference on language variation in Europe (ICLaVE 8), Leipzig 2015*, 113–124. Amsterdam: John Benjamins.

Pernot, Hubert Octave. 1905. La dissimilation du Σ dans les dialectes néo-grecs. *Revue des Études Grecques* 18. 253–276.

Pernot, Hubert Octave. 1910. Le verbe être dans le dialecte tsakonien. *Revue des Études Grecques* 23. 62–71.

Pernot, Hubert Octave. 1914. Notes sur le dialecte tsakonien. *Revue de Phonétique* 4. 153–188.

Pernot, Hubert Octave. 1933. Tsakonie, Italie mériodinale, Péloponnèse. *Revue des Études Grecques* 46. 15–19.

Pernot, Hubert Octave. 1934. *Introduction à l'étude du dialecte tsakonien* (Société d'édition "Les Belles Lettres". Collection de l'Institut Néo-Hellénique de l'Université de Paris. Vol. 2). Paris: Université de Paris.

Pernot, Hubert Octave & Thanasis P. Costakis. 1933. *Sýntomos grammatikḗ tês Tsakōnikês dialéktou* [A brief grammar of the Tsakonian dialect]. Athens: I. Karanasou.

Petakos, Christos D. 2003. *O Tsakónikos Chorós* [The Tsakonian dance]. Athens: Educational association of Leonidio.

Petris, Georgios. 2014. Ídrysē kai leitourgeía tōn scholeíōn stēn Tsakōniá 1829–1848 [Establishment and operation of public schools in Tsakonia 1829–1848]. *Tsakonian Chronicles* 22 (3). 7–102.

Pitsinos, Dimitrios. 1951. Tsakṓnia kaí Malebós [Tsakonia and Malevo]. *Deltíon tôn Tsakṓnōn* [Bulletin of Tsakonians] 1. 3–5.

Pitsios, Theodoros K. 1986. Anthropologische Untersuchung der Bevölkerung des Peloponnes unter besonderer Berücksichtigung der Arwaniten und Tsakonen. *Anthropologischer Anzeiger* 44 (3). 215–225.

Pouqueville, François. 1820. *Voyage dans la Grèce.* Vol. 4. Paris: Chez Firmin Didot, Père et Fils.

Pritchett, William Kendrick. 1991. *Studies in Ancient Greek topography. Vol. 7.* Amsterdam: J. C. Gieben.

Ralli, Angela. 2006. Syntactic and morphosyntactic dialectal phenomena in Modern Greek: the state of the art. *Journal of Greek Linguistics* 7. 121–159.

Reiske, Johann Jakob (ed.). 1829. *Constantinus Porphyrogenitus. De ceremoniis aulae Byzantinae: Libri duo graece et latine 1* [Book of Ceremonies of Constantine vii Porphyrogennetos: Two books in Greek and Latin 1] (Bekker, Immanuel, Ludwig Schopen & Guilielmus Dindorfius (eds.), Corpus scriptorum historiae Byzantinae). Bonn: Impensis Ed. Weberi.

Romaios, Constantinos A. 1956. Archaîa toponýmia tês Tsakōniâs [Ancient toponyms of Tsakonia]. *Tsakonian Chronicles* 1. 7–9. Reprinted 2006.

Rylik, Polina A. 2012. K voprosu o svi̇azi novogrecheskikh govorov ostrova Karpatos s doriĭskim dialektom [On a connection between the Modern Greek idioms used on the island of Karpathos and the Dorian dialect]. *Indoevropeiskoe iazykoznanie i klassicheskaia filologia* [Indo-European Linguistics and Classical Philology] 16, 730–741.

Salminen, Tapani. 2007. Europe and North Asia. Ch. 3. In Christopher Moseley (ed.), *Encyclopedia of the world's endangered languages*, 211–280. London & New York: Routledge.

Sarris, Theodoros. 1956. Perí Tsakṓnōn kaí Tsakōniâs [On Tsakonians and Tsakonia]. *Tsakonian Chronicles* 1. 25–28. Reprinted 2006.

Sarris, Theodoros. 1984. Apó tēn istoría tou Leōnidíou [On the history of Leonidio]. *Tsakonian Chronicles* 6. 147–148.

Schwyzer, Edward. 1921. Die junglakonische Genitive auf HP. In *Aphiérōma eis G. Chatzidákin. Diatribaí phílōn kaí mathētṓn epí tê triakostê pémtē epéteiō tês en tô panepistḗmiō kathēgesías autoû* [Festschrift in honor of G. Hatzidakis. Articles by his friends and students dedicated to 35th anniversary of his professorship at the University], 82–88. Athens: P. D. Sakellarios.

Scutt, Cecil A. 1912–1913. The Tsakonian dialect – I. *The Annual of the British School at Athens* 19. 133–173.

Scutt, Cecil A. 1913–1914. The Tsakonian dialect – II. *The Annual of the British School at Athens* 20. 18–31.

Siakotos, Basileos D. 2011. Ho epoikismós tês Kastánitsas toû Párnōna mé plēthysmoús hypó tēn Chalkidikḗ (1081–1118) [Colonization of Parnon's Kastanitsa by migrants from Halkidiki]. *Peloponnēsiaká* [Peloponnesian Studies] 30 (1). 343–350.

Simpson, Adrian P. 2009. Phonetic differences between male and female speech. *Language and Linguistics Compass* 2 (3). 621–640.

Sitaridou, Ioanna & Maria Kaltsa. 2014. Contrastivity in Pontic Greek. *Lingua* 146. 1–27.

Sjuzjumov, Michail Ia. 1974. Symeōnídēs Ch. P. Oí Tzákōnes kai ḗ Tzakonía [Symeonidis Ch. P. The Tsakonians and Tsakonia] (review). *Vizantiyskiy Vremennik* 36. 210–212.

Spratt, Thomas A. B. 1865. *Travels and researches in Crete*. Vol. 1. London: John van Voors; Paternoster Row.

Symeonidis, Charalampos P. 1972. *Hoi Tsákōnes kaí ē Tsakōniá. Symbolḗ stḗn hermēneía tôn onomátōn kaí toû omṓnymou byzantinoú thesmoû tôn kastrophylákōn* [The Tsakonians and Tsakonia. Contribution to the interpretation of names and the homonymic Byzantine institution of the fortress-guards]. Thessaloníki: Centre for Byzantine Studies.

Tachydromos 2015: Phōtiés anáboun ta mikrá aeróstata [Small balloons cause fire]. *Tachydrómos* [Postman]. Daily newspaper. 13 August: http://www.taxydromos.gr/Τοπικά/187816-Φωτιές-ανάβουν-τα-μικρά-αερόστατα.html (accessed 15 March, 2021).

Taloş, Ioan. 1997. *Meșterul Manole* [The master builder Manole]. Vol. 2. București: Cultura Națională.

Thiersch, Friedrich Wilhelm, von. 1832. Über die Sprache der Zakonen. *Abhandlungen der philosophisch-philologischen Klasse der Königlich Bayerischen Akademie der Wissenschaften* 1. 513–582.

Thumb, Albert. 1894. Die ethnographische Stellung der Zakonen. *Indogermanische Forschungen* 4. 195–213.

Triantafyllidis, Manolis. 2009. *Lexikó tēs Koinḗs Neoellēnikḗs* [Dictionary of Modern Greek]. 8th edn. Thessaloniki: Aristotle University of Thessaloniki. Institute of Modern Greek Studies. Manolis Triandafyllidis Foundation.

Trubachev, Oleg N. 1975. *Etimologicheskiĭ slovar' slavi͡anskikh i͡azykov. Praslavi͡anskiĭ leksicheskiĭ fond* [Etymological dictionary of Slavic languages. Proto-Slavic vocabulary]. Vol. 2. Moscow: Nauka.

Trubachev, Oleg N. 1984. *Etimologicheskiĭ slovar' slavi͡anskikh i͡azykov. Praslavi͡anskiĭ leksicheskiĭ fond* [Etymological dictionary of Slavic languages. Proto-Slavic vocabulary]. Vol. 11. Moscow: Nauka.

Trudgill, Peter. 2003. Modern Greek dialects. A preliminary classification. *Journal of Greek Linguistics* 4. 45–64.

Tsakonas, Michail. 1974. Hē Tsakōnía stá 1851 [Tsakonia in 1851]. *Tsakonian Chronicles* 4. 157–158.

Tsakonas, Michail. 1980. Tó empóreion tôn Tsakṓnōn [Tsakonian commerce]. *Tsakonian Chronicles* 5. 123–124.

Tzitzilis, Christos. 2013. Archaisms in Modern Dialects. In Georgios K Giannakis & Vít Bubeník (eds.), *Encyclopedia of Ancient Greek language and linguistics*. http://dx.doi.org/10.1163/2214-448X_eagll_COM_00000034 (accessed 15 March, 2021).

Vagena, Eleni Th. 1984. O períphēmos 'tsakṓnikos' chorós [On the famous Tsakonian dance]. *Tsakonian Chronicles* 6. 105–106.

Vagenas, Thanos K. 1969a. Dioikētikḗ hypagōgḗ tês Tsakōniás mésa stá chrónia tês Henetokratías [Administration of Tsakonia during Venetian rule]. *Tsakonian Chronicles* 3. 85–90.

Vagenas, Thanos K. 1969b. Tó ónoma tês póleōs toû 'Leōnidíou' kaí ho 'Hágios Leōnídēs' [The name of the town of Leonidio and Saint Leonidas]. *Tsakonian Chronicles* 3, 33–40.

Vagenas, Thanos K. 1971. *Istoriká Tsakōniás kaí Leōnidíou* [History of Tsakonia and Leonidio]. Athens: Municipality of Leonidio.

Vagenas, Thanos K. 1974. Hē syllogḗ Tsakṓnikōn toponymíōn [A collection of Tsakonian toponyms]. *Tsakonian Chronicles* 4. 155–156.

Vagenas, Thanos K. 1980. 'Tsakōniá' kaí hoi 'Tsákōnes' mesaiōnikés polyethnikés léxeis ["Tsakonia" and the "Tsakonians" Medieval polyethnic terms]. *Tsakonian Chronicles* 5. 97–100.

Vagenas, Thanos K. 1984. Períphēmoi giatroí tês Tsakōniás [Famous physicians of Tsakonia]. *Tsakonian Chronicles* 6. 41–46.

Vagiakakos, Dikaios B. 1963–1964. B' – Anthrōpōnýmia [2 – Personal names]. *Athina* 67. 145–369.

Vagiakakos, Dikaios B. 1986. Koiná glōssiká stoicheîa eis tḗn dialékton tês Tsakōniâs kaí tês Mánēs [Common linguistic features of Tsakonia and Mani]. *Tsakonian Chronicles* 7. 76–126.

Vasmer, Max. 1941. *Die Slaven in Griechenland* (Aus den Abhandlungen der Preußischen Akademie der Wissenschaften. Jahrgang 1941. Phil.-hist. Klasse 12). Berlin: Verlag der Akademie der Wissenschaften in Kommission bei Walter de Gruyter u. Co.

Vergis, Nikos. 2012. Women, language and stereotypes: evidence from a rural community of Greece. Ch. 6. In Georgia Fragaki, Thanasis Georgakopoulos & Charalambos Themistocleous (eds.), *Current trends in Greek linguistics*, 148–176. Newcastle: Cambridge Scholars Publishing.

Vocabolario 2020: *Vocabolario veneto-italiano*: http://www.dialetto-veneto.it/Vocabolario-veneto.htm (updated 23.01.2020, accessed 15 March, 2021).

Vyzantios Skarlatos D. 1874. *Lexikón tês kath' ēmâs ellēnikḗs dialéktou methērmēneuménēs eis tó archaîon hellēnikón kaí tó gallikón. Metá geōgraphikoû pínakos tôn neōtérōn kaí palaiôn onomátōn* [Dictionary of Greek dialects translated into Ancient Greek and French. With a geographical map including modern and ancient names]. 3rd edn. Athens: Andreas Koromilas.

Witczak, Tomasz Krzysztof. 2015. On the chronology of the loss of *λ in Tsakonian (Late Laconian). *Graeco-Latina Brunensia* 20 (2). 177–188.

Zarbanos, Michail K. 1956. Perí toû Leōnidíou [On Leonidio]. *Tsakonian Chronicles* 1. 63–64. Reprinted 2006.

Brian D. Joseph
Convergence and Failure to Converge in Relative Social Isolation: Balkan Judezmo

Abstract: This chapter[1] on Judezmo shows how easily some features can penetrate into a language system, especially those aspects of the lexicon and morphosyntax most tied to conversation and the habits of pronunciation acquired via heavy use of the socially dominant language. The mix of Balkan features in Judezmo sharpens a sense of what it means to be peripheral within a Sprachbund. Some of the developments of Judezmo, with either sources or parallels elsewhere in Ibero-Romance, show that both timing and environment — here the Balkan chronotope — are crucial in helping to distinguish between that which is convergent and that which is parallel.

1 Historical background

From ancient times, it is clear that there were Jewish inhabitants on the Iberian peninsula, even if it is not entirely clear whether the first evidence of their presence dates to Biblical times or later, during the period of the Roman Empire and its control of the entire Mediterranean. Whatever their origins there, by Medieval times, Jews constituted a flourishing, intellectually lively, and generally well-to-do population within a predominantly Christian environment in both Spain and Portugal. By some estimates, by the 15th century, there were as many as 300,000 Jews in the area.

After 1492, however, this population was nearly entirely wiped out, due to the Alhambra Decree (the Edict of Expulsion, enacted 2 August), which required practicing Jews to leave Spain and Portugal. Most of those expelled from Spain were Spanish-speaking, "Sephardic" Jews,[2] and they relocated to various points in the Mediterranean and Europe, including North Africa, France, The Netherlands, and the Balkans, which were then largely under the control of the Ottoman Turks. These Jews were invited by Ottoman sultan Beyazit II, and the

---

[1] This chapter would not have been possible without the considerable input of my good friend and collaborator Victor Friedman, specifically knowledge that I gained about Judezmo in the Balkans from working with him on Friedman & Joseph (2014; 2021). My debt to the general work on those pieces is hereby acknowledged.
[2] This label is based on the Hebrew word *sefarad* (a Biblical location that was identified by Jews as Spain).

Ottoman Empire in general was attractive because it offered a greater degree of religious tolerance than they might have enjoyed elsewhere. In the late 15th and early 16th centuries, these Spanish Jews came to populate urban centers all over the Balkans, first in Greece, Macedonia, and Turkey. In Greece, the Sephardim settled mainly in the north, with the two large cities of Thessaloniki and Ioannina being the major loci, although islands both in the Ionian Sea, especially Corfu, and in the Aegean Sea, such as Chios, also came to have significant Sephardic populations. In Macedonia, the cities of Bitola, Skopje, and Štip ended up being home to significant numbers of Sephardim; and in Turkey, Constantinople (later known as Istanbul) was the major focal point for Spanish Jewish in-migration. There were more scattered settlements in Serbia, Bosnia-Hercegovina, Dalmatia, and Bulgaria, and later movement from Bosnia and Bulgaria in the 19th century brought a considerable number of Sephardim to Romania, primarily to Bucharest.

It is difficult to be certain about the numbers of those who re-settled in the Balkans, but working from various sources, one can develop the following figures for some of the largest Jewish cities in the early 20th century:

- c. 50,000 Jews in Constantinople
- c. 60,000 Jews in Bucharest
- c. 75,000 Jews in Thessaloniki

Most of these were Spanish Jews, though in Bucharest, many Jews came from Russia due to pogroms there. These populations suffered almost total annihilation at the hands of the Germans in the Holocaust before and during World War II, so that Balkan cities now are almost empty of their former Jewish populations, with only some 3,000 in Bucharest, and less than 1,500 in Thessaloniki. Most of the survivors have settled in Israel, with c. 100,000 there now, many of whom actively continue the use of their language.

The Sephardic Jews brought with them as their native Spanish language, actually in what can be considered an ethnolectal form that can be referred to as "Jewish Spanish", or perhaps better, "Judeo-Spanish". This variety co-existed with other non-Jewish and Jewish languages in Spain (e.g., Arabic and a Jewish form of Arabic, Judeo-Arabic), as Wexler (1981) makes clear.

But separation from the Iberian homeland post-1492 gave the opportunity for the development of other differences, resulting both from changes that Iberian Spanish underwent that the newly separated Jewish Spanish did not and from changes that Jewish Spanish underwent in its new settings that Iberian Spanish did not. The resulting variety of Spanish is thus recognized as a distinct language, and is known as Judezmo, Judeo-Spanish, Judeo-Espagnol, or

Ladino,³ and in its North African (mainly Moroccan) form, Haketia. As far as the Balkans are concerned, two major dialects can be recognized for the language, Eastern Judezmo and Western Judezmo. The eastern dialect includes the speech of the Turkish Sephardic communities of Istanbul and Izmir, the Greek island of Rhodes, and the largest Greek city in the north, Thessaloniki. Western Judezmo includes the dialects of Sephardic speakers in Bulgaria (Sofia). Romania (Bucharest), Macedonia (Bitola), Serbia (Belgrade), and Bosnia (Sarajevo). The language is relatively well documented from various periods, and there is a large and important body of scholarship on it in all its geographic varieties; this includes bibliographic compilations such as Studemund (1975) and Bunis (1981), as well as the overviews provided by Sala (1976) and Sephiha (1986), and essays such as Bunis (1983; 2011), as well as lexical studies such as Bunis (1993). Some sources that are specifically on Balkan varieties of Judezmo are Bunis (1999), Crews (1935), Gabinskii (1992), Luria (1930), Sala (1970; 1971), Sephiha (1996–1998), Symeonides (2002), Walter (1920), Wagner (1914; 1923; 1925; 1930).⁴

2 Importance of Judezmo for Balkan linguistics

It is well known that the Balkans have always been a hotbed of multilingualism and language contact. The particularly intense and sustained multilingualism and contact among speakers of different languages there led, beginning in the Medieval period during Ottoman times, to a structural and lexical convergence in the languages in question. The resulting convergence zone, with striking similarities in both structural features and lexical elements across several languages defines what is usually referred to in the literature as a "Sprachbund" or "linguistic area". These languages include: Albanian (in northern Gheg and southern Tosk dialects); the Balkan Romance languages made up of Aromanian, Meglenoromanian, and Romanian; Balkan Slavic made up of Bulgarian, Macedonian, and the southeastern ("Torlak") dialects of Serbian; Greek, Romani, and Balkan (Western Rumelian) Turkish. The features that characterize the Sprachbund are known as "Balkanisms" and they range over all components of grammar – phonology, morphology, morphosyntax, syntax, and even semantics – as well as the lexicon.⁵

---

3 The name *Ladino* is used by some specialists for a written form of the language used in translating religious texts in Hebrew in a word-for-word fashion. Following Bunis (2018: 185–187), I primarily use the name Judezmo here.
4 Wexler (1981) is a detailed overview of the phenomenon of Jewish languages more generally, with a number of references to Judezmo specifically.
5 See Friedman & Joseph (2021) for details on the Balkan Sprachbund more generally.

A key question to ask about Judezmo vis-à-vis these other languages is the extent to which it participates in the convergence that characterizes the Balkan Sprachbund. In other words, to what extent does Judezmo show "Balkanisms" (i.e., Balkan convergent features)? This is an interesting and important question to ask for several reasons, all having to do with illuminating the nature of the contact situation in the Balkans. First, because Judezmo was a relatively late arrival on the Balkan contact scene, compared to the other convergent languages, it is possible to determine the chronology of some features and in some cases to weigh the relative importance of timing and structure to outcomes of language contact. Second, the relative social isolation of the Judezmo-speaking Jewish communities scattered across the central areas of the region gives a social index for the feature. Finally, the existence of both Spanish and Judezmo dialects outside the Balkans (e.g., for Judezmo, in North Africa) makes it possible to decide between contact-related Balkan convergence and simple coincidence (or other scenarios) to explain the presence of various features in Judezmo and other languages in the region.[6]

2.1 Relevance of these Questions Illustrated

The relevance of these questions can be illustrated through a consideration of various case studies. For instance, from the domain of morphosyntax one can point to the analytic comparison of Balkan Judezmo; e.g., *mas blanko* 'more white; whiter'. In particular, although this Judezmo structure matches the parallel structure found in various languages of the Balkan Sprachbund, e.g., Greek *pjo ómorfo* 'more beautiful', Albanian *më interesant* 'more interesting', the convergence is completely coincidental, as this feature is found all over non-Balkan Judezmo and all over Spanish dialects (and in Romance more widely, for that matter). It is thus best treated as part of the linguistic inheritance that Sephardim brought with them to the Balkans, though contact with Balkan languages having such a structure could well have reinforced the continuation of this inherited feature.

A phonological example that serves as a similar case regarding the questions in Section 2 pertains to the raising of unstressed /e, o/ to /i, u/. This development is found in northern Greek, eastern Macedonian, eastern Bulgarian, and Aromanian. Intriguingly, mid-vowel raising is also found in several regional varieties of Judezmo, e.g. in Bitola (southern Macedonia), Veroia (Northern Greece), Kastoria (northern Greece), areas that are co-territorial with some of the other Balkan languages showing this vowel development. The contiguity of the Judezmo vowel

---

[6] See also Friedman & Joseph (2014), and Friedman & Joseph (2021: Chapters 1 and 8), as well as Joseph (2019) for discussion of Judezmo as a Balkan language.

raising area with these other languages naturally raises the specter of language contact being responsible, so that the Judezmo raising would be evidence of its "participation" in Balkan Sprachbund structural convergences. However, some varieties of Judezmo raise these vowels only word-finally, while others have the raising of /o/ only pretonically, while still others show raising also of /a/ to /e/. Thus there is less convergence on details of the raising than one might expect if the Judezmo and Balkan phenomena were connected. Moreover, the Judezmo of Bitola has had significant influence from Portuguese, via the expulsions from Iberia of 1497, and Portuguese is a language in which raising occurs as well. Thus this is most likely a coincidental convergence, with pre-Balkan roots as far as Judezmo is concerned. This feature, therefore, cannot be attributed to the Balkan context in which Judezmo came to exist.

As a consequence of examining features such as these two, one cannot take a similarity between Judezmo and other Balkan languages at face value. Each must be subjected to the same sort of diachronic qualitative investigation as these examples have been.

2.2 Balkanisms in Judezmo

Despite the "near-misses" in Section 2.1 that turn out not to show Balkan language contact influence, there are a number of legitimate Balkanisms in Judezmo, features that show Judezmo to be like Balkan Sprachbund members in various ways that moreover have the mark of having begun via language contact after Judezmo entered the Balkans. These convergent features range over all components of the language, from phonology to morphosyntax to syntax proper and the lexicon, as outlined in the sections that follow.

2.2.1 Phonology

Like other languages in the Balkans, at least some Balkan Judezmo varieties, especially that of Bucharest (Sala 1971), show multiple affricates, and they have a hissing/hushing opposition, specifically [c] / [tʃ], (roughly: apico-dental / alveo-palatal). As far as Balkan languages are concerned, this feature is found in the more central Balkan northern dialects of Greek, in Albanian, in Balkan Slavic, and in Balkan Romance. Importantly, such an affricate presence is not found in other Spanish dialects.

Other varieties of Balkan Judezmo, e.g., that in Thessaloniki, have only the hushing affricates, [tʃ] versus [dʒ], but in that case, the occurrence of the voiced affricate is important as it is absent as such from most Iberian Spanish dialects, yet present in Turkish, in Bulgarian and Macedonian, though to a quite limited extent, and in Greek in a systematically altered form to the hissing affricate [dz].

Still, it must be noted that Old Spanish did have a [dʒ], and this remains in Judezmo while in Modern Castilian it underwent a change to [ʃ] and later [x]. This change took place probably around the end of the 16th century or the start of the 17th century, so that it was too late to have affected Judezmo. However, any potential incipient tendency affecting [dʒ] at the time of the departure of the Jews from Spain would have been suppressed in the Balkans with the abundance of affricates in the various languages there.

2.2.2 Morpho-Syntactic

In the domain of morpho-syntax, there are several widespread Balkan structural features that can be found in the Judezmo of various locales in the Balkans. These are discussed in the subsections that follow.

Evidentiality

Many Balkan languages, in particular Turkish, South Slavic, Albanian, and even some varieties of Aromanian, show special verbal forms that mark "evidentiality", indicating the source of information, especially whether one knows something by seeing it oneself or instead by hearing about it from someone else; this is thus a "witnessed" ('seen') versus "unwitnessed" ('unseen', 'reported', 'unconfirmed') distinction, encoded in the grammar,

Interestingly for the question of Judezmo as a Balkan language, some Judezmo speakers of Istanbul are reported to use the pluperfect as a calque on the Turkish use of perfect marker *–miş* as a non-confirmative, reported, or unwitnessed past; an example is given in (1):[7]

---

[7] I take these examples from Varol (2001). They are cited elsewhere in the literature; e.g., by Friedman (2003), Friedman & Joseph (2014), and Slobin (2016), as illustrative of evidentiality marking in some Judezmo. Still, there is reason to believe (based on information from an anonymous, but clearly well-informed reviewer of Joseph (2019)) that such marking may be an idiolectal phenomenon and not a feature that ever was or is now widespread within the Istanbul Judezmo community. Nonetheless, even if produced by a single speaker, and even if a one-off, nonce phenomenon, these examples show how contact with Turkish can affect the production of Judezmo by some speakers.

(1) *Kuando estavan   en l'   Amérika, les   **aviya***
    when they.were.IMP in the America them.DAT had.IMP
    ***entrado**   ladrón*
    enter.PTCP thief
    'When they were in America [i.e., not at home], a thief (apparently) broke into their house.'

A comparable sentence in Turkish, somewhat simplified, would be as in (2), with the -*miş* verbal form:

(2) *Onlar yok-ken,   hırsız gir-miş* (Turkish)
    they not.exist-while thief enter-REP.PRF
    'While they weren't there, a thief (apparently) entered'

Similarly, Judezmo has sentences such as (3):

(3) *Dos ermanos eran,   uno salyó   doktor dişçi, el*
    two brothers were.IMP one became.PRET doctor dentist the
    *otro salyó   dahilkiye después s'   **aviya   etcho***
    other became.PRET internist afterwards REFL had.IMP made.PST.PTCP
    doktor de bebés (Judezmo)
    doctor of babies
    'There were two brothers, one became a dentist and the other became an internist, afterwards he seems to have become (lit. had become) a pediatrician'

This example is a statement about an unwitnessed, thus reported event, and like (1), uses a pluperfect. It is important to note that pluperfects used in this way would not be grammatical in (Castilian) Spanish, so that contact with Turkish is a reasonable hypothesis as the cause of this innovation.

Marking for evidentiality in this way does not occur in Iberian Spanish, but it does occur in some forms of Spanish. Importantly, though, it is only in those varieties of Spanish that have been influenced by languages with evidential systems or usages that evidentiality marking occurs. For instance, in the Spanish of Peru, the pluperfect is used to give evidential effects, much as in the examples cited here, and substratal influence of Quechua's evidential system is the likely source of that innovation.

Therefore, to the extent that these examples reflect usage for some speakers of Judezmo (see footnote 7), evidentiality marking can be taken as a Balkan-inspired innovation in the language.

Conditional sentences

Montoliu & van der Auwera (2004) point out that Judezmo can have both a protasis and an apodosis in conditional sentences with an indicative imperfect, possibilities not found in either Old or Modern Spanish, as is exemplified in (4). This is a feature, however, that is found in Turkish and in Greek, the latter illustrated in (5):

(4) *Si me yamavan ya iva* (Judezmo)
    If me call.IMPF.IND.3PL PTCL go.IMPF.IND.1SG
    'If they called me/were to call me, I would go.'

(5) *An ebenes, ton evlepes* (Greek)
    if enter.IMPF.2SG him see.IMPF.2SG
    'If you went in / were to go in, you would see him'

Judezmo also can use the anterior past, the pluperfect, in the apodosis, again like Turkish and Greek. Importantly, this usage of the pluperfect is unlike Modern or Old Spanish, so that this seems to be a legitimate instance of influence from a Balkan language on Judezmo.

Future tense

Judezmo has a synthetic future tense formation that derives from a univerbation of a Late Latin periphrasis consisting of an infinitive followed by conjugated forms of the present tense of 'have', e.g. *diré* 'I will say', from earlier *dicere habeō* (literally "say.INF have.1sg").[8] This is a potentially interesting fact from a Balkanological standpoint as there are some 'have'-based futures in Balkan languages; however, such forms occur also in Spanish, so that they could well reflect a feature Sephardim brought with them to the Balkans. As for the Balkans, *have*-forms occur primarily in Romanian, e.g., *am să scriu* 'I will write', literally "I.have that I.write", but this structure reflects a Romanian inheritance from the Late Latin periphrasis, with the replacement of the infinitive by finite complementation, as found throughout Balkan syntax (see Section 2.2.3). As such, this type would be equatable to the Spanish and Judezmo type, differing only in the fate of the infinitive. Moreover, the *have*-future found elsewhere in Balkan Romance, in particular northern Aromanian, does not make for a significant point of comparison for understanding the Balkanological status of Judezmo because it is found

---

8 The fact that this future tense derives historically from a phrasal, analytic, formation is no obstacle to calling it "synthetic", since from a synchronic point of view, it functions as a single word and is not analyzable in the way that the construction was in Late Latin.

only in negated forms, e.g. *noare s' neadzim* (not.have.1sg that go.1sg) 'I will not go', and is thus a pattern that matches Macedonian (and Bulgarian); this means that it is a likely structural borrowing (calque) from Balkan Slavic. Thus the synthetic future tense of Judezmo, even though formed with 'have' like some other Balkan languages, is of no Balkanological significance in and of itself.

However, in Spanish (and other Romance languages), and in Judezmo, there is also an analytic future based on the verb 'go', e.g. *voy a escribir* 'I will write' (literally "I.go to write.INF") that competes with the synthetic future form from infinitive + 'have', as in Spanish. This type turns out to have Balkanological significance in an indirect but important way. In particular, Balkan languages have an analytic future based on the verb 'want', e.g. Greek *θa yrapso* 'I will write', based on an earlier *θe(li) na yrapso* (literally "it.will that I.write", where 'will' is originally the 3sg present form of 'want'), Albanian *do të shkruaj*, where *do* is the 3sg present of *dua* 'want', Aromanian *va s-cântu* 'I will sing', where *va* is based on the 3sg form of 'want' and the *s* is a subordinating particle. Even though Greek, for instance, in its present state, might be best treated as a synthetic form, i.e. with *θa* as a prefix and not a separate word (see Sims & Joseph 2018: 118 on this), the more clearly analytic type persisted into the late 19th century (see Thumb 1964).

This situation with the Judezmo future becomes significant with respect to Judezmo and the Balkan Sprachbund because of the way the competition between the analytic future with 'go' and the synthetic future is being resolved. In particular, Judezmo favors the analytic 'go' future over synthetic 'have' future. In a text-based study, Kramer & Perez-Leroux (2007) found that a text count reveals that only 2 out of 40 futures in their corpus were synthetic, and they were both in more formal contexts. The favouring of an analytic type could be attributed to influence from neighboring Balkan languages, as they have had, and some still have, an analytic future to serve as a model. Some caution is necessary here, for the analytic 'go'-future is common everywhere in colloquial Spanish, especially in Latin America, where it is preferred and where the synthetic ('have') future is increasingly rare.

Thus, these facts suggest that the *timing* of the separation of Latin American Spanish from Iberian Spanish coincided roughly with the separation of Judezmo, so that perhaps contact in each case favored such a development, pushing each variety of Spanish by chance, in the same direction. Yet, studies of Latin American Spanish (see Orozco 2007), show that Judezmo has gone significantly farther than any Spanish dialect in Latin America in favoring the analytic 'go'-future. This analytic structure is very frequent colloquially in Iberian Standard Spanish, but the synthetic future is more common in written texts. Thus, influence from its Balkan linguistic neighbors may well be responsible for the extent to which the analytic type is found in Judezmo. In this way, the Judezmo future, even if not comporting to the widespread Balkan 'want'-based type, nonetheless shows considerable relevance for the consideration of Judezmo as a Balkan Sprachbund language.

2.2.3 Syntax

We now move to a slightly different domain of grammar and examine the evidence from syntactic Balkanisms for the degree of convergence Judezmo shows to Balkan structural norms.

Object reduplication

In a construction that can be referred to as "object reduplication", Balkan languages allow so-called "weak" object pronouns[9] to occur together with full objects, as in (6), from Greek; there are concomitant pragmatic effects associated with topicality and focus which the parenthetical translations attempt to capture:

(6) a. *Me   θelis   emena?* (Greek)
       me.ACC.WK want.2SG me.ACC.STRNG
       'Do you want me?' (= 'Am I the one you want?')
    b. *Tus   vlepume ton jani   ke ti maria* (Greek)
       them.ACC.WK see.1PL the-Yani.ACC and the-Maria.ACC
       'We see Yani and Maria.' (= 'Yani and Maria are the ones we see')

Similar patterns can be found in Albanian, Aromanian, Bulgarian, Macedonian, among others.

Both Spanish and Judezmo allow for object reduplication and thus have sentences parallel to (6). However, Wagner (1914) observed that reduplicated object pronouns occur more frequently in Constantinople Judezmo than in Spanish, and Kramer & Perez-Leroux (2007) found much greater pragmatic conditioning for object reduplication in Judezmo than in Spanish. In (7a) and (8a) are given two Judezmo proverbs from Bitola with their Macedonian equivalents, (7b) and (8b), respectively, each one showing object reduplication typical of the Balkans but not of Spanish:

---

9 These pronominal forms are most usually referred to as "clitics", but as I have argued elsewhere (Joseph 1988, Joseph 2002) that they are best treated as affixes, I use the more neutral term "weak pronoun" here (and correspondingly, "strong" for fuller forms).

(7) a. *Il palu tuertu la lumeri lu indireche* (Judezmo)
the stick crooked the fire it.ACC straightens
b. *Kriv stap ogn-ot go ispravuva* (Macedonian)
crooked stick fire.DEF it.ACC straightens
'A crooked staff is straightened in the fire'
(literally: "the crooked stick the fire it straightens")[10]

(8) a. *Al hamor kwandu mas l' aroges mas alvante*
to.DEF donkey how.much more it.ACC beg.2SG more raises
las urezhes (Judezmo)
the ears
b. *Magare-to kolku poveḱe go moliš poveḱe gi*
donkey-DEF how.much more it.ACC beg.2SG more them.ACC
diga ushi-te (Macedonian)
raises ears-DEF
'The more you beg the donkey, the more it raises its ears.'
(literally: "(to.)the donkey how.much more you beg it, (so much) more it.raises its ears").[11]

The Iberian Spanish equivalents of (7) and (8) either would not have the weak pronoun reduplicating the object, or if occurring with such a weak pronoun, would sound distinctly odd. Their presence in Balkan Judezmo is thus a good candidate for a feature that can be attributed to influence from Macedonian, or conceivably also Greek.

Infinitives and finite subordinate clauses

Balkan languages show a reduction or total loss of the infinitive and the parallel expansion of finite subordinate clauses in functions that were once typical of infinitives, such as purpose clauses or complementation; these twin developments are seen most robustly in Aromanian, Greek, and Macedonian.

Balkan Judezmo preserves the Ibero-Romance infinitive (as noted in Joseph (1983: Chp. 7) for the Judezmo of Thessaloniki), still seen quite robustly in Iberian Spanish. Some examples are given in (9):

---

[10] This proverb occurs also in Greek, and also has object reduplication: *kirto ravði to isioni i fotja*.
[11] This proverb also occurs in Greek, also with object reduplication: *oso to rotas to yaiðaro, toso anevasi t' aftja*.

(9) a. *Tienes una vos mui buena para kantar* (Judezmo)
　　　have.2SG a　voice very good　for　sing.INF
　　　'You-have a voice (that is) very good to-sing-with / for singing'
　b. *Ke pueda fazer* (Judezmo)
　　　what can.3sg do.INF
　　　'What might-he-be-able to-do?'
　c. *¿Puede recontar historia?* (Judezmo)
　　　is.possible tell.INF story
　　　'Can I tell the story?' (literally: "Is-it-possible (for someone) to-tell (the) story?")[12]

Thus, in this regard, Balkan Judezmo is decidedly un-Balkan in its syntax. However, there is some expansion of finite subordination where one might expect infinitives, and there is one aspect of the use of subjunctive mood forms in particular that parallels somewhat the syntax of finite verbs in Balkan languages that are co-territorial with Judezmo.

In particular, the Judezmo use in (10a) of the subjunctive (SBJV) by itself in modal questions, such as 'When might we come to get you?', has a direct parallel in Balkan languages (e.g. Greek and Macedonian, in (10b) and (10c), respectively) with a subordinating marker (SM):

(10) a. *Kwando ke te vengamoz a tom-ar?* (Judezmo)
　　　　when　SM you.ACC we.come.SBJV to take-INF
　　b. *Póte na 'rθúme na se párume?* (Greek)
　　　　when SM we.come SM you.ACC we.take
　　c. *Koga da ti dojdeme da te zememe?* (Macedonian)
　　　　when SM you.DAT we.come SM you.ACC we.take

The Judezmo in (10a) can be compared with its Iberian Spanish equivalent in (11), where a controlling verb (*quieres*) is needed to introduce the subjunctive of 'come', as is also the case in North African Judezmo:

(11) *Cuándo quieres que vengamos a recog-er-te?*
　　　when　you.want SM we.come.SBJV to take-INF-you.ACC
　　　'When do you want us to come to get you?'

---

12 This example has impersonal active *puede* (as opposed to *se puede*, with a reflexive marker, in Standard Spanish), modeled on impersonal Macedonian *može* 'it.can' and/or Greek *borí* 'it.can'.

Thus this bare use of the subjunctive without a controlling verb is a way in which finite subordination in Judezmo has moved in the direction of the norm for the Balkan Sprachbund languages. So even with the retention of an infinitive in Judezmo, the language shows Balkan-like syntax as far as subordination is concerned.

2.2.4 Lexicon

Given that the lexicon is typically one of the first components of a language that is affected by language contact, in the form of loanwords (borrowings), it is not surprising to find a considerable number of Turkish culture words in Judezmo. Reflecting the fact that Turkish was the key language of urban areas in the Balkans during Ottoman rule, loanwords occur that cover administrative and religious terms, terminology for food, names for items of material culture, and the like. A sampling of such words is given in (12):[13]

(12) *aboyadear* 'to paint' (Turkish *boya-* 'paint')
     čorap 'stocking' (Turkish *çorap*)
     čorba 'soup' (Turkish *çorba*)
     jaği 'pilgrim' (Turkish *hacı*)
     jendek 'ditch' (Turkish *hendek*)
     talašis 'wood chips' (Turkish *talaş*)
     tavan 'ceiling' (Turkish *tavan*)
     tenğere 'pot' (Turkish *tencere*)

What is more telling regarding Judezmo and the Balkan lexicon is the penetration of a particular class of Balkan elements into the Judezmo lexicon. Friedman & Joseph (2014) argue that an essential tool for understanding the Balkan Sprachbund is the recognition of a class of conversationally-based loans which they refer to as "E.R.I.C." loans, an acronym for loanwords that are "Essentially Rooted In Conversation". The term is intended as a tribute to Eric Hamp, Balkanist par excellence, but it is a useful notion in itself and offers insight into the nature of language contact in the Balkans. Such loans are ones that go beyond simple informational needs and the object orientation of speakers of different languages interacting with one another. And borrowing them is not a matter of prestige or need per se, to focus on two of the most commonly cited motivations

---

13 See Subak (1906) for other examples, as well as Friedman & Joseph (2014; 2022).

for borrowing. Rather, they are forms that can only be exchanged through actual conversational interaction; e.g., discourse particles, terms of address, greetings, exclamations, interjections, and the like, reflecting a more human orientation of speaker-to-speaker interactions. Friedman and I argue that the close and sustained sort of contact leading to this sort of lexical convergence is precisely the social context in which Sprachbund-like structural convergence can take place as well. Thus E.R.I.C. loans are indicative of Sprachbund-conducive conditions.

E.R.I.C. loans are all over the Balkans, as we document (Friedman & Joseph 2021: Ch. 4), and while many are from Turkish, they are not limited to Turkish sources. Significantly, they are found in Judezmo. In (13), a sampling of such conversational loans is given:

(13) *bre* 'hey you' (ultimately from Greek *more*; see Joseph 1997)
ayde 'c'mon!' (ultimately from Turkish *haydi*)
ná 'here (it is); here ya go!' (ultimately from Slavic; see Joseph 1981)
aman 'oh my; mercy!' (ultimately from Arabic, but via Turkish (and Greek))
asiktar 'scram; go to hell' (from Turkish, actually a stronger curse)

E.R.I.C. loans can also add color and affect to conversation; the highly expressive and mildly dismissive *m*-reduplication of Turkish, e.g. *kitap mitap* 'books (*kitap*) and such', is an example of such an affective borrowing into Judezmo:

(14) *livro mivro* 'books and such'
zapatos mapatos 'shoes and such'

In addition, borrowed bound morphology, usually felt to be fairly resistant to borrowing except under conditions of highly intensive contact, here involving suffixes of Turkish origin, can be found in Judezmo in words and expressions of both Hebrew and Spanish origin. Examples include the qualitative or concrete suffix *-lik*, adjectival *-li*, privative *-siz*, locational *-ana* (< *hane* 'place (of)'), and onomastic *-oğlu* 'son of', all highly common in conversational contexts:

(15) *hanukalik* 'Chanukah present'
purimlik 'Purim gift'
benadamlik 'good deed'
azlahali 'profitable' / *azlahasiz* 'useless'
perrana 'kennel' (cf. *perro* 'dog')
gregana 'Greek quarter'
basinoğlu 'son of a urinal' (a term of abuse)

E.R.I.C. loans are found all over the Balkans and bespeak an intense sort of contact at a very human and personal level. In this way, therefore, even the lexicon provides some insight into the degree of Balkan integration shown by Judezmo.

3 Causes of Judezmo convergence or failure to converge

Based on this material concerning Judezmo vis-à-vis the Balkan languages and Balkan linguistic features, it can be stated that, consistent with its later arrival in the Balkans, some of the older features that are widespread among Balkan languages are not found in Judezmo, for instance the absence of a postposed definite article. Just as the presence of a well-established definite article in Greek seemed to have averted the adoption of this particular Balkanism, so was the well-developed article in Iberian usage retained.

Further, it can be observed that local geography matters. For instance, there are ways in which Judezmo diverges phonologically from Balkan languages, including development of vowel nasalization for the Judezmo of Salonica with sequences of *a/o* + *n* developing into nasalized vowels word-finally. This runs counter to the usual claim of a "clear" vowel system with no overlay features such as length or nasalization.[14] But such divergences are actually to be expected, under the view of Balkan phonology as a highly *local* phenomenon. As Friedman (2008) puts it: "there is no Balkan phonology, rather only Balkan phonologies". This is seen also in the shift from *ty/dy* (or palatalized dentals) to *ky/gy* (or palatalized velars) precisely in Bosnia and Macedonia; e.g., *Ingiltyerra* > *Ingilk'erra* 'England', where the same change took place in the local Slavic (and, in Macedonia, also Albanian) dialects. Moreover, some features found in Balkan Judezmo deviate in detail from other Balkan languages or have other possible origins, as with vowel raising.

Nonetheless, there are features of Balkan Judezmo that converge with those in Balkan languages that occur in the same place, so that there is some local linguistic assimilation – convergence – just not the more complete assimilation/convergence that other languages show.

Sociolinguistics serves to illuminate the situation here. With regard to the countervailing tendencies regarding the infinitive, for instance, we can note the

---

14 This feature is admittedly problematic as vowel length is found in a number of Albanian dialects, and nasalization characterizes Geg Albanian. However, this is a claim that is commonly made in the handbooks, e.g., Schaller (1975).

social — specifically, in this case here, religious — associations that non-infinitival languages have, in that Greek is largely associated with Orthodox Christianity, and Macedonian with official atheism. Moreover, Jewish languages in general are likely to preserve archaisms different from those of the co-territorial languages they are in contact with (cf. Wexler 1981). Given the general local and social segregation of Jewish communities, Jewish speakers would have less exposure to and less access to linguistic innovations found in the usage of non-Jewish speakers in the same area. Thus the persistence of the use of infinitives in at least some Balkan Judezmo varieties probably reflects a lower degree of contact between Jews and non-Jews in the Balkans than among the non-Jewish speakers of various languages in the region.

Furthermore, one has to reckon in the relative social isolation in which the Jewish speakers would have lived relative to their non-Jewish neighbors in Balkan cities. Without consistent, regular, and sustained contact with non-Jewish speakers of the local majority languages, Balkan Jews would not have had the opportunities nor have been subject to the pressures that could have lead to full convergence of their speech with the linguistic structures of their non-Jewish neighbors. Relevant here too is the fact of one-way bilingualism: for the most part, Jews learned other languages but speakers of other languages did not learn Judezmo. This one-way bilingualism as far as Judezmo is concerned is reflected in the anecdotal tales contained in Cepenkov's (1972) 19th century collection of Macedonian materials. As reported by Friedman (1995) (and note also Friedman & Joseph (2014: Section 10.4)) out of 155 such tales, 24 show code-switches into Turkish, 4 into Greek, 3 into Albanian, 2 into Aromanian and 1 into Romani, but there are none into Judezmo. Characters in these tales representing all the other languages show code-switching into their ethnic languages – Greeks into Greek, Albanians into Albanian, and so on – the code-switching from the Macedonian matrix language of the tales that Jews exhibit is into Turkish, offering another indication of how marginalized speakers of Judezmo were in the Balkan linguistic social hierarchy.

4 Lessons for Balkan Linguistics from Judezmo

There are several lessons, in part of a methodological nature, that the case of Judezmo in the Balkans offers for those investigating the Balkan linguistic scene. First, a simple catalogue of features is not enough to offer the best insight into the Balkan Sprachbund; rather, a qualitative assessment of each feature is needed. The complex contact situation demands consideration of the social setting and the dynamics of interaction. Second, despite the attention on structural and grammatical features in the handbooks on Balkan linguistics (e.g. Schaller 1975), the lexicon is not extraneous to phonology and morphosyntax when discussing Sprachbund phenomena and in fact complements it in important ways.

We can now address the motivating question for this investigation: is Judezmo a "Balkan language"? The answer is "Yes, in some respects, but no in other respects!" Such a response is perhaps unsatisfyingly uncertain, but maybe it is illuminating just because it is unsatisfying. In some instances, the sociolinguistic environment can be invoked as a reason for Judezmo's divergence from other Balkan languages, as with infinitival developments. In other instances, chronology is responsible, as with the absence of a postpositive article, under the assumption that that feature is due to a substratum absorbed before Sephardim arrived in the Balkans, along with the recognition that the chronology of the entry of Sephardic Jews into the Balkans gave enough pre-Balkan-contact time for a (preposed) article system to develop in Spanish.

Thus Judezmo shows how easily some features can penetrate into a language, especially those aspects of the lexicon and morphosyntax most tied to conversation and to the habits of pronunciation acquired via heavy use of the socially dominant language. And, overall, the mix of Balkan features in Judezmo sharpens a sense of what it means to be peripheral within a Sprachbund. Some of the developments of Judezmo, with either sources or parallels elsewhere in Ibero-Romance, show that both timing and environment — here the Balkan chronotope — are crucial in helping to distinguish between that which is convergent and that which is parallel.

References

Bunis, David M. 1981. *Sephardic Studies: A research bibliography incorporating Judezmo language, literature and folklore, and historical background.* New York: Garland Publishing.
Bunis, David M. 1983. Some problems in Judezmo linguistics. *Mediterranean Language Review* 1. 103–138.
Bunis, David M. 1993. *A lexicon of the Hebrew and Aramaic elements in modern Judezmo.* Jerusalem: Magnes Press.
Bunis, David M. 1999. *Voices from Jewish Salonika.* Jerusalem-Thessaloniki: Misgav Yerushalayim, National Authority for Ladino Culture, Ets Ahaim foundation of Thessaloniki.
Bunis, David M. 2011. Judezmo: The Jewish Language of the Ottoman Sephardim. *European Judaism* 44 (1). 22–35.
Bunis, David. 2018. Judezmo (Ladino/Judeo-Spanish): A historical and sociolinguistic portrait. In Benjamin Hary & Sarah Bunin Benor (eds.), *Languages in Jewish Communities, Past and Present*, 185–238. Berlin & Boston: De Gruyter Mouton.
Cepenkov, Marko. 1972. *Narodni umotvrobi* [Folklore]. Vol. 6, ed. by K. Penušliski. Skopje: Kultura.

Crews, Cynthia M. 1935. *Recherches sur le judéo-espagnol dans les pays balkaniques* (Société de publications romanes et françaises XVI). Paris: E. Droz.

Friedman, Victor A. 1995. Persistence and Change in Ottoman Patterns of Codeswitching in the Republic of Macedonia: Nostalgia, Duress and Language Shift in Contemporary Southeastern Europe. In Durk Gorter, Hendrik E. Boeschoten, Pieter C. Muysken, and Jacomine M. Nortier (eds.), *Summer school: code-switching and language contact*, 58–67. Ljouwert/Leeuwarden: Fryske Akademy.

Friedman, Victor A. 2003. Evidentiality in the Balkans with special attention to Macedonian and Albanian. In Alexandra Y. Aikhenvald & Robert M. W. Dixon (eds.), *Studies in Evidentiality*, 189–218. Amsterdam: John Benjamins.

Friedman, Victor A. 2008. Macedonian Dialectology and Eurology: Areal and Typological Perspectives. *Sprachtypologie und Universalienforschung* 61 (2). 139–146

Friedman, Victor A. & Brian D. Joseph. 2014. Lessons from Judezmo about the Balkan Sprachbund and contact linguistics. *International Journal of the Sociology of Language* 226: 3–23.

Friedman, Victor A. & Brian D. Joseph. 2021. *The Balkan languages*. Cambridge: Cambridge University Press.

Friedman, Victor A. & Brian D. Joseph. 2022. Eastern and Western Romance in the Balkans – The contrasting but revealing positions of the Danubian Romance languages and Judezmo. To appear in *Romance languages and the others: the Balkan Sprachbund*, ed. by Francesco Gardani & Michele Loporcaro, Special Issue of *Journal of Contact Linguistics*.

Gabinskii, Mark A. 1992. *Sefardskij (evrejsko-ispanskij) jazyk: Balkanskoe narečie* [Judezmo. The Balkan dialect]. Chişinău: Ştiinca.

Joseph, Brian D. 1981. On the synchrony and diachrony of Modern Greek NA. *Byzantine and Modern Greek Studies* 7. 139–154.

Joseph, Brian D. 1983. *The Synchrony and Diachrony of the Balkan Infinitive: A Study in Areal, General, and Historical Linguistics*. Cambridge: Cambridge University Press.

Joseph, Brian D. 1988. Pronominal Affixes in Modern Greek: The Case Against Clisis. In Diane Brentari et al. (eds.), *Papers from the 24th Regional Meeting*, 203–215. University of Chicago: Chicago Linguistic Society.

Joseph, Brian D. 1997. Methodological Issues in the History of the Balkan Lexicon: The Case of Greek vré/ré and its Relatives. In Victor Friedman, Masha Belyavski-Frank, Marc Pisaro & David Testen (eds.), *Studies Dedicated to the Memory of Zbigniew Gołąb 19 March 1923 – 24 March 1994. Balkanistica* 10. 255–277.

Joseph, Brian D. 2002. Defining "Word" in Modern Greek: A Response to Philippaki-Warburton & Spyropoulos 1999. In Geert Booij & Jap van Marle (eds.), *Yearbook of Morphology 2001*, 87–114.

Joseph, Brian D. 2019. Can there be Language Continuity in Language Contact? In Edit Doron, Malka Rappaport Hovav, Yael Reshef & Moshe Taube (eds.), *Linguistic Contact, Continuity and Change in the Genesis of Modern Hebrew*, 257–285. Amsterdam: John Benjamins

Kramer, Christina E. & Ana Teresa Perez-Leroux. 2007. Balkan lives, Jewish voices: Judezmo in the context of the Balkan Sprachbund. Paper presented at the Third Biennial Conference of the Southeast European Studies Association, The Ohio State University, 26–28 April.

Luria, Max A. 1930. *A study of the Monastir dialect of judeo-spanish based on oral material collected in Monastir, Yugo-Slavia*. New York: Instituto de las Españas en los Estados Unidos.

Montoliu, César & Johan van der Auwera. 2004. On Judeo-Spanish conditionals. In Olga M. Tomić (ed.), *Balkan syntax and semantics*, 462–474. Amsterdam: Benjamins.

Orozco, Rafael. 2007. Social constraints on the expression of futurity in Spanish-speaking urban communities. In Jonathan Holmquist, Augusto Lorenzino & Lot Sayahi (eds.), *Selected proceedings of the third workshop on Spanish sociolinguistics*, 103–112. Somerville, MA: Cascadilla Proceedings Project.
Sala, Marius. 1970. *Estudios sobre el judeoespagnol de Bucarest*. Flora Botton-Burlá (trans.). Mexico: Universidad Nacional Autónoma.
Sala, Marius. 1971. *Phonétique et phonologie du judéo-espagnol de Bucarest*. The Hague: Mouton.
Sala, Marius. 1976. *Le judéo-espagnol*. The Hague: Mouton.
Schaller, Helmut W. 1975. *Die Balkansprachen. Eine Einführung in die Balkanphilologie*. Heidelberg: Carl Winter.
Sephiha, Haim Vidal. 1986. *Le judéo-espagnol*. Paris: Editions entente.
Sephiha, Haim Vidal. 1996–1998. Le judéo-espagnol de l'ex-Empire ottoman: musée de cinq cents ans d'histoire. Problématique et programmatique. *Elinikē dialektologia* 5. 83–112.
Sims, Andrea D. & Brian D. Joseph. 2018. Morphology versus syntax in the Balkan verbal complex. In Iliyana Krapova & Brian Joseph (eds.), *Balkan Syntax and Universal Principles of Grammar*, 99–150. Berlin & Boston: De Gruyter Mouton.
Slobin, Dan I. 2016. Thinking for speaking and the construction of evidentiality in language contact. In Mine Güven, Didar Akar, Balkız Öztürk & Meltem Kelepir (eds.), *Exploring the Turkish Linguistic Landscape. Essays in Honor of Eser Erguvanlı-Taylan* [Studies in Language Companion Series 175], 105–120. Amsterdam: John Benjamins.
Studemund, Michael. 1975. *Bibliographie zum Judenspanischen*. Hamburg: Helmut Buske.
Subak, Julius. 1906. Zum Judenspanischen. *Zeitschrift für romanische Philologie* 30. 129–185.
Symeonides, Haralambos. 2002. *Das Judenspanische von Thessaloniki* (Sephardica 2). Berlin: Peter Lang.
Thumb, Albert. 1964. *A Handbook of the Modern Greek Language. Grammar, Texts, Glossary*. Chicago IL: Argonaut (reprint of 1912 edn.).
Wagner, Max L. 1914. Beiträge zur Kenntnis des Judenspanischen von Konstantinopel. *Schriften der Balkankommission, Linguistische Abteilung. II, Romanische Dialektstudien, Hft. III*. Vienna: A. Hölder.
Wagner, Max L. 1923. Algunas observaciones generales sobre el judeo-español de Oriente. *Revista de Filología Española* 10. 225–244.
Wagner, Max L. 1925. Los dialectos judeo-españoles de Karaferia, Kastoria y Brusa. *Homenaje a Menéndez Pidal*, II. 193–203. Madrid.
Wagner, Max L. 1930. *Caracteres generales del judeo-español de oriente*. Madrid: Librería y Casa Editorial Hernando.
Walter, Simon. 1920. Charakteristik des judenspanischen Dialekts von Saloniki. *Zeitschrift für Romanische Philologie* 40 (6). 655–689.
Wexler, Paul. 1981. Jewish interlinguistics. *Language* 57 (1). 99–149.

Andrey N. Sobolev
Balkan Sprachbund Theory as a Research Paradigm

Abstract: This chapter[1] deals with the theoretical foundations of Balkan Sprachbund studies: their purpose and aims, terminology and methods, and the areal and intralinguistic evidence for the regularity of contact-induced Balkanization processes on the peninsula. Instead of deconstruction, Balkan Sprachbund theory is supported by positivism, historicism, structuralism, social relevance and sufficient field data. These together demonstrate that it is possible to acquire new and profound insights into linguistic convergence in general and to provide Balkan linguistics with paradigms for research and models of interpretation. The concepts of linguistic boundary, dialect, regular correspondences in the functions of linguistic units, parallel grammaticalization, lexicalization, and semantic neutralization are stressed as crucial for understanding the nature of linguistic and cultural convergence and divergence that may manage to either evade or intensify identity loss. I argue that a facts-on-the-ground-based Sprachbund theory is capable of making predictions on the basis of the regularity of linguistic convergence in the Balkans. It is further argued that, for the first time in Balkan linguistics, thorough attention is being paid to bilingual symbiotic groups in zones of ongoing intimate contact on the part of the language and speech behaviour of their members.

1 Introduction

The Balkan (South Eastern European) linguistic and cultural community,[2] notorious the world over for its ethnic, confessional and linguistic conflicts, provides an exceptionally valuable case of linguistic and cultural convergence which *preserves the identity as well as the ethnic and linguistic diversity of groups of people*.[3]

---

[1] This research was made possible by a grant from the Russian Science Foundation (the projects "From separation to symbiosis: South Eastern European languages and cultures in contact", No. 14-18-01405 and "Balkan bilingualism in dominant and equilibrium contact situations in diatopy, diachrony and diastraty", No. 19-18-00244). The author wishes to thank prof. Alexander Yu. Rusakov for his engaging discussion of a range of controversial arguments put forth in this chapter. The chapter draws partially on Sobolev (2016).
[2] It is fully justified to speak of a Balkan *community* as a group of people living in the same place, having linguistic and cultural characteristics in common, and perceived as such both by the populations themselves and researchers.
[3] A clearly noticeable disappearance of various historically attested groups that results from assimilation or migration is certainly not specific to the Balkans.

The central problem of Balkan linguistics and Balkan Sprachbund research, Balkan cultural anthropology, and ethnic history is the unresolved issue of determining the general, shared, or specific processes (strategies, scenarios, agents, mechanisms, or outcomes) of linguistic and cultural divergence and convergence that either evade or intensify identity loss.

Among others, Balkan linguistics in general, and this book in particular, addresses the following **theoretical and methodological questions:**

1. Sources such as Sandfeld (1930), Asenova (1989), MDABL (2003–2018) show that we have sufficient evidence to account for the outcomes of parallel grammaticalization and semanticization in the spoken languages of South Eastern Europe; yet the paucity of historical linguistic and social evidence does not allow us to convincingly reconstruct the scenarios, agents and mechanisms that led to these outcomes. Can we then definitively prove that these developments were indeed contact-induced? Is there a "Sprachbund theory" which is capable of making predictions on the basis of the regularity of Balkan linguistic convergence? Can the expected outcomes be attested with the addition of new historical or field data?

2. What are the outcomes of the language contact phenomena (matter and pattern borrowing, mutual reinforcement, code-switching, code-mixing, and others) in the different contact situations under study? What can be accounted as "native" and "borrowed" in relation to structural and substantial elements? What is the degree of mutual isophonetism, isogrammatism and isosemanticism in the idioms in contact? What are the proportions of inherited and acquired elements in the speech of bi- and multilingual speakers? What are the scenarios, agents, and mechanisms that contribute to outcomes (substratum, non-dominant adstratum, donor, recipient, and others) and is there any causal relationship between the observable contact settings and the outcomes of the demonstrated contact-induced language change?

3. What are the socio-linguistic, cultural, religious and other factors that influence linguistic and social processes of separation and integration in the communities under investigation? Are there any contact situations among those in our study that can be regarded as responsible for Balkan linguistic convergence in general? Taking into consideration the following groups: (a) Greeks and Albanians (Himara and Tsakonia), (b) Greeks and Romance speakers (Tsakonia), (c) Greeks and Slavs (Tsakonia), (d) Albanians and Slavs (Mrkovići, Golloborda, Prespa), (e) Slavs and Romance speakers (Krk/Dalmatia, Karashevo, Prespa) in South Eastern Europe, can we regard ethnic and linguistic contact (up to symbiosis) between them as responsible for synchronic and diachronic linguistic convergence? How can the data on Judezmo contribute to our understanding of the Sprachbund?

4. What can be gained in the observation of very little-known Balkan symbiotic societies with non-dominant bilingualism, such as that in Montenegro? Are the L1 and L2 of supposedly symbiotic multiethnic multilingual groups of people in South Eastern Europe allophonetic, allogrammatical, allolexical, etc., to the same degree as all the other idioms of those languages? What kind of intercultural dialogue takes place within such societies?

2 Discoursive deconstruction of Balkan linguistics

In its active engagement with the most important developments[4] in 21st century language studies, Balkan linguistics is, in addition to determining the dominant features of Balkan languages themselves, devoted to such issues as: defining its own aims and methods, establishing its theoretical and methodological foundations, determining general sets of terms, and identifying areal and internal linguistic constants. Balkan linguistics is likewise a testing ground for establishing general and specific theories in the humanities, for linguistic theories and their heuristic value, the typology of contact situations, the history of linguistic communities and the individual speakers that comprise them.

The theoretical and methodological basis of contemporary comparative-historical and areal-typological Balkan linguistics as it is conducted at the Russian Academy of Sciences' Institute for Linguistic Studies and at St. Petersburg State University, is a continuation of Russian traditions of positivism, structuralism, and attention to relations between language and society (see Selishchev 1925; Trubetskoy 1928; Desnitskaya 1990; Desnitskaya & Tolstoi 1998; compare Asenova 2002; Friedman & Joseph 2017). Maintaining the position of preserving, transmitting, and developing Balkan linguistic traditions stands sharply at odds with a tacit impression that is widespread among a significant portion of the scientific community,[5] namely that:

---

[4] These include the "digital turn" in humanities in general (including geoinformatics, corpus studies and aggregate dialectology in linguistics) and the "anthropological turn" in linguistics (including primary data collection technologies, research on socially-conditioned language variation and change, sophisticated methods of research on bilingual speech production).
[5] This can be attributed to Hilary Putnam's "scientific realism" and the thesis that: a) the world does not consist of a fixed set of objects independent from consciousness, we fractionalize the world with objects by introducing different, alternative conceptual schemes, b) the truth is a particular type of idealized rational acceptability whose criteria allows for operational applicability, coherence, simplicity, internal consistency, and the like, c) it is possible that there are many true descriptions of the world (Vilinbakhova 2015).

1. knowledge of the world does not accumulate;
2. substantialization of the denotations of linguistic signs should *ipso facto* be condemned;
3. the meaning of a term is always dependent on context (thus if two different theories have one and the same term, for example, dialect A, then the meaning of that term varies depending on the theory);
4. a term's use should focus on the social norms to the extent that it is determined by the whole of the language collective;
5. it is useful to eliminate categorization, that is to reject the perception of concrete entities as individual cases of more abstract phenomena.

This approach, conscious and unconscious, affects discourse in humanities in general, linguistics as a whole, contact and Balkan linguistics and the theory of Sprachbund in particular and has a range of destructive consequences. For one, old information is constantly being rewrapped in new terminological boxes, such as in generativist analysis (Kosta 2009; Manzini & Savoia 2018). Other achievements have been ignored, as in the areal-typological projects of the *Linguistic Atlas of Europe* (Alinei 1983–) and the *Obshchekarpatskii dialektologicheskii atlas* (Carpathian General Dialectological Atlas) (Bernshtein & Klepikova 1988) which engaged in geographical mapping of structural linguistic markers decades before that of the *World Atlas of Language Structures* (Dryer & Haspelmath 2005). Competing researchers in the field are at pains to accuse one another of "substantializing" the objects of their research. It is interesting to note the appearance of alarmist accusations that Balkan studies is somehow hermetically sealed and resistant to comparison, that its existence reveals the dangers (!) of regional studies in general: "The concept behind Balkan studies was, due to this implied postulate of its own singularity, closed off hermetically and resisted comparison for decades. [...] Balkan studies reveal all too clearly the dangers of regional studies, namely the rejection of comparative and, in turn, innovative approaches that necessarily results in essentialization of one's own object of study" (Voss 2015: 144–145). Europeanization and internationalization have hence been proposed as important forms of influence on language variation in South Eastern Europe (Hinrichs 2014, especially pp. 241–378, 409–434). This theory, as in the time of Jernej Kopitar in the 19th century (Sobolev 2011b), again openly politicizes Balkan studies and formalizes the attempt to unify a discourse about this part of the world (compare the similar course of affairs in cultural anthropology, as shown in Čapo (2014)). There is a drift toward the social norms of a research team's dominant language. For example, the term *linguistic union* is deemed inappropriate in American English (Joseph 2011), and the word *Balkan* has negative connotations in western European languages (Hinrichs 2010), a connotation absent in Russian and even in many of the region's languages themselves (e.g., Serbian, Macedonian, Bulgarian, Albanian, and Aromanian). Furthermore, in Germany alone three handbooks have been published over the last 15 years reflecting, on the part of German experts, this trend toward negative connotations in western European reality, mass media and academic discussions regarding "Balkanistics (Balkanology)" (Reiter 1994). This began with "Southeast European Linguistics", then on to the ideologically appropriate "Eurolinguistics"[6] and its no less ideological critique (Voss 2014: 145–147). Finally, there is a thrust towards absolutizing a single or constructive intentional prototype which itself has no denotative value (see Wiemer's (2014: 432–434) discussion). This position leads, in particular, to sets of inferences such as "linguistic areas are, in the last resort, constructed by linguists" (Wiemer 2014: 440) and to a rather facile poststructuralist rejection of definitions and the employment of semantic oppositions.[7] Let us give as an example a terminological problem related to a central subject in Balkan studies: the definition and theory of a Sprachbund. In 2001, the debate over identifying "linguistic area" and "Sprachbund" can be illustrated with two citations:

1. "The term 'linguistic area' is an English translation of the more colourful German term 'Sprachbund' (literally, 'language union'), which was apparently introduced by Nikolai S. Trubetzkoy in 1928" (Thomason 2001: 99).
2. There is "evidence for a linguistic area (or *Sprachbund*) in Europe that comprises the Romance, Germanic and Balto-Slavic languages, the Balkan languages, and more marginally also the westernmost Finno-Ugrian languages (these will be called *core European languages* in this article)" (Haspelmath 2001: 1492).

After decades of conceptual discussions (Friedman 2021), the following contestation is more than valid: "I argue that too much effort has been wasted on trying to define the concept, that little progress has been made, and that it would be more productive to investigate the facts of linguistic diffusion without the concern for defining linguistic areas" (Campbell 2017: 27).

One should only welcome a deepening dialectological and geolinguistic study of binary *contact zones* as well as multilingual areas in all their possible variety. For example, contact points such as the Romano-Germanic (Domashnev

---

[6] For example: Hinrichs, Uwe et al. (eds.) (1999) *Handbuch der Südosteuropalinguistik*. Hinrichs, Uwe et al. (eds.) (2010) *Handbuch der Eurolinguistik*, and Hinrichs, Uwe et al. (eds.) (2014) *Handbuch Balkan*.

[7] Terms and concepts are used with shifts in their reference dependent on context (cf. Haspelmath (2001) on clitics, or metaphorically (cf. Hinrichs (2004) on creoles).

1988–1993; Smirnitskaya & Kosheleva 2002), Balto-Slavic (Wiemer et al. 2014), "Black Seminoles" (Opala 2000), west African (Rolle 2015) or Amazonian (Birchall 2015; Epps 2015) all typify the situation of language contact and the changes wrought by such contact. However identifying a "contact area", "linguistic area",[8] or a "Sprachbund" is a terminological and theoretical step backwards, an unprofitable, severely insufficient form of differentiation between what constitutes the geographical and the linguistic, but also the genetic and the typological, synchronic and diachronic, discrete and continuous[9] down to the complete abolishment of the concept of linguistic kinship whatsoever. Here one can speak of the "European sister languages of English", conflating genetic and areal criteria including Balto-Slavic, Balkan and even Western Finno-Ugric languages.

No less futile is the exclusion of the sense of *linguistic boundary* from the terminology of European linguistics. The use of the term "European language continuum" is simply erroneous and disregards the linguistic knowledge that Europe has at pains accumulated.[10] In particular, area-based linguistic research of the European continent conducted by the *Linguistic Atlas of Europe* (Alinei et al. 1983; Viereck 2003), exposed a continent-wide landscape of distinct individual ethnic languages which, in a most authentic manner, are engaged in contact in zones marked by linguistic boundaries and beyond.

The concept of linguistic boundary – extremely relevant for Western European linguistic landscapes in general – is especially so in the case of the Swiss (Zimmerli 1891–1899), as Norbert Furrer, the historian of the sociology of language, has shown in great detail. His term *Sprachbarrierenforschung* launched a new direction in research (Furrer 2002). Language boundaries – the boundaries between communities of speakers – do actually exist despite continuous contact between representatives of these communities. This is also true despite territorial, institutional and individual multilingualism. Boundaries can be conceived as both filters and bottlenecks. A "shift" in their position raises anxiety among

---

8 "A linguistic area, to the extent that the concept may be of any value, is merely the sum of borrowings among individual languages in contact situations" (Campbell 2017: 23).
9 Compare the proposed synonymy of the terms: "Standard Average European" (SAE), "Sprachbund in Europe", "linguistic area in Europe", and "SAE Sprachbund", as well as the announcement of the SAE kernel: the "Charlemagne Sprachbund" (Haspelmath 2001: 1504).
10 Traditional German philology noted, no less than a century ago, that the ethnically mixed and bilingual character of the Merovingian and Carolingian states likely led to a number of morphosyntactic phenomena that served to combine Old French with Old High German. This, in particular, led to the formation of analytic verb forms: perfects, pluperfects, the future, the passive voice, the development of definite and indefinite articles, and other features (Brinkmann 1931). Yet it is presumed, for example, that the Rhine-Moselle area of the Romano-Germanic linguistic *boundary* was formed by the 10th century.

speakers of "Romanisation" or "Germanisation" and so forth. Diatopic boundaries can be opposed to isotopic ones. Among the latter one may profitably distinguish between the 1) the diacratic (e.g., the German-speaking government over Swiss cantons with Romance speakers. It was the case in 1795 that *"L'Allemand est comme la langue nationale."*), 2) the diadoxological (differences in language between Catholics and Protestants), 3) diataxical (the difference between the various classes that make up the social group), 4) diatechnical (professional distinctions), 5) diagenic, 6) diachronic, 7) diaphasal (written and spoken, sacred and profane, official and private).

Modern dialectology, like other linguistic disciplines, places great importance on combining traditional and new research methods into one set of combined approaches. These mostly involve combinations of descriptive and comparative-historical dialectology (Sobolev 2014), linguistic geography (Lameli et al. 2010), dialectology of perception (Preston 2002), sociolinguistics and corpus linguistics. This is the approach which is most useful for the study of linguistic boundaries, an approach that, among others, involves dialectal phenomena and their areal distribution, objective and subjective differentiation among dialects along a border area (Sauermilch et al. 2019), and a typology of the diglossia and diaglossia respective to it (Furrer 2002: 135–153; Auer 2011: 487–494).

The phenomena that characterize border language space, that can allow us to understand the essence of language change and contact, have been previously quite insufficiently examined. Trenchant political debates over the ethnic affiliation of speakers have left many relevant questions completely unanswered over the last century of research. In particular, to date almost nothing is known about the following: 1) the extent to which linguistic variants precede a border or are the consequences of it; 2) the effect of boundaries on linguistic structure at all linguistic levels; 3) "socio-pragmatic" or extralinguistic phenomena along with the perceptions of linguistically naive speakers of the region's dialect landscape (here we must admit that we are still quite far from the use of mental maps, listening tests, or value judgments of dialect speakers); 4) the speaker's inherent cognitive acts that construct the otherness of what, and whom, is on the other side of the border in relation to their own social group; 5) the dynamics of the development of local language variants in relation to "synchronizing macro-processes in society" along with political, cultural, economic, and educational differences between groups of people; 6) processes of linguistic convergence, advergence and divergence taking into account the formation and functioning of regiolects; 7) the applicability of language contact and multilingualism taking into account different high and prestigious forms of languages (Germ. *Überdachung*); 8) linguistic profiles of dialect speakers in the region, including the questions: What role does polyglossia play here? What motivates the choice of the language of communication? What distinguishes dialect competencies on the both sides? Where do dialects persist and where do they disappear? To what extent are old dialect isoglosses preserved? What defines the circle of individuals that maintains competence in a dialect? Is there the development of a regional koine? What are the repertoires of dialectal, regional, and standard language variants, and in which domains are they used? How can the language situation be qualified in each individual case – as diglossia, in the sense of (Ferguson 1959), or diaglossia? What role have cross-border marriages and family ties played in the past and present?

As for **state borders**, some linguists hold the opinion that: "Divergence at state borders is not ... a consequence of political barriers that were hinderances to movement and communication [*Verkehrsbehindernd*], (as the old dialectology held), but a consequence of the cognitive structuring of diatopics, which orders and regulates language heterogeneity according to a national ideological pattern. It is not the political border that establishes the language area, but the imagined presence of the language area that establishes the dialect's borders" (Auer 2004: 177). This generalization that territorial language variation is an imagined state within communities of speakers is, in the Balkan material, still subject to verification. But be that as it may, it is useful for Balkan studies to begin to establish a distinction between borders that are systemic-linguistic (Germ. *linguistisch-systemische*) and individual-subjective (Germ. *individuell-subjektive*). The first "denotes contrasts between instances of variation that represent variants that are differently normative for different groups where each demonstrates its own patterns of usage. As such, they are derivatives of specific configurations of features, norms, and situations, as well as specific patterns of language structure, language attribution, and praxis." The second "denotes contrasts between instances that are, for speakers, perceptually different and reflect situationally significant and acceptable ways of speaking in interaction. As such, they are derivatives of specific interpretations of features, norms, and situations, as well as specific samples of language competence, language evaluation, and language understanding in practice" (Purschke 2019: 23, 25).

From the methodological point of view, aside from juxtaposing speakers' "facts on the ground" with "artifacts of dominant discursive processes", it is very useful when studying borders of the first type to distinguish between those open to movement and communication between divided population groups and those that hinder such movement. It is important to contrast "horizontal", that is, linguistic-geographical dialect differences, with "vertical" ones that result from the influence of literary languages or (supra)regional koine, so-called "standardizing changes" (Trudgill 1974). In the second case, the dialect is "moving closer, from a distratic-structural point of view, with the standard language" (Smits 2019: 33), that is, it adverges. Furthermore, situations of particular interest are those involving a change in the dialect system or standard language, those in which one and the same dialect is affected by different standard languages. It must be emphasized that creating massive corpora of dialect texts is the best way to document the entire range of phenomena that are of interest to us.

In the field of *perceptual dialectology* one may already raise the question as to whether speakers regard old and new political borders as being language ones. One can get information about personal experiences in connection with the border and stereotypical conceptions, including borrowed characteristics, all of which can be acquired by means of metalinguistic commentaries. What must be considered separately is whether the fact that the interviewer is not a member of the speaker's community has an effect on the results of such investigations. In any case, it is important to recognize that the methods of perception research in the Balkans today do not always allow us to obtain quantitatively relevant information and go beyond the boundaries of "professional opinion".

In addition to other theoretical and terminological innovations in contact and Balkan linguistics, Uwe Hinrichs, inspired by the work and ideas of Ulf Hannerca and Salikoko Mufwene, has sought to enlarge *the concept of creolization* and, in particular, to identify it with a Sprachbund (Hinrichs 2002; 2004). In the latter case, it is useful to refer to terminological details which we find to be telling, such as the following. While arguing that Balkan languages should be viewed as creoles, Uwe Hinrichs emphasized that an essential part of his argument puts forward "particle-based analyticity (*Partikel-Analytismus*)". He illustrates this with an example from Bulgarian: "Щял съм да съм чел (*Schtyal săm da săm chel*)" (Hinrichs 2004: 237), an analytic verbal form with the meaning 'Reportedly I read'. From our point of view, out of the five given constituents only one – *da* – is a particle, an *indeclinable* auxiliary word.[11] For the number of particles, this form does not exceed the form of the conditional mood in Russian with the particle бы /bi/.[12] The deconstruction of traditional linguistic theories and terminology in Balkan studies, and in contact linguistics in general, is accompanied by the construction of "social situations that enable hybridization" and

---

11 Just as only one particle – *a* – can be seen in the Romanian perfect passive with the infinitive and its auxilliary: "*A fi fost făcut*", meaning 'To be done'.

12 Perhaps announcing that the term "clitic" is *grammatical* may serve as another example: "many grammatical terms (including the term 'clitic')..." (Haspelmath 2015: 273). What makes something clitic, in our view, is not dependent on the level of grammar, but on its suprasegmental phonetic features. A clitic is usually understood as a word that must always be without an accent and is attached to words which must have an accent (orthotonic words). The deliberate lack of distinction between phenomena at different levels of language leads to aporia.

"speakers' cognitive processes" taking place in scientific research in general.[13] Certain organizing dichotomies such as symmetries and asymmetries of power, prestige, prevalence, as well as metaphors such as acquisition, imposition and assimilation (Michaelis & Haspelmath 2014) bring contact linguistics to the loss of its own problematics, models and methods, and finally to the marginalization of our science which transforms into an auxiliary humanitarian sub-discipline.

In Balkan studies there are longstanding "internal" problems. The year 2014 saw the return of such inveterate topics as "the oft-used term "Balkan language", "Balkanism", "Balkan Sprachbund", and "Balkan linguistics" (*die oft benutzten Termini Balkansprache, Balkanismus, Balkansprachbund und Balkanlinguistik*)" (Steinke 2014, 435). Klaus Steinke provided two, to my mind, conflicting distinctions according to which "Balkan languages" denotes all the languages of the Balkans whilst "Balkan linguistics" is the study of the languages which participate in the Balkan Sprachbund.

(a) Balkan languages ("*Balkansprachen*") are "all languages spoken on the Balkan Peninsula (*alle Sprachen, die auf der Balkanhalbinsel gesprochen werden*)" (Steinke 2014, 437);
(b) Balkan linguistics (to be more precise, *Balkanhalbinsellinguistik*) examines "the languages of the Balkans as not inherently separate from one other and not complete in themselves, but from the perspective of the features that make them members of the Balkan Sprachbund" (*die Balkansprachen nicht jeweils separat für sich und auch nicht in ihrer Gänze, sondern nur in Hinblick auf die Eigenschaften, die sie zum Mitglied des Balkansprachbundes machen*)" (Steinke 2014: 435).[14]

This noteworthy problem arises from the fact that Balkan studies regards itself as a narrow investigation of the Balkan Sprachbund, which is to say, those languages which, to a greater or lesser extent, exhibit convergent features called Balkanisms (Friedman & Joseph 2017: 57). Yet for decades a confrontation has been raging between linguists who justifiably believe that no relationship can be established between Balkanisms (for example, between those in Miklosich's traditional listing) (Steinke 2014: 440) and those that exhibit a systemic and hierarchical relationship with one another (Asenova 2018).

---

13 Compare this with the more traditional understanding of creolization expressed by Zuzanna Topolińska. She came to the conclusion that the Balkan and creole language situations are not subject to proper comparison, though they share similarities in some of their results (for example, the isomorphism of content and expression) (Topolińska 1995).
14 Furthermore, they hold that "membership in a Sprachbund is typically a matter of degree" (Haspelmath 2001).

From our point of view, "Balkan linguistics can be understood as the summation and as the result of such disciplines as Greek, Albanian, Romanian, Slavic, Indo-European, and Turkic linguistics, history of language and dialectology, theoretical and historical-comparative linguistics, linguistic arealogy, linguistic typology, sociolinguistics, ethnolinguistics, language policy, comparative cultural studies and anthropology as applied to the languages and cultures of the Balkan Peninsula that form, or once formed, an *areal* or *convergent group*" (Rusakov & Sobolev 2008: 11). Over the last quarter-century, contact linguistics in particular and Balkan studies in general have been actively developing the methods of areal and diachronic typology as well as methods associated with contact linguistics itself and those of other fields. Contact linguistics has been examining language areas, code switching and mixing, types of contact situations, language contacts and their outcomes (in particular when one language is preserved or replaced by another), grammaticalization, metatypy, and, most recently, hybridization (see Brown & Joseph 2018).

3 Testing a General theory against the Balkan Language material

All Balkan languages and dialects and their groupings may and must be examined without any ideological restrictions,[15] but with full consciousness of the limitations of each of the *methods* applied in the field, namely: comparative-historical (including linguistic geography), areal-typological contactology, as well as general linguistic formal and functional, including general typological methods, and discourse analysis.

Yet not all of modern linguistic theories that may lay claim to identifying and interpreting individual facts, dominants or constants *may pass the test of the Balkan linguistic material*. For example, generative linguistics as applied to Balkan languages, (see Tomić (2006) and Kosta (2014), and the balanced criticism of the

---

15 There are enough examples of Balkan languages and dialects that have been neglected for decades *in situ* exactly for political and ideological reasons: Romanian (Serb. *vlaški jezik* the 'Vlach language') and Bulgarian (Serb. *šopski jezik* the 'Shop language') in Eastern Serbia; Macedonian (Greek *ta ndopia* 'local language') in Northern Greece; Macedonian (Maced. *goranski* the 'Gora patois', *golobordski* 'the Golo Bordo patois') in North-East and East Albania; Greek in Himara, Delvina and Saranda in South Albania, Turkish in Bulgaria to name just the most evident cases. In these and similar cases, the international research community silently obeyed, and in the case of Greece still obeys, the national taboo that forbade "endangering the nation's homogeneity by research on officially unrecognized minorities".

former in Joseph (2011)) loses its explanatory and predictive force. As applied to this material it reduces analysis to mere description as it is unable to explain variability of word order, in particular the positioning of clitics in Balkan dialects, nor can it predict the grammaticality of such positioning in a particular idiom. For example, in the concluding chapter of his handbook on Slavic linguistics, Peter Kosta writes on clitics and negation in Bulgarian: "the Bulgarian system seems to prefer a position (of Neg[ative]) higher in the clause than the other Slavic languages... Neg[ative] has also some prosodic features in Bulgarian and Macedonian relevant for the description of syntax of clitics" (Kosta 2009: 309).

On the contrary, comparative-historical and areal-typological methods that point to both the combination of archaic (even proto-Slavic) and innovative features, as well as to the facts of areal proximity, find economical means of justifying compelling hypotheses in resolving such issues (MDABL 2003, Map No. 43; Sobolev 2001a). For example:

(1) Eastern Serbia
    t'i   mu   ne=s'i   d'a-l   p'are.
    2SG.NOM   3SG.DAT   NEG=be.2SG   give-PTCP.M   money
    'You didn't give him money.'

(2) Rhodope
    ĭ'ê   go   səm   ne=r"ukʌ-lʌ.
    1SG.NOM   3SG.ACC   be.2SG   NEG=call-PTCP.F
    ĭ'ê   nə=s'ôm   go   r"ukʌ-lʌ.
    1SG.NOM   NEG.=be.2SG   3SG.ACC   call-PTCP.F
    'I didn't call him.'

    nə=m"ô   sʌ   ml'ogu   tr'ôsə-lə.
    NEG=1SG.ACC   be.3PL   a lot   search-PTCP.PL
    'They didn't look for me long.'

In contrast to formally oriented methods, functional ones applied to Balkan languages and dialects have a great heuristic potential and allow us not only to observe the *internal linguistic constants and dominants* of a language system, for example, redundancy in grammatical marking (Sobolev 2012), or different degrees of donation from languages and 'borrowing' in language structure and matter (Sobolev 2011a; Rusakov 2013), but also provide economical and consistent *explanations* of the observed facts (Rusakov, this volume).

4 Theoretical postulates of the Petersburg School of Balkan Studies

From our point of view, the accumulation, consolidation and presentation of reliable knowledge about the world is not only possible but is, in fact, the principal aim of scientific activity. An enterprise is truly scientific only so long as a preponderance of facts are established by observation, so long as the segments selected for analysis reveal a systemic relationship between individual facts, so long as a systemic relationship is also revealed between the selected segment and the world, so long as this activity is conducted with consideration for the variability of facts and relations in time and space, and so long as this activity is directed toward the explication of the role selected segment plays in the language as a whole and toward verifiable explication of the motives of the linguistic behaviour of persons and groups. The truth that can be accessed by such an enterprise is not contextual, consensual or socially determined, rather it is referentially correlated. Substantialization (referentialization) of the denotations of linguistic signs and categorization are, therefore, both inevitable and desirable.

The *purpose* of scientific study of the languages of the Balkan Peninsula is, in our view, a description of reality that is comprehensive, system-oriented, that uses modern technologies (such as data collection through elicitation and recording narratives, electronic databases, linguistic corpora, computer mapping), theoretically grounded in geographic linguistics in the wider sense (for example, Cyxun (1981) on Balkan Slavic), and that involves deep research in a single language category (for example, Mladenova (2007) on definiteness in Bulgarian). It is also an explanation of the manner in which such a description has historically formed out of the fullness of past and present knowledge about linguistic, historical, and social reality (Sobolev 2013). After Agniya V. Desnitskaya and Norbert Reiter noted in, respectively, the 1970s and 1990s, the "appalling dearth of material resources" in Balkan studies, data collection acquired new importance. A researcher in Balkan languages who sets *scientific fact* (the actual, real state of affairs) above *discourse* puts value on data-based case studies (e.g., Adamou 2006; Sandry 2013; Steinke & Ylli 2007–2013) above biased political analysis (Steinke & Voss 2007; Gal & Irvine 2019).

As shown already by Cyxun (1981: 212–217), the Balkan Sprachbund, as another scholar writes: "arises from an accumulation of individual cases of 'localized diffusion'; it is the investigation of these specific instances of diffusion, and not the pursuit of defining properties for linguistic areas, that will increase our understanding and will explain the historical facts" (in Campbell 2017: 27). With the obvious inability of scientific research to embrace all the fullness in the facts of 'localized diffusion' as given, we study Balkan languages – together and individually – as a category. We compare their respective members and establish a hierarchy through identifying comprehensive, prototypical examples which we call representative dialects. On one side, it is important to avoid any inflationary usage of the term "dialect" and to escape from the absurd qualification of any speech production or inclusive standard, as dialectal (Szmrecsanyi & Anderwald 2018). On the other side, it also must be noted that *juxtaposing dialect and language* is as irrelevant for comparative and historical linguistics (Sobolev 2014) as it is for areal linguistics and general typology (Haspelmath 2005). It should be noted that the term "dialect language" was developed in Russian research to account for a large set of dialects that are grouped together into a non-codified form (Avanesov & Orlova 1965). In my understanding, there is no gap between Balkan dialectology and Balkan linguistics in general. The identification of representative dialects, for example, is done by means of intentional descriptions (Domosiletskaia et al. 1998; Sobolev 2001c: 55–57, Sobolev 2004a) in order to establish a network in the *Minor Dialectological Atlas of Balkan Languages* (MDABL 2003–2018).[16]

We maintain that our science needs *definitions of terms*, above all:

1. a strict distinction in the understanding of language families (divergent groups of languages and dialects), language areas (areal groups of languages and dialects), and Sprachbünde (convergent groups of languages and dialects) and the various different issues lying behind them,
2. a clarification of the question into how areal groups of languages and dialects integrate into convergent ones and under what circumstances do they do so,
3. establishing the role of each of the languages and dialects involved in these processes as:
    a) linguistic superstrates, adstrates and substrates,
    b) contact donors and recipients. This includes situations in which a language that is wholly or partially isolated in its system is neither the donor or recipient (see, for example, Joseph 2010; Rusakov 2013).

---

[16] A representative territorial dialect of a particular language is a dialectal unit, purposefully selected by implementing a linguistic procedure. This unit belongs to the core of a large dialectal area of a single language and, consequently, exhibits all the characteristic developmental tendencies associated with the area in question. Our list of representative Balkan dialects includes the Croatian Neo-Štokavian younger i-dialect, Serbian Zeta-Lovćen dialect, Serbian Timok dialect, West Macedonian Ohrid dialect, South-West Bulgarian Pirin dialect, Bulgarian Rhodopi dialect, Bulgarian Moesia dialect, Albanian Gheg Dibra dialect, Albanian Tosk Skrapar dialect, North Greek West-Macedonian dialect, South Greek Peloponnese dialect, South Arumanian Pindus Non-Farsherot dialect (in contact with a Greek superstratum).

We maintain that the *cause* for the integration of a language group into a convergent one is not the widely understood phenomenon of "intimate language contact" (a designation that, so far as I am aware, has not yet received its generally accepted definition, see Thomason (2001) and Matras (2009)), but bilingualism among large groups of people (larger than the typical patriarchal Balkan clan) that have engaged in lifelong contact over generations, and then are subsequently subject to monolingualization.

Let us repeat several proposals that we have previously advanced.

We can regard a group of languages as being pertinent for linguistics when virtually any two have been brought together on any basis. This includes geography (such as the languages of the Macedonian geographical region), a governmental structure (the languages of the Republic of North Macedonia), religion (the languages of Muslims, Jews, and others), and diachronic-genetic groupings (Indo-European or Turkic languages), among others. However, from the point of view of linguistics per se, language groups are more interesting when their members exhibit similarities that are not the result of genetic similarities or mere lexical borrowing. For example, for recognizing languages as being in a *convergent* group one must consider the existence of regular *correspondences in the functions of linguistic units* at all language levels (substantial convergence will then be an inevitable accompanying characteristic). If languages whose speakers are in direct territorial proximity do not demonstrate such systematic correspondences, they should be recognized as a (geographical) areal group. One may allow that a (geographical) areal group can be integrated into a convergent group and the opposite – that a convergent group be de-integrated into a (geographic) areal group – as, apparently, is happening and has happened in the Balkans. For the Balkan convergent group the term "Balkan linguistic union" has been traditionally used... (Rusakov & Sobolev 2008: 11–12).

"The existence of regular *correspondences in the functions of linguistic units* at all language levels" certainly must be distinguished from a situation of clear, overarching, unilateral *influence* from the socially dominant prestige language, for example, the influence of German on Sorbian (Lusatian).

5 Regular functional correspondences between Balkan languages

The types of regular correspondences that we have in mind are, for example, in functional (distributional or semantic) amplitudes of units and in categories of Balkan languages and dialects at all linguistic levels: in phonetics and phonology, grammar, lexicon, and text. Demonstrating their dependence on areal and not typological features is one of the principal aims of the linguistic study of the Balkans.

Granting full respect to "the importance of our examining the minute details provided by dialects" (Drinka 2017: 278), the MDABL with its extensive data on grammar and a lexicon from a minimal number of maximally representative Balkan dialects, provides for singular observations of the areal and systemic distribution of linguistic features across the peninsula. The areal (diatopic), systemic, and diachronic criteria alone serve as a reliable *proof of the contact-induced character* of some prior structural changes.

Regarding lexicon, Kristian Sandfeld (1930: 35–41) has noted the plethora of examples of *inter-language isosemy, parallel derivational motivations*, *lexical conflation*, and *lexical neutralization* (cf. Sobolev 2001a: 65–67, 86–89). The maps of the MDABL lexical series have shown the areal dependence of variation in dozens of parallel semantic motivations or internal forms. Just to name two examples: 'an onion bulb' ~ 'root', 'veins', 'beard' and 'mustache' (MDABL 2013, vol. 6, Map No. 37); 'braided onions (saved for winter)' ~ 'crown', 'garland', 'pony-tail (hairstyle)' and 'wire, string' (MDABL 2013, vol. 6, Map No. 39). There are numerous, newly discovered structural parallels in syntax as well. For example, map No. 85 (MDABL 2005a) illustrates just one of the isoglosses between Albanian and Macedonian, where the verb 'to fear' requires an indirect object in the dative, as opposed to a direct object in Greek and ablative prepositional constructions in Aromanian, Bulgarian, Serbian and Croatian. Considering the diachronic Old Church Slavonic data (*bojati sę* 'to fear' cum gen. et cum *otъ* + gen. (Kurz 1966: 136–137)), the specific and innovative structural property of Macedonian can be best explained by contact with Albanian:

(3) Maced. dial.
 ne mu se=plaʃam na=kut͡ʃeto.
 NEG PRON.DAT REFL=fear on=dog.SG.DAT/GEN.DEF
 'I don't fear the dog.'

(4) Alb. dial.
 nuk i trəmbem t͡ɕenit.
 NEG PRON.DAT fear dog.SG.DAT.DEF
 'I don't fear the dog.'

Both in lexicon and in grammar contact results in parallels in the distribution of morphemes (see, especially for morphosyntax, Asenova 2002). For instance, there is a movement toward greater grammaticalization (i.e., from morphemic function that shifts from lexical to grammatical or from less grammatical to more grammatical) and vice versa.[17] It also involves a "simple" extension of the range of functions of grammatical morphemes (also including a kind of semantic homogeny and neutralization), perhaps reflecting the progress of its value from less to more abstract. A good example is the regular isomorphy in expression of simple preterite, remote past, immediate past, resultative perfect, experiential perfect, evidentiality and admirativity in Macedonian, Albanian and Aromanian dialects in the Prespa area in North Macedonia (Makarova, this volume).

As is well known, *parallel grammaticalization* has been observed across the historical development of a number of classic Balkanisms. For example, particles that historically have their etymological origins in adverbs, prepositions and prefixes are now taken to build analytical comparative forms of adjectives: Alb. *më* ~ *mâ* < IE **məies* 'bigger' (Orel 1998: 258; Çabej 1976–2014 (2014): 322); Arom. *ma* < Lat. *magis* 'bigger' (Papahagi 1974: 762; Ciorănescu 2001: 484); SSlav. *po* < Protoslav. **pa*, **pa-* (preposition and prefix with many meanings) (BER V: 394–395); Gr. *pió* < AncGr. *pléon* 'big' (Andriótēs 1995: 281). Identical processes that have been well documented and understood at least in part occurred during the formation of the category of definiteness with its primary marker – the postpositive article – originating in demonstrative pronouns. To this also may be added the acquisition of the modal verbs 'want' and 'have' that have taken on the grammatical status of auxiliary verbs in the analytical form of the future tense. Here can be added a typical suffix for mass nouns now used as a grammeme to mark a plural and many other similar phenomena:

(5) Maced.
od   d'əbot l'is-je-to   p'adv-et d'olu
from oak   leaf-COLL-DEF.SG fall-PL down
'The leaves fall down from the oak' (MDABL 2005 I, Map No. 18).

The opposite of grammaticalization can be observed in a process of phrase formation or **lexicalization.** In phrasing the names for digits between ten and twenty the history of the Balkan languages reveals the formation of a free compound '*in/on + ten*'; this stem then takes on derivative forms in the meaning of 'between ten

---

[17] For contemporary discussions about the phenomenon of grammaticalization and the so-called 'theory of grammaticalization', see (Mengden, Simon 2014). Ultimately, the focus of the question is on the distinction between lexical and grammatical meanings. See, in particular, (Melchuk 1997: 241–246). We must especially emphasize that parallel grammaticalization in Balkan languages does not always result in phonological erosion, fusion at morphemic boundaries, or the loss of prosodic independence or morphosyntactic autonomy.

and twenty'. This also includes the so-called 'associative plural' which is a grammeme that has shifted its meaning from plurals of proper names to a patronymic suffix that means 'the family of so-and-so' (see Alb. Leshnjë *nasipll'arët* '1. several people named Nasip; 2. the Nasip family') (MDABL 2005 I, Map No. 24; compare: Map No. 30).

Parallel *semantic neutralization* is reflected, for example in:

1. the lack of distinction between the roles of possessor and beneficiary (forms of genitive and dative in their functional-semantic ranges), e.g., the use of enclitic dative forms of personal pronouns with both possessive and indirect object functions,
2. correspondences along the scope of direct, figurative and modal usages of verb tenses (e.g. the aorist of the indicative oscillating from a true aorist sense to future and conditional senses), among others.

Interesting, non-trivial, regular correspondences also exist in the functions of such classic Balkanisms as the phoneme /ə/. This has been observed in Balkan dialects where it is not a part of their basic phonemic inventory but rather has a peripheral status, in particular, as a mark of Turkic loans (found in some Serbian, Macedonian, Bulgarian, Gheg Albanian and Greek dialects).

Glancing over other classic Balkanisms such as *"the loss of the infinitive"* and its replacement by "syntactically equivalent" finite and non-finite forms and constructions clearly attests to the general heterogeneity in grammatical solutions that are, one after the other, implemented by respective Balkan dialects (on the principles by which this is achieved and, in particular, on the conjunctive see (Joseph 1983; Gabinskii 2002; Sveshnikova 2003; Arapi 2010; Schumacher & Matzinger 2013: 95 ff., 185–188; MDABL 2003, Maps No. 26, 30)). Noteworthy is the fact that Romanian and Bulgarian dialects did *not* lose the non-finite forms of the verb normally used for predication in the position of the nominal parts of the sentence (for example, to denote the predicate dependency from a modal or phase verb). Rather, while some of these dialects lacked the marker (Rom.) -*re* and (Slav.) -*ti*, along with their morphogenetic function, these forms adopted a syntactic function, comp. Rom. *pot face-* 'I can do it', and Rhodope Bulgarian *nəštôt pravə-* 'They don't want to do it' (Sobolev 2001a). In analytical substituents of an old synthetic infinitive, prepositions are grammaticalized into particles: Rom. *trebue a face* and *trebue de făcut* 'It must be done'; Arom. *ptui di intrai* 'He could (have) come'; Alb. *duhet me bâ* 'It needs to be done' (Rom. *a* < Lat. *ad*, Rom. *de* < Lat. *de*, Alb. *me* < Proto-Alb. **me(t)* (Ciorănescu 2001: 15; 280–281; Orel 1998: 254; Çabej 2014: 312–313; Sobolev 2004b: 254)). There is natural matching in the functions of the participle and verbal noun:[18] as well as the 'substitute infinitive': Rom. *trebue făcut* and Alb. *duhet bâ* 'It must be done', Megl.-Rom. *lipseaşte neardzire* and Maced. *treba odenje* 'One must go'; Arom. *va lucrari* and Maced. *saka rabotenje* 'It needs lot of work' (Nastev 1988: 97–99; Gabinskii 2002: 194; Sobolev 2004b). The same position may be taken by the finite form of the verb, as in Rhodope Bulgarian *i gu nə mužaxmə fanəm* 'And we couldn't catch him' (Sobolev 2001b: 185) and Alb. *sun dalim jasht mâ* 'We couldn't go outside any longer' (Ylli & Sobolev 2003: 208). Paratactical constructions can also be observed, for example, Gr. *thélō kai se pistévō* 'I believe you, because I want to (literally, I want and I believe you)' (Leluda-Voss 2006: 208) and Rom. *şî io vreu şi mă duc la ię* 'And I want to follow her'; *şî dup-aia poţ şî-l fači* 'And later you can do this' (Sveshnikova 2003: 75).

The factual (material) base for modern Balkan studies is solid. Even in the small number of monographs on subdialects that deal with individual items in the MDABL, there is enough authentic material to establish valid comparisons, including large volumes of transcribed authentic oral texts in each dialect (Sobolev 2001a; Ylli and Sobolev 2002; 2003; Bara et al. 2005; Leluda-Voss 2006). Furthermore, MDABL's lexical and grammatical mapping clearly demonstrates the distribution of full and partial inter-Balkan **regular correspondences in the function of linguistic units**. An incomplete list of such mappings includes, for example:

- lifting restrictions on the distribution of the definite article in formal contexts with a demonstrative pronoun or with prepositions, with proper names and kinship terms for nearest relatives (MDABL 2003, Map No. 9 ff.; MDABL 2005 I, Map No. 96 et seq.),
- neutralization of the dative and accusative as a means of expressing the status of subject in impersonal sentences (for example, in Arom. Kraniá / Turia *a ɲ'ia* (Gen.-Dat.) *arise'aſti ſi k'əndu* // *m'ini mi* (Acc.) *arise'aſti ſi kəndu* 'I like singing.') (MDABL 2003, Map No. 18),
- neutralization of the instrumental and sociative (comitative) (Sobolev 2006; MDABL 2005 I, Map No. 77),
- neutralization of transitivity and intransitivity (for labile verbs) (MDABL 2003, Map No. 19),
- neutralization of the future in the past and the habitualis (MDABL 2003, Map No. 25), among many others.

---

18 There is a very interesting question about the complementarity of phase verbs denoting the completion of an action. These have a special verbal noun in Albanian (Gabinski 1967; Morozova 2015).

Despite the abundance of examples of neutralization of opposing pairs, we are not inclined to consider *ambivalence* to be a fundamental feature, or even a basic distinctive feature, of Balkan languages. We likewise do not believe that "reconciling" the contrasting members of opposing pairs "results in a new meaning, a new category [...] where the fact of opposition is subsumed under a unity of a dialectal character that facilitates through opposition recognizing the means of a complete description of the object so as to achieve greater semantic volume where ambivalence is implicit and implied." (Tsiv'ian 2009 (1992): 23–24). Just as it is the case that Russian two-aspect verbs such as жениться (*zhenit'sya*) 'to marry' do not give rise to new categorical meanings, but bring to bear specific characteristics in their appropriate contexts: буду жениться (*budu zenit'sya*) 'I shall marry', imperfect aspect, so it is the case that Balkan neutralizations do not go on to create new metacategories. But if dissection of ambivalence as characteristic of the Balkan languages is useful for scientific aims, scientific ambivalence in theory and terminology is directly harmful to the extent that scientific knowledge is replaced by other symbolic forms, myth, or lip service.

Regular correspondences in function are, in our opinion, sufficient criteria for establishing a *Sprachbund* (see a different view in Friedman & Joseph (2017: 67)) and their *regularity*[19] provides Balkan Sprachbund theory with predictive power similar to those of sound laws. Like in comparative-historical linguistics, where the regularity of sound corespondences in synchrony is the ultimate proof for the diachronic claim on linguistic kinship, the regularity of functional correspondences accross linguistic boundaries is the proof of a Sprachbund. As the MDABL shows, the Balkan linguistic landscape is a continuum with no gaps between neighbouring languages and dialects, not only those related to each other, but also those unrelated (Rusakov & Sobolev 2008; Sobolev 2019). Mutual intelligibility through bilingualism makes this continuum true where a "language border has to be crossed" for an innovation to spread. Once we know the functional amplitude of a unit or a category in language/dialect A, we can predict the amplitudes of the unit's equivalents in the convergent languages/dialects B, C, D... from the same area, even in the case when B, C, D... are not closely related to A. As in the Mendeleev's Periodic Table of Elements we can predict the properties and behaviour of an element or category according to its place among its neighbours. This is true for distribution rules in phonology (Sawicka 1997), lexicon and grammar. For example, we were able to predict that the lexical item '(the day of)

---

19 The study of convergent linguistic groups, including territorially-based dialectology, aims to establish the *linguistic constants and dominants of the Balkan Peninsula* (Rusakov & Sobolev 2008). Such constants and dominants may be areal in nature (for example, the centuries-long juxtaposition of the Balkan East and West) or involve (inter-)linguistic features.

St. Andreas' will have a second meaning "December" in at least one Western Macedonian patois, leaning on the geographic distribution of this semantic neutralization (colexification) in Albanian, Northern Greek, and Aromanian representative dialects (MDABL 2005: 19, Map Nr. 2); and this fact was indeed attested in Golo Bordo as *j'odrej* 'December' (Sobolev & Novik 2013: 139).[20] Another example was the prediction that Aromanian verbal substantives with an indefinite article could build polypredicative taxis constructions of immediate consequence, leaning on Albanian usage; and indeed it was attested as *ună videari, una irotipsiri* 'Loved at a first sight' (MDABL 2003: 74, Map Nr. 29). We expect a similar phenomenon to be found in Macedonian. Indeed, the initial inspiration for this volume came from questioning the extent, limits, and regularity with which signs in Balkan languages can develop parallel functions in bilingual communities, especially in those with non-dominant bilingualism.

6 Zones of ongoing intimate language contact and Balkan bilingual (symbiotic) societies

In this volume, ethnic groups from a number of west-Balkan *krajinas* have been selected that were the site of manifold instances of positive linguistic and cultural integration across confessions. These were put together with those which, on the contrary, exhibited differing levels of separation on account of confession, language and traditional culture. As opposed to the above-mentioned "representative dialects", we were forced to ostensibly define the areas of ongoing intimate language contact, pointing to communities that can be eventually qualified as Balkan pre-industrial bilingual *symbiotic societies*:

1. The Roman Catholic Christian population of the regions of Istria and the Kvarner Archipelago (Croatia), where Croatian Čakavian dialects, Greek, Latin, Dalmatian, and Istroromanian have been in interaction from the Middle Ages to the present (Kozak 2015),
2. The Roman Catholic Christian population of Carașevo in Romanian Banat (with Slavic as L1 and Romanian as L2, except the village of Iabalcea with Romanian as L1 and Slavic as passively known L2 (Konior 2016; Konior & Makarova 2015; Konior & Sobolev 2017)),

---

[20] Previous literature on the patois listed *d'orvar* as 'December', for which we were unable to find an attestation.

3. The Orthodox Christian Macedonians, Orthodox Christian Aromanians and Sunni Muslim Albanians of Prespa in the Republic of North Macedonia (in the village of Arvati with Slavic or Albanian as L1 or L2 of male speakers respectively (Makarova 2016; 2017)),
4. The Muslim Gollobordas in Albania (with Slavic as L1 and Albanian as L2 (Sobolev & Novik 2013; Asenova 2016; 2018); see the situation in Gora (Dugushina et al. 2013)),
5. The Muslim Mrkovići and Ana e Malit population in the Montenegrin Coast and Krajina regions (with Slavic as L1 and Albanian as L2, except the village of Velja Gorana with Slavic as L1 of male speakers and Albanian as L1 of female speakers (Sobolev 2015; Novik & Sobolev 2016; Morozova 2017a; 2019)),
5. The Orthodox Christian population of the Tsakonia region in Greece, where Greek, Slavonic, Albanian, and Romance have been present from the Middle Ages (Kisilier, this volume),
6. The Orthodox Himariotes in Albania (in the village of Palasa with Greek as L1 of the majority and Albanian as L1 of the minor part of population, especially women (Novik & Sobolev 2016; Sobolev 2017)).

Special attention has been paid to phenomena we call "the Krk phenomenon", "the Iabalcea phenomenon", "the Arvati phenomenon", "the Velja Gorana phenomenon", and "the Palasa phenomenon". At these localities we have actually witnessed, observed, or tried to reconstruct the ethnic symbiosis of bi- and multilingual Slavs, Romanians, Albanians and Greeks.[21] May we perhaps draw conclusions regarding prior contact-induced changes by making use of the effects of contact in speech behaviour involving actual interference?

The notion of ethnic symbiosis was used in this book in a broad and, *de facto*, non-specialized fashion. Actually we subsume under the term "symbiosis" any coexistence of groups of people on the same definable territory, starting with a very narrow case where groups are additionally distributed (Barth 1969; Smith 2000), continuing with the relatively rare cases of linguistic exogamy (Jackson 1983; Fleming 2016), and eventual cases of non-dominant bilingualism, and ending at the most common case of minority groups in a modern European state, excluding situations with no direct interference through oral contact between the alloglottic speakers. None of these situations is presented in the Balkans in

---

21 Compare this with the recent conclusion of our American colleagues: "... because of the variety of sociolinguistic circumstances that Slavic interactions have occurred in Albanian, it is vital to consider individual areas of contact for understanding the effects of language contact. Ideally this would be at a very local level, such as individual families, tribes, or villages" (Curtis 2012: 381–382).

its pure form. Previously, Balkan linguistics has never paid thorough attention to symbiotic groups and the field possesses insufficient information on the languages and speech behaviour of their members.

Materials for researching the languages of symbiotic groups are being collected by MDABL programmes and, consequently, they are complete, systematic, and fully compatible with data presented and charted in the publications of the grammatical, lexicographic, and ethnolinguistic issues of the *Atlas*.

7 Conclusion

With the classic problem of creating a Balkan grammar, Balkan dictionary and major Balkan atlas still unsolved, nonetheless the research prospects for the next few decades are good. Recent developments in the theory of language contact include, for example, a discussion of the possible limits of influence of contact languages on each other, the scientific issue of capturing the nature of this assimilation, and interest in the language history of individual native speakers within contact situations. This theoretical progress has made apparent the need for a detailed study of the *types of contact situations* in the Balkans that form a continuum from separation to symbiosis (Curtis 2012; Sobolev & Novik 2013; Sobolev 2015). Furthermore, *anthropological adjustments* must be applied – knowledge about the ethical attitudes of large groups of people, their beliefs regarding the prestige of their own or someone else's realia and lifestyles, including their language, and the behaviour of a range of native Balkan language and dialect speakers who have prestige in comparison with the behaviour of other native speakers. We consider, on our part, the desire for freedom and, in particular, the desire to free oneself from linguistic and cultural dictates to be the most important anthropological constant.

The "Sprachbund theory" is capable of making predictions on the basis of the regularity of linguistic convergence in the Balkans. Expected outcomes can be attested when new historical or field data are added and regular correspondences in the function of linguistic units (phonemes, lexicon, grammar markers, text) are revealed. These likewise may illustrate possible correspondences between the language situation itself and the type of linguistic change.

References

Adamou, Evangelia. 2006. *Le Nashta. Description d'un parler slave de Grèce en voie de disparition*. Munich: Lincom Europa.
Andriṓtēs, Nikólaos. 1995. *Etēmologikó leksikó tēs koinḗs neoellēnikḗs* [Etymological dictionary of Modern Greek]. Thessaloniki: Institute of Modern Greek Studies.
Alinei, Mario et al. 1983. *Atlas Linguarum Europae. Volume I: Premier fascicule. Cartes et Commentaires*. Assen: van Gorcum.
Arapi, Ina. 2010. *Gebrauch von Infinitiv und Konjunktiv im Altalbanischen mit Ausblick auf das Rumänische*. Hamburg: Dr. Kovač.
Asenova, Petya. 2003. *Balkansko ezikoznanie: osnovni problemi na balkanskiia ezikov s"iuz*. [Balkan linguistics: the basic problems of the Balkan Sprachbund]. Sofia: Faber.
Asenova, Petya. 2016. Les interférences dans le dialecte de Golo bărdo – Albanie. In Petya Asenova (ed.), *Izbrani statii po balkansko ezikoznanie* [Selected papers in Balkan linguistics], 282–309. Sofia: Faber.
Asenova, Petya. 2018. Balkan Syntax: Typological and Diachronic Aspects. In Brian Joseph & Iliana Krapova (eds.), *Balkan syntax and universal principles of grammar*, 13–36. Berlin & Boston: De Gruyter Mouton.
Auer, Peter. 2004. Sprache, Grenze, Raum. *Zeitschrift für Sprachwissenschaft* 23 (2), 149–179.
Auer, Peter. 2011. Dialect vs. standard: a typology of scenarios in Europe. In Bernd Kortmann & Johan van der Auwera (eds.), *The languages and linguistics of Europe. A comprehensive guide*, 485–500. Berlin, Boston; de Gruyter.
Avanesov, Ruben I. & Varvara G. Orlova. 1965. *Russkaia dialektologiia* [Russian dialectology]. Moscow: Nauka.
Bara, Maria, Tede Kahl & Andrey N. Sobolev. 2005. *Iuzhnoarumynskii govor sela Tur'ia (Pind). Sintaksis. Leksika. Etnolingvistika. Teksty.* [The South Aromanian subdialect of Turia in the Pindus. Syntax. Lexicon. Ethnolinguistics. Texts]. München: Biblion Verlag.
BER – Vladimir Georgiev et al. (eds.). 1971–2010. *Bŭlgarski etimologichen rechnik*. [Bulgarian etymological dictionary]. 7 Vols. Sofia: BAN.
Bernshtein, Samuil B. & Galina P. Klepikova (eds.). 1988. *Obshchekarpatskii dialektologicheskii atlas [Atlas dialectologique des Carpathes]*. Vol. 1. Moscow: Nauka.
Birchall, Joshua. 2015. Reexamining Amazonia as a linguistic area: A view from morphosyntax. Paper presented at ALT 2015. *11th Conference of the Association for Linguistic Typology*. August 1–3, 2015. University of New Mexico. Albuquerque. Abstract booklet. 17–18.
Brown, Christopher G. & Brian D. Joseph. 2018. On Hybrid Forms in Language Contact: Some evidence from the Greek of Southern Albania. *Albanohellenica* 6. 49–58.
Campbell, Lyle. 2017. Why is it so Hard to Define a Linguistic Area? In Raymond Hickey (ed.), *The Cambridge Handbook of Areal Linguistics*, 19–39. Cambridge: Cambridge University Press.
Çabej, Eqrem. 1976–2014. *Studime etimologjike në fushë të shqipes* [Etymological studies in Albanian]. Vols. 1–7. Tirana: Academia e Shkencave e Shqiperisë.
Čapo, Jasna. 2014. Ethnology and Anthropology in Europe. Towards a Trans-National Discipline. In Waldimar Hafstein & Peter Jan Margry (eds.), *What's in a Discipline?* (Cultural Analysis 13), 51–76.
Ciorănescu, Alexandru I. 2001. *Dicţionarul etimologic al limbii române* [Romanian etymological dictionary]. Bucureşti: Editura Saeculum I.O.
Curtis, Matthew Cowan. 2012. *Slavic-Albanian Language Contact, Convergence, and Coexistence*. Ohio State University Doctoral Dissertation.

Desnitskaya, Agniya V. (ed.). 1990. *Osnovy balkanskogo iazykoznaniya. Iazyki balkanskogo regiona. Chast' I (novogrecheskii, albanskii, romanskie iazyki)* [Foundations of Balkan linguistics. Languages of the Balkan region. Part I (Modern Greek, Albanian, Romanian languages)]. Leningrad: Nauka.
Desnitskaya, Agniya V. & Nikita I. Tolstoi (eds.). 1998. *Osnovy balkanskogo iazykoznaniya. Iazyki balkanskogo regiona. Chast' II. Slavianskie iazyki* [Foundations of Balkan linguistics. Languages of the Balkan region. Part II. Slavic languages]. St. Petersburg: Nauka.
Domashnev, Anatolii I. (ed.). 1988–1993. *Romano-germanskaia kontaktnaia zona* [The Romance-Germanic contact zone]. Vol. 1–3. Leningrad: Nauka.
Domosiletskaia, Marina V., Anna A. Plotnikova & Andrey N. Sobolev. 1998. Malyi dialektologicheskii atlas balkanskikh iazykov [Minor Dialectological Atlas of Balkan Languages]. In *Slavianskoe iazykoznanie. XII mezhdunarodnyi s"ezd slavistov. Doklady rossiiskoi delegatsii*, 196–211. Moscow: Nauka.
Drinka, Bridget. 2017. *Language Contact in Europe: The Periphrastic Perfect through History*. Cambridge: Cambridge University Press.
Dryer, Matthew & Martin Haspelmath (eds.). 2005. *The World Atlas of Language Structures Online*. Oxford: Max Planck Institute for Evolutionary Anthropology. http://wals.info.
Dugushina, Alexandra S., Maria S. Morozova & Denis S. Ermolin. 2013. Etnograficheskie nabludeniya v oblasti Gora (Albaniya, Kosovo) [Ethnographic observations in the region of Gora (Albania, Kosovo)]. In Elena G. Fedorova (ed.), *Materialy polevykh issledovaniy MAE RAN* 13, 50–65. St. Petersburg: MAE RAN.
Epps, Patience. 2015. Exploring the relationship between linguistic diversity and language contact: An Amazonian perspective. Paper presented at ALT 2015. *11th Conference of the Association for Linguistic Typology. August 1–3, 2015*. University of New Mexico. Albuquerque, New Mexico, USA. Abstract booklet. 50–51.
Ferguson, Charles. 1959. Diglossia. *Word* 15, 325–340.
Friedman, Victor. 2021. The Balkans. In Evangelia Adamou & Yaron Matras (eds.), *The Routledge Handbook of Language Contact*, 385–403. London & New York: Routledge.
Furrer, Norbert. 2002. *Die vierzigsprachige Schweiz. Sprachkontakte und Mehrsprachigkeit in der vorindustriellen Gesellschaft (15.–19. Jahrhundert)*. Zürich: Chronos.
Gabinskii, Mark A. 2002. *Posobie po morfologii dakoromanskogo glagola* [Textbook of Daco-Romanian verbal morphology]. Kishinev: Academy of Sciences.
Gal, Susan & Judith T. Irvine. 2019. *Signs of Difference: Language and Ideology in Social Life*. Cambridge: Cambridge University Press.
Haspelmath, Martin. 2001. The European linguistic area: Standard Average European. In Martin Haspelmath, Ekkehard König, Wulf Oesterreicher & Wolfgang Raible (eds.), *Language typology and language universals* (Handbücher Zur Sprach- Und Kommunikationswissenschaft), Vol. 2, 1492–1510. Berlin & New York: Mouton de Gruyter.
Haspelmath, Martin, Matthew S. Dryer, David Gil & Bernard Comrie (eds.). 2005. *The World Atlas of Language Structures*. Oxford & New York: Oxford University Press.
Haspelmath, Martin. 2015. Defining vs. diagnosing linguistic categories: a case study of clitic phenomena. In Joanna Baszczak, Dorota Klimek-Jankowska & Krzysztof Migdalski (eds.), *How categorical are categories?: New approaches to the old questions of noun, verb, and adjective*. 273–304. Berlin & Boston: De Gruyter Mouton.
Hinrichs, Uwe. 2002. Können Balkanlinguistik und Kreolistik voneinander profitieren? *Linguistique balkanique* 42 (2). 147–157.

Hinrichs, Uwe. 2004. Ist das Bulgarische kreolisiertes Altbulgarisch? In Uwe Hinrichs (ed.), *Die europäischen Sprachen auf dem Weg zum analytischen Sprachtyp*, 231–242. Wiesbaden: Harrassowitz.
Hinrichs, Uwe (ed.). 2010. *Handbuch der Eurolinguistik*. Wiesbaden: Harrassowitz.
Hinrichs, Uwe & Uwe Büttner (eds.). 1999. *Handbuch der Südosteuropa-Linguistik* (Slavistische Studienbücher). Vol. 10. Wiesbaden: Harrassowitz.
Hinrichs, Uwe et al. (eds.). 2014. *Handbuch Balkan*. Wiesbaden: Harrassowitz.
Joseph, Brian D. 1983. *The synchrony and diachrony of the Balkan infinitive: a study in areal, general, and historical linguistics*. Cambridge: Cambridge University Press.
Joseph, Brian D. 2010. Language contact in the Balkans. In Raymond Hickey (ed.), *The Handbook of Language Contact*, 618–633. Malden, MA: Wiley-Blackwell.
Joseph, Brian D. 2011. Review of Olga Mišeska-Tomić (ed.). Balkan Sprachbund Morpho-syntactic Features. *Acta Slavica Iaponica* 67 (29). 123–132.
Joseph, Brian & Victor Friedman. 2017. Reassessing sprachbunds: A view from the Balkans. In Raymond Hickey (ed.), *The Cambridge Handbook of Areal Linguistics*, 63–90. Cambridge: Cambridge University Press.
Konior (Koner), Daria V. 2016. Leksicheskaya realizatsiya predmetnogo koda karashevskoi svad'by ["Objective code" of the Krashovani wedding vocabulary and its lexical manifestation]. *Acta linguistica Petropolitana. Trudy Instituta lingvisticheskih issledovaniy* 12 (3). 629–649.
Konior (Koner), Daria V. & Anastasia L. Makarova. 2015. Osobennosti etnoyazykovoy situacii v regione Karashevo (Rumyniya) [On the ethnolinguistic situation in the community of Karashevo (Romania)]. *Poznańskie studia sławistyczne* 8. 83–91.
Konior (Koner), Daria V. & Andrey N. Sobolev. 2017. Osobennosti neravnovesnogo bilingvizma u rumynoyazychnyh karashevtsev v sele Yabaltcha [On some aspects of nonequilibrium Romanian-Slavic bilingualism in the village of Iabalcea]. *Indoevropeyskoye yazykoznaniye i klassicheskaya filologiya* 21. 985–1001.
Kosta, Peter. 2009. Targets, Theory and Methods of Slavic Generative Syntax: Minimalism, Negation and Clitics. In Peter Kosta, Karl Gutschmidt & Sebastian Kempgen (eds.), *Die Slavischen Sprachen, ein internationales Handbuch zu ihrer Struktur, ihrer Geschichte und ihrer Erforschung*, Vol. 1, 282–316. Berlin & New York: Mouton de Gruyter.
Kozak, Vyacheslav V. 2015. Otrazhenie slaviano-romanskikh kontaktov v leksike glagolicheskikh nadpisei s ostrova Krk XI–XVIII vv. [Reflections of Slavo-Romance contacts in the lexicon of Glagolitic inscriptions of the 11th to the 18th centuries on the island of Krk]. *Indoevropeyskoye yazykoznaniye i klassicheskaya filologiya* 9. 401– 10.
Kurz, Jozef (ed.). 1966. *Slovník jazyka staroslověnského* [Lexicon linguae palaeoslovenicae]. Vol. I. Praha: Československá Akademie Věd.
Labov, William. 2020. The regularity of regular sound change. *Language* 96 (1). 42–59.
Lameli, Alfred, Roland Kehrein & Stefan Rabanus (eds.). 2010. *Language and Space : Language Mapping : An international handbook of linguistic variation*. Vols I–II. Berlin & New York: Mouton de Gruyter.
Makarova, Anastasia L. 2016. Neka zapažanja o etnojezičkoj situaciji u dvojezičnim makedonsko-albanskim selima u regionu Prespa: fenomen Arvati [Some observations on the ethnolinguistic situation in the bilingual Macedonian-Albanian villages of the Prespa region: the case of Arvati]. *Studia Slavica Academiae Scientiarum Hungaricae* 61 (1). 115–130.
Makarova, Anastasia L. 2017. Interferentsiia v rechi bilingval'nykh nositelei dialektov regiona Prespa (Makedoniia). [Discourse Strategies of Bilingual Speakers of Macedonian, Aromanian and Albanian Dialects. the Prespa Region]. In Sergey Monakhov, Irina Vasilyeva &

Maria Khokhlova (eds.), *Social Science, Education and Humanities Research* (ASSEHR) 122. 364–367.

Manzini, Rita M. & Leonardo Savoia. 2018. *The Morphosyntax of Albanian and Aromanian Varieties. Case, Agreement, Complementation.* Berlin & Boston: De Gruyter Mouton.

Matras, Yaron. 2009. *Language Contact.* Cambridge: Cambridge University Press.

MDABL – Andrey N. Sobolev (ed.). 2003–2018. *Malyi dialektologicheskii atlas balkanskikh iazykov. Probnyi vypusk (2003). Seriia leksicheskaia. Tom I. Leksika dukhovnoi kul'tury (2005). Tom II. Chelovek. Sem'ia (2006). Tom III. Zhivotnovodstvo (2009). Tom IV. (Avtor: M. V. Domosiletskaia). Landshaftnaia leksika (2010). Tom V. (Avtor: M. V. Domosiletskaia). Meteorologiia (2012). Tom VI. Polevodstvo. Ogorodnichestvo (2013). Tom VII. (Avtor: M. V. Domosiletskaia). Pčelovodstvo (2018). Seriia grammaticheskaia. Tom I. Kategorii imeni sushchestvitel'nogo (2005)* [Minor dialect atlas of the Balkan languages. Test launch (2003). Lexical series. Vol. 1. Cultural vocabulary (2005). Vol. 2. The person and human relations (2006). Vol. 3. Animal husbandry (2009). Vol. 4. (M. V. Domosiletskaia, author). Landscape (2010). Vol. 5 (M. V. Domosiletskaia, author). Meteorology (2012). Vol. 6. Field-tending and Gardening (2013). Vol. 7. (M. V. Domosiletskaia, author). Apiculture (2018). Grammatical series. Vol. 1. Noun categories (2005)]. St. Petersburg, München: Nauka, Verlag Otto Sagner.

Michaelis, Susanne M. & Martin Haspelmath. 2014. Introductory remarks. *Grammatical hybridization and social conditions. Workshop.* Leipzig. https://www.eva.mpg.de/linguistics/conferences/grammatical-hybridization-and-social-conditions/index.html (accessed 15 March, 2021).

Mladenova, Olga. 2007. *Definiteness in Bulgarian. Modelling the Processes of Language Change* (Trends in Linguistics. Studies and Monographs 182). Berlin & New York: Mouton de Gruyter.

Morozova, Maria S. 2017. Albanskii govor ili govory Gorany? Genezis i funktsionirovanie [Albanian subdialect or subdialects of Gorana? Origins and function]. *Vestnik Sankt-Peterburgskogo gosudarstvennogo universiteta. Iazyk i literatura* 14 (2). 222–237.

Morozova, Maria S. 2019. Language contact in social context: Kinship terms and kinship relations of the Mrkovići of southern Montenegro. *Journal of Language Contact* 12 (2). 305–343.

Nastev, Božidar. 1988. *Aromanski studii. Prilozi kon balkanistikata* [Aromanian Studies. Contributions to Balkanology]. Skopje: MANU.

Novik, Aleksandr A. & Andrey N. Sobolev. 2016. Traditional wedding costume of the Mrkovići in Montenegro: between real heritage and folk construction (materials of the Russian expeditions in 2012–2014). *Folklore* 66. 15–36.

Opala, Joseph A. 2000. *The Gullah. Rice, Slavery and the Sierra Leone-American Connection.* Freetown: USIS.

Orel, Vladimir. 1998. *Albanian etymological dictionary.* Leiden; Boston & Köln: Brill.

Palliwoda, Nicole, Verena Sauer & Stephanie Sauermilch (eds.). 2019. *Politische Grenzen – sprachliche Grenzen? Dialektgeographische und wahrnehmungsdialektologische Perspektiven im deutschsprachigen Raum.* Berlin & Boston: De Gruyter Mouton.

Papahagi, Tache. 1974. *Dicţionarul dialectului aromân general şi etimologic [Dictionnaire Aroumain (Macédo-Roumain) général et étymologique].* 2nd edn. Bucureşti: Editura Academiei Republicii Socialiste România.

Poplack, Shana & Suzanne Robillard, Nathalie Dion, John C. Paolillo. 2020. Revisiting phonetic integration in bilingual borrowing. *Language* 96 (1). 126–159.

Preston, Dennis R. 2002. Perceptual dialectology: Aims, methods, findings. In Jan Berns & Jaap van Marle (eds.), *Present-Day Dialectology: Problems and Findings*, 57–104. Berlin & New York: Mouton de Gruyter.

Purschke, Christoph. 2019. Vom Sprechen zur Sprache. Versuch über die variationslinguistische Praxis des Begrenzens. In Palliwoda, Nicole, Verena Sauer & Stephanie Sauermilch (eds.), *Politische Grenzen – sprachliche Grenzen? Dialektgeographische und wahrnehmungsdialektologische Perspektiven im deutschsprachigen Raum*, 9–29. Berlin & Boston: De Gruyter Mouton.

Reiter, Norbert. 1994. *Grundzüge der Balkanologie. Ein Schritt in die Eurolinguistik*. Wiesbaden: Harrassowitz.

Rolle, Nicholas. 2015. An areal typology of nasal vowels in West Africa. Paper presented at ALT 2015. *11th Conference of the Association for Linguistic Typology. August 1–3, 2015*. University of New Mexico. Albuquerque. Abstract booklet. 116–117.

Rusakov, Alexander Yu. & Andrey N. Sobolev. 2008. *Substantsial'no-funktsional'naia teoriia balkanskogo iazykovogo soiuza i slavianskie iazyki* [A substantial and functional theory of Balkan Sprachbund and Slavic languages]. XIV *Mezhdunarodnyi s"ezd slavistov v Okhride, Makedoniia*. St. Petersburg: ILI RAN.

Rusakov, Alexander Yu. 2013. Nekotorye izoglossy na albanskoi dialektnoi karte (k voprosu o vozniknovenii i rasprostranenii balkanizmov albanskogo iazyka) [Some isoglosses on the Albanian dialectical map (toward the question of the emergence and distribution of Balkanisms in Albanian)]. In Viacheslav V. Ivanov (ed.), *Issledovaniia po tipologii slavianskikh, baltiiskikh i balkanskikh iazykov* [Research on typology of Slavic, Baltic and Balkan languages], 113–174. St. Petersburg: Aleteia.

Sandfeld, Kristian. 1930. *Linguistique balkanique. Problèmes et résultats*. Paris: Champion.

Sandry, Susan. 2013. *Phonology and Morphology of Paševik Pomak with Notes on the Verb and Fundamentals of Syntax*. London: University College London. School of Slavonic and East European Studies Master's Thesis.

Sawicka, Irena. 1997. *The Balkan Sprachbund in the Light of Phonetic Features*. Warszawa: Wydawnictwo Energeia.

Schumacher, Stefan, Joachim Matzinger & Anna-Maria Adaktylos. 2013. *Die Verben des Altalbanischen. Belegwörterbuch, Vorgeschichte und Etymologie*. Wiesbaden: Harrassowitz.

Selishchev, Afanasii M. 1925. Des traits linguistiques communs aux langues balkaniques: Un balkanisme ancien en bulgare. *Revue des Études slaves* 5 (1–2). 38–56.

Smirnitskaya, Svetlana V. & Irina S. Kosheleva. 2002 [1980] Romano-germanskaya kontaktnaya zona v svete dannykh regional'nykh atlasov [Romance-germanic contact area in the light of the regional language atlases]. In Svetlana V. Smirnitskaya (ed.), *Trudy po germanistike i istorii iazykoznaniia*, 139–146. St. Petersburg: Nauka.

Smits, Tom F. H. 2019. Die Grenzdialekte des Deutschen. In Nicole Palliwoda, Verena Sauer & Stephanie Sauermilch (eds.). 2019. *Politische Grenzen – sprachliche Grenzen? Dialektgeographische und wahrnehmungsdialektologische Perspektiven im deutschsprachigen Raum*, 31–45. Berlin & Boston: De Gruyter Mouton.

Szmrecsanyi, Benedikt & Lieselotte Anderwald. 2018. Corpus-based approaches to dialect study. In Charles Boberg, John Nerbonne & Dominic Watt (eds.), *The Handbook of Dialectology*, 300–313. Malden, MA: Wiley-Blackwell.

Sobolev, Andrey N. 2001a. Balkanskaia leksika v areal'nom i areal'no-tipologicheskom osveshchenii [Balkan lexicon in the the light of areal and areal-typological study]. *Voprosy iazykoznaniia* 2. 59–93.

Sobolev, Andrey N. 2001b. *Bolgarskii shirokolykskii govor. Sintaksis. Leksika dukhovnoi kul'tury. Teksty* [The Bulgarian Shiroka Lyka dialect. Syntax. Cultural lexicon. Texts]. Marburg: Biblion Verlag.

Sobolev, Andrey N. 2001c. Das Sankt Petersburger Projekt eines dialektologischen Atlasses der Balkansprachen. *Studien zum Südosteuropasprachatlas* (Grundfragen eines Südosteuropa-Sprachatlas. Geschichte. Problematik. Method. Pilotprojekt), Vol. 1, 55–68. Marburg: Biblion Verlag.

Sobolev, Andrey N. 2004a. Analytische Tendenzen in den balkanslavischen Dialekten vor dem allgemeinbalkanischen Hintergrund. In Uwe Hinrichs (ed.), *Die europäischen Sprachen auf dem Weg zum analytischen Sprachtyp*, 243–262. Wiesbaden: Harrassowitz.

Sobolev, Andrey N. 2004b. On the areal distribution of syntactical properties in the languages of the Balkans. In Olga Mišeska-Tomic (ed.), *Balkan Syntax and Semantics*, 59–100. Leiden: Benjamins.

Sobolev, Andrey N. 2006. Iuzhnoslavianskii instrumental i ego balkanske ekvivalenty (instrumental'nost' v pole pritiazheniia agentivnosti i patsientivnosti) [The South-Slavic instrumental and its Balkan equivalents (instrumentality in the poles of attraction toward the agent or patient)]. *Prilozi na Makedonskata akademija na naukite i umetnostite* 2. 59–71.

Sobolev, Andrey N. 2011a. Antibalkanizmy [Antibalkanisms]. *Južnoslovenski filolog* 67. 185–195.

Sobolev, Andrey N. 2011b. Rumynskie shtudii Kopitara i vozniknovenie akademicheskoi balkanistiki [Kopitar's Romanian studies and the emergence of academic Balkan studies]. *Studia linguistica et philologica. Omagiu profesorului Nicolae Saramandu*, 713–724. Bucharest: Editura Universităţii.

Sobolev, Andrey N. 2012. On redundancy in Albanian. In Domosiletskaia, Marina V., Alvina V. Zhugra, Maria S. Morozova & Alexander Yu. Rusakov (eds.), *Sovremennaia albanistika: dostizheniia i perspektivy* [Contemporary Albanology: Achievements and Perspectives], 407–412. St. Petersburg: Nestor-Istoriia.

Sobolev, Andrey N. 2013. *Osnovy lingvokul'turnoi antropogeografii Balkanskogo poluostrova. Tom I. Homo balcanicus i ego prostranstvo* [Foundations of linguocultural anthropogeography on the Balkan peninsula. Vol. 1. Homo balcanicus and his space]. St. Petersburg, München: Nauka, Otto Sagner Verlag.

Sobolev, Andrey N. 2014. Theoriebildung in der Dialektologie: historisch-vergleichende Beschreibung. In Peter Kosta, Karl Gutschmidt & Sebastian Kempgen (eds.), *Die Slavischen Sprachen, ein internationales Handbuch zu ihrer Struktur, ihrer Geschichte und ihrer Erforschung*, Vol. 2, 2067–2074. Berlin & Boston: De Gruyter Mouton.

Sobolev, Andrey N. 2015. Mrkovichi (i Gorana): iazyki i dialekty chernogorskogo Primor'ia v kontekste noveishikh balkanisticheskikh issledovanii [Mrkovići (and Gorana): Languages and dialects of the Montenegro coast in the context of recent Balkan research]. In Demiraj Bardhyl (ed.), *Sprache und Kultur der Albaner: Zeitliche und raumliche Dimensionen. Akten der 5. Deutsch-albanischen kulturwissenschaftlichen Tagung (Albanien, Buçimas bei Pogradec, 5.–8. Juni 2014)*, 533–556. Wiesbaden: Harrassowitz.

Sobolev, Andrey N. 2016. Sravnitel'no-istoričeskoe i areal'no-tipologičeskoe izučenie balkanskih dialektov: aktual'nye voprosy teorii. [Comparative-historical and areal-typological research in Balkan dialects]. *Linguistique Balkanique* 1. 53–74.

Sobolev, Andrey N. 2017. Iazyki simbioticheskikh soobschestv Zapadnykh Balkan: grecheskii i albanskii iazyki v sele Paliasa v kraine Himara, Albaniii [Languages in the Western Balkan Symbiotic Societies: Greek and Albanian in Palasa, Himara, Albania]. *Vestnik Sankt-Peterburgskogo gosudarstvennogo universiteta. Iazyk i literatura* 14 (3), 421–442.

Sobolev, Andrey N. 2019. Slavic dialects in the Balkans: unified and diverse, recipient and donor In Motoki Nomachi & Andriy Danylenko (eds.), *Slavic on the Language Map of Europe. Historical and Areal-Typological Dimensions*, 315–346. Berlin & Boston: De Gruyter Mouton.

Sobolev, Andrey N. & Novik, Aleksandr A. 2013. *Golo Bordo (Gollobordë), Albaniia. Materialy balkanskoi ekspeditsii RAN i SPbGU 2008–2010 gg.* [Golo Bordo (Gollorbordë), Albania. Materials from the Balkan expedition of the RAN and SPSU, 2008–2010]. St. Petersburg: Nauka; München: Verlag Otto Sagner.
Steinke, Klaus & Christian Voss (eds.). 2007. *The Pomaks in Greece and Bulgaria. A model case for borderland minorities in the Balkans.* München: Verlag Otto Sagner.
Steinke, Klaus & Xhelal Ylli. 2007–2013. *Die slavischen Minderheiten in Albanien (SMA).* Vol. 1–4. München: Verlag Otto Sagner.
Steinke, Klaus. 2014. Balkanlinguistik. In Uwe Hinrichs et al. (eds.), *Handbuch Balkan*, 434–451. Wiesbaden: Harrassowitz.
Sveshnikova, Tat'iana N. 2003. *Sintaksis rumynskogo glagola. Kon"iunktiv i ego transformy* [Syntax of the Romanian verb. The conjunctive and its forms]. Moscow: RAN.
Thomason, Sarah G. 2001. *Language contact.* Edinburgh: Edinburgh University Press.
Tomić, Olga Mišeska. 2006. *Balkan Sprachbund. Morpho-Syntactic Features.* Dordrecht: Springer.
Trubetzkoy, Nikolai S. 1928. Proposition 16. In *Actes du Premier Congrès International de Linguistes du 10–15 avril, 1928*, 17–18. Leiden: Sijthoff.
Trudgill, Peter. 1974. *Sociolinguistics. An introduction.* Harmondsworth: Penguin Books.
Tsiv'ian, Tat'iana V. 2008. Kontsept iazykovogo soiuza i sovremennaia balkanistika [The concept of Sprachbund in contemporary Balkan studies]. In Tat'iana V. Tsiv'ian (ed.), *Iazyk: tema i variatsii*, Vol. 2, 13–47. Moscow: Nauka.
Viereck [Firek], Wolfgang [Vol'fgang]. 2003. Lingvisticheskii atlas Evropy i ego vklad v evropeiskuiu istoriiu kul'tury: rezul'taty issledovanii v ramkakh proekta Atlas Linguarum Europae [The Linguistic Atlas of Europe and its contribution to the European history of culture: results of research in the *Atlas Linguarum Europae* project]. *Voprosy iazykoznaniia* 5. 30–39.
Vilinbakhova, Elena L. 2015. *Lingvisticheskoe izuchenie stereotipov. Materialy k kursu lektsii* [The linguistic study of stereotypes. Materials for a lecture series]. St. Petersburg, manuscript.
Voss, Christian. 2015. South Slavic Studies in Germany. In Christian Promitzer, Siegfried Gruber & Harald Heppner (eds.), *Southeast European Studies in a Globalizing World*, 141–152. Berlin: LIT-Verlag.
Wiemer, Björn. 2014. Quo vadis grammaticalization theory? Why complex language change is like words. In Ferdinand von Mengden & Horst Simon (eds.), *Refining grammaticalization (Folia Linguistica* 48 (2)), 425–468.
Wiemer, Björn et al. 2014. Convergence in the Baltic-Slavic Contact Zone. Triangulation approach. https://www.researchgate.net/publication/ 341151684_Convergence_in_the_ Baltic-Slavic_Sontact_Zone_Triangulation_approach (accessed March 15, 2021).
Ylli [Iully], Xhelal [Dzhelial'] & Andrey N. Sobolev. 2002. *Albanskii toskskii govor sela Leshnia (Kraina Skrapar). Sintaksis. Leksika. Etnolingvistika. Teksty.* [The Albanian-Tosk subdialect of the town of Leshnia (Skrapar Krajina). Syntax. Lexicon. Ethnolinguistics. Texts]. Marburg: Biblion Verlag.
Ylli [Iully], Xhelal [Dzhelial'] & Andrey N. Sobolev. 2003. *Albanskii gegskii govor sela Mukhurr (Kraina Dibyr). Sintaksis. Leksika. Etnolingvistika. Teksty.* [The Albanian-Gheg subdialect of the town of Mukhurr (Dibyr Krajina). Syntax. Lexicon. Ethnolinguistics. Texts]. München: Biblion Verlag.
Zimmerli, Jacob. 1891–1899. *Die deutsch-französische Sprachgrenze in der Schweiz.* Basel. Genève: Georg.

Abbreviations

Language names

Alb	Albanian	Lat	Latin
AncDor	Ancient Doric	Lesb	Lesbian
AncGr	Ancient Greek	Maced	Macedonian
Arom	Aromanian	MeglRom	Megleno-Romanian
AttGr	Attic Greek	MGr	Modern Greek
Azov	Azov Greek	MS	Montenegrin/Serbian
Balt	Baltic	NGr	Northern Greek
Ban	Banat Romanian	NTGr	New Testament Greek
BCMS	Bosnian/Croatian/Montenegrin/Serbian	OChSl	Old Church Slavonic/Slavic
		Pal	Greek idiom of Palasa
Bulg	Bulgarian	Proto-Alb	Proto-Albanian
Cret	Cretan	Protoslav/PSl	Proto-Slavic
Cypr	Cypriot	Rom	Romanian
Eng	English	Rus	Russian
Fr	French	Serb/Sr	Serbian
Germ	German	Serb-Cr	Serbo-Croatian
Gr	Greek	Slav	Slavic
Hung	Hungarian	SSlav	South Slavic
It	Italian	Thess	Thessalian
KDG	Krashovani Dialect Group	Tr	Turkish
KrSl	Krashovani Slavic	Tsak	Tsakonian
Lac	Laconian	Ven	Venetian Italian

Interlineal glosses

1	first person	INDF	indefinite
2	second person	INF	infinitive
3	third person	INSTR	instrumental
ACC	accusative	IPF	imperfect
ADJ	adjective	IPFV	imperfective
ADV	adverb	LOC	locative
AOR	aorist	M	masculine
AUX	auxiliary	N	neuter
COM	comitative	NEG	negative (particle)
DAT	dative	NF	any gender, except feminine
DEF	definite	NGEN	any case, except genitive
F	feminine	NN	any gender, except neuter
FUT	future	NOM	nominative
GEN	genitive	NUM	numeral, number
IMP	imperfect	OBL	oblique
INACT	inactive (voice)	PFV	perfective

PL	plural	PTCP	participle
POSS	possessive	REFL	reflexive
PP	past participle	REP	reported
PREP	preposition	SBJV	subjunctive
PRES	present	SG	singular
PRET	preterite	SM	subordinating marker
PRF	perfect	STRNG	strong
PRO	pronoun	VOC	vocative
PRS	present	WH.Q	wh-question
PST	past	WK	weak
PTCL	particle		

Other abbreviations

BER	*Bŭlgarski etimologičen rečnik* [Bulgarian Etymological Dictionary]
comp.	compare
DER	*Dicţionarul etimologic al limbii române* (Ciorănescu 2001)
DEX	*Dicţionarul explicativ al limbii române* (DEX 2009)
dim.	diminutive
DLRLC	*Dicţionarul limbii romîne literare contemporane* (DLRLC 1955–1957)
DOB	date of birth
GI	Glagolitic inscriptions
HJP	*Hrvatski jezični portal* (HJP 2018)
lit.	literally (word for word translation)
MDABL	*Minor Dialectological Atlas of Balkan Languages*
pop.	popular
prob.	probably
reg.	regional
RPSSh	*Republika Popullore Socialiste e Shqipërisë* [People's Socialist Republic of Albania]
VS	*Statute of Vrbnik*

Index of names

Adamou, Evangelia 32, 41, 66, 143, 149, 217, 297
Ahmetaj, Mehmet 60
Aikhenvald, Alexandra Y. 8, 10, 90
Alinei, Mario 288, 290
Anderwald, Lieselotte 298
Andriṓtēs, Nikólaos 148, 301
Arapi, Ina 302
Asenova, Petya 21, 72, 73, 193, 286, 287, 294, 300, 306
Auer, Peter 291, 292
Auwera, Johan van der 272
Avanesov, Ruben I. 298

Babe, Σpiro 140, 147
Baciuna 173
Balša III 94
Balšići 94
Bara, Maria 81, 163, 303
Barth, Fredrik 138, 140, 158, 191, 306
Bernshtein, Samuil B. 288
Beul 162, 173
Beyazit II, Sultan 265
Birchall, Joshua 290
Bisang, Walter 28, 35, 51
Bjeletić, Marta 48
Bógkas (Mpógkas), Euángelos Ath. 137
Bolizza, Mariano 94, 95
Borgia, Nilo 136, 140
Bosanich (Bosanig), Nicolaus 201
Božanić, Barić 202
Brown, Christopher G. 137, 139, 295
Buchholz, Olga 81, 237
Bunis, David M. 267
Burkhart, Dagmar 137

Çabej, Eqrem 148, 301, 302
Çaçi, Elpiniqi Kosta 147
Çaço 140
Campbell, Lyle 5, 8, 28, 289, 290, 297
Čapo, Jasna 288
Ceapă 173
Ceaușescu, Nicolae 163
Cepenkov, Marko 280
Charalampopoulos, Agathoclis 217, 227, 233, 235

Chatzipanagiotis, Costas 223
Chioru 173
Ciorănescu, Alexandru I. 175, 177–179, 250, 301, 302
Coetsem, Frans van 7, 8, 18, 41, 92, 117
Constantine Porphyrogenitus 222
Constantinopoulos, Christos G. 224
Costakis, Thanassis 218, 222, 226, 227, 231, 232, 242
Crews, Cynthia M. 267
Crnojevići 94
Curtis, Matthew Cowan 9, 77, 98, 106, 122, 138, 306, 307
Cvetanovski, Goce 63
Cvijić, Jovan 61
Cvitović, Marin 202
Cyril 192
Cyxun, Gennadiy A. 29, 297

Dahl, Östen 14
Dapčevići (family) 96
Deanović, Mirko 191
Deffner, Michael 217, 224, 226–228, 231
Demiraj, Shaban 5, 72
Desnitskaya, Agniya V. 7, 63, 103, 135, 136, 138, 193, 226, 287
Dibre 96
Dion, Nathalie 168
Domashnev, Anatolii I. 289
Dombrowski, Andrew 29, 31, 138
Domosiletskaia, Marina V. 29, 50, 142, 298
Drinka, Bridget 5, 13, 28, 300
Drusinich, Gerga 201
Dryer, Matthew 288
Dugushina, Alexandra S. 91, 96, 99, 306

Epps, Patience 290
Erdeljanović, Jovan 97, 161, 162
Ermolin, Denis S. 91
Eugene of Savoy 160
Evliya Çelebi 226
Evreinova, Anna M. 193

Fallmerayer, Jakob Philipp 216
Fedchenko, Valentina 225, 231, 232, 235, 240, 246

Ferguson, Charles 292
Fiedler, Wilfried 5, 237
Fielder, Grace E. 77, 81
Filka 173
Fine, John V. A. 31, 94
Fleming, Luke 306
Friedman, Victor A. 1, 2, 4, 5, 8, 9, 13, 19, 21, 28, 90, 265, 267, 268, 270, 277–280, 287, 289, 294, 304
Fryd, Marc 79
Fučić, Branko 193
Fugošiĉ 189, 208
Fugossich, Mattheus 201
Furrer, Norbert 139, 290, 291

Gabinskii, Mark A. 267, 302, 303
Gaidova, Ubavka 63
Gal, Susan 297
Gardani, Francesco 18
Gâscă 173
Gashi, Skënder 138
Georgiev, Petŭr 60
Ghersanus 201
Ghițoi 173
Giakoumis, Konstantinos 136
Gjikuri, Arianti Spiro 147
Gjinajt 140
Gjinari, Jorgji 5, 45, 47, 63, 102, 103, 105, 111, 116
Gjin 140
Gołąb (Golomb), Zbigniew (Zbignjev) 3, 7, 64, 84, 138
Golant, Natal'ia G. 225
Graves, Nina 77, 82
Gregorič Bon, Nataša 137
Grillo, Helena 136

Hadži-Vasiljević, Jovan 61
Hallig, Rudolf 189
Hannerca, Ulf 293
Harris, Salome 9
Hasani, Liri 140
Haspelmath, Martin 8, 41, 66, 73, 120, 197, 199, 200, 204, 239, 288–290, 293, 294, 298
Heine, Berndt 21
Hesseling, Dirk Christiaan 217
Hinrichs, Uwe 28, 34, 73, 137, 138, 158, 288, 289, 293

Holtus, Günter 137

Ianachieschi-Vlahu, Iancu 81
Ibrahim Pasha of Egypt (Ibrahim) 223
Ifca, Nicușor 170, 173
Irvine, Judith T. 297
Ismajli, Rexhep 7, 137
Ivanovići 96
Ivanov, Jordan N. 60
Ivanov, Valeriy V. 164
Ivanov, Vyacheslav 225

Jackson, Jean 306
Jireček, Konstantin 60
Johansson, Lars 30
Joseph, Brian D. IX, 1, 2, 4, 5, 8, 9, 17–19, 21, 28, 90, 135–137, 139, 168, 217, 237, 241, 265, 267, 268, 270, 273–275, 277, 278, 280, 287, 288, 294–296, 298, 302, 304
Jovanovski, Vlado 59–62, 68
Jovićević, Andrija 9, 37, 91, 99
Jusufi, Lumnije 61, 63

Kahl, Thede 81
Karanastasis, Athanasios 244
Kashta, Dhimitrulla 147
Kaufman, Terrence 6, 68, 90, 115, 129, 209
Kisilier, Maksim L. IX, 4, 14, 47, 50, 137, 215–218, 224–232, 234, 238–241, 243, 244, 246, 247, 306
Klepikova, Galina P. 158, 288
Kniesza, István 160
Koka, Pavllo 139, 140, 147
Kokavēsē, Eleonṓra-Elénē 137
Kokora 173
Kola, Gjeto 136
Kondis, Basil 135
Koneski, Blaže 62, 76, 77
Konior (Koner), Daria V. VII, IX, 3, 6, 14–17, 19–21, 36, 41, 64, 65, 157, 158, 161, 163, 164, 171–174, 181, 183, 215, 305
Konomi 144
Kontomíchēs, Pantazḗs 148
Kontosopoulos, Nikolaos 217, 230, 244, 246
Kopitar, Jernej K. 34, 72, 288
Koptjevskaja-Tamm, Maria 5
Kosheleva, Irina S. 290

Kosta, Peter 147, 288, 295, 296
Kovačevići 97
Kozak, Vyacheslav V. VII, IX, 6, 47, 50, 189, 305
Kramer, Christina E. 273, 274
Kramer, Johannes 137
Kuči, see *Index of places*
Kukudis, Asterios 64
Kulo, Llazar Marko 147
Kŭnchov (Kŭnčov), Vasil 60, 64, 68
Kurz, Jozef 300
Kuteva, Tania 21
Kuzmić, Boris 208
Kyriazḗs, Dṓrēs K., see *Qirjazi, Dhori*

Labov, William 234
Lackul 162
Lakovići 96
Lameli, Alfred 291
Leake, William Martin 135, 221
Lehman, Rosa 138, 158
Leluda-Voss, Christina 148, 303
Ligorio, Orsat 191, 197
Lindstedt, Youko 2, 72, 73, 79, 82, 90
Liosis, Nikos 226, 228–230, 235, 239, 241, 242, 250
Lítsios, Fílippas 136
Loma, Aleksandar 160
Lüpke, Friederike 9, 11, 91
Luria, Max A. 267

Makarova, Anastasia L. VII, 5, 12, 13, 20, 21, 46, 59, 64, 65, 91, 164, 301, 305, 306
Makartsev, Maxim M. 73, 77
Malltezi, Luan 136
Manta, Eleutheria 135
Manzini, Rita M. 288
Marković, Marjan 72, 73, 81
Marku, Xristina 21
Massey, Victoria W. 81
Matras, Yaron 7, 15–17, 20, 21, 90, 109, 123, 182, 299
Matzinger, Joachim 302
Mëhilli 140
Mehmet the Conqueror 222
Melich, János 160
Memushaj, Rami 103, 136
Mendeleev, Dmitrii I. 304

Mërkot, see *Index of places*
Methodius 192
Michaelis, Susanne M. 41, 294
Miklosich (Miklošić), Franz R. 72, 294
Mikulčić, Ivan 60
Milaj 140
Milin, Jiva 165, 166
Miloradović (Miloradovich), Sofia 110
Milu, Fevronia 142
Milu, Paraskevula 142
Mindak, Jolanta 62
Mladenova, Olga 297
Momeva, Viktorija 62
Montoliu, César 272
Morozova, Mariia S. VIII, 2, 6, 9, 11, 16–22, 36, 41, 47, 48, 50, 89–91, 96, 97, 99–101, 103, 104, 115–117, 122, 125, 126, 129, 138, 303, 306
Moschos, John 239
Mrkovići, see *Index of places*
Mufwene, Salikoko 139, 293
Muljačić, Žarko 138, 190, 191
Muysken, Pieter 31, 41, 66, 90, 92, 102, 138, 143, 144

Narumov, Boris 64, 72, 190, 191
Nasi, Lefter 37, 136
Nastev, Božidar 303
Nevaci, Manuela 81
Newton, Brian 244
Nikdedaj 140
Novik, Alexander A. 3, 10, 32, 41, 47, 50, 91, 115, 119, 135, 137, 138, 144, 216, 217, 305–307

Opala, Joseph A. 290
Orel, Vladimir 148, 301, 302
Orlova, Varvara G. 298
Orozco, Rafael 273
Osmani, Zihni 63, 72, 83
Osmanovići 97

Paço 140
Padineanț 173
Pjanka, Vloǵimjež 61
Papadhates 140
Papahagi, Tache 81, 249, 301
Pausanias 220, 222

Pavković, Nikola 160, 161
Pavlović, Cvetko 60
Pavlović, Milivoj 35
Perez-Leroux, Ana Teresa 273, 274
Pernot, Hubert 227, 230, 244, 246
Pešikan, Mitar 94
Petrović, Dragoljub 103
Petrovici, Emil 158, 160, 162–166, 170
Pitsios, Theodoros 221
Pižurica, Mato 110
Plotnikova, Anna A. 70, 142, 175
Poloska, Agim 63
Poplack, Shana 40, 167, 168
Popović, Ivan 161, 162
Prendergast, Eric Heath 29
Preston, Dennis R. 291
Pulaha, Selami 91, 94
Purschke, Christoph 292
Pușcă 173
Putnam, Hilary 287

Qirjazi, Dhori, alias *Kyriazḗs, Dṓrēs K.* 137, 138, 143

Rackovići 96
Radan, Mihai 157, 158, 160–167, 169, 181
Ralli, Angela 241, 244
Rebegila 173
Reiter, Norbert 289, 297
Rolle, Nicholas 290
Ross, Malcolm D. 21
Rusakov, Alexander Yu. VII, VIII, 1, 2, 8, 9, 13, 18–20, 30, 31, 36, 41, 73, 89–91, 97, 99–102, 122, 126, 138, 215, 285, 295, 296, 298, 299, 304

St. Andreas 305
St. Andrew 146
St. Barbara 146
St. Francis 201–203
St. Ignatius 146
Sala, Marius 267, 269
Salminen, Tapani 233
Samuel, king 60, 64
Sandfeld, Kristian 72, 286, 300
Sandry, Susan 297
Sankoff, David 167, 168

Saramandu, Nicolae 81
Sauermilch, Stephanie 291
Savoia, Leonardo 288
Sawicka, Irena 304
Schaller, Helmut W. 73, 279, 281
Scheiner, Walther 160
Schirò, Joseph 136
Schumacher, Stefan 302
Schutz (Schütz), Ishtvan 137
Schwyzer, Edward 227, 229
Šekularac, Božidar 60
Selishchev (Seliščev), Afanasii M. 61, 287
Sephiha, Haim Vidal 267
Shishko, Arqile 147
Shkurtaj, Gjovalin 103
Sichinava, Dmitrii V. 82
Silva-Corvalán, Carmen 51
Sims, Andrea D. 273
Simu, Traian 162, 164, 181
Sinanaj 140
Singer, Ruth 9
Skanderbeg 3
Šklifov, Blagoi 63
Skok, Petar 137, 175–178, 181, 191
Slobin, Dan I. 270
Smirnitskaya, Svetlana V. 290
Smith, Norval 138, 306
Smits, Tom F. H. 292
Sobolev, Andrey N. VII–X, 1, 3, 5, 9, 10, 12, 19–21, 27–52, 60, 70, 81, 84, 90, 91, 93, 95, 98, 99, 102, 105, 106, 110, 115, 117, 119, 121, 122, 125, 135–150, 158, 164, 171–173, 190, 193, 216, 217, 285–307
Sokolski, Metodija 60
Sotiri, Natasha 136, 140
Spiro, Maylinda 135, 137, 142
Spiro (Spýrou), Aristotélēs H. 135, 137, 142
Stanišić, Vanja 117, 120
Steinke, Klaus 10, 294, 297
Stern, Dieter 34, 138
Strabo 222, 224
Straică 173
Studemund, Michael 267
Subak, Julius 277
Šufflay, Milan 138
Sukhachev, Nikolai L. 29
Sveshnikova, Tat'iana N. 302, 303

Sveti Ilija 168
Symeonides, Haralambos 267
Syrku, Polihroniy A. 37, 170
Szmrecsanyi, Benedikt 298

Tadmor, Uri 199, 200, 204
Tahiri 97
Tahirovići 97
Tekavčić, Pavao 191, 197
Theseus 225
Thomason, Sarah G. 6–8, 13, 18, 28, 49, 68, 90, 92, 115, 129, 209, 289, 299
Thomo, Pirro 139
Thucydides 222
Thumb, Albert 224, 273
Tirta, Mark 136, 143, 145
Todoriani, Maria 142, 144
Tolstoi (Tolstoy), Nikita I. 180, 287
Toma 173
Tomici, Mile 173
Tomić, Olga Mišeska 5, 164, 173, 295
Torres Cacoullos, Rena 50
Totoni, Minella 136
Travis, Catherine E. 50
Trimble, Walker X
Trubetzkoy, Nikolai S. 289
Trudgill, Peter 22, 216, 229, 244, 245, 292
Tsiv'ian, Tat'iana V. 304
Ture, Ivan od' 208
Tzitzilis, Christos 227, 229, 238, 239

Ursul 173

Vagiakákos, Dikaíos V. 137
Valcich, Jurchus 201
Valkouich, Nicolaus 201
van Coetsem, Frans 7, 8, 18, 41, 92, 117

Vekarić, Nenad 138
Velkovska, Snežana 79
Vidoeski, Božidar 62, 63, 72
Viereck (Firek), Volfgang (Vol'fgang) 290
Vilinbakhova, Elena L. 287
Villoison, Jean-Baptiste-Gaspard d'Ansse de 226
Vinja, Vojmir 191
Vlčijiĉ, Matij 208
Voss, Christian 288, 289, 297
Vrabie, Emil 81
Vučići 97
Vujović, Luka 48, 91, 95, 96, 98, 99, 102, 103, 105, 106, 108, 109, 111, 115, 119, 122
Vuletić, Nikola 191

Wagner, Max L. 267, 274
Wahlström, Max 29
Wälchli, Bernhard 5, 22
Walter, Simon 267
Wartburg, Walter von 189
Weigand, Gustav 64, 160
Weinreich, Uriel 7, 21, 116
Wexler, Paul 266, 267, 280
Wiemer, Björn 5, 22, 74, 289, 290
Winford, Daniel 8
Winnifrith, Tom J. 64

Xhelilaj 140

Ylli (Iully), Xhelal (Dzhelial') 10, 47, 147, 297, 303

Zheltova, Ekaterina A. 12, 137
Zimmerli, Jacob 290
Županović, Šime 191
Zutinis, Jacobus de 201

Index of places

Achaea 220, 222
Adriatic Sea V, 92, 137, 190, 191
Aegean Sea 266
Agios Andreas 218, 219, 224, 230, 231, 234, 236
Agrafa 229
Albania V, VI, VIII, IX, X, 4, 11, 12, 22, 27, 31, 32, 34, 36, 39, 41, 42, 47, 49, 60, 64, 81, 92, 95, 96, 99, 135–139, 141, 144, 145, 150, 168, 216, 217, 295, 306
Alpine region 190
Ana e Malit VI, 92, 93, 95–99, 306
Anatolia 4
Anina 157, 163
Arad 157
Arkadia 218
Arvati 12, 13, 61–63, 68, 69, 306
Asamati 61
Asia Minor 217, 218, 225, 229, 230, 237
Athens 223, 229, 244–246
Australia 223
Austria 163, 172
Austro-Hungarian Empire 2, 166, 181
Azov Sea 216, 226, 238, 241, 244–246

Bačka 106, 160, 163
Balasa, see *Palasa*
Balkan Peninsula V, 4, 28, 29, 41, 59, 60, 73, 158, 160–162, 192, 193, 209, 294, 295, 297, 304
Balkans V, VII, VIII, 1–6, 10, 14, 21, 22, 27–35, 41, 45, 51, 90, 91, 116, 121, 137–139, 141, 158, 159, 162, 182, 190, 225, 265–274, 277–281, 285, 293, 294, 299, 300, 307
Banat (Romanian Banat, Serbian Banat) IX, 3, 106, 157–167, 169, 171, 175, 180–183, 305
Bar 89, 92, 94–96, 99, 103, 115
Belareca 160
Belgrade 267
Berlin 95
Bitola 61, 266–269, 274
Bojana (Bunë) 92, 95
Bolno 61
Borkeš 178

Bosnia and Herzegovina 163
Bosnia-Hercegovina 266
Brajčino (Braichino) 70
Brda 96
Bregu i Poshtëm 136
Bregu i Sipërm 136
Bucharest 266, 267, 269
Budva 103
Bulgaria V, 5, 31, 266, 267, 295
Bunë, see *Bojana*
burimi i Dhikules 139

Carașova, see *Karaševo*
Cetatea Turcului (Turski grad, Castrum Crassou) 162
Cetinje 96
Checea 165
Chicera Comării 159
China 225
Chios 266
Cimarra, see *Himara*
Clocotici 157, 164
Čoka (Șoacă) 178, 179
Constantinople 222, 223, 266, 274
Corfu 136, 266
Cres 190
Crete 237
Crimea 216, 222
Crnogorsko Primorje, see *Montenegrin Coast*
Croatia VI, IX, X, 31, 39, 163, 164, 189, 305
Cumgni 95
Cuptoare 162
Cutina 160
Cyclades 245
Cyprus 226

Dabezići 92, 94, 95
Dacia 158
Dafnon 219
Dalmatia 6, 14, 163, 190–192, 198, 208, 209, 266, 286
Danube 158–160, 162
Dapčevići (Dobčevići) (clan and village) 92, 95, 121

Dealu Lipondij 178, 179
Debar (Dibër, Dibra) VI, 4, 27, 32, 33, 41, 96, 298
Delvina 136, 295
Dhërmi (Dhermi) 136, 142, 143
Dinaric region 190
Dobra Voda 92, 95, 96
Dobrinj 208
Dolina 178
Dolna Prespa 60, 63
Doman 162
Dos 178, 179, 271
Drimades, see also *Dhërmi* 140
Dropull VI, 136, 216, 217
Dubova 160
Dubrovnik 191
Dukati 139–141

Eastern Albania VI, 27, 295
Eastern Serbia VI, 183, 295, 296
Egypt 223
England 279
Epirus 135
Eratyra 237, 249
Europe V, VII, X, 34, 52, 64, 120, 158, 265, 286–290

Faca Mikula 178
faqja e Abjenbrit 139
faqja e Gjipogës 139
faqja e Pandaleos 139
faqja e Pirit 139
faqja e Pjerivallos 139
faqja e Qerashes 139
France 223, 265
fráŋgo 220, 250

Gabrova 178
Geraki 221
Germany 70, 163, 223, 289
Glâmboaca (Glâmboca) 158
Golloborda VI, 3, 10–12, 14, 15, 19–22, 27, 32, 33, 41–43, 47, 49, 50, 286, 306
Gönen 218
Gora 295, 306
Gorana VIII, 2, 4, 8–11, 15–22, 42, 48, 49, 89, 91–109, 111–115, 117–119, 121–130, 306

Gorna Bela Crkva 61, 63
Gorna Belica 19, 74
Gorna Prespa 19, 62, 63, 68
Grahovac 97
Grahovo 97
Grdovići (Gradojevich) 92, 95
Great Prespa Lake VIII, 2, 59, 60, 62
Greece V, VI, IX, X, 4, 22, 39, 60, 64, 81, 135, 215–219, 221–223, 225, 234, 237, 244, 266, 268, 295, 306
Grnčari (Grnchari) 61
Gusinje 98

Havoutsi (Havousi) 218
Himara (Himarë, Cimarra) VI, IX, 3, 11, 12, 15, 16, 21, 22, 36, 39, 121, 135–144, 149, 150, 168, 217, 286, 295
Hungary 158–160
  Kingdom of ~ 160

Iabalcea VI, IX, 3, 14, 15, 19, 20, 22, 157, 159, 162, 164, 167, 170–175, 177–182, 305, 306
Iberia 269
Indol 158
Ioannina 266
Ionian (Sea) 148, 246, 266
Israel 266
Istanbul 17, 76, 78, 82, 266, 267, 270
Istria 192, 305
Istrian peninsula 190
Italy 163, 217, 223, 237
Izmir 267

Kalimani 95
Kameno polje (Poiana Stâncoasă) 178
Karaševo (Karasheno, Caraşova) VI, IX, 3, 14–22, 36, 37, 39, 157, 159, 162, 164, 165, 171, 173–175, 177, 179–182, 286
Karpathos 229
Kastanitsa 218, 219, 221, 223, 230–232, 234, 235
Kastelli 148, 249
Kastoria 268
Katërkollë (Vladimir) 97
Kičer 178
Klezna 99
Klisura 165

Kobilina Gropa (Groapa lepii) 178
Koći (Kojë) 97
Kod studenci 178
Komarnik 178
Korlan 179
Kosovo 31, 34, 110, 165
Kotor 103
Kraja (Krajë) 41, 92, 95, 96, 103
Krajina 41, 94, 306
Krajište 178
Krani 12, 61–63, 69, 70, 79
Krashovani villages 14, 157, 159, 162, 164, 166, 167, 170, 171, 173, 174, 179, 182
Krъguja 179
Kriči 95
Krk (island) VI, IX, 1, 4, 14, 189–195, 198, 201, 204, 209, 286, 306
Krk (town) 190
Krno polje 178
Krstin hrt 179
Kruče 95
Kruja 140
Kruševac 161, 162
Kruševo (Krushevo) 64, 71, 81, 161
Kuči (community, or *pleme*, and area) 94, 96, 97
Kunje 92, 95, 105, 124
kurrizi i Fajevos 139
kurrizi i Skantavës 139
Kvarner 190, 192, 305
Kvarner Archipelago 305
Kynouria 218

Laberia (Labëria) VI, 136, 140, 141, 143, 150
Laconia 218, 219
Lake Skadar 92, 94, 103
Lefkadia 148
Leonidio 218, 219, 221–223, 225, 230, 233, 234, 251
Lika 163, 192
Lisinj 92
Livadi 233
Lješanska Nahija 96
Lješkovac 92, 93, 95, 99
Lošinj 190
Lovćen 298
Lugoj 160

lumi i Vreshtirës 139
Lunje 92, 117
Lupac 157, 164

Macedonia VI, VIII, X, 4, 12, 17, 31, 41, 59, 60, 63, 64, 68, 70, 73, 74, 79, 81, 138, 218, 221, 229, 266–268, 279, 299, 301, 306
Mala Gorana 92, 94, 95, 103, 108, 109, 127
Malesia (Malësia) 32
malet e Mesofijes 139
Malevišta (Malevishta) 61
Malevos 220, 250
mali i Paliskës 139
mali i Plepit 139
mali i Thanasit 139
Mali Kaliman 95
Mali Mikulići 92, 95
Mani 229
Marmara (Sea of) 218
Mediterranean 198, 208, 265
Međureč 92, 93, 95, 99
Melana 218, 220, 230–233, 235
Mërkot, see *Mrkovići*
Metohija 32
Michulichi (Mikulići) 95
Mide (Millë) 97
Military Frontier 160
Mirdita 140
Moçal 139
Moesia 298
Montenegrin Coast 52, 103, 306
Montenegro (Republic of) VI, VIII, X, 27, 28, 36, 41, 42, 49, 50, 89, 91–98, 102, 103, 105, 106, 115, 120, 128, 129, 144, 286
Morarul 159
Morava 162
Morea 221, 222
Moscopole 64, 73
Možura 92, 93
Mrkovići (Mrkojevići, Mërkojeviqi, Marchoeuich, Mërkot) (community, or *pleme*, clan, village, and area) VI, 2, 9, 10, 15–20, 22, 28, 36, 39, 41–43, 47– 50, 52, 89, 91–112, 115–117, 119–124, 127–130, 144, 286, 306
Muke 178
Mureş 159
múzya 220

Myrtoon Sea 219

Nădlac 161
Nafplio 222, 223, 226
Nahija Mërkodlar 94
Nakolec 61
Nermed 157, 164, 173
Netherlands 265
Nikšić 97
Niš 162
North Africa 265, 268
North-East Albania 61, 63, 94, 295
Northern Albania 7, 96, 117, 120, 135, 267
North Kynouria 218
North Macedonia (Republic of) VI, VIII, X, 4, 12, 59, 60, 64, 70, 73, 74, 79, 81, 221, 229, 299, 301, 306

Ohio VIII
Ohrid 2, 72, 73, 81, 298
Old Montenegro 94
Omišalj 208
Oriontas 220
Ottoman Empire 94, 95, 97, 160, 223, 266
Ouranoupoli 221

Padina saka 179
Pag 190
Palasa (Palasë) IX, 121, 135, 136, 139–149, 168, 306
Pannonian region 190
Parnon 218
Pašak 178
Pečurice 92, 95
Pelinkovići 93, 95, 99
Peloponnese VI, 140, 148, 216, 218, 220–226, 247, 249, 250, 298
Përmet 136
përroi i Thatë 139
përroi Radhimës 139
Peru 271
Pindos (Pindus) 229, 298
Piperi 94
Pirin 298
Plava 98
Poda 92, 96
Podgorica 98

Podmočani (Podmochani) 61
Pogon 136
Poiana Rusca 159
Polje (Câmp) 178
Portugal 265
Poulithra 220
Požarevac (Passarowitz) 160
Pragmateftis 218, 230, 231, 233
Prasíai (Brasíai) 222
Prastos 218, 220, 222–225, 230–236, 250, 251
Prespa VI, VIII, 2, 12, 13, 15, 18–20, 22, 59–65, 68, 69, 72, 74, 76, 77, 79, 83, 84, 286, 301, 306
Priština 162
Prizren 162
prroi i Parapotameos 139
prroi i Qerashës 139
pylli i Aljatheos 139
pylli i Dushkut 139
pylli i Shalceve 139

qafa e Shën Gjergjit 139

Rab 190
Rafnic 157, 164
Ravanj (Racé) 95
Ravnište 178
Recaș (Rekaš) 165, 166
Resava 111, 165
Resen 61, 64, 69–71, 81, 82
Resița (Ričica) 162
Rhine-Moselle 290
Rhodes 267
Rhodopi 298
Riza 136
Roman Empire 265
Romania VI, IX, X, 36, 157–159, 161, 163, 170, 221, 223, 266, 267
Rumija 92
Russia 223, 266
Russian Federation VII

Saint Petersburg VII, VIII, 89, 91, 135, 218, 287
Salonica 279
Sanjak of Scutari 94
Sapounakeika 218, 230–237
Sarajevo 267

Saranda 136, 295
serbetsía 220
Serbia VI, X, 96, 98, 106, 158–160, 163, 183, 266, 267, 295, 296
sern⁾áli 220
Severin county 158
Shestan 92, 95, 96
Shkodra 99
Sibiu county 158
Sitena 218–220, 230, 234, 235, 250
Sjenica 98
Skopje 64, 70, 162, 266
Skrapar 47, 147, 298
Skyros 246
Small Prespa Lake 60
Şoacă cu apă 179
Sofia 64, 267
South Eastern Europe V, VII, X, 34, 64, 286–288
South Kynouria 218
South Western Macedonia 63, 64
soxá 220
Spain 265, 266, 270
Srem 160
St. Achilles island 60
State Union of Serbia and Montenegro 96
Štip 266
Studenac 178
Sumbrak (Sumrak) 178
Sviniţa 164, 165
Symi 229

Tepelenë 140
Tërbaçi 139–141
Thessaloniki 266, 267, 269, 275
Thessaly 225
Timiş 161
Timişoara 157, 160
Timok 298
Tirol (Tilori) 157
Tisa 159, 160
Toplica 178
Transylvania 159
Trebisht (Trebišta) 42, 47, 49
Tsakonia IX, 215, 217–225, 232–234, 237, 238, 250, 251, 286, 306
tʃárko 220
Tuđemili 92, 96
Turda 158

Turkey 237, 266
Turopolje 163
Tyros 218–220, 222, 223, 230–237

Ulcinj 89, 92, 94–96, 99–101
Ulići 95
USA VIII, 135

Vaskina 218, 219, 222, 230–234, 236, 237
Vatika 218
Velebit 190
Velika čoka (Şoacă mare) 179
Velika Kapela 190
Velja Gorana VIII, 2, 4, 8–11, 15–22, 42, 48, 49, 89, 91–109, 111–115, 117–119, 121–130, 306
Velje Selo 92, 94, 95
Velji Kaliman 95
Velji Mikulići 92, 95
Venetian Republic 94
Venice IX, 198, 202, 209
Veroia 268
Vinodol 192
Vladimir, see Katërkollë
Vlora 136
Vodnic 157, 164
Vojvodina 160
Vranishti 139–141
Vranje 162
Vrbnik 189, 192, 193, 202, 207, 208
Vukići 93, 95, 99
Vulići 95
Vuno 144

Wallachia V
West Balkans V
West Macedonia 218

Yugoslavia (Federal Republic of, Socialist Federal Republic of) 2, 11, 95, 96, 123

Zadar 192
Zaggoli 220, 250
Zagreb 164, 193
Zaritse 220, 250
Zeta 98, 298
Zetska Ravnica 94
Župa Dubrovačka 192

Authors' profiles

Joseph, Brian D.
Born 22 November 1951, USA. Specialist in historical linguistics, language change, Greek linguistics, Balkan linguistics, and morphological theory. Distinguished University Professor of Linguistics and the Kenneth E. Naylor Professor of South Slavic Linguistics at The Ohio State University. Member of the American Philosophical Society (2019). President of the Linguistic Society of America (2019).

Profile: https://www.asc.ohio-state.edu/joseph.1

Kisilier, Maxim Lyvovich (Maxim L. Kisilier)
Born 14 May 1977, Leningrad, USSR. Specialist in Modern Greek Studies and Modern Greek dialectology, Candidate of Philological Sciences (PhD, Russia, 2003), Associate Professor at the St. Petersburg State University, Philological Faculty, Director of the Hellenic Institute of St. Petersburg State University, senior researcher at the Institute for Linguistic Studies at the Russian Academy of Sciences in St. Petersburg. Awarded a Badge of Honour from the Tsakonian Archive for contribution to preservation and description of the Tsakonian dialect of Modern Greek.

Profiles: https://spbu.academia.edu/MaximKisilier
https://www.researchgate.net/profile/Maxim_Kisilier

Morozova, Maria Sergeevna (Maria S. Morozova)
Born 11 September 1986, USSR. MA in Balkan Studies from Saint Petersburg State University (2010), PhD in Comparative, Typological and Contrastive Linguistics (diss. "The dialect of the Albanians of Ukraine: Evolution of the dialect system in language contact situation") from the Institute for Linguistic Studies of the Russian Academy of Sciences (2013). Senior researcher at said institute and teaches Albanology at the Department of General Linguistics in the Philological Faculty, St. Petersburg State University. Keynote projects include research in the Albanian villages of Ukraine (2005–2013); the Balkans (Albania, the area of Golloborda, Dibër, 2009–2010; Albania and Kosovo, the Gora (2011); southeastern Korça, Devoll, and Kolonja, Albania (2011–2013); Mrkovići, Montenegro (2012–present). Active in the development of the Albanian National Corpus (2012–present, see http://web-corpora.net/AlbanianCorpus/search). Research interests include language contact and bilingualism in Balkan speech communities, dialectology of the Balkan languages, and corpus studies of Albanian grammar.

Profile: https://iling-spb.academia.edu/MariaMorozova

Konior, Daria Vladimirovna (Daria V. Konior)
Born 19 March 1990, Leningrad, USSR. BA in Romanian Linguistics (2011), master's degree in Balkan Linguistics (2013, Saint Petersburg State University), PhD in Comparative, Typological and Contrastive Linguistics (2020, Institute for Linguistic Studies of the Russian Academy of Sciences). Specialist in Slavic and Romance linguistic and cultural contacts in the Balkans, bilingualism, linguistic anthropology, and field research.

Profile: https://iling-spb.academia.edu/DariaKonior

Kozak, Vyacheslav Viktorovich (Vyacheslav V. Kozak)

Born 26 January 1988, Leningrad, USSR. Slavicist and Balkanologist, MA in linguistics with specialization in palaeoslavistics (the St. Petersburg State University, 2012), PhD in Comparative, Typological and Contrastive Linguistics (2019, Institute for Linguistic Studies of the Russian Academy of Sciences in St. Petersburg). Research interests: paleo-Slavonic studies, Old Russian, history and dialectology of Croatian, Medieval Latin, lexicology, language contact.

Profile: https://iling-spb.academia.edu/ViacheslavKozak

Makarova, Anastasia Leonidovna (Anastasia L. Makarova)

Born 4 December 1988, Leningrad, USSR. Researcher at University of Zürich and at the Institute for Linguistic Studies of the Russian Academy of Sciences. Graduate of Faculty of Philology at the St. Petersburg State University, Department of Classical Philology (2011). Master's thesis on Balkan studies (2013). PhD in Comparative, Typological and Contrastive Linguistics (2018, Institute for Linguistic Studies of the Russian Academy of Sciences in St. Petersburg). Research interests: Balkan (Serbian, Macedonian, Albanian) dialectology, paleo-Slavonic studies, Medieval Latin.

Profile: https://iling-ran.academia.edu/AnastasiaMakarova

Rusakov, Alexander Yuryevich (Alexander Yu. Rusakov)

Born 28 August 1957, Leningrad, USSR. Albanologist, Candidate of philological sciences (PhD, USSR, 1985), Doctor of philological sciences (Russia, 2005), principal researcher at the Institute for Linguistic Studies at the Russian Academy of Sciences in St. Petersburg (1985), Professor of Albanology and General linguistics (2006) at the St. Petersburg State University, Philological Faculty.

Sobolev, Andrey Nikolaevich (Andrey N. Sobolev)

Born 13 July 1965, Leningrad, USSR. Slavicist und Balkanologist, Candidate of philological sciences (PhD, USSR, 1991), Doctor habilitatus (Germany, 1997), Doctor of philological sciences (Russia, 1998), chief researcher at the Institute for Linguistic Studies at the Russian Academy of Sciences in St. Petersburg, Professor of Balkan Linguistics (2007–2019) and Professor of Slavic Linguistics (2015–2019) at St. Petersburg State University (SPSU), Philological Faculty, extranumeral Professor at the University of Marburg, Germany (from 2003).

Profiles: https://iling.spb.ru/people/sobolev.html.ru
https://igpran.academia.edu/AndreySobolev

www.ingramcontent.com/pod-product-compliance
Lightning Source LLC
Chambersburg PA
CBHW071735150426
43191CB00010B/1579